Introduction to
Scientific Psychology

APPLIED CLINICAL PSYCHOLOGY

Series Editors:
Alan S. Bellack
University of Maryland at Baltimore, Baltimore, Maryland
Michel Hersen
Pacific University, Forest Grove, Oregon

A Continuation Order Plan is available for this series. A continuation order will bring delivery of each new volume immediately upon publication. Volumes are billed only upon actual shipment. For further information please contact the publisher.

Introduction to Scientific Psychology

Henry D. Schlinger, Jr.
Western New England College
Springfield, Massachusetts

and

Alan Poling
Western Michigan University
Kalamazoo, Michigan

Plenum Press • New York and London

Library of Congress Cataloging-in-Publication Data

Schlinger, Henry D.
    Introduction to scientific psychology / Henry D. Schlinger, Jr.
and Alan Poling.
        p.   cm. -- (Applied clinical psychology)
    Includes bibliographical references and index.
    ISBN 0-306-45728-8
    1. Psychology.   I. Poling, Alan D. II. Title.   III. Series.
    [DNLM: 1. Psychology.   2. Psychology, Experimental.   3. Behavior.
4. Psychology, Applied.   5. Human Development.   6. Behavior Therapy.
BF 139 S344i 1998]
BF121.S335   1998
150--dc21
DNLM/DLC
for Library of Congress   98-9986
                                                                      CIP

ISBN 0-306-45728-8

©1998 Plenum Press, New York
A Division of Plenum Publishing Corporation
233 Spring Street, New York, N.Y. 10013

http://www.plenum.com

10 9 8 7 6 5 4 3 2 1

Printed in the United States of America

To Julie and Kristal

Preface

We humans are faced with an interesting problem: That which we think we understand the most—our own behavior—we probably understand the least. On the eve of a new millennium, the planet is beset by a host of problems that are, for the most part, caused by human behavior. Ironically, although it seems that the greatest impact of our behavior is on the planet and its other inhabitants, we may actually be threatening our own future the most. For example, we have caused untold harm to the air we breathe, to the water we drink, and, by extension, to much of the food we eat. More important perhaps, we have created a society in which, among other things, many people are anxious and depressed, young women starve themselves, and alcohol and cigarette use are responsible for hundreds of thousands of cases of illness and death every year. And humans still murder one another at an astounding rate, while at the same time continuing to affirm the value of human life. At a time when it is critical that our children become educated, more and more children are not learning the basic skills they will need to think logically so that they can begin to solve the world's problems. The question may be not "Can the planet survive?" but, rather, "Can we humans survive and change our own destructive actions?"

Although many scholars, philosophers, and theologians have suggested solutions to the problems caused by human activity, it seems clear that understanding our own behavior is the first priority. However, human behavior, like other natural phenomena, is remarkably complex and, therefore, difficult to understand and explain. Nevertheless, we regularly create explanations for our behavior. Often, explanations for the same behavior differ from individual to individual. Everyone, it seems, wants to believe that he or she is an expert when it comes to explaining human behavior. It should be obvious, however, that some of the conflicting explanations are wrong. But how is one to tell the good explanations from the bad, the right from the wrong, or the logical from the illogical?

Although there is more than one way to understand the natural world, one approach—science—has proven especially effective. Simply speaking, the success of science is evident in the technologies it has generated for improving many features of the world. At the same time, science has been blamed for many of the world's ills. In truth, neither science nor technology is harmful in and of itself; it is their use by humans that may render them either helpful or harmful. Thus, we are brought back to the problem of understanding our own behavior. From a scientific perspective, the extent to which we can understand our own behavior will determine the degree to which we can change it and, therefore, whether we can save ourselves from ourselves. The picture is optimistic, but we have work to do. On the eve of the next millennium, understanding our own behavior is our most pressing task. A scientific study of behavior is the first step.

Goal of the Book

Although many disciplines concern themselves with human behavior, the discipline dedicated to studying and explaining human behavior is psychology. We define "psychology" as *the scientific study of behavior*, although much that passes for psychology today is neither scientific nor directly concerned with behavior. Thus, our goal in *Introduction to Scientific Psychology* is twofold. First, we introduce a *natural science* approach which endeavors to study the objective variables that determine behavior. Second, we provide an overview of some of the traditional content areas in psychology and describe what psychologists in these areas have done. In many instances, we show how these areas can be better understood according to a natural science approach.

We emphasize three general themes throughout the book. The first is that all behavior is determined by a combination of evolutionary, physiological, and environmental variables. The second is that many traditional explanations of behavior are fundamentally inadequate and therefore will likely not produce an effective behavior-change technology. The final theme of the book is that an effective behavior-change technology derived from a natural science approach and based, in large part, on manipulation of environmental variables has been developed. Our overall objective in this book is to teach students of psychology to think critically (i.e., scientifically) about the topic of behavior.

Organization of the Book

Introduction to Scientific Psychology contains 13 chapters grouped into three general sections. Part I, "Scientific Psychology" (Chapters 1–3), introduces the relationship between psychology and science. It lays the foundation for the rest of the book by providing the student with the standards by which to judge the information received from a variety of sources, such as newspapers, magazines, television, and other college courses, in order to determine whether such information is based on sound scientific practice. This part of the book will not and cannot cover everything that scientists do, but it presents an overview of the most important practices. Specifically, Chapter 1 describes the historical origins of the two contrasting approaches to explaining natural events, including behavior—science and philosophy. Chapter 2 describes the general features of the natural science approach adopted by psychologists, including the kinds of activity scientists engage in. Chapter 3 describes some different approaches to research, including observational studies, correlational studies, archival studies, and surveys, but emphasizes experimentation as the method proven to be most successful in revealing functional relationships.

Part II, "Behavioral Causation" (Chapters 4–7), considers at three different levels—genetic (evolutionary), physiological, and environmental—what causes humans and other organisms to behave as they do. Specifically, Chapter 4 provides an introduction to evolution by natural selection and considers its significance for the study of behavior. Like most scientists, scientific psychologists accept the evolution of humans and other species as fact. Evolution is important to scientific psychologists because it determines the range of behaviors that members of a species can acquire and their ease of acquisition. In a real sense, all of the behavior we exhibit is dependent on evolutionary history. We would not, for example, be able to learn about scientific psychology had not central nervous systems adequate to the task evolved in our ancestors. Chapters 5 and 6 examine how behavior is affected by events outside the organism, that is, by environmental variables (the general topic of learning). In particular, Chapter 5 describes Pavlovian conditioning and Chapter 6 describes operant conditioning. The principles introduced in these two chapters are then used throughout the book in an effort to understand a variety of behaviors. Chapter 7 deals with the role that the central nervous system and other physiological structures play in determining behavior. Changes in behavior cannot occur without changes in physiology; hence there is good reason to explore brain–behavior interactions.

Part III, "Applications of Scientific Psychology" (Chapters 8–13), builds on principles introduced in the first six chapters to deal with topics traditionally of importance to psychologists. Chapter 8 describes human language from a natural science perspective and contrasts that with some traditional approaches. Chapter 9 discusses some of the cognitive phenomena, including memory, consciousness, and mental imagery, that have fascinated psychologists, philosophers, and laypeople alike. Because of the inherent problems in observing cognitive phenomena, they are difficult to study scientifically. Scientific psychologists, however, can study the behavior from which cognitive phenomena are inferred and then explain them according to evolutionary, physiological, and environmental variables. Chapters 10 and 11 address human development: evolutionary and prenatal development (Chapter 10) and behavioral development through early childhood (Chapter 11). Chapter 12 discusses how humans behave in both similar and dissimilar ways and considers three traditional content areas of psychology—intelligence, personality, and social psychology—that have attempted to understand these similarities and differences. Chapter 13 deals with what is traditionally referred to as abnormal behavior, but is also called troublesome behavior to reflect the fact that it is behavior that causes problems for people. The chapter considers the diagnoses, causes, and treatments of troublesome behaviors associated with mental illness, drug abuse, and mental retardation.

Because of its natural science orientation, *Introduction to Scientific Psychology* is somewhat more limited in scope than most standard introductory textbooks in psychology. Most texts cover numerous minor contributions to psychology that have often already been disproven or found unhelpful in the understanding or treatment of behavior. In contrast, this book is not intended as an encyclopedia but, rather, as a primer in the scientific achievements in psychology. As such, this book covers many of the important and relevant topics in psychology without losing the scientific focus.

A Caveat

Some of the material in this book may prove difficult. Human behavior is remarkably diverse and complex, so it should come as no surprise that it is not easy to explain. In fact, "quick and dirty" explanations of behavior are usually suspect. As you will discover, science is hard work, but work that ultimately pays large dividends. Although we have endeavored to emphasize fundamentals, not details, and to write without unnecessary embellishment, the concepts of a science of behavior are no less challenging or complicated than, for example, those of biology.

Unlike the concepts of biology, which generally do not conflict with commonsense notions, the concepts of scientific psychology may tend to clash with everyday conceptions in which behavior is assumed to be solely the result of mental activity—thoughts, feelings, desires, cognitions, and so on. In order to benefit most from *Introduction to Scientific Psychology,* two things are required from the student. The first is a willingness to accept an analysis of human behavior that shares little with folklore or commonsense notions. The second is a willingness to accept the fact that even though human behavior is complex, it can still be explained as a function of objective variables.

Acknowledgments

Obviously a book such as this cannot be written without the help of many individuals. We would like to acknowledge some of them. First, we are grateful to Mariclaire Cloutier, Kathleen Lucadamo, Mary Curioli, Jeff Leventhal, Clay Boswell, and all the others at Plenum Press for their help and cooperation throughout all phases of the book's development. We would like to thank Matthew Normand and Dennis Kolodziejski for reading and commenting on early versions of various chapters, and Britt Bousman for his fine adaptation of S. L. Washburn's figure of the anthropoid evolutionary tree. We are especially grateful to Bryan Riggott for his many excellent drawings and illustrations and to Julie Riggott for proofreading the entire book numerous times, and for her help in constructing and labeling some of the illustrations. Finally, we want to thank both Kristal Ehrhardt and Julie Riggott for their patience, support, and encouragement during this project.

To the Student

Our main goal in writing *Introduction to Scientific Psychology* is for your behavior to be changed as a result of reading and studying it, in the sense that you will be better able to talk or write about many of the issues presented in the book. Therefore, we have tried to design the book in a way that will increase the chances for learning. First, we have put all important terms in **bold face**. We have also included a glossary of terms at the end of the book. Second, we have included a chapter outline at the beginning of each chapter and a summary of the main points at the end of each chapter. Third, we have provided study questions at the end of each chapter.

In order to maximize your learning, we recommend the following steps. First, look over the chapter outline to see what topics are covered and in what order. This will give you a basic familiarity with the chapter and prepare you to read it. Although this next suggestion sounds illogical, we recommend that you read the summary at the end of the chapter *before* as well as after you read the chapter.

After you have followed these steps, you can sit back and read the chapter without diving into it "cold." We suggest that you simply read the chapter without taking notes or underlining too much. The reason is that you need to read the entire chapter so that you understand its essential thrust. After you have read the chapter, you should begin to answer the study questions. You can do this by finding the answer to each question and then writing it down in your notebook. Remember to make your answers as brief but complete as possible so that you will be more likely to learn and remember them for a quiz or test.

As you well know, simply reading a chapter doesn't necessarily mean that you can talk about what you have read or that you can answer questions about the material. Therefore, your studying has to be active. Talk out loud to yourself and write down answers to the study questions. Use the study questions as mock test questions by asking yourself the question and providing the answer without looking at your written notes. Then, open your notebook and check to see if your answer was correct. If not, do it again until you can say the answer to a question without looking.

When learning many new technical terms, as is the case in any science, it is helpful to construct flash cards. The easiest way to do this is to take the terms from the glossary, and any important terms in the chapters that may not be included in the glossary, and write the term on one side of the flash card with the definition on the other side. When you study the cards, you should first go through them by reading the definition and then saying the corresponding term, which you then check by turning the card over. After doing this, turn all the cards over and read the term and try to state the definition. In addition, you should time yourself so that you can go through the terms for a given chapter very quickly. Finally, shuffle the cards occasionally so that you are not learning the order of the cards. When you are able to do all of this, you have learned the material and are ready for a quiz or test. The more you study this way, the more you will learn. We hope you like the book and enjoy learning about a science of behavior!

Hank Schlinger
Al Poling

Contents

Scientific Psychology

I

Historical Origins

1

This chapter introduces some of the historical developments that influenced the evolution of psychology as a natural science. Those developments include (a) the philosophy of Descartes; (b) the evolution of the scientific method by such notable scientists as Copernicus, Galileo, Newton, and Darwin; and (c) the beginnings of modern scientific psychology with contributions by Pavlov, Thorndike, Watson, and Skinner.

Early Philosophical Origins

Humans have probably wanted to understand their own behavior and the behavior of other living things since they began to talk early in their evolutionary history. Their prescientific attempts to explain the world constituted the earliest **philosophy**, which is the term used to designate *inquiries into the nature of reality based on logic and reason,* rather than experimental findings.

Animism

Although we cannot be certain, many of the explanations humans developed to explain the behavior of animals probably involved appealing to spirits or life forces residing within the animal. Even the word "animal," derived from the Latin, *anima*, or soul, and *animalis,* to animate, reflects this. The view that all living things contain a life force or soul that cannot be explained by natural laws has been called **animism,** or **vitalism.** Animistic explanations can even be extended to inanimate objects. For example, a rock tumbles down a mountain because it "desires" to get to the bottom, or a tree falls because it is "tired." Animistic explanations are no longer used to explain the behavior of inanimate objects (except poetically). They are still used to explain the behavior of organisms, but not without problems.

Aristotle's Souls

Many historians of psychology view ancient Greece as the source of the philosophy of psychology. Although many Greek philosophers, including Plato and Socrates, were influential, only Aristotle (384–322 BCE[1]) is considered here. Aristotle said that souls (he used the word *psyche,* which is Greek for soul) are what distinguish living from nonliving beings. In other words, according to Aristotle, things that are alive have souls that make them alive.

Aristotle drew distinctions among different kinds of souls. He concluded that all life forms—plants, animals, and humans—have *nutritive* souls, which enable them to find nourishment and to grow and reproduce. Animals and hu-

---

[1]Before the Common Era.

mans also have *sensitive* souls, which enable them to sense events in the environment. Only humans, however, have *rational* souls, or minds (Greek *nous*), as Aristotle called them; minds enable humans to reason.

Despite the appearance of being animistic, Aristotle's view of the soul was consistent with the view of **naturalism,** which states that all natural entities, including humans, are to be understood in the same basic, naturalistic, terms (Bolles, 1993, pp. 48–49). Thus, Aristotle's souls were really inseparable from the natural functions of the body, such as eating, sensing, and reasoning. With the decline of Greece as a great intellectual center, and the ascendance of Christianity, Aristotle's naturalistic souls were replaced by a spiritual soul that was not bound by the laws of nature.

Descartes's Philosophy of Mind

We now beg the historian's pardon for our large leap of time and move to another great philosopher, René Descartes (1596–1650), to explain where the modern psychological concept of mind originated. Descartes (pronounced day-cart) was a Renaissance man, both literally and figuratively. He is remembered for inventing analytic geometry, developing a mechanistic physiology and a theory of reflexes, and crafting a philosophy of mind that even today underlies most people's view of human nature.

In a sense, Descartes condensed Aristotle's three souls (nutritive, sensitive, and rational) into just two. The nutritive and sensitive souls were combined into all the functions of the body that could be explained and understood naturally and mechanistically, that is, in terms of physical laws. Descartes's approach to understanding all of the body's (physiological) functions according to natural laws is called **mechanistic physiology.** Descartes agreed with Aristotle, however, that human reason (and human language used to express it) could not be understood in the same terms as the other bodily functions. According to Descartes, reason reflected the action of the rational soul or mind. He believed that the rational soul also explained the fact that humans, but not animals, had volition, or will. Descartes considered animals to be automatons (i.e., machines) that were completely bound by reflexive, mechanistic principles and, thus, had no free will. In contrast, humans could go beyond reflexes and behave freely and consciously.

Our own personal, subjective experience seems to confirm Descartes's belief that humans do indeed have free will. For instance, we seem to be able to do whatever we wish, whenever we want to do it. We can even override basic reflexes, as when we consciously prevent ourselves from blinking at the sudden approach of an object or from coughing when our throat is irritated. Descartes believed that voluntary behavior was distinctly human and could not be explained mechanistically. It required another level of explanation, which involved the rational soul. This explanation is still used today by many psychologists and other people as well, although the term *mind* is used instead of *soul*.

Cartesian Dualism

One implication of Descartes's philosophy of mind was that the mechanistic body and the rational soul had different contents. The body was physical and subject to natural laws; the mind was not a physical entity and therefore could not be explained by natural laws. It could, however, influence the body, as in the previous example of consciously preventing a cough. The suggested interaction between the mind and body caused what has now become an age-old philosophical problem: how could a nonmaterial entity—the mind—affect a material entity—the body?

Philosophers throughout the centuries have attempted to solve this problem, with a notable lack of success. Nevertheless, many modern people believe that humans possess both a physical body and a nonphysical mind (soul). This position is called **mind–body** or **Cartesian** (from Des-*cartes*) **dualism.** For many dualists, the study of the body—anatomy and physiology—is biology, whereas the study of the mind is psychology, which means literally the study, or science, of the soul (from Greek *psyche*, for soul).

Because the mind–body problem is unanswerable, it should probably be left to philosophers to debate. For scientific psychologists, **psychology** is *the study of interactions between behavior and the environment in which it occurs.* Therefore, it is also a part of biology. Defined in this way, psychology is a natural science, and many questions about human behavior can be answered with the methods of science. Several factors have influenced the development of scientific psychology.

Early Scientific Influences

The seventeenth century (1600s) is usually considered to be a turning point in Western history for a number of reasons. One of the most important was the enormous growth in science, especially astronomy and physics. The growth in science beginning in the late sixteenth century was certainly built on earlier ideas and discoveries. Nevertheless, modern science often is said to have begun with Nicholas Copernicus's (1473–1543) claim (which had actually been proposed by some ancient Greek philosophers) that the earth revolved around the sun.

Copernicus's Heliocentric View

The prevailing view of the time (and the preceding fourteen centuries) was that the earth was the center of the universe and that the sun and all the planets and stars revolved around it. This **geocentric** (earth-centered) **view** had been described by Aristotle and Ptolemy and then embraced by the Church because it placed humans and, thus, God, at the center of the universe. Copernicus's heliocentric (sun-centered) view of the solar system was important, in part, because it correctly rejected the geocentric view.

One major implication of Copernicus's heliocentric position was that it removed humans from their self-appointed central place in the universe. Of course, this idea caused a problem with the Church for Copernicus and others who followed his lead, although in the end, as we all know, his view prevailed.

The Discoveries of Kepler, Galileo, and Newton

Copernicus's views were strengthened by Johannes Kepler (1571–1630), who used geometry to show that the planets moved in elliptical orbits around the sun, not in perfect circular orbits around the earth, as Aristotle and many religious scholars believed. The most convincing evidence for Copernicus's heliocentric view of the solar system, which provided the "death blow to the Aristotelian/Ptolemaic theory" (Hawking, 1988, p. 4), came from Galileo Galilei (1564–1642), who in 1609 built a new telescope and with it made direct observations of moons orbiting around the planet Jupiter.

As Hawking tells us, one implication of these observations was that not everything had to orbit the earth (and humankind). Although it might have been possible to fit these new observations into a geocentric worldview, Copernicus's theory was a simpler way of accounting for the same data, and consequently to be preferred. Acceptance of the doctrine of **parsimony,** which means that given any two explanations of some phenomenon, the one that explains it with the fewest assumptions is to be preferred, is a cornerstone of science. Copernicus's heliocentric theory was accepted largely because it required fewer assumptions to explain new astronomical observations than did the older geocentric theory.

Further confirmation of Copernicus's theory and Kepler's refinement of it was provided by Isaac Newton (1642–1727) in his book *Philosophiae Naturalis Principia Mathematica,* published in 1687, which Hawking (1988) has called "probably the most important single work ever published in the physical sciences" (p. 4). In it, Newton described mathematically the laws of motion discovered by Galileo.

Although it is commonly believed that Galileo dropped objects of different weights from the leaning tower of Pisa (Italy), it is more likely that he rolled objects (polished balls) down the grooves of inclined planes in order to slow them down, thereby making it easier to time their movements. By doing so, he found that the speed with which an object falls is determined by how long it has been falling, not by its weight. Newton summarized mathematically Galileo's discovery of the relationship between the speed of falling objects and the length of time they have been falling, and used his mathematical summaries (laws) to describe the motion of all objects, including planets. These observations, and the mathematical laws that describe them, form the basis of the theory of gravity, for which Newton is best remembered.

The Practice of Science

The experiments by Galileo, and their mathematical description by Newton, illustrate four important points about how science is practiced. First, a scientist makes an observation that sparks his or her interest to learn more about that observation and others like it. For example, Bolles (1993) tells us that Galileo's interest in the movement of objects began when he observed candle lamps in the great cathedral in Pisa swaying back and forth. Bolles writes about the singular importance of Galileo's initial observation: "We might think of that moment of contemplation as the beginning of modern science" (p. 20).

Second, after an initial observation is made, scientists characteristically design experiments in which one variable is manipulated in systematic, measurable ways while changes in another variable (affected by the first variable) are observed and measured.[2] Galileo manipulated the duration of an object's fall by using inclined planes of varying lengths and measured the speed of the objects as they rolled down the planes. In this way, he discovered cause-and-effect relationships between the length of the inclined plane and the speed with which the objects rolled. In other words, one variable—the speed of a falling object—was a function of another variable—the duration of its fall.

Third, after cause-and-effect relationships are discovered, scientists describe those relationships either mathematically or verbally. Newton, in his own words, "stood on the shoulders of giants" (i.e., Copernicus, Kepler, and Galileo, among others) and described the results of their work in mathematical terms. The mathematical or verbal description of cause and effect relationships between different sets of variables is known as a **scientific law.**

Fourth, after scientific laws are formulated, those laws are used to explain as wide a range of phenomena as possible. For example, Newton's law of gravity was a general law that could be used to describe the motion of all sorts of different objects, including falling rocks, pendulums, the movement of the ocean tides, and the orbits of planets.

In short, scientists make initial observations that suggest that certain variables are related, conduct experiments that search for the cause-and-effect relationships among those variables, and describe those relationships in general terms called laws. They then use those laws to understand other phenomena in addition to those initially observed.

Later Scientific Influences

Although numerous discoveries in biology and chemistry influenced the development of scientific psychology, none is as important as Charles Darwin's theory of evolution. Darwin's theory of how life on earth originated and changed over time by natural selection was a watershed event in the history of the biological sciences, of which scientific psychology is a part.

---

[2]A variable is a clearly defined object or event that can be measured in physical units.

Darwin's Theory of Evolution

Charles Darwin (1809–1882) developed the main ideas of his theory of evolution as a result of his five-year ocean voyage on the *H.M.S. Beagle*. Twenty-three years after the voyage ended, he described that theory in a book entitled *On the Origin of Species by Means of Natural Selection, or the Preservation of Favoured Races in the Struggle for Life* (1859). Darwin's delay in presenting his theory occurred, in part, because he had continued to collect and interpret observations in support of his new and revolutionary hypothesis about the origin of life on earth.

When Darwin's younger friend, the naturalist Alfred Russel Wallace (1823–1913), sent Darwin a copy of his own paper outlining essentially the same theory of natural selection, Darwin was forced to speed up his own efforts. In fairness to Wallace, Darwin proposed to present both his and Wallace's papers at a meeting of scientists. Afterward, Darwin worked quickly to complete his book. In it, Darwin presented a very detailed case, supported by an enormous amount of data, for natural selection as an explanation of the development of the variety of life forms.

Evolution by natural selection (covered in detail in Chapter 4), like many great scientific theories, is, at least on the surface, simple, yet elegant. In essence, it proposes that:

1. Life on earth has existed for a very long time (millions of years).
2. Organisms vary, and some variations can be inherited.
3. On average, offspring that vary most strongly in directions favored by the environment will survive and propagate.
4. Over time, characteristics that help organisms to survive and propagate will accumulate in the population.
5. The environment in which organisms live changes from time to time.
6. As variations that are favorable in a changed environment accumulate, new species evolve from existing species.[3]

Evolution, therefore, is neither planned nor purposeful, but rather the result of largely random changes in the environment. Some of these changes have been the direct result of such chance occurrences as asteroids striking earth, drastic changes in temperature, or availability of oxygen, and even the result of human beings' effect on the environment, such as overfishing and deforestation.

Darwin's ideas about the origin of species and natural selection as the mechanism of evolution were heavily influenced by the life forms he observed on the Galápagos Islands 600 miles off the coast of Ecuador in the Pacific Ocean. The Galápagos Islands are a relatively recent (about 1 million years old) product of a "volcanic hot spot." They lie at the juncture of three tectonic plates (large sections of the earth's crust which are in constant, although slow, motion) (C. Patterson, 1978).

---

[3] A species comprises all actually or potentially interbreeding organisms.

Darwin did not know these geological facts about the Galápagos Islands. He did discover, however, that life forms on the islands differed somewhat from those on mainland South America. Of all the species that Darwin encountered on the Galápagos Islands, he was most fascinated by the sparrow-sized birds called finches. The finches intrigued Darwin because they were so varied not only from island to island, but also sometimes on the same island. Darwin's finches, as they have come to be known, differed mainly in the size and shape of their beaks, which appeared to Darwin to be dependent on the type of food they ate. For example, those that fed on hard seeds had hard, flat beaks, those that fed on plants had long, curved beaks, and those that fed on insects had narrow beaks.

The fact that the characteristics of the species on the Galápagos Islands differed from those of the same species on the mainland suggested to Darwin that the environmental forces operating on the islands had shaped these different traits. By observing the finches, Darwin obtained good evidence that the characteristics of species seemed to be logical adaptations to the demands of the environment.

Species Continuity and Human Uniqueness

An important implication of Darwin's theory for scientific psychology is that his account of evolution implied **species continuity.** This means that all species are related in the sense that at any given time during evolution, all existing species could be traced back to earlier ones. The idea of species continuity is also known as **common descent,** which means that all life forms descended from a common ancestor. Considering the vast amounts of time in which life has been evolving, this common ancestor (the first life form on the earth) must have lived a very long time ago. Scientists speculate that it was probably about 3.6 billion years ago.

Obviously, Darwin's account of the origin of species was quite different from the concept of fixed or unrelated species that heretofore had prevailed in Western thought. In that conception, all species were created separately in their present form, and humans were fundamentally different from, and given dominion over, all other species. Darwin's theory of evolution, like Copernicus's theory of the universe before it, forced humans to reconsider their place in nature. Copernicus's theory removed humans from the center of the universe, and Darwin's theory removed humans from their separate, if not central, place on earth.

Animal Research and Comparative Psychology

The idea of species continuity meant, among other things, that scientists might be able to learn something about humans from the study of nonhumans.

Prior to Darwin, when the prevailing belief was that humans were fundamentally different from other animals, no one would have thought to study the physiology (or behavior) of animals in the hope of shedding light on similar processes in humans. But because of Darwin, this practice not only has become commonplace in all of the biological and chemical sciences, but has formed the foundation for scientific psychology.

In his book, *The Descent of Man* (1879), Darwin wrote that "there is no fundamental difference between man and the higher animals in their mental faculties" (p. 66). Darwin believed that the differences that could be shown were a matter only of degree, not of kind. He contended that humans and nonhumans were similar not only in physical characteristics, but in mental ones as well. What he meant was essentially that the higher animals (e.g., apes) possess the same kind of intelligence as humans, but not as much. The occurrence of similar patterns of behavior in different species was evidence for this position.

George Romanes (1848–1894) supported Darwin's notion of the cross-species continuity of intelligence by collecting stories about animal behavior and examining those anecdotes for signs of human-like intelligence. Darwin contributed many observations to Romanes, and encouraged his efforts to demonstrate mental continuity from animals to humans. Darwin appeared to believe that similar behavioral processes occurred in many species. Prior to meeting Romanes, Darwin had published a book called *Expression of the Emotions in Man and Animals* (1872), in which he postulated that emotional expressions in humans were remnants of similar emotional expressions in animals. For example, the curling of the human lips in a threatening sneer seems like the baring of canine teeth exhibited by carnivores under similar conditions.

Although Romanes tried to be careful in selecting anecdotes that were real and reliably reported, he made the mistake of relying on secondhand stories. Also, Romanes often interpreted the animals' behavior too freely in terms of human qualities; this is known as **anthropomorphism,** a term for attributing human characteristics to nonhumans. For example, dogs were described as exacting "revenge," or moths as showing "curiosity." Despite his anthropomorphism, Romanes made many positive contributions to the development of scientific psychology (F. S. Keller, 1973).

First, he is generally credited with being the first to use the term **comparative psychology,** which is the study of the behavior of different species in search of similarities and differences. Second, Romanes's criterion for inferring mental attributes in animals was a fairly objective one; namely, whether their behavior was modifiable as a result of experience. In other words, the process that we would call learning is what Romanes used to infer that animals have minds and intelligence. Later, we will see that we can compare humans and nonhumans in terms of basic learning capacity, just as Romanes did, but without considering the status or existence of minds. The first step in this direction was taken by Morgan, whom we will meet next.

Lloyd Morgan and His Canon

The new field of comparative psychology begun by Romanes was furthered by C. Lloyd Morgan (1852–1936). In his writings, Morgan described numerous learning experiments with animals. Despite the fact that Morgan, perhaps more than anyone else, was responsible for getting the new field of comparative psychology under way, he is perhaps better known for his canon, or rule, which had to do with parsimony. Remember that parsimony in science means explaining some phenomenon in the simplest terms possible. Morgan advanced his canon in reaction to the blatant anthropomorphism of Romanes and others who tried to explain animal behavior in terms of human characteristics without first considering simpler explanations. Bolles (1993) paraphrased Lloyd Morgan's canon as follows: "We must not interpret a behavior as due to a higher level process if it can be interpreted as the result of a psychologically lower process" (p. 298).

Morgan conducted numerous experiments showing that many animal behaviors, including those that seemed to be innate (e.g., drinking) could be modified by experience. Although Morgan was careful not to anthropomorphize when explaining animal behavior, many of his explanations had their own problems. For example, after describing how his dog learned to open the latch of a gate, he talked about the conscious mental processes necessary for the behavior to occur (F. S. Keller, 1973). Inferring unobservable mental processes in a dog was not much better than attributing human qualities to the same animal. Nevertheless, Morgan's descriptions of animal behavior were unusually objective for the time.

Both Romanes and Morgan extended Darwin's idea of species continuity and in so doing established a new field of scientific study that was soon to be taken up by experimenters in Russia and the United States.

Natural Selection and Scientific Explanations of Behavior

Darwin's theory of natural selection also gave scientists a new mode of explanation in the sense that it required no unobservable entities, such as minds or souls, and no intentions or purposes (Bolles, 1993). In other words, it was a more parsimonious explanation than alternative views. According to Darwin's account, evolution resulted from the success of certain physical traits in the changing environment and did not move purposely toward some goal of perfection, as many before Darwin had believed.

As we will see, the theory of learning known as reinforcement theory is very similar to natural selection theory in its statement that learning occurs as a function of whether individual behavior is successful in a particular environment. Reinforcement theory, like natural selection theory before it, offers a mode of explanation that is environmentally dependent, and both theories suggest hypotheses about observable events (Bolles, 1993).

Darwin's theory of evolution by natural selection set the stage for the development of psychology as a science of behavior. Herman Ebbinghaus is reported to have remarked that "psychology has a long past, but only a short history"; and the same can be said of scientific psychology, as outlined in the following section.

The Beginnings of Scientific Psychology

In Ivan Pavlov (1849–1936), we find all of the characteristics of the physical scientists (e.g., Galileo, Newton) previously described. Pavlov was an eminent Russian physiologist (he won the 1904 Nobel Prize in physiology), not a psychologist, but his best-known contribution is in the field of psychology.

Pavlov and Classical Conditioning

Pavlov was interested in how the digestive system worked, and he used dogs as experimental subjects. Consistent with the notion of species continuity à la Darwin, he believed that he could learn something about human digestion by studying nonhuman subjects. Pavlov was remarkable in many ways. For one, he devised new apparatuses to make the previously unobservable processes of digestion observable and, thus, measurable. One such device was a tube attached to the salivary ducts of dogs. Pavlov could observe the flow of saliva into the tube as his dogs were exposed to different conditions (see Figure 1-1).

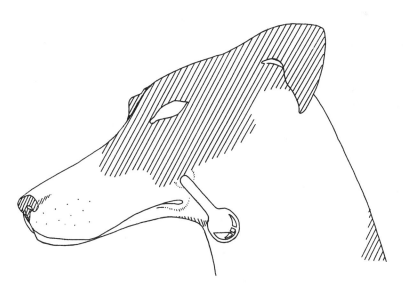

Figure 1-1. The procedure used by Pavlov to collect saliva from dogs.

Pavlov presented various stimuli, such as a dilute acid solution or dry food, to dogs and measured the amount of saliva produced. Some stimuli (e.g., food) reliably elicited salivation, as long as the dogs were hungry. Pavlov noticed that salivation was also produced by stimuli that reliably preceded food delivery, such as the sound of his footsteps or the laboratory light being turned on. Pavlov initially called salivation controlled by such stimuli *psychic reflexes,* or *psychical secretions,* but came eventually to term them *conditional* (or *conditioned*) *reflexes.* Pavlov spent much of his life studying conditioned reflexes (Chapter 5 discusses this work and its implications for human behavior).

The Importance of Pavlov's Work

Three features of Pavlov's work were important for the development of scientific psychology. First, Pavlov did not set out to study conditional reflexes, but he was prepared for the unexpected. The willingness to follow up on chance observations often results in important scientific discoveries, and appears to be a characteristic of many prominent scientists. A second feature of Pavlov's work that was important to scientific psychology followed from Darwin's idea of species continuity. Specifically, Pavlov used nonhumans (dogs) to learn about humans. Third, and most important, Pavlov studied observable events—environmental stimuli and behavior—and explained his findings parsimoniously, that is, without speculating about unobservable mental or cognitive processes.

Thorndike's Law of Effect

Edward L. Thorndike (1874–1949) is remembered, in part, for a series of experiments on problem solving in cats that he conducted while at Columbia University in the last years of the nineteenth century. In those experiments, Thorndike placed individual cats in large cratelike boxes (he called them puzzle boxes), from which the cats could escape by either pulling a string that was tied to a latch on the door, or by pushing down on a pedal that would likewise open the door (see Figure 1-2).

If either response was made, the cats could get out of the box and get food. Thorndike found that all cats eventually made the response that opened the door, and on successive trials it took progressively less time for the response to occur. To clarify his findings, Thorndike plotted the time-to-escape in a series of trials. Because these *learning curves* (see Figure 1-3) showed a gradual continuous improvement in performance instead of sudden jumps, Thorndike proposed that it was not necessary to postulate any mental processes to account for the learning. (Presumably, mental processes, such as the insight that a particular response might work, would be reflected in a sudden jump on the learning curve.) For Thorndike, all that was necessary for learning to occur was the connection between the response (pulling the string or pressing the pedal) and the effect (getting out of the box and getting food).

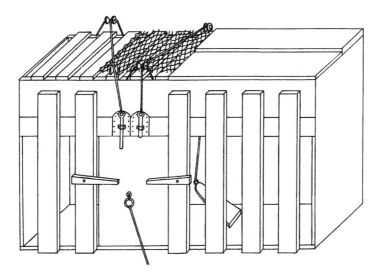

Figure 1-2. The puzzle box devised by Thorndike to measure learning. From Thorndike (1898).

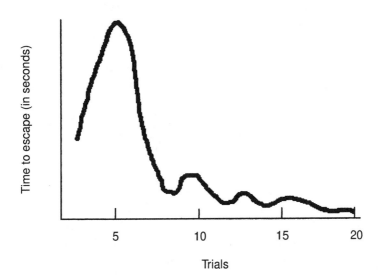

Figure 1-3. A typical learning curve depicting the time it took for a cat to engage in the behavior that caused the door to open (on the vertical axis) and the number of trials (on the horizontal axis). From Thorndike (1898).

After many experiments with different animals in the puzzle boxes yielded similar findings, Thorndike (1911) formulated one of the first psychological laws, which he called the **law of effect.** It may be paraphrased as follows: Of the many responses made to a situation, the ones that are closely followed by satisfaction will be more strongly connected to the situation and will be more likely to recur, while those that are followed by discomfort will be less likely to recur. More simply, the law of effect states that behavior in a certain situation is determined by the consequences of the behavior in such situations.

The Importance of Thorndike's Work

Although a few historians consider Thorndike to be a significant figure in the development of scientific psychology, his influence generally has been underrated (F. S. Keller, 1973). Keller speculates that this may be because Thorndike was not like his peers. Thorndike never taught a standard course in psychology or worked within a standard university department. Moreover, by his own admission he did not work well with laboratory equipment or animals, even though he conducted many studies. Despite the unique aspects of his career, Thorndike made four significant contributions to scientific psychology.

First, Thorndike did actual experiments in which he manipulated objective events. Second, he discovered regularities in his data that he described in terms of laws. Third, he explained his findings in objective terms instead of speculating about things he could not see, like mind or consciousness. Fourth, Thorndike's experiments, like Pavlov's, demonstrated the importance of the environment in determining behavior. In a sense, Thorndike "emptied the head" by showing that environmental variables, not mental events, are responsible for behavior. The fundamental importance of "emptying the head of mental events" as explanations for behavior was strongly emphasized by John B. Watson, whom we now consider.

Watson and the Beginning of Behaviorism

John B. Watson (1878–1958) is remembered for many things. Probably his most enduring contribution to the development of scientific psychology occurred in 1913, when he published an article entitled "Psychology as the Behaviorist Views it." In that article, which many believe represents the formal founding of behaviorism, Watson called for psychology to be a natural science, like biology and chemistry, with the goals of predicting and controlling its subject matter (human behavior).

Watson further asserted that psychologists should be interested in understanding and explaining behavior without considering it as an expression of mental events, like consciousness. Watson did not deny the existence of mental events, but he thought that they were unnecessary to explain behavior.

Although Watson conducted many interesting experiments, he did not discover any laws of behavior, and was at something of a loss to explain many human actions. Watson knew of Thorndike's analysis, but dismissed it as being too subjective, because Thorndike emphasized the "satisfaction" or "annoyance" produced by a behavior. As an alternative to Thorndike's approach, Watson emphasized the importance of Pavlov's work on conditional reflexes and attempted to explain behavior in terms of them.

Although this attempt was doomed to failure, Watson was a powerful advocate for scientific psychology, and his arguments in favor of it proved persuasive for many people. Watson emphasized that the environment played an important role in determining how people behaved. Therefore, by changing the environment in appropriate ways, human behavior (and the human condition) could be dramatically improved. Such a message was very optimistic at a time when many people believed that how a person behaved, and what she or he eventually became, was determined primarily by inheritance, and was therefore fixed at birth.

Skinner and Operant Conditioning

When he died in 1990, B. F. Skinner (1904–1990) was arguably the best-known psychologist ever. A few months before he died, the American Psychological Association (APA) awarded him its Lifetime Achievement Award, the only such award ever given. At the ceremony during which Skinner received the award, he lamented that psychology still had not become a natural science, and that many psychologists continued in their attempts to explain behavior by appealing to mental or cognitive events. B. F. Skinner's contributions to modern scientific psychology are numerous and we will discuss many of them throughout this book. For now, our goal is to show how Skinner contributed to the development of scientific psychology.

Although Thorndike had paved the way for the discovery of a type of learning different from Pavlovian conditioning, it remained for Skinner to complete the process. After spending much time in his laboratory at Harvard tinkering with equipment, Skinner stumbled on an apparatus that enabled him to discover a type of learning that he called **operant conditioning.** Skinner's apparatus was a small enclosed chamber, called an operant conditioning chamber (although many refer to it as a Skinner box), with a metal lever extending from one of the walls (see Figure 1-4). In addition, there was a small cup into which food could be delivered, and a light that could be turned on and off.

Skinner arranged the box so that when a rat pressed the lever downward, a pellet of food dropped into the cup. In Skinner's conditioning chamber, rats could respond (press the lever) at any time and at any rate, whereas Thorndike's cats could respond only once, after which he had to put them back into the box.

Skinner also invented a device called a *cumulative recorder* (see Figure 1-5), which was like a polygraph (lie detector) in that a pen would draw a straight line on the paper if nothing happened, but if the rat pressed the lever, the pen would move upwards slightly. The advantages of Skinner's operant conditioning chamber over Thorndike's puzzle box become clear when one looks at the data as registered on a cumulative recorder. One can actually see conditioning (learning) taking place; that is, the more the responses, the steeper the line and, conversely, the fewer the responses, the flatter the line.

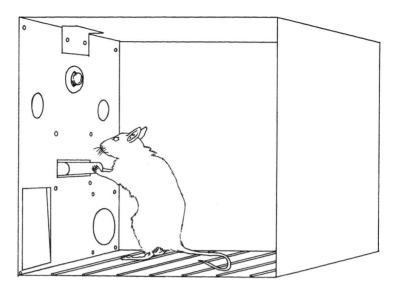

Figure 1-4. A typical operant conditioning chamber for rats invented by Skinner. A metal lever extending from the panel can be pressed down; this causes food (or water) to be delivered into the opening at the bottom left. The chamber is equipped with a light and a speaker which can present visual and auditory stimuli respectively.

In his experiments, Skinner manipulated objective variables (e.g., food deliveries) and directly observed their effect on behavior. He could, for instance, see how response rate changed if food delivery followed every response, or every tenth response, and what happened when food was no longer delivered.

By examining how changes in events that occurred before and after a response affected the likelihood of such behavior recurring, Skinner achieved his main goal as a scientist, which was to discover the orderliness in behavior and its relationship to environmental variables. In 1938, Skinner described the results of his early experiments in his first book, *The Behavior of Organisms,* and concluded that operant conditioning differed from classical conditioning (which Skinner called respondent conditioning). In addition, he described the scientific laws of behavior called **reinforcement, extinction,** periodic reinforcement, discrimination learning, and **punishment,** among others. Skinner maintained until his death that the behavior of humans and other animals could be explained adequately without talking about mental or cognitive or even physiological events, although he acknowledged that the latter would one day help scientific psychologists understand *how* operant conditioning occurred at the level of the nervous system.

Skinner's career provides a case study in the practice of science, with four noteworthy features. First, like Pavlov, he made accidental discoveries and followed up on those chance occurrences. Second, he did experiments in which he manipulated objective events. Third, he formulated laws summarizing the regularities revealed in his experiments. Finally, he explained the results in the simplest terms possible (i.e., parsimoniously), by referring to objective events,

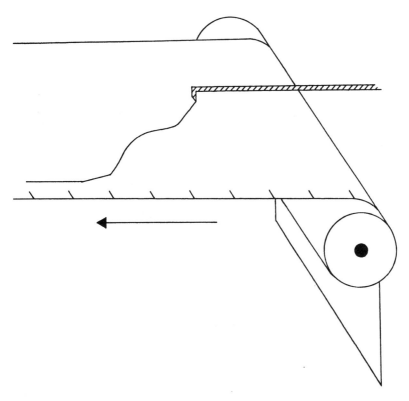

Figure 1-5. A cumulative record of responses per time as drawn by a cumulative recorder. The paper moves in the direction of the arrow and each response is recorded by the pen making an upward movement on the paper. No responding would be indicated by a flat line.

not mental or cognitive events, as determinants of behavior. These practices have repeatedly proven valuable in other areas of natural science and, as we will see, have formed the basis for an emerging science of human behavior.

Beginning with Pavlov and Thorndike and then Skinner (and since then, thousands of others), psychologists have finally become scientific like their peers in chemistry, biology, and physics. As a result, they have made discoveries about behavior that were not previously possible. The rest of this book will describe what scientific psychologists have done for the past 50 years or so, and what they are doing today.

Summary

1. In an attempt to understand the world, including their own behavior and the behavior of other living things, humans first began to use reason, which had to await the evolution of verbal behavior (language). This was the beginning of

philosophy. Early philosophical explanations of behavior probably included some form of *animism,* the belief that all living things contain a life force or soul that cannot be explained by natural laws.

2. One of the most prolific and influential of all philosophers was Aristotle (384–322 BCE), who postulated that differences between plants, animals, and humans were due to different souls that were each responsible for different bodily and behavioral functions. Aristotle's view reflected a naturalistic approach whereby all natural entities, including humans, were to be understood in the same basic, naturalistic terms.

3. The philosopher who perhaps more than any other most influenced modern philosophy and psychology was Descartes. He was responsible for formalizing a dualistic view of humans. *Cartesian dualism* is the name for the belief that humans possess both a physical body and a nonphysical mind (soul).

4. The scientific approach began when humans began to try to explain nature by using observation. Modern science may be said to have begun with Nicholas Copernicus's (1473–1543) hypothesis that the earth revolved around the sun, the so-called *heliocentric view* of the solar system. Discoveries by Kepler, Galileo, and Newton confirmed Copernicus's theory and showed it to represent a more parsimonious (that is, a simpler) explanation of the facts than had the previous, *geocentric* (earth-centered), view of the solar system.

5. The scientific discovery that perhaps was the most influential for the development of modern scientific psychology was Darwin's theory of evolution by natural selection which, like Copernicus's theory of the observed facts of astronomy at the time, was a more parsimonious explanation of the known facts of natural history than were other views.

6. Darwin's theory had at least three implications for scientific psychology: (1) the idea of functionality; (2) the suggestion that behavior is a product of evolution by natural selection; and (3) the idea of species continuity.

7. Darwin's ideas about behavior were taken up by comparative psychologists such as Romanes and Morgan, who attempted to explain animal behavior by comparison with human behavior.

8. The modern history of scientific psychology included the scientific accomplishments of Pavlov, Thorndike, and Skinner, who used naturalistic approaches to the study of behavior and explained the results of their scientific experiments in parsimonious, nonmentalistic terms.

Study Questions

1. What kinds of explanations of behavior might early humans have constructed, and how were these explanations animistic?

2. How did Aristotle account for the various functions of living things?

3. How did Descartes modify Aristotle's view of souls and how did he explain human voluntary behavior?

4. How did Descartes's philosophy of mind influence later thinking about human behavior?

5. How did the discoveries of Kepler, Galileo, and Newton support Copernicus's theory?

6. How did the discoveries of Galileo and Newton illustrate the scientific method?

7. What are the essential features of Darwin's theory of evolution by natural selection and what did the theory explain?

8. What are three implications of Darwin's theory of natural selection for the development of scientific psychology?

9. What is meant by species continuity and what was the common effect of Darwin's and Copernicus's theories on the place of humans in nature?

10. How did Romanes and Morgan extend Darwin's theme of species continuity to develop a comparative psychology?

11. How did Darwin's theory of natural selection provide a new mode of explanation, especially for scientific psychology?

12. What did Pavlov do with dogs and how did he discover conditioned reflexes?

13. What were the three features of Pavlov's work that were important for the development of scientific psychology?

14. What did Thorndike do with cats and what law of behavior did he name as a result?

15. How was Thorndike's work important to the development of scientific psychology?

16. What was John B. Watson's role in the development of scientific psychology?

17. What did B. F. Skinner do with rats and what did he discover as a result?

18. How was Skinner like Pavlov (and Galileo and Newton)?

Science and Psychology

2

As we saw, Pavlov, Watson, Skinner, and several other pioneering psychologists argued that the best way to understand human behavior is to study it from the perspective of the natural sciences. As indicated in Chapter 1, this approach to understanding human behavior was offered as an alternative to traditional approaches, which had their roots in, and were inextricably linked to, philosophy. Chapter 1 suggested that philosophy, as a human activity, came into being when people began talking about themselves and their world. Science, on the other hand, came into being when people began trying to understand the natural world systematically by observing it and using the experimental method. Like philosophy, then, **science** is also a human activity, but one that is characterized by the search for regularities in the natural world.

In this chapter, we describe the general features of the scientific approach adopted by psychologists, including the general characteristics of scientific activity, psychological theories, and explanations of behavior.

What Is Science?

Characteristics of Scientific Behavior

What is science? The simplest answer is that science is what scientists do and the resulting accumulation of what they learn from that scientific activity. Thus, to understand what science is, we must look at the behavior of scientists. What we find is that scientists do many different things. First, it is necessary to understand that scientists are behaving individuals, and their actions are affected by the same kinds of variables that affect the behavior of other people. All scientists are influenced by the specific training that they receive and the culture in which they live and work. Legitimate scientists often disagree with one another, and differ dramatically in their personal styles, interests, and ethics. Nonetheless, there are limits to the kinds of phenomena that can be investigated scientifically, and to the strategies employed by scientists. So, what is it that scientists do? In general, we may describe the behavior of scientists according to five characteristics.

1. *Scientists deal primarily with empirical phenomena.* The natural world is the source of all scientific information, and that world consists of **empirical phenomena.** These are objects and events that can be detected through observation (through our senses). Most scientists agree that in science one should only use empirical phenomena that are objective, reliable, and quantitative. They are **objective** if they can be observed by more than one person, **subjective** if they cannot. They are **reliable** if two or more observers can agree as to whether or not the events occurred. And they are **quantitative** if they can be measured in physical units.

Psychology, historically, has been plagued by subjective and unreliable observations (data), in part because many phenomena of interest to psychologists can be observed directly only by the person who experiences them. For example, only you are directly aware of your thoughts and feelings (i.e., they are subjective), although you can report them to other people who may be able to observe behaviors that accompany them (e.g., the public act of cursing may accompany the more subjective "feelings" we have learned to call anger). The fact that some events are not directly available for public observation does not mean that they do not exist or that they are trivial or uninteresting. It does, however, pose serious problems for a scientific analysis that puts a premium on objective data.

The long-standing religious and philosophical tradition, formalized by Descartes (see Chapter 1), in which humans are considered **dualistic** beings, made up of body and mind (or soul), also poses problems for a science of behavior. The main reason is that if the mind is a nonphysical entity (as Cartesian dualism demands), and therefore beyond the realm of science (i.e., not objectively observable), then a science of the mind or its effects on behavior is impossible. Of course, no one can truly evaluate the role of the nonphysical in human behavior. If, however, one acknowledges that at least *some* aspects of behavior are lawfully related to physical (i.e., objectively observable) events, then those aspects can in principle be analyzed scientifically.

2. *Scientists attempt to disclose orderly relationships between classes of events, and then use these relationships to explain natural phenomena.* All people, scientific or not, gather information about their world. What sets scientists apart is the way in which they collect and order the information. For scientists, understanding an event requires specifying the variables that cause it to occur. What lay people term cause-and-effect relationships are called functional relationships by scientists. In a **functional relationship,** the value of one event, termed a **variable,** is determined by (or is a function of) the value of a second variable. For example, there is often a functional relationship between the duration and intensity of crying in children and the attention they get from others (e.g., parents) when they cry: The more attention for crying, the more they cry.

How do scientists determine functional relationships between two variables? In psychology, as in the natural sciences, scientists determine functional relationships by doing experiments in which the value of one variable (termed the **independent variable**) is manipulated, and changes in the value of another variable (termed the **dependent variable**) are observed and measured. If the value of the dependent variable changes systematically with the value of the independent variable, the two are said to be functionally related: B is a function of A [or B = f(A)].

Functional relationships between variables are the raw material of science, but to be of value in understanding the world these relationships must be organized and classified according to the common features they share. When this is done, scientific laws are the result. Scientific laws are descriptions of relatively constant, repeatable relationships between certain kinds of phenomena, which may be in sentence form or symbolic form such as an equation (McCain & Segal, 1988, p. 51). For example, as described in Chapter 1, beginning with Thorndike and Skinner, scientific psychologists have repeatedly demonstrated that the consequences of behavior powerfully influence whether such behavior will recur. Some kinds of consequences make behavior more likely, whereas others make it less likely to occur. This general relationship has been observed in many species with a wide range of behaviors and consequences and was first stated years ago in Thorndike's Law of Effect. Nowadays, the Law of Effect is also called the law, or principle, of reinforcement and reflects the accumulation of approximately 60 years of extensive experimentation.

Scientific laws are based on observation. Before a statement can be accepted as a scientific law, it must satisfy certain criteria. For example, the statement must show a functional relationship between two or more kinds of events and is not only about a simple event, and there must be a large amount of data confirming the law and little or none disconfirming it (McCain & Segal, 1988). If the Law of Effect described only a relationship between one response in an animal and one consequence, then it would be about a single event and would not qualify as a scientific law. Because the Law of Effect describes functional relationships between many kinds of responses and consequences in many different species, and under many different circumstances, it is accepted as a scientific law.

3. *Scientists attempt to predict, control, and understand their subject matter.* When experimentation reveals that an independent variable is functionally related to a dependent variable, scientists have demonstrated control over their subject matter. In other words, the value of the dependent variable can be controlled (determined) by manipulating the value of the independent variable. Once scientists are able to control a dependent variable, they are in a better position to predict it. Thus, prediction of dependent variables follows from controlling them and is possible precisely because the value of the independent variable determines the value of the dependent variable. For example, when some scientists (called behavioral pharmacologists) discovered that nonhuman animals, including rats and monkeys, would learn to make a response if doing so produced an injection of cocaine, they were in a position to predict such responses under similar conditions.

Once scientists are able to control the value of variables in the laboratory through experimentation, control of variables outside the laboratory becomes possible. For scientific psychologists, this means that they are able to apply what they have learned in the laboratory to try to correct problem behaviors in the real world. Science has practical value when scientists can isolate independent variables and then manipulate them to change important parts of the world (i.e., dependent variables) in a manner that benefits humans or the world in which they live. For example, scientific psychologists have successfully applied the Law of Effect to the treatment of children with autism. Intensive interventions, begun at an early age, and based in large part on manipulating the consequences of their behavior, enable many such children to live relatively normal and happy lives (e.g., Lovaas, 1987, 1993).

Although we may not like the term, whenever we act to affect the behavior of someone else, we are acting as controllers. This happens in everyday and seemingly trivial interactions. For example, if laughing at someone's jokes increases the likelihood that the person will again tell you a joke, then you have affected or in some way controlled that person's joke-telling behavior, particularly if you are the only one laughing at her jokes. For some people, such as teachers and therapists, it is their specific job to control or change the behavior of others (i.e., students and clients, respectively). For example, when a teacher successfully teaches a child to read or write, the teacher is changing (controlling) the child's behavior. Consider an alcoholic who comes to a clinical psychologist seeking treatment. In order for the clinician to help the alcoholic, he or she will most likely suggest or implement some type of intervention designed to change (control) the client's behavior with respect to the consumption of alcohol. Most of us are not opposed to this kind of control, or to the kind of control that helps autistic children, particularly if it works. What we object to is control that involves unpleasant means or that leads to undesirable ends. Therefore it is not the control per se that is bad, but how some people might use it. As B. F. Skinner repeatedly stated, *if we understand how behavior is caused, then we will be in a better position not only to recognize unpleasant behavior control and avoid it, but also to change behavior using positive practices.*

4. *Scientists assume the phenomena they study are orderly and deterministic.* As noted previously, scientists are able to make predictions precisely because they are able to show that some variables are lawfully related to other variables: If A has occurred, then B will almost certainly follow. Knowing this allows one to predict that B will occur each time A occurs. Such knowledge is dependent on an orderly world, one in which relationships revealed in the past (e.g., B follows A) can be shown to occur again. Moreover, it requires a deterministic world, one in which the value of some events depends upon (i.e., is determined by) the value of other events. This holds true regardless of the subject matter of the individual science. As B. F. Skinner (1953) noted:

> If we are to use the methods of science in the field of human affairs, we must assume that behavior is lawful and determined . . . that what a man does is the result of specifiable conditions and that once these conditions have been discovered, we can anticipate and to some extent determine his actions. (p. 6)

At present, no one is able to predict accurately all of human behavior. In fact, behavior sometimes appears chaotic rather than orderly. Nearly every day we hear of upstanding citizens who, without warning, kill themselves and their loved ones. We also hear of individuals raised in the worst of conditions (e.g., poverty, abuse) who manage to overcome these adversities and become successful citizens. Moreover, each of us is aware of being confronted with behavioral alternatives from which we seem free to select an option. Should I study for the exam or go skiing? Is J.B. or B.J. a better date for the party? We mull our options, talk to ourselves and others about them, agonize, and eventually choose. The choice, when made, appears to be ours alone—we typically are aware of what we did and felt immediately prior to making the choice, but not of the historical events that affected the process. The fact that we are not aware of the historical events that determine our behavior does not mean that they did not influence our behavior. Although it is not possible to demonstrate that *all* human behavior is caused by historical events, it is abundantly clear that much of what we do is determined by our past experiences. A science of human behavior is possible only with respect to those actions that are determined, in the sense of being lawfully related to other empirical variables, because they can be described in terms of functional relationships, and therefore can be predicted and controlled.

Knowing that behavior is lawfully related to specifiable events leads to optimism, because such knowledge often suggests ways of changing a person's actions in desired directions. Scientific knowledge characteristically is practical knowledge: It lets us change our world and develop useful technologies. The truth of this assertion is evident in the dramatic medical advances made within the past 100 years. For millennia, the causes of infectious diseases were not known, and the diseases were not treated effectively. As a science of medicine arose, it became clear that microorganisms caused infectious diseases and that these tiny invaders could be thwarted with antibiotic drugs, serums, and vaccines. These interventions produced dramatic results. In 1900, for example, pneumonia, tuberculosis, infections of the gastrointestinal tract, and diphtheria were among the ten leading causes of death in the United States, collectively accounting for more than one-third of all fatalities. Whooping cough, measles, scarlet fever, meningitis, and typhoid fever also killed an impressive number of people (Dowling, 1977). Though these scourges have not been completely eradicated, relatively few people die from them today, because scientists have discovered how to prevent or treat these diseases effectively.

5. Scientists make claims that are tentative and testable. Recall that observations of real events are the raw material of science and that relationships among these observations form the basis of scientific laws. These laws in turn are organized into scientific theories. Scientists recognize, however, that observations are not exact and that it often is not easy to detect or to summarize important relationships among variables. Therefore, scientific claims do not reflect absolute truth at all levels, but are instead tentative and subject to revision.

This does not mean that scientists know nothing or that scientific claims are so imprecise as to be useless. On the contrary, there are many useful and well-established scientific laws, including the laws of gravity and motion discovered by Newton, the laws of inheritance discovered by Mendel, and the Law of Effect discovered by Thorndike and Skinner. The statements and equations that summarize these and other scientific laws enable scientists to predict with very good accuracy the phenomena described by the laws. In fact, when it comes to predicting natural phenomena, scientific information is far superior to any other kind. In large part, this is so because scientific knowledge is not fixed, but changes over time to reflect observations more accurately. Science is fallible, but it is self-correcting. Scientific statements made at a given time are usually incomplete, or even in error, and they may subsequently be modified or rejected. Science is self-correcting because these changes lead to a progressively refined worldview, one that provides better integration of observations and allows for better prediction of important phenomena. For example, as described in Chapter 1, scientists such as Copernicus, Kepler, Galileo, and Newton developed an increasingly refined view of the solar system based on improvements in their observations.

However, as stated previously, scientists are human organisms and, just like the rest of us, it is sometimes difficult for them to give up old beliefs. The reluctance of some scientists (and indeed most people in general) to give up old beliefs is well stated in the physicist Max Planck's maxim: "Educated, intelligent, successful adults rarely change their most fundamental premises" (Snelson, 1995, p. 54). The reluctance with which physicians accepted the germ theory of disease provides one good example of the truth of this maxim (Snelson, 1995).

Characteristics of Established Sciences

The end result of the scientific behaviors of many scientists over long periods of time is the evolution of a mature, or established, science. What makes a science mature? A mature science is **internally consistent:** Its assumptions, laws, and general principles hold together and make sense in light of the observations it attempts to explain. Moreover, its findings do not violate those of other scientific disciplines. For example, theorizing that the earth is only 10,000 years old violates the archaeological findings of the carbon dating of fossils. Likewise, theorizing that genes determine most human behavior violates the findings from thousands of published experiments showing that changing environmental conditions affect human behavior.

A mature science is also **deductively ordered**, which means that the laws and other general statements permit accurate predictions to be made about particular happenings. As Sir Peter Medewar (1984) notes:

> [A] property that sets the genuine sciences apart from those that arrogate to themselves the title without really earning it is their predictive capability: Newton and cosmology generally are tested by every entry in a nautical almanac and corroborated every time the tide rises or recedes according to the book, as it is also corroborated by the periodic reappearance on schedule of, for example, Halley's comet (due, 1986). [It appeared on schedule.] I expect that its embarrassing infirmity of prediction has been the most important single factor that denies the coveted designation "science" to, for example, economics. (p. 4)

If we currently hold psychology to the test of accurate prediction outside the laboratory, then psychology is not scientific. No psychologist, regardless of his or her theoretical persuasion, can consistently and accurately predict human behavior, although some can make accurate predictions in certain circumstances. Whether psychologists will ever succeed in building a science of human behavior that is more like the mature physical sciences in predictive utility and emergent technology remains to be seen. But, as you will see, they have at least taken substantial steps in that direction.

Psychological Theories

People use the term **theory** in different ways. For some it simply means "guess" or "conjecture," as in "What is your theory of why the boy threw a tantrum?" In science, however, "theory" is used more consistently. In general, the term theory refers to a system of rules and assumptions used to explain and predict observations. Some psychological theories are formal, detailed, and specific, whereas others are loose and informal. All of them are designed to make sense of, that is, to organize, observations.

But how do scientists use scientific theories? The purpose of theory in science "is to describe and explain observable and observed events and to predict what will be observed under certain specified conditions" (McCain & Segal, 1988, p. 96). This means that a good theory should be able to explain what has already happened and to predict what will happen given certain preconditions. Suppose you are a student teacher and you witness a child throwing a tantrum in a classroom. A sound psychological theory should be able to explain that behavior in such a way that its future occurrence under similar circumstances can be accurately predicted. If the explanations generated by the theory point to observable, objective functional relationships, it will be easier to predict behavior and, more importantly, to correct it. Many theories, including some in psychology, do not fulfill the purpose of a theory; they simply borrow hypothetical constructs from other disciplines and make comparisons to human behavior. These theories are considered analogical.

Theories Based on Analogy

Theories based on analogy involve describing something by comparing it with something else. For example, earlier in this century a hydraulic theory of motivation was popular among **ethologists** (scientists who study species-specific behavior). In this model, motivation is represented as a fluid that is stored in a reservoir. The fluid, when released, causes certain behaviors to occur much as hydraulic pressure causes mechanical devices to operate (e.g., brakes to close). Certain stimuli act to open a valve and release the motivational fluid, or it can simply build up and eventually leak out. In that case, the behavior would occur in the absence of a stimulus. The model, which resembles a flush toilet, is easy to understand and to talk about. Despite these appealing features, the hydraulic theory of motivation is of only historical interest to modern scientists.

An example of analogy in psychology is comparing the function of the central nervous system to that of a telephone switchboard or, more recently, to that of a computer. Perhaps the main advantage of such analogies is that they make things more familiar or understandable. For example, the nervous system seems easier to understand if we think of it as a telephone switchboard or as a computer: There is input, which resembles stimuli affecting our senses; some kind of internal processing, which resembles the workings of the brain; and then output, which resembles behavior. The problem is that such analogies do not explain the phenomena of interest because we must then use another science, model, or even another analogy to explain them (Eacker, 1972).

Despite these problems, computer models of brain function (or of mental activity) are quite popular today (see Chapter 9). These models use a diagram of electronic circuitry to represent "cognitive architecture." Although a model based on the modern computer has more appeal than one based on a telephone switchboard or a flush toilet, the fact remains that the brain does not contain either electronic circuitry or plumbing fixtures.

Criteria for Evaluating Theories

Although models based on analogy may help us to talk about and predict how an organism will function in a given situation, they should be viewed with caution for the reasons just described. Instead of building theories based on elaborate models, many scientific psychologists prefer to account for behavior by summarizing observed relationships between real events, usually environmental, and changes in behavior. They do so with a minimal use of analogies and without proposing mental or cognitive events that do not have an empirical basis. For example, if we want to understand why a teacher constantly yells at his students, we can use the principle of reinforcement, which summarizes thousands of experimental findings showing that behavior is determined by its immediate consequences. We can thus explain the teacher's yelling in terms of the immediate reinforcing consequences of that behavior, which may include the students' becoming quiet or sitting down after he yells at them to do so. Does this explanation work? In order to answer this question, scientific psychologists must be able to evaluate a theory. Theories can be evaluated according to several criteria (e.g., Bachrach, 1972). Five of particular importance that we will discuss throughout the book are discussed below.

1. *Empirical Support.* In judging a theory, one must consider whether there are any observations that relate to it. If there aren't, the theory is automatically suspect. If there are, the observations must support the theory, not contradict it. A theory is also suspect if it is framed so generally or so imprecisely as to be able to account for any possible set of observations. Such theories are deemed **untestable.**

2. *Logical Support.* The mechanisms proposed by a theory must be plausible. If, for instance, a theory accounts for some behavior in terms of structures in the brain, then these structures must be consistent with what is known about the brain. Moreover, the explanations of behavior associated with a theory must be fundamentally adequate. In other words, they must not involve reification, circularity, nominal fallacy, or teleology (see the following discussion).

3. *Generality.* The **generality** of a psychological theory refers to the range of behaviors it purports to explain, and the range of conditions under which it does so. A theory of learning that attempts to account for the acquisition of many kinds of behavior is, for instance, more general than one that attempts to account for verbal behavior alone. Similarly, a theory of depression that explains the phenomenon in all depressed humans is more general than one that explains it only in adult children of alcoholics. Usually, general theories are preferable to specific ones.

4. *Parsimony.* As mentioned in Chapter 1, good theories do not invoke complex mechanisms when simple ones will suffice to explain a phenomenon. **Ockham's** (also spelled Occam) **razor,** named after the English philosopher William of Occam (c. 1285–1350), is the name assigned to the principle dictating that all else being equal, the simplest explanation of a phenomenon is the best one. Or, in terms more akin to those of Occam's day, "what can be done with fewer (assumptions) is done in vain with more" (Thomas, 1981, p. 979). As mentioned in Chapter 1, the principle of parsimony was restated by Lloyd Morgan in his canon which specifically applied to explaining behavior.

5. *Utility.* As noted previously, the goals of scientific analysis are the prediction and control of the subject matter. If psychology is to be scientific, an accepted theory must allow for accurate prediction of the behaviors it covers. Depending on the nature of the events assumed to control behavior, it may also suggest strategies for changing behavior in desired ways. In evaluating a psychological theory, it is useful to ask, "Does knowledge of this theory suggest any procedures for changing behavior in desired ways?" In other words, is it useful? If the answer to this question is "Yes," then the theory has practical value. A significant strength of the theories of behavior advanced by Thorndike, Skinner, and their colleagues is their practical utility, for these theories have spawned many effective interventions (e.g., J. O. Cooper, Heron, & Heward, 1987; Miltenberger, 1997). Such interventions are carried out by applied psychologists.

Applied psychologists, who include clinical psychologists, school psychologists, and industrial/organizational psychologists, use their understanding of human behavior to generate solutions to a wide variety of behavioral problems. Sometimes these individuals are directly involved in implementing treatments, as when a therapist uses systematic desensitization to treat a phobia (see Chapter 13). Other times, they act as consultants to help people select treatments that they can use to treat their own problems or problems evident in people in their charge, as when an obese person is trained to use contingency contracting to lose weight or the owner of a company is taught to use incentives to increase productivity.

Ideally, applied psychologists select treatments based on the results of controlled experiments, and use the general procedures of scientific analysis to quantify behavioral problems and to evaluate the success of chosen treatments in alleviating those problems. The term scientist-practitioner is used to refer to psychologists who proceed in this fashion (Barlow, Hayes, & Nelson, 1984). Such individuals have a sound rationale for selecting the treatments they use, and empirical evidence of the effectiveness of those treatments in their own everyday practices.

Unfortunately, many applied psychologists are not affected by research findings, and do not systematically evaluate the results of the treatments that they use. Although such individuals undoubtedly sometimes provide valuable services, they also waste a great deal of their clients' time and money. In some cases, such as the tragedy of facilitated communication (described in Chapter 3), their misguided efforts do much harm. Given the problems associated with intuitive, nonempirical approaches to treatment, these approaches should be used with caution. Good applied psychologists are neither artists nor sorcerers. Instead, they are skeptical and informed mental health professionals. Figure 2-1 illustrates the steps involved in treating any kind of behavioral problem. The first step, initial assessment, involves determining what, exactly, is wrong. The second step is selecting and implementing a treatment. The third is evaluating the effects of the treatment. The fourth, if necessary, is modifying and reevaluating the treatment until the desired changes in behavior are produced. In addition, several general variables determine the intervention employed by an applied psychologist (see Table 2-1). To see how the scientist-practitioner model might be used to treat a relatively simple behavior problem—thumb sucking in a 9-year-old girl—read Sidebar 2-1.

STEPS IN TREATING A BEHAVIORAL PROBLEM

STEP 1: DETERMINE THE ASPECTS OF BEHAVIOR THAT ARE CAUSING A PROBLEM AND SET TREATMENT GOALS.

STEP 2: DETERMINE HOW THE BEHAVIORAL PROBLEM SHOULD BE TREATED AND BEGIN THE TREATMENT.

STEP 3: EVALUATE BEHAVIOR TO DETERMINE WHETHER THE PROBLEM IS SOLVED.

STEP 4: IF THE PROBLEM PERSISTS, MODIFY THE TREATMENT AND AGAIN EVALUATE ITS EFFECTS.

Figure 2-1. The four primary steps involved in treating any kind of behavioral problem.

Table 2-1
Four Variables Determining Psychological Intervention

1. *Professional training and experience of the clinician.* A psychologist's history determines how she or he construes a behavior problem and the interventions that will be deemed appropriate. For example, a clinician trained in the client-centered therapy developed by Carl Rogers (see Chapter 12) will favor different treatment strategies than one trained in behavior analysis.
2. *The nature of the problem.* The treatment employed obviously depends upon the desired changes in a patient's repertoire. Among the variables to be considered in selecting an intervention are the kind and number of behaviors to be changed, the direction and magnitude of the desired changes, and the apparent cause of the problem.
3. *Legal and ethical considerations.* Interventions must be instituted with the patient's well-being held foremost. As a rule, applied psychologists begin with the least restrictive (i.e., least harmful) treatment likely to prove beneficial, then proceed to progressively more restrictive interventions if necessary. *Primum no nocere*—first of all, do no harm—is an ancient precept of the medical profession, and good advice for psychologists as well.
4. *Practical considerations.* All interventions use resources like time, money, personnel, and equipment. Psychologists always should consider what is feasible in the situation at hand.

Sidebar 2-1
The Scientific Approach to Treatment

Susan is a 9-year-old girl who often sucks her thumb. Her parents have had no success in dealing with the problem, and seek help from a child psychologist. The psychologist's first task is to determine the severity of thumb sucking and the conditions under which it occurs. In their first meeting with the psychologist, the parents report that thumb sucking occurs "all the time" while Susan is watching TV, but not often at other times.

Of course, "all the time" may actually mean "most of the time" or "some of the time," and a cautious psychologist would request that the parents actually quantify Susan's thumb sucking. They might, for instance, record at 2-minute intervals whether or not she was thumb sucking while watching TV and at selected other times, and provide the psychologist with this information one week after the initial visit. Assume that this was done and, on average, Susan sucked her thumb on 91% of the observations while watching TV, and on 4% of other observations. Given this, the adults know what they are up against. The parents were right, Susan essentially sucks her thumb "all the time" while watching TV.

The next task is for the psychologist and parents to select an intervention. Research has revealed that several procedures are often successful in treating thumb sucking, including response prevention; placing bad-tasting substances on the thumb; delivering rewards dependent on the passage of a specified period of time without thumb sucking; and habit-reversal, which involves training the person to engage in behaviors incompatible with thumb sucking (Miltenberger, 1997). After discussing the options, the parents decide to try a habit-reversal procedure. The psychologist demonstrates the procedure, which involves one of the parents physically guiding the child's hand away from the mouth and providing verbal praise when no thumb sucking is observed. The parents then practice implementing the procedure in a role-play situation under the psychologist's direction. When they are comfortable, the session ends with the recommendation that the parents try habit reversal for one week, while continuing to count the occurrences of thumb sucking.

One week later, the parents report that the procedure was fairly easy to use, and that thumb sucking occurred on 77%, 68%, 54%, 46%, 49%, 34%, and 46% of observations across the last seven days when habit reversal was arranged. Though this is encouraging, the problem is not solved. Given this, the psychologist asks the parents to demonstrate how they are using the procedure, provides corrective feedback, and emphasizes the importance of implementing the procedure consistently. They agree to try it another week, and come back to report that thumb sucking has dropped to 20% of observations.

Of course, the parents and psychologist agree that they would like to see thumb sucking totally eliminated. They decide to add another component to the treatment: placing a safe, but bad-tasting, substance on Susan's thumb. With this addition, thumb sucking is essentially eliminated and the problem is solved. Over time, the bad-tasting substance is eliminated, and the habit-reversal procedure is gradually terminated, but thumb sucking does not recur.

Explanation in Science

Discovering the causes of natural phenomena through experimentation increases our understanding of those phenomena. Theories enable scientists to understand phenomena by organizing information gained through experimentation. Scientists are then able to apply that understanding to phenomena not specifically studied in the laboratory. As a result, scientists are able to offer explanations of the phenonmena in which they are interested. When we are asked to explain why a particular phenomenon occurred, our verbal reply is called an **explanation** (from the word *explain*, which means *to give the cause of*). Explanatory statements usually include the word "because" (which literally means *by cause*), as, for example, when we say that life on earth became so varied *because* of natural selection operating on random variation, or that the earth revolves around the sun (and not the other way around) *because* of the relatively greater mass of the sun.

When discussing behavior, explanations also point to causes and usually use the word "because," as when we say, for example, that a child hits other children *because* of the attention that she gets from teachers for that behavior. As already mentioned, scientists explain phenomena (behavior) by determining functional relationships between presumed causes and effects. This is why functional relationships are also called cause-and-effect relationships.

Explanation and Prediction

As stated previously, prediction in science is intimately related to control: The more precisely one can control events, the better one can predict the future occurrence of those events. In a laboratory where scientists can control independent variables (i.e., causes) exactly, they can accurately predict the resulting dependent variables (i.e., effects). For example, in a laboratory chemists can accurately control the amount of hydrogen and oxygen that flows into a combustion chamber and then can measure the effect on the amount of heat and light produced. Chemists can make very accurate predictions about the nature of combustion, such as when and under what conditions we can expect an explosion, how destructive it will be, and so on. Applied chemists have made use of this knowledge to produce controlled explosions by the millions every day in the engine of your car.

Explaining events in the laboratory is fairly easy because scientists can manipulate independent variables and measure the changes they produce in the dependent variable. Thus, their explanation of changes in the dependent variable is in terms of the value of the independent variable. For example, the chemist explains combustion—the increase in heat and light—in terms of the relative amounts of hydrogen and oxygen. When scientists try to explain events in the natural world, they must assume that those events will obey the same laws they obey in the laboratory. Scientific explanations of events in nature are called *interpretations* or *extrapolations* (to extrapolate means to expand into an area not known). Scientists use the laws discovered in the laboratory to understand events in the natural world. For example, as mentioned in the quotation by Medawar, Sir Isaac Newton explained the ocean tides using his laws of motion even though he obviously never did direct experiments on ocean tides. Nevertheless, we accept his interpretation as a plausible explanation based on the strength of the laws of physics he discovered under more controlled laboratory conditions (Palmer, 1991). Similarly, a chemist could explain (and even predict) a naturally occurring gas explosion based on the strength of the laws of combustion discovered in the laboratory if he or she knew the levels of hydrogen and oxygen present.

Explaining and, thus, understanding events outside the laboratory is more difficult; not because the same laws don't apply in the "real world," but because scientists don't have the same degree of control over the variables. When a scientist offers a prediction about some natural event, the prediction is based on what scientists have discovered in the laboratory, where the variables can be precisely controlled and measured. Thus, the prediction is always based on what scientists learn from experiments that are done under tightly controlled (or ideal) conditions. For example, suppose you decide to ask a physicist friend of yours to predict exactly where a particular leaf from a tree will fall and the exact path it will take. Obviously your friend will tell you that he or she is unable to predict either event with much accuracy. What does this mean? Do you now doubt that the science of physics can predict more complex events in nature like the formation of stars if it can't predict something as simple as where a leaf will fall? No. Why not? Because you know that your friend could predict where the leaf would fall if he or she knew all of the variables that affected its fall, such as the weight and shape of the leaf, the current wind velocity, and so on. Those are the kinds of variables that can be controlled in the laboratory. Using such knowledge, scientists have designed machines, such as airplanes, that can move through the air without falling.

Now consider a similar example in psychology. You are asked to consult with a teacher in a classroom. Upon entering the classroom, the teacher asks you to predict when a particular child in his classroom will hit another child. Of course, you are unable to do so. In fact, the teacher and the other children could more accurately predict what the child will do than you could, even though you are the behavioral scientist. Is there something wrong with your science? Of course not. In fact, you could predict the child's behavior if you knew something about her particular history, including the circumstances under which she has hit in the past and what the consequences of that behavior have been. The more you know about her past behavior and the environmental variables associated with it, the better you will be able to predict what her behavior will be and when it is likely to occur. With such knowledge, you might be able to design a program that would decrease the probability of hitting.

In summary, the difference between explaining events inside and outside the laboratory is simply that in a laboratory scientists can control the causes more precisely, which is exactly what is needed to discover precise rules and laws. Also, explanations of natural events can be scientifically valid if the explanations are based on (extrapolated from) what is discovered in the laboratory. Much of the time, scientific psychologists are expected to explain the behavior of a large variety of organisms in their natural settings. Scientific psychologists are not alone with respect to the expectation to explain behavior; each of us has been asked on any number of occasions to give explanations for behavior. We are typically asked questions like, "Why did that behavior occur?" "What made her do that?" or "What caused him to behave that way?" People always seem to have an answer (an explanation), but the explanation is almost never one that would satisfy a scientist. People get their explanations from a variety of sources, but mostly from their own personal experiences, from parents or friends, from things they have read, or, more likely nowadays, from television. Rarely, however, do people admit that they really don't know why a particular behavior occurred, that is, what caused it. In fact, many psychologists also err in this way. Rarely will a psychologist admit that he or she doesn't always know the answer to the question, "Why did she or he do that?"

People who always have an explanation for behavior are able to get away with it because most of the time no one asks for evidence. And, let's face it, most of the time it doesn't really matter what kind of explanation someone offers. Understanding and explaining behavior scientifically becomes more important if we want to change troublesome behavior (see Chapter 13), as, for example, when a child's behavior threatens the child's or someone else's safety, when a person abuses drugs, when an autistic child lacks functional language skills, or when two people fight constantly. In instances like these, it matters very much how we explain behavior, because if we offer explanations that are not scientifically valid, then we will be less successful in changing the troublesome behavior.

The question for any science, including scientific psychology, is whether the explanations offered for a particular phenomenon (behavior) are scientifically adequate. Unfortunately, explanations for behavior by both ordinary people and psychologists are often scientifically inadequate. Before we discuss the characteristics of scientifically adequate explanations of behavior, we discuss several common inadequate explanations.

Inadequate Explanations of Behavior

Inadequate explanations occur because of the ways in which we have all learned to talk about behavior. As such, they are really just ordinary, or commonsense, ways of talking about behavior and not well-reasoned explanations based on scientific evidence or logic. Consider a preschool girl who hits other children. Parents and teachers seek an answer to the question, "Why does the child hit other children?" or, more generally, "What causes hitting?"

Because our culture teaches us to classify behaviors when naming them, we usually classify hitting as *aggressive* behavior. When asked why a child hits, we might answer: "That is aggressive behavior," or, simply, "That's aggression." That is the correct answer to the question: "How would you classify hitting?" but it does not answer the question, "Why does that child hit other children?" Simply naming the behavior as an explanation is called a **nominal fallacy** (*nominal* comes from "naming"). This naming strategy is a fallacy because naming alone does not explain why the behavior occurs, nor does it allow us to predict, control, or understand the behavior.

Sometimes we change the answer slightly: "The child hits because she is aggressive." An explanation such as this may sound good to the untrained listener, but it provides no new information. We have moved ever so slightly from labeling the behavior, "That is aggressive," to labeling the child, "She is aggressive." In order to discover the flaw in this explanation, we must ask the following question: "What is the evidence for her aggression?" In other words, how do you know the child is aggressive? If the only evidence for the aggressiveness is the hitting, then we are providing what is known as **circular reasoning**, in which the only evidence for the explanation is simply the behavior to be explained. We are essentially saying that "The child hits because the child hits," and everyone should recognize the error in this line of reasoning. There is simply no independent evidence for the child's aggressiveness other than the aggressive behavior (hitting) itself. We are still left not knowing what causes the hitting. And if we don't know what causes it, we will not be very successful in changing it. As you can see, nominal fallacy and circular reasoning sometimes combine to give us what looks like a reasonable explanation (cause) for behavior, but on closer inspection, proves to be inadequate.

Some psychologists go one step further and say that "the child hits because she has an agresssive personality." Of course, this sounds even more impressive to the untrained listener, but hasn't really moved us much further in our search for the causes of the behavior. Just as there wasn't much difference in going from naming the behavior ("That's aggression") to naming the child ("She is aggressive"), we haven't accomplished any more by saying that the child has a *personality* (which cannot be observed independently from the child's behavior) and then naming it ("She has an aggressive personality"). We have simply added another scientifically inadequate explanation to nominal fallacy and circular reasoning, known as reification. In **reification,** an abstraction (in this case the term *personality*) is treated as if it were a real thing and then used as an explanation or cause for behavior. Although we think we know what we mean by the commonsense term *personality,* it is nonetheless an abstraction; that is, a term invented to describe a set of behaviors. As such, it has no physical existence. In science, all causes have to be real things that have material or physical existence.

It is understandable how psychologists as well as ordinary people may commit this error. After psychologists invent these terms, repeated usage of them can lead people (even psychologists) to believe that the terms refer to actual entities inside the individual. For example, to help explain some of the behaviors in his patients Freud used the terms *id, ego,* and *super ego* to refer to abstract forces. Someone whose behavior conformed very strictly to the rules and mores of the culture was said to be governed by her super ego, whereas someone who often showed impulsive behavior without regard for its effect on others was said to be governed by her id. There is certainly nothing inherently wrong with using these terms to classify certain behaviors but not to explain them. To say that a child hits because her id has overpowered her ego is to treat these abstractions as if they were real entities, which is an example of reification. Attempts to explain behavior in terms of reified entities are fundamentally flawed, because the reifications have no physical status and consequently cannot possibly affect behavior.

These explanations are flawed because they are untestable. An untestable explanation is one that cannot be disproven by observation. Because no one can see or hear the id, ego, superego, or personality, we obviously cannot ascertain how, or if, it affects the child's behavior. Problems with untestable explanations are especially common in psychology, and include many other terms (abstractions) that have come, after repeated usage, to be treated as real physical entities that can cause behavior; for example, self or self-esteem (whether high or low), personality traits, mind, cognitions, and so on.

One other inadequate explanation often offered for behavior is termed a **teleological explanation**. In a teleological explanation, a future event is assumed to cause a current event. Returning to our example of the preschool girl who hits other children, suppose someone explains the behavior by saying that the child hits other children in order to get their attention. In this explanation the presumed cause of hitting occurs in the future, which is indicated by the phrase *in order to*. This is obviously illogical because causes must precede effects. It is reasonable to speculate that the little girl hits other children because doing so *in the past* has resulted in attention from the other children or the teacher. But it is teleological to speculate that the little girl hits other children *in order to* gain attention.

Perhaps the best advice that can be given in evaluating any explanation of behavior is expressed by Snelson (1995) in the Principle of Scientific Skepticism: "The less scientific verification for an explanation of causality, the more skeptical one can afford to be; and the more scientific verification the less skeptical one can afford to be" (p. 55).

Now that we have discussed some of the most common types of inadequate explanations of behavior, we turn to those that are considered scientifically adequate.

Adequate Explanations of Behavior

Scientifically adequate explanations of behavior involve specifying the variables that are necessary and sufficient for a particular kind of behavior to occur. In general, scientifically adequate explanations point to observable variables that precede and cause behavior. To be accepted, such explanations must be supported by observations and be consistent with what is known in general about the kind of behavior in question.

Although the number of variables that may influence human behavior is enormous, they can be conveniently categorized as *genetic, physiological,* and *environmental.* We may further classify the causes of behavior according to when they occur in relation to behavior. **Proximate causes** are events that occur shortly before the behavior that they control, and consist of both environmental events (called stimuli) and physiological processes (nerve impulses). **Ultimate causes** (ultimate here means "first") are historical environmental happenings that make proximate causes effective, and always consist of environmental events.

Proximate Causation

Consider a simple example of proximate causation. A telephone ringing causes you to answer it. The sound of the ringing is a proximate cause of answering. Because the sound of the ringing is an environmental stimulus, it is classified as a *proximate environmental cause*. At the neurophysiological level, the sound of the ringing initiates a process in the brain that results in the behavior. Scientific psychologists classify these as *proximate physiological causes*. In fact, the neurophysiological processes that occur between the stimulus and the response are the most immediate cause of behavior in that they occur closest in time to the behavior. When describing the effect of proximate causes on behavior, scientific psychologists use the term *evoke*, which means "to call forth." Thus, proximate causes evoke behavior in the sense that they immediately cause it. Think about what behaviors are evoked by the following environmental proximate causes: a teacher's command to sit down; the sound of the can opener for a cat; a traffic light turning from green to red; and a sudden loud noise.

It is probably best to think about proximate causes as a chain of events. The first link in the chain are environmental events (stimuli), which evoke the second link, the physiological events (nerves), which then evoke the final link, behavior. We can diagram this chain of events with our example of answering the telephone simply as follows:

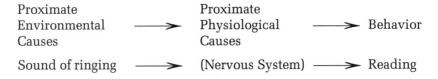

We see only the proximate environmental cause(s) and the behavior it produces, but we could measure the physiological cause(s) if we had the proper recording and measuring instruments, such as an electroencephalogram (EEG) that measures brain waves.

Ultimate Causation

Ultimate causes make proximate causes effective and are thus considered to be the first causes of behavior. There are two categories of ultimate causes, *ontogenetic* and *phylogenetic*. Let us deal with ultimate ontogenetic causes first by going back to the example of answering the telephone. How did the sound of the ringing telephone come to have its effect on you in the first place? The general answer is that it was your having been taught to answer ringing telephones. Consider the fact that the same stimulus won't evoke the response in a preverbal infant or a non-human animal, both of whom lack the same experience you have. The experiences which occur in the lifetime of individuals and establish proximate causes are called ultimate ontogenetic causes. (The term *ontogenetic* comes from *ontogeny,* which refers to the development of an individual organism.) Ultimate ontogenetic causes are also termed **learning** (discussed in detail in Chapters 5 & 6) and help us understand *why* a certain stimulus (such as the sound of a ringing telephone) evokes behavior (such as answering the telephone).

The second category of ultimate causes is *ultimate phylogenetic causes.* (The term *phylogenetic* comes from *phylogeny,* which refers to the development of a genetically related group of organisms, called a **species.**) Like ultimate ontogenetic causes, ultimate phylogenetic causes also result from experience, not of an individual during his or her lifetime, but of the species over evolutionary time. Darwin referred to these causes as natural selection. Thus, ultimate phylogenetic causes are responsible for characteristics that all members of a given species have in common. For example, a stimulus such as a sudden loud noise will evoke an increase in heart rate, among other physiological responses, in all humans. The ultimate cause of this relationship is that in our evolutionary history, individuals who reacted this way were better prepared to face threatening events and survive to pass on that trait. Thus, in a real sense, ultimate phylogenetic causes are the most ultimate (meaning fundamental or basic) causes. They are truly the first causes.

As you can see, determining the causes of any behavior is not as easy as you may have thought. The foregoing discussion should help to prepare you to look for the causes of behavior either in the individual's genes (phylogeny; see Chapter 4), physiology (see Chapter 7), or past and present environment (ontogeny; see Chapters 5 and 6).

Summary

1. Science is a distinctly human activity that is characterized by the search for regularities in the natural world through observation and experimentation. In other words, science is what scientists do. In particular, they:

- deal primarily with empirical phenomena.
- disclose functional relationships between classes of events.
- attempt to predict and control and, thus, understand their subject matter.
- assume the phenomena that they study are orderly and deterministic.
- make claims that are tentative and testable.

2. The term *theory* in science refers in general to a system of rules and assumptions used to explain and predict observations which, in psychology, include behavior.

3. There are several criteria for evaluating psychological theories, including *empirical support, logical support, generality, parsimony,* and *utility.*

4. Explanations in science, including a science of psychology, point to causes, or functional relationships between variables, and usually employ the word "because."

5. Explaining, understanding, and predicting events in the laboratory is relatively easy because scientists can precisely control events in the laboratory. Explaining and understanding events outside the laboratory (called interpretation or extrapolation) is more difficult because scientists don't have the same degree of control over the variables.

6. There are at least four types of scientifically inadequate explanations of behavior, including *nominal fallacy, circular reasoning, reification,* and *teleology.* All of these are untestable explanations and, therefore, cannot be disproven by observation.

7. Scientifically adequate explanations involve specifying the variables that are necessary and sufficient for a particular kind of behavior to occur. They specify observable variables that precede and cause the behavior.

8. The variables that may influence human behavior can be conveniently categorized as genetic, physiological, and environmental. The variables can be further classified according to when they occur in relation to behavior. *Proximate causes* are events that occur shortly before the behavior that they control; they may be environmental or physiological events. *Ultimate causes*, which may be phylogenetic or ontogenetic, are historical happenings that make proximate causes effective.

Study Questions

1. How is science best described as what scientists do?

2. What are empirical phenomena and what does it mean to say that data are objective, reliable, and quantitative?

3. What are some problems with the scientific analysis of subjective, unreliable phenomena?

4. What are functional relationships, how are they related to scientific laws, and how do scientists use them to understand natural phenomena?

5. What is the relationship between control and prediction in science?

6. What is the doctrine of determinism and what are some implications for human behavior?

7. How are scientific claims tentative, how is science self-correcting, and why are these characteristics strengths of the scientific approach to understanding?

8. What is meant by *theory* in science? What should a sound scientific theory be able to do? What are theories based on analogies, and what are the problems with them?

9. What are the five criteria used to evaluate scientific theories?

10. What is the difference in predicting and explaining events inside and outside the laboratory?

11. What is scientific interpretation and what makes an interpretation more plausible?

12. What are the four types of scientifically inadequate explanations of behavior? What makes an explanation untestable?

13. What constitutes a scientifically adequate explanation of behavior?

14. What are proximate and ultimate causes of behavior and how can proximate causes be thought of as a chain of events?

Research
Methods

3

How do scientists know what they know? The answer isn't as easy as it appears at first glance. For example, consider the following questions:

1. Is nicotine addictive?
2. Is homosexuality, or alcoholism caused genetically?
3. Does cocaine addiction produce withdrawal symptoms like those in heroin addiction?
4. Does parental neglect of infants cause autism?

Social psychologist Thomas Gilovich (1991) points out that most people believe they know the answers to these and many other questions, regardless of scientific evidence. How do scientists get their evidence? By conducting research, especially experimentation. Chapter 1 described how the use of experimentation by early scientists such as Galileo and Newton laid the groundwork for other sciences. Chapter 2 stated that science is what scientists do and then described generally what they do—research—in the search for orderly cause-and-effect, or functional, relationships between events. This chapter describes some different approaches to doing research, but emphasizes one—experimentation—that has proven to be most successful in revealing functional relationships. The term *research* is used by different people to describe a wide range of activities that sometime bear little resemblance to one another. Therefore, we begin by defining the term.

What Is Research?

In general, the term **research** refers to *a systematic way of asking questions and gaining information,* with an emphasis on the word *systematic.* Many people ask questions and attempt to answer those questions by looking for information. Only scientists do so in a systematic manner and according to certain guidelines. It is in following certain rules of conduct that the scientific approach to doing research is different from other approaches. The information gained through scientific research, called **data** (a plural noun; the singular is *datum*), forms the foundation of all of the sciences, including psychology.

In psychology, as in the other natural sciences, research can be classified as either applied or basic. The sole purpose of **basic research** in psychology is to gain information about behavior and the variables that affect it. The purpose of **applied research,** on the other hand, is to gain information that directly and immediately benefits others. If, for example, a psychologist attempts to answer the question "Can high blood pressure be lowered by teaching patients self-relaxation?" it is *applied research* because it directly addresses a clinical problem (hypertension). In contrast, a study designed to evaluate whether an experimental drug improves memory in monkeys would be considered *basic research*, because the results of such a study have no immediate clinical

Much of the material in this chapter is based on Poling, Methot, & LeSage (1995).

significance for humans. Basic research may, however, yield findings that are clinically important. If, for instance, the experimental drug improved monkeys' memory without producing adverse reactions, one might reasonably suggest a future role for it in treating Alzheimer's disease and other conditions involving deterioration of memory. Testing that speculation would require further research with Alzheimer's patients, which would make the research applied because of its direct and immediate benefit to people suffering from the disease. Table 3-1 provides some examples of basic and applied research.

We have indicated that there are many ways to conduct psychological research. Moreover, the types of research strategies employed by a psychologist are influenced by many things; perhaps the most important is the *researcher's training and experience.* For example, the research questions and methods favored by a cognitive psychologist are likely to differ substantially from those used by a behavioral psychologist. The research question influences how a study is conducted. Although it rarely dictates specific procedures, the research question does limit the range of general strategies that are justifiable. Another factor that influences how research is conducted is the *availability of resources*—personnel, time, money, equipment, and subjects. In the last several years, shrinking budgets, both in university and government settings, have seriously affected the amount and kind of research that psychologists conduct. *Ethical and legal considerations* also affect how research is conducted. A researcher interested in the effects of child abuse on subsequent sexual activity obviously could not conduct a controlled investigation in which some children were intentionally abused and others were not. Rather, existing groups would have to be examined, and the nature of the study would be determined, in part, by legal and ethical concerns. In this case, the researcher would be forced to

Table 3-1
Examples of Basic and Applied Research

Basic Research:
1. A study evaluating the effects of room temperature on the air speed of honeybees.
2. A study using Pavlovian conditioning procedures to condition eye blinks in humans to a tone.
3. A study demonstrating that the "runner's high" can be blocked by administration of the drug naloxone.
4. A study showing that monkeys deprived of maternal attention early in life fail to develop normal patterns of sexual behavior as adults.
5. A study evaluating whether electroconvulsive brain stimulation interferes with short-term memory in dogs.

Applied Research:
1. A study using nicotine fading procedures on smokers to eliminate cigarette smoking.
2. A study showing that a self-monitoring procedure can be used by students to increase time spent studying.
3. A study employing contingency contracting to increase the productivity of factory employees.
4. A study demonstrating that the drug naloxone dramatically reduces self-injury in autistic children.
5. A study showing that electroconvulsive brain stimulation is effective in reducing depression in adult humans unaffected by other treatments.

---

rely on nonexperimental methods, which are one of two general tactics of scientific investigation. The other general tactic, experimentation, is preferred whenever possible, and is discussed first and in greater detail.

Experimentation

As noted in Chapters 1 and 2, scientific psychologists search for variables that lawfully influence behavior. Experimentation aids in this search by providing an especially powerful method for determining relationships between behaviors of interest and other events.

In **experimentation,** researchers systematically alter one variable, called the **independent variable,** and look for changes in another variable, called the **dependent variable.** Thus, we may say that changes in dependent variables *depend* on changes in the independent variable. In psychological experiments, behavior is always the *dependent variable* (DV), and any event that can be manipulated by the experimenter in an attempt to alter behavior is the *independent variable* (IV). In applied research, dependent variables often are referred to as **target behaviors** and independent variables are termed **treatments** or **interventions.** Table 3-2 lists several experimental questions in which the independent variable is underlined and the dependent variable is italicized. It is important to recognize that the terms *independent* and *dependent variable* are appropriately applied only when a variable is actually manipulated. If this is not the case, as occurs in nonexperimental research, there is no independent variable or dependent variable. For example, in some developmental research (see Chapter 11), researchers are interested in the relationship between a child's age and the onset of certain developmental changes, such as the initial age at which children begin to walk or talk. Researchers measure the ages of children and observe whether the behavior of interest occurs or not. Because someone's

Table 3-2
Research Questions with the Independent Variable Underlined
and the Dependent Variable Italicized.

1. How is *rate of lever pressing* in food-deprived rats influenced by <u>amount of food delivered</u>?
2. How does <u>Ritalin</u> influence *attention span* in normal adults?
3. Does <u>participating in an exercise program</u> alter *self-ratings of mood* in mildly depressed college students?
4. Does *reported condom use* by male homosexuals change as a result of <u>reading a pamphlet about AIDS</u>?
5. What is the relationship between <u>number of violent episodes in a cartoon</u> viewed by preschool children and their subsequent *physical aggression* toward peers?
6. Does *water intake* by rodents change as a function of <u>electrical stimulation of the ventromedial hypothalamus</u> in the brain?
7. Does *amount of merchandise stolen* from a convenience store change as a function of <u>posting warning signs</u>?
8. What is the relationship between <u>amount of sleep deprivation</u> and *reaction time* in adult humans?

age cannot be manipulated, age cannot be an independent variable, and researchers cannot conduct true experiments, but must rely instead on correlational methods (see below).

Although specific experiments differ widely and some are quite complex, the logic of the experimental method is straightforward: One determines whether an independent variable affects a behavior by manipulating different values of the independent variable, or treatment, and measuring the effects they may or may not have on the behavior of interest.[1] The researcher controls the value of the independent variable and also ensures that **extraneous variables,** which are factors other than the independent variable that might alter the dependent variable, are eliminated or held constant across conditions. Therefore, if values of the dependent variable differ when the independent variable is or is not operative (or is operative at different values), it is logical to assume that the independent variable determined (or caused) changes in the dependent variable (the effect).

Functional Relationships

If the value of a dependent variable varies systematically with the value of an independent variable, the two are said to be **functionally related.** Figure 3-1 shows several types of functional relationships. Once experimentation reveals that a dependent variable is functionally related to (controlled by) an independent variable, prediction of the dependent variable becomes possible.

Once the value of the dependent variable can be controlled in an experimental setting (through basic research) it can then be changed by manipulating the value of the independent variable in other settings (through applied research). The practical value of basic scientific research stems from the isolation of independent variables that can be manipulated in the natural environment and thus can change behavior (the dependent variable) in a clinically significant fashion.

Steps in Experimentation

Although something of an oversimplification, it is convenient to think of experimentation as involving a sequence of seven kinds of activities

1. Making Initial Observations

The scientific researcher, like the ordinary person, initially gains information about a general phenomenon of interest through day-to-day activities. For the researcher, these may include contact with other scientists (in person or

---

[1]Researchers often measure two or more dependent variables in a single study. This complicates data analysis, but does not change the logic of experimentation. To simplify for explanation, we will emphasize studies in which the effects of one independent variable on one dependent variable are evaluated.

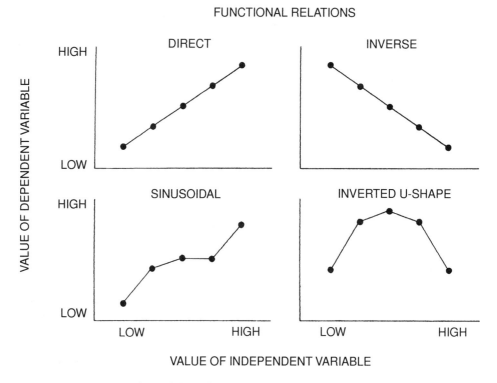

Figure 3-1. Hypothetical data showing four types of functional relationships.

through reading scientific journals or books), specialized training, or naturalistic observation. The difference between the scientist and the ordinary person, however, is that the scientist's specialized training usually makes her or him a more astute observer of events. For example, after doing decades of physiological research, Pavlov was perhaps in a better position to notice his subjects' learned reflexes (salivation before the food was presented). The information scientists gain suggests that some measurable variable may affect behavior in an interesting fashion. Pavlov's observation suggested that some other stimulus, such as the sound of a tone, might elicit salivation. The researcher then decides to explore whether there is, in fact, a relationship between the behavior and the independent variable.

2. Formulating the Experimental Question

The next step in experimentation is formulating an experimental question. The experimental question is "a brief but specific statement of what the researcher wants to learn from conducting the experiment" (J. M. Johnston & Pennypacker, 1993, p. 366). The formula of such questions may be as simple as "I wonder what will happen to B if I manipulate A." Questions may also hypothesize an answer: "I predict B will change in a certain direction if A is manipulated in a certain way." During B. F. Skinner's early career as an experimenter, the device that he used to deliver food to the rats when they made a response malfunctioned, resulting in a dramatic decrease in the response, which Skinner termed operant "extinction" (see Chapter 6). Skinner then intentionally tried to re-create the situation perhaps by asking the question "I wonder if I can produce the same effect by withholding food for responding"? The experimental question thus orients the study and dictates the kind of data to be collected. Table 3-3 provides examples of several experimental questions that scientific psychologists have examined recently.

3. Designing the Study

In designing a study, one deals with issues of selecting subjects, arranging conditions, collecting data, and analyzing data. The independent and dependent variables are carefully and objectively defined, and an experimental design is chosen that will provide the desired information concerning the relationship between those variables. To avoid ambiguity about particular independent and dependent variables, researchers typically use **operational definitions**, which define variables in terms of how they are measured. A clinical researcher interested in treating depression as a dependent variable might, for example, define depression in terms of a client's score on the Schedule for Affective Disorders and Schizophrenia for School-Age Children (Puig-Antich & Ryan, 1986), which is a semistructured clinical interview schedule. This is, of course, not the only way to define depression. Several other tests/inventories are available, and one could also use self-evaluations, ratings by significant others, or direct observations of behaviors believed to be related to depression (e.g., sleep disturbance, negative self-statements, crying). These different measurement systems would not necessarily

Table 3-3
Examples of Experimental Questions

---

1. What are the effects of behavioral parent training on parent and child feeding-related behaviors in the child's natural environment (Werle, Murphy, & Budd, 1993)?
2. How does performance under a piece-rate system in which 100% of the subject's pay is incentive-based differ from performance under a base-pay plus incentive system (Dickenson & Gillette, 1993)?
3. How does delayed reinforcement affect operant conditioning in untrained rats (Lattal & Gleeson, 1990)?
4. What are the effects of amphetamines on operant conditioning with immediate and delayed reinforcement (LeSage, Byrne, & Poling, 1996)?
5. What are the effects of Ritalin and a contingency-management intervention, alone and in combination, on the disruptive behavior of children with mental retardation (Blum, Mauk, McComas, & Mace, 1996)?
6. Does intermittent food delivery produce defecation in pigeons (Jarema, LeSage, & Poling, 1995)?
7. Does incentive pay improve the performance of garbage truck drivers (LaMere, Dickinson, Henry, & Poling, 1996)?

---

yield comparable information. Therefore, it is imperative that the researcher specify exactly the technique(s) used to quantify the dependent variable.

In psychology, researchers typically differentiate two general kinds of experimental designs, within-subject and between-subjects. Some psychologists refer to these designs as single-subject and group designs, respectively, which suggests that in the former typically only one subject is studied, whereas in the latter groups of subjects are used.

In a **within-subject experimental design,** the same subject is exposed to different levels of the independent variable, and the effects of that variable are determined by comparing the subject's behavior across different conditions. For instance, a researcher might test how different doses of alcohol might affect a college student's reaction time. The minimum number of subjects in a within-subject design is one, but the researcher may study any number of individual subjects. It is important that each subject be exposed to all values of the independent variable. In a **between-subjects experimental design,** different subjects are exposed to different levels of the independent variable and the effects are determined by comparing the behavior of the different subjects. In a between-subjects design the minimum number of subjects is equal to the number of different values of the independent variable, because each subject is exposed to only one value of the independent variable. Typically, however, several subjects (i.e., a group) receive one value of the independent variable. Hence, the name *between-subjects* designs.

Consider our experimental question "How does alcohol affect college students' reaction times?" An experiment could be designed as a within-subject configuration, in which researchers test students individually under conditions in which each student consumes different amounts of alcohol (e.g., 0 oz, 1 oz, 2 oz, 3 oz, and 4 oz), and then compare each person's reaction time across the different conditions (alcohol doses). In a between-subjects design, 50 students could be used in the study (although the experiment could be carried out with just 5 students—one for each value of the IV), with 10 of these students being tested at each alcohol dose (e.g., 0 oz, 1 oz, 2 oz, 3 oz, and 4 oz), and results compared across, or between, subjects (or groups).

Both within-subject and between-subjects designs have legitimate applications in a science of behavior, but within-subject designs are generally preferred whenever possible (Johnston & Pennypacker, 1993; Poling, Methot, & LeSage, 1995; Sidman, 1960). This is so, in part, for two reasons: (1) The only way to determine whether a given person responds favorably (DV) to a clinical treatment (IV) is to compare her or his behavior in the presence or the absence of the treatment, which demands a within-subject design; and (2) individuals often vary in their sensitivity to particular independent variables, which makes it harder to detect the effects of those variables with between-subjects designs.

There are some experimental questions that require a particular design (within- or between-subjects). For example, a researcher interested in the effects of different reading strategies on children learning to read would have to use a between-subjects design. This is because once a particular teaching strategy is used, even if it is only minimally effective, an individual child would have already learned how to read and would not be a good subject to test using another strategy. A researcher interested in four different reading programs would have to use at least four different subjects.

4. Conducting the Study

The researcher carries out the investigation, often changing the design across the course of the study as he or she encounters interesting data or unexpected problems. In many experiments, it is not possible during the design phase to specify exactly the conditions to which particular subjects will be exposed or the duration of their exposure to those conditions. The manner in which scientific research is conducted characteristically depends, in large part, on incoming data.

5. Evaluating the Data

The researcher examines the data in light of the experimental question and determines whether and how the independent variable affected the dependent variable. Data can be analyzed through visual inspection or statistical analysis. Although statistics can be used appropriately in scientific psychology, simple visual inspection of graphed data often is preferred (Johnston & Pennypacker, 1993; Poling et al., 1995; Sidman, 1960).

6. Determining Theoretical and Practical Implications

The researcher examines the study in its totality—the question asked, the design employed, the data obtained, the problems encountered—and makes a judgment concerning its importance and, consequently, whether the study should be presented to other scientists and the method of doing so. A given study is not often of earth-shaking importance, but a series of studies can have important implications and benefits for society at large. For example, after an initial report that monkeys not physically dependent on morphine would self-administer this drug (Thompson & Schuster, 1964), researchers have gone on to demonstrate that animals will self-administer most of the drugs that humans abuse (e.g., Poling, 1986). This finding suggests that humans use drugs because their short-term effects are rewarding (technically, they serve as positive reinforcers; see Chapter 6), not because the user is mentally ill, weak willed, or morally degenerate. It also suggests that changing the consequences of drug-related behaviors should be useful in treating drug abuse, a proposal that has been proven (e.g., Higgins et al., 1991).

7. Sharing Findings with Others

A study can benefit the culture that pays for it only when its results reach members of that culture. Data that are not disseminated cannot cause people to take action. Therefore, there is considerable pressure for scientists to share

Table 3-4
Five Features of a Meaningful Experiment

1. The experimental question must be reasonable.
2. The dependent variable must be adequately defined and measured.
3. The independent variable must be adequately defined and consistently manipulated.
4. Conditions must be sufficiently controlled to confirm that the independent variable, not something else, was responsible for observed changes in the dependent variable.
5. The results must be analyzed in an appropriate manner to determine whether the independent variable truly affected the dependent variable.

findings that they deem to have noteworthy theoretical or practical implications. Research projects usually culminate in the formal dissemination of findings. This is accomplished through conference presentations and publications. Conferences are professional gatherings, such as the annual American Psychological Society meeting, where people share information through posters, oral presentations, and discussion panels. Conference presentations allow for relatively rapid dissemination of information.

It is, however, the peer-reviewed journal article that provides the most important outlet for scientific findings. The information contained in an article accepted for publication is deemed to be of scientific importance by the editorial board of the journal (peer review), and scientific psychologists are judged, in large part, according to the quantity and quality of the articles that they publish.

There is, in principle, nothing especially difficult about designing and conducting a psychological experiment. The essential features of a meaningful study, however, can be reduced to five (summarized in Table 3-4). If these features are present, and if the relationship between the independent and dependent variables is reasonably clear, then the experiment has advanced our understanding of behavior and its controlling variables.

Important Features of Research Findings

Before scientists make any claims about their results, they must take care to answer two important questions concerning the **reliability** and **generality** of those results: (1) Can similar results be reproduced under conditions essentially equivalent to those of the original study? and (2) Can similar results be produced under conditions that differ in one or more aspects from those of the original study? There is no way to know whether experimental findings are reliable except through conducting **direct replications** of the study, which are studies that essentially duplicate the conditions of the original investigation. Therefore, the results of any single study must be interpreted with caution. *In science, repeatability is tantamount to believability.* Relationships that can be reproduced are accepted; those that cannot are rejected. As you will recall from Chapter 2, science is fallible, but self-correcting. For example, cold fusion generated considerable attention in the media a few years ago, but it is ignored today because other scientists could not replicate the findings of the original study.

Once it becomes clear that particular experimental findings are reliable, the issue of generality arises: Under what other conditions can those findings be reproduced? Regardless of how a study is conducted, it is impossible to know, without further testing, the range of conditions under which its results can be reproduced. The only way that this generality can be evaluated is through a series of systematic replications of the original study. In a **systematic replication,** the independent and dependent variables are similar to those examined in the original investigation, but the studies differ in at least one significant aspect. That aspect constitutes the dimension along which generality is being assessed. Psychologists are often interested in whether similar results can be obtained with different subjects, different behaviors, and different settings (generality across subjects, behaviors, and settings), among others. Researchers should not speculate about the possible generality of their findings, because educated guesses are not very convincing to scientists. Rather, generality should be demonstrated by providing clear experimental evidence and showing exactly how systematically manipulating the variable affects the results (Johnston & Pennypacker, 1993, p. 355).

An Example of Experimental Research: Facilitated Communication

To illustrate the activities necessary in experimentation, we will consider a study conducted by Wheeler, Jacobson, Paglieri, and Schwartz (1993) which was one of the earliest rigorous evaluations of a popular technique used primarily with people with autism to help them to communicate. The technique is called facilitated communication (FC). Before we describe the Wheeler et al. experiment, we present a little history of FC.

Facilitated communication is a procedure in which a facilitator provides physical assistance to enable a client with severe communication impairments to spell words by touching letters on a computer keyboard or similar device (Biklen, 1990). The assumption is that the words spelled are initiated by the disabled person, who is cognitively able to communicate but is not physically able to do so without assistance.

Facilitated communication was developed in the 1970s by an Australian teacher, Rosemary Crossley. In the late 1980s, her methods came to the attention of Douglas Biklen, a professor of education at Syracuse University. Biklen was greatly impressed with the utility of FC, and was largely responsible for popularizing it in the United States and Canada. In a 1990 article based on observations of 21 Australian citizens said to be autistic, Biklen reported that their facilitated communications often were sophisticated in structure and content, which indicated to him that autism was not really a problem of cognition, but of voluntary motor control. His message, in essence, was that people with autistic impairment were essentially like everyone else, except for physical limitations that prevented them from communicating normally. According to Biklen, FC enabled autistic individuals to overcome their physical limitations, revealing previously hidden intellectual capacities. It thereby allowed autistic people, and others with communication disorders, to reveal their true thoughts and feelings. Green (1994) summarizes the initial impact of FC:

> Biklen's message was well received in many quarters: Soon after publication of Biklen's article, special education personnel . . . adopted FC [facilitated communication] enthusiastically. Scores of children with disabilities were placed in regular classrooms doing grade-level academic work with "facilitation." Decisions about the lives of adults with severe disabilities—living arrangements, medical and other treatments, use of hearing aids, and so on—were based on "facilitated" messages. . . . In many cases FC supplanted other communication modes. . . . [Some professionals] began to give IQ [and other] tests with "facilitation," changing diagnoses and program recommendations in accordance with the "facilitated" results. Individuals who had significant delays before FC were proclaimed to have average or above-average intelligence. "Facilitated" counseling and psychotherapy were promoted to help FC users deal with personal problems. Millions of tax dollars were invested in promoting its widespread adoption. (p. 73)

The news media was quick to report seemingly miraculous successes achieved through the use of FC, and Biklen, Crossley, and their associates published several journal articles describing remarkable verbal outputs by people diagnosed with severe autism, mental retardation, and other conditions. Some of the messages revealed through the FC stated that the autistic individuals had been abused (sexually or in other ways). This led to a variety of harsh actions against the alleged abusers. School personnel lost their jobs, family members were required to leave the home where the autistic person lived, and criminal charges were brought against accused parties.

From the time FC first became popular in Australia, critics suggested that the facilitator, not the client, was responsible for the content of the messages. Many professionals raised this point even as FC exploded in popularity in North America. They further contended that Biklen and other advocates of FC had failed to provide experimental proof that the client, not the facilitator, was responsible for the content of the messages (e.g., Mulick, Jacobson, & Kobe, 1992; Prior & Cummins, 1992; Thompson, 1993). Wheeler and his associates decided to put the validity of FC to the experimental test.

1. Making Initial Observations

Wheeler and his colleagues (1993) had witnessed the use of FC at an autism program where 25 clients used facilitated communication. The researchers also were aware of the dramatic claims made for FC, and the observations that supported those claims. In essence, those observations repeatedly seemed to indicate that messages of remarkable sophistication and significant content were produced by client-facilitator teams. Wheeler and his associates themselves initially assumed that the clients were responsible for the content of messages.

2. Formulating the Experimental Question

Wheeler and his colleagues (1993) were aware of two possible explanations for those observations. One was that the clients were primarily responsible for the content of spelled messages (their initial assumption). The other, of course, was that the facilitators were primarily responsible. Either of these possibilities was tenable. Fortunately, experimentation provides a ready way of testing the alternative predictions, and several researchers, among them Wheeler and his colleagues, set out to do the necessary tests. They did so in the context of a picture-naming task, and their experimental question was "Are the clients or are the facilitators primarily responsible for the content of messages in a picture-naming task?"

3. Designing the Study

The researchers selected from those clients the 12 people who were the most competent producers of FC. The experimental task involved having a researcher present pictures of objects and ask clients to name the objects. The client and facilitator sat side by side at one end of a table and the researcher sat at the other end. Partitions were arranged so that the client could not see the picture presented to the facilitator and vice versa. Three different experimental conditions were arranged. In one, the client was presented with a picture, no picture was presented to the facilitator, and the client was asked to identify the picture through FC. In a second, the client was presented with a picture, no picture was presented to the facilitator, and the client was asked to identify the picture without the use of FC. Here, the facilitator could use verbal prompts, but could not provide physical assistance. In a third condition, both the client and the facilitator were presented with cards. On half of the trials, the cards were the same; on the other half, they were different. Each client took part in two sessions under each of the three conditions, with each session composed of a total of five trials (picture presentations). The same 30 pictures, which showed common objects (e.g., a pair of shoes, a jacket) were used with all clients. The order of exposure to conditions differed across subjects, as did the pictures presented during particular conditions.

4. Conducting the Study

The design of the study was simple, and the researchers appeared to encounter few problems in carrying it out. They did, however, report that it was not always possible to present five pictures per session (one block of trials) and to arrange a single session per day for each client, because of the clients' limited attention span or distractibility. They also indicated that it was occasionally difficult to determine whether objects were named correctly, as when the word "food" was typed and the picture viewed by the client showed bread, or when "vehicle" was typed and the picture depicted a van. This was not a serious problem, because it occurred so rarely that it did not alter the interpretation of results.

A simulation of the facilitated communication technique (bottom) and one form of a double-blind research design in which the facilitator and client each view different cards (top). Photos courtesy of Gina Green and the New England Center for Children.

5. Evaluating the Data

Data were described in terms of the number of correct responses (the dependent variable) that occurred under the various experimental conditions. Comparing the accuracy of performance across the three conditions of interest (the independent variable) supported three conclusions. In general, with respect to the objects shown to the client:

1. Objects were named correctly only when they appeared in both the picture shown to the client and in the picture shown to the facilitator.
2. Objects were never named correctly when they appeared only in the picture shown to the client.
3. Objects were never named correctly when different pictures were presented to the client and the facilitator. In this case, object names reflected the picture presented only to the facilitator (i.e., were accurate from the facilitator's perspective).

Although Wheeler and colleagues (1993) provided a statistical analysis of their data, such analysis was not necessary to detect the patterns in the data that supported the foregoing conclusions. For instance, with respect to clients' accuracy in naming objects that they alone viewed, Wheeler and colleagues indicated, "Of these 180 trials [15 for each of 12 participants], there were no clear correct responses to the participant's stimulus card [picture]" (p. 54). This is overwhelming evidence in support of the second conclusion listed above, that is, the facilitators were primarily responsible for the content of spelled messages.

6. Determining Theoretical and Practical Implications

The implications of this study are far-reaching. Obviously, under the conditions arranged by Wheeler and colleagues (1993), the facilitated communications (naming pictures) were authored by the facilitator, not by the client. That is, the facilitator, not the person with autism, was responsible for the content of the typed messages. Wheeler and his colleagues were careful to point out that their findings did not suggest that facilitators intentionally controlled the content of messages, and emphasized that facilitators appeared to be unknowingly determining what was typed.

Nonetheless, their results indicate that information revealed through FC should not be accepted as originating from the client unless there is other objective evidence to support the claim. Evaluating the content of messages under anything other than controlled conditions is inadequate to determine authorship and provides no compelling proof of validity.

7. Sharing Findings with Others

Wheeler and colleagues (1993) published a description of their study in the journal *Mental Retardation*. Articles that appear in *Mental Retardation* are likely to be read by researchers and academics, but not by teachers and parents.

Further Reports on Facilitated Communication

Although the study by Wheeler and colleagues (1993) casts serious doubt on the validity of FC, it is of course possible that for unknown reasons their findings are limited in reliability or generality. Given this, and the obvious implications of FC for the treatment of people with autism and other handicapping conditions, it is fortunate that several related studies have also appeared. These studies differ substantially in many respects, including the kinds of tasks involved, the characteristics of clients and facilitators, and the type of experimental design; in other words, they are all *systematic replications* of the Wheeler et al. study. And they are consistent in their outcome, as Green (1994) relates:

> Recently I analyzed reports of 17 controlled evaluations of FC that have appeared or have been accepted for publication in peer-reviewed professional journals, and 8 presented at scientific conferences. . . . None of these controlled evaluations produced compelling evidence that FC enabled individuals with disabilities to demonstrate unexpected literacy and communication skills, free of the facilitator's influence. Many messages were produced over numerous trials and sessions, but the vast majority were accurate and appropriate to context only when the facilitator knew what was to be produced. The strong inference is that facilitators authored most messages, although most reported that they were unaware of doing so. Fifteen evaluations found no evidence whatsoever of valid productions. A total of 23 individuals with various disabilities in 10 different evaluations made accurate responses on some occasions when their facilitators did not know the answers, but most of those productions were commensurate with or less advanced than the individuals' documented skills *without* FC. (pp. 76–77; emphasis in original)

In short, FC is not a significant advancement in the treatment of people with autism and other challenging conditions, and there is every reason to be skeptical of the contents of messages produced through this method. Those communications characteristically reveal far more about the facilitator than about the client. In recognition of this state of affairs, several organizations concerned with the proper treatment of people with disabilities have issued cautionary statements concerning FC. Among those organizations are the American Psychological Association, the Association for Behavior Analysis, and the National Association of School Psychologists.

Tragically, Biklen and his colleagues, as well as many parents, teachers, and others who work with children with autism, continue to argue that FC is a valuable technique. They contend that all of the experimental tests that have failed to validate the procedure are in one way or another flawed, and point to the remarkable successes obtained with the method. For reasons that can only be guessed at, perhaps including the personal gains they have realized by popularizing FC, they refuse to be swayed by the overwhelming preponderance of experimental evidence.

Experimental findings are of value only if people take them seriously and know how to interpret them. Unfortunately, many people know little about the methods of science, and are apt to be more swayed by apparent, though unsubstantiated, miracles than by experimental tests and skeptical analyses. The real tragedy is that such people may be unable to act in the best interest of themselves or their loved ones.

Nonexperimental Methods

Practical or ethical constraints sometimes make it difficult or impossible to conduct an actual experiment in which the value of an independent variable is manipulated and its effects on a dependent variable are observed directly. In such cases, nonexperimental methods may be used to gain meaningful information about behavior and the variables that influence it. Nonexperimental investigations serve to describe relationships among variables as they exist in the natural environment, but it is generally accepted that they are not adequate for supporting strong assertions about functional (or causal) relationships. Therefore, their role in a science of behavior is limited. Four types of nonexperimental methods are described here.

Correlational Studies

Unlike their experimental counterparts, researchers who conduct **correlational research** do not intentionally alter the environment of the subjects that they are studying. That is, the researcher does not manipulate the value of an independent variable. Instead, the researcher attempts to determine the relationship between two existing variables in a population. The general purpose of correlational research is to determine whether and to what extent the value of one variable is related to the value of the second. Does the value of A increase with the value of B? Does it decrease? Or are their values independent? In general, though, even if the presence of A is highly correlated with (predictive of) the presence of B, it does not mean that A *causes* B.

If the value of one variable increases with the value of the other, the two are said to be positively correlated. They are negatively correlated if the value of one decreases as the other increases. If there is no systematic relationship between them, the variables are uncorrelated. The degree and direction of correlation is expressed by a statistic that can range from −1.0 to 0 to +1.0. If the correlation is close to −1.0 or +1.0, the relationship is strong, and one can accurately predict the presence of one variable given another variable. As the correlation approaches 0, the accuracy of prediction decreases. If, for instance, the correlation between alcohol consumption (milligrams consumed per kilogram of body weight) and reaction time is 0.76, then squaring the correlation gives us the percentage of the observed variation in one variable that can be *explained statistically* in terms of the other. Thus, 58% ([0.76 × 0.76] × 100) of the variation in speed of reaction can be explained in terms of alcohol consumption. The remaining variance (42%) is the result of other, unknown, factors. So, because of other knowledge (experimental evidence) that we have about alcohol and its effects, it seems reasonable to assume that the positive correlation does reflect cause and effect.

But consider the situation in which a moderately high positive correlation (0.56) exists between the number of bars and the number of churches in United States cities. How can this finding be interpreted? Cautiously. Would we say that the number of bars causes the number of churches? Probably not. The reason for this relationship is uncertain. Perhaps the values of both variables are determined by the action of some other, unknown variable or set of variables (termed the *problem of the third variable*). This is probably the case: most people in U.S. cities both drink and go to church, and so as the size of the city increases so does the number of bars and churches.

As a general rule, *causality cannot be inferred from simple correlation alone*. Nonetheless, there are surely instances where a correlational relationship can *suggest* a causal one. This occurs when the relationship is a strong one and there is a plausible (and testable) mechanism whereby the value of one variable could determine the value of another, as in the alcohol and reaction time correlation. Another example would involve the possible adverse effects produced by various drugs and toxins. If a significant positive correlation exists between the adverse effect and exposure to the drug, then there is good reason to examine further the possible further effects of the substance and, in the interim, to institute steps limiting exposure to it. When ethical or practical constraints prevent researchers from conducting actual experiments to examine the substance further, trials with animals are often arranged. This was the approach taken to demonstrate that cigarette smoke actually is carcinogenic (cancer causing). Epidemiological studies found a high positive correlation between the level of exposure to cigarette smoke and the incidence of lung cancer, and subsequent experiments with nonhuman subjects confirmed the causal relationship that was implied in the correlation (Ray & Ksir, 1995).

Our culture is plagued by the misuse and misunderstanding of correlational strategies by certain researchers. The above mentioned dictum—causality cannot be inferred from simple correlation alone—is frequently violated. Consider the following example. Some have shown that scores on intelligence tests are correlated with height. And, more controversially, intelligence test scores have been compared in people of different races. Although statistically significant results have been reported—height and intelligence are positively correlated, and on average people of different races score differently on intelligence tests—the former result is a meaningless trifle. The latter result is subject to many conflicting interpretations, and has generated more heat than light, as the controversy over *The Bell Curve* (Herrnstein & Murray, 1994) so dramatically illustrates.

As stated previously, one problem with correlational data is providing a testable interpretation of them. Just as we can't manipulate height in a true experiment to test whether it really *causes* different scores on intelligence tests, we can't manipulate race in a true experiment to see whether it *causes* different scores on intelligence tests. In addition, it is possible (indeed, likely) that these correlations are better explained by the problem of the third variable. For instance, proper nutrition could be the third variable that causes both differences in height and different scores on intelligence tests. And with respect to race and scores on intelligence tests, the small correlational differences between the races can be better explained by variables such as proper nutrition, socioeconomic status, differing cultural variables, genetic susceptibility to disease, prenatal and postnatal care, the availability and quality of daycare, the quality of the schools, the availability of books or reading materials, the parents' educational levels. After all, we do know that many of these socioeconomic and cultural variables have an even larger correlational coefficient and, therefore, greater potential as causal agents.

Observational Studies

In an **observational study,** no experimental manipulation occurs and data are simply recorded under the conditions that occur in the natural environment. These conditions may differ substantially, however, and observational studies are often mistaken for true experiments. Observational studies provide less compelling demonstrations of relationships between variables than can be provided by true experiments. Observational studies have been carried out by well-known researchers such as Jane Goodall (with chimpanzees), Diane Fossey (with gorillas), Margaret Mead (with other cultures), and Jean Piaget (with children, see Chapter 11). In all of these instances, the research was almost purely descriptive, the what and the when, but not the how or the why; for that we need experiments, as in the FC case.

The previously mentioned reports by Biklen and his associates, in which messages produced via FC were described, provide a good example of observational studies. In this case, observational methods provided accurate information about *what* behaviors occurred—that facilitator–client pairs regularly type messages of remarkable sophistication under uncontrolled conditions is a fact—but those procedures were inadequate for indicating *how* or *why* those behaviors occurred. Either the client or the facilitator could be primarily responsible for the content of the messages, and observation alone does not allow one to certify or falsify either possibility. Controlled experimentation does so, however, and has allowed researchers to determine what actually occurs in facilitated communication.

Archival Studies

Archival studies make use of existing documentation as a data source. Usable information can be obtained from clinical records, quarterly reports, census banks, or any other permanent records kept by clinics, hospitals, businesses, governments or other organizations. Such sources sometimes provide meaningful information about behavior, and looking at data from such sources may suggest how behavior was affected by a particular environmental event. (Remember that archival data only suggest a cause; other evidence, usually experimental, would be necessary to confirm a cause-and-effect relationship.)

For example, Lavelle, Hovell, West, and Wahlgren (1992) used archival data in a study of child protection and law enforcement. They examined archival records of the number of tickets issued by police officers for nonuse of child safety seats. Police records from two communities were examined, one in which a program to target child safety-seat use was implemented and one in which no program existed. In the intervention community, officers were instructed on the importance of safety-seat use and were told to give drivers coupons redeemable for safety seats and waivers for fines (good if the recipient attended a special safety class) when issuing tickets for seat infractions. Three years of baseline data were examined for the intervention community, followed by 6 months under the safety-seat program and 12 subsequent months after withdrawal of the program. A second community, in which conditions did not change systematically across time, was monitored over the same period (i.e., 54 months). The archival data, presented graphically in Figure 3-2, show that officers in the intervention community had a much higher rate of issuing tickets for nonuse of child safety seats during the intervention period compared to baseline levels.

Levels of ticket writing dropped during the reversal phase but were maintained at a higher rate than during the initial baseline period. Officers in the

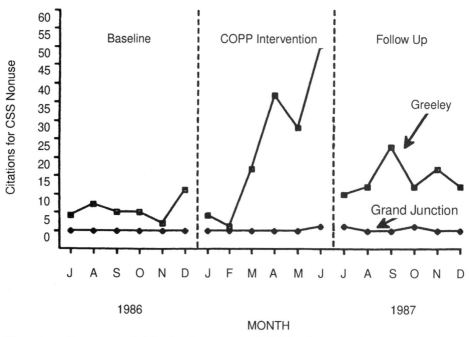

Figure 3-2. Frequency of ticketing for nonuse of child safety seats (CSS) by Greely (intervention site) and Grand Junction (control site) officers for the 6-month baseline, intervention, and follow-up periods. Officer training began at the beginning of the intervention (COPP) phase for the Greely group only and was completed within 8 weeks. (From "Promoting Law Enforcement for Child Protection: A Community Analysis," by J. M. Lavelle, M. F. Hovell, M. P. West, and D. R. Wahlgren, 1992, *Journal of Applied Behavior Analysis, 25,* 885–892. Copyright 1992 by The Society for the Experimental Analysis of Behavior. Reproduced by permission.)

comparison community maintained low levels of citations for nonuse of safety seats throughout the 54 months. These results certainly suggest, as Lavelle and colleagues (1992) pointed out, that the program affected ticket-writing behavior. This conclusion is reasonable, even though the investigators themselves did not manipulate an independent variable, or even plan a prospective study. Rather, they took advantage of an existing body of information to draw their conclusions.

Although archival data can support meaningful conclusions, one should be aware of the limitations of such data. First, the content included in archival records should always be held suspect. What goes into a permanent record is often as much a function of who creates the document as of what actually occurred. Second, the completeness of records as they are maintained over time should be questioned. Documents are lost, thrown away, misfiled, and otherwise disappear, sometimes selectively (e.g., those that contain information that makes an organization look bad may be especially likely to turn up missing), making archival records incomplete, and potentially biased, sources of data. Third, errors in recording and transcribing can occur. Therefore, the accuracy of information contained in archival records should be verified wherever possible.

Surveys

A fourth type of nonexperimental investigation, the **survey,** is an organized way of obtaining information directly from people by asking them questions concerning their current and historical practices, opinions, and demographic characteristics. Either open-ended or closed questions can be used in survey research, and those questions can be asked in interviews or in questionnaires. Open-ended questions require respondents to supply answers in their own words. Closed questions limit response options through the use of checklists (e.g., check the foods that you eat weekly), Likert-type scales (e.g., circle a number from 1 to 10 indicating how satisfied you are with your job), ranking (e.g., list your top three fears), or yes/no options (e.g., have you ever smoked marijuana?).

The primary advantage of survey methods is that they are easy to use in obtaining anonymous information from large and widely distributed groups of individuals. Because survey methods can provide respondents with anonymity, they are often used to gain information about troublesome behaviors for which interventions are needed. For example, nationwide surveys of drug use indicate that cigarette smoking peaked in the United States in 1963 and has declined steadily since then (Maisto, Galizio, & Connoer, 1995). Nonetheless nearly 30% of respondents in the 1992 survey reported cigarette use in the past month (U.S. Department of Health and Human Services, 1993). Hence, further attention to stop-smoking and don't-start-smoking programs is warranted.

A serious disadvantage of survey methods is that the information reported may not be an accurate reflection of the actual behaviors of interest. The primary reason for this is that people's self-reports often are either inaccurate or untruthful. Moreover, surveys can be constructed so as to get certain "desired" responses from people to whom the survey is administered. For example, the question "Who will you vote for in the upcoming election?" will likely get a different response than "If the election were held today, who would you consider voting for as president?"

Like other nonexperimental methods, surveys can play a legitimate role in understanding human behavior. Such methods are valuable for obtaining information about how people behave and in suggesting why they behave as they do. They do not, however, provide especially convincing evidence of particular explanations of behavioral phenomena. As the example of facilitated communication demonstrates, controlled experiments provide far more convincing tests. Remember that where practical or ethical considerations do not allow for the use of experimental methods, proposed explanations of observed behaviors should be accepted tentatively and with caution, especially when other, equally plausible, explanations are possible.

Summary

1. The term *research* refers to a systematic way of asking questions, and the information obtained is called *data*. The purpose of *basic research* is to gain information about behavior and the variables that affect it, and the purpose of *applied research* is to directly and immediately benefit human beings.

2. In one tactic of research, called *experimentation,* researchers systematically alter one variable, called the *independent variable*, and look for changes in another variable, called the *dependent variable.* If the value of a dependent variable varies systematically with the value of an independent variable, the two are said to be *functionally related.*

3. The seven steps in experimentation are:

- Making initial observations.
- Formulating the experimental question.
- Designing the study, by using either a *within-subject* experimental design or a *between-subjects* experimental design.
- Conducting the study.
- Evaluating the data.
- Determining the theoretical and/or practical implications of the findings.
- Sharing findings with others.

4. Two important measures of the utility of a study are *reliability* and *generality.* A study is reliable if similar results can be produced under conditions essentially equivalent to those of the original study. A study has generality if similar results can be produced under conditions that differ in one or more aspects from those of the original study.

5. Experimental analysis revealed the treatment technique for people with autism called *facilitated communication* to be invalid and, thus, not the miracle cure its proponents claimed it to be.

6. Nonexperimental methods include *observational studies, archival studies, surveys,* and *correlational studies.*

Study Questions

1. What is the difference between basic and applied research and what are the factors that influence how a researcher carries out research?

2. What are the features of the research strategy called *experimentation* and how does it aid in discovering functional relationships?

3. What are the seven steps in experimentation?

4. What are the two important questions concerning the results of a study, how do researchers answer them, and what is the relationship between repeatability and believability in science?

5. What is facilitated communication and what is the point of discussing the experiment by Wheeler et al. (1993)?

6. What are nonexperimental methods of research, including observational studies, archival studies, surveys, and correlational studies, and what kinds of information can they produce?

Behavioral Causation

II

Phylogeny: Evolution and Behavior

4

Chapter 1 introduced Darwin's theory of evolution by natural selection and its corollary, the principle of common descent, which states that all species evolved from a common ancestor. That chapter also described how Darwin's theory of natural selection paved the way for a science of behavior, especially human behavior. Specifically, some researchers, including Pavlov, Thorndike, and Skinner, began to study nonhuman behavior in order to learn about human behavior. Doing so was based on the assumption that species differed from one another only by degrees, and not in fundamental ways. As a result, scientific psychologists discovered that humans and nonhumans possesssed similar learning processes confirming the evolutionary relatedness of all species.

But all species of animals also behave in ways that are distinctly their own, because such behavior results from an evolutionary history that is different from other species. Such behavior is called **species-specific** and it cannot in principle be studied using any other species. Both species-specific and non–species-specific behavior is influenced by evolution. The present chapter describes how evolution by natural selection—**phylogeny**—can influence behavior.

The Study of Individual Differences

Darwin's theory of evolution by natural selection dramatically changed the way we view human behavior. Before Darwin, scholars were mostly interested in how humans were similar to one another, that is, in their fundamental human nature. As we will see, interest in a biologically determined human nature has recently resurfaced in the discipline called evolutionary psychology. After Darwin, however, interest shifted to how humans were similar to nonhumans, at first in terms of mind and then, as mentioned in Chapter 1, in terms of behavior. Interest also shifted to how individual humans differed from one another, which became the study of individual differences.

Francis Galton

The person most responsible for the shift of interest in psychology to the study of individual differences was Charles Darwin's younger cousin, British psychologist Francis Galton. From his own experiences in school, Galton observed that not everyone had the same intellectual ability. Moreover, differences in intelligence, as measured by scores on tests, appeared to Galton to be inherited. As a case in point, even though Galton himself came from a very privileged background, he did not score as well on an important test at Cambridge University as did other students, some of whom presumably had less fortunate backgrounds. This and other experiences convinced Galton that intelligence must be, to a significant degree, inherited. Galton devised methods for studying intelligence (e.g., intelligence tests, statistical correlations), explained differences in intelligence in terms of inheritance, and suggested controversial social policies to increase positive psychological traits in humans (Fancher, 1996). Those policies merit attention.

Eugenics

In 1883, Galton introduced the term **eugenics** to describe attempts to improve human characteristics by selective breeding. Galton claimed that many desirable human characteristics, including intelligence, are inherited, and that inherited characteristics cannot be altered. Hence, attempts to educate intellectually inferior people are doomed to failure, and the only way to stop the menace of intellectual degeneracy is to prevent such people from reproducing. This analysis was claimed to be consistent with evolutionary theory as advanced by Charles Darwin, although it is not. Galton, however, argued his position convincingly and even offered evidence (such as the failure of persons with mental retardation to improve in institutions) in support of it.

Pedigree research in the vein of Henry Goddard's infamous Kallikak study was also used in support of the eugenics movement. In that study, Goddard described the descendants of "Martin Kallikak" (Goddard, 1912). Kallikak, a name fabricated by Goddard from Greek words meaning "good" and "evil," was a Revolutionary War soldier who fathered an illegitimate son by a feeble-minded girl. Goddard claimed to have identified 480 descendants of this son. Of them, 143 supposedly were mentally retarded. There was a high incidence of alcoholism, criminality, and promiscuity among the retarded and other descendants of Martin Kallikak and the feeble-minded girl. In contrast, these problems were not evident in the descendants of Kallikak and a woman of normal intelligence whom he married.

Goddard's study was egregiously flawed (see Gould, 1981) and, even if it were not, the fact that the two lineages were reared in very different environments prevents one from attributing any observed differences to genetic variables. Nevertheless, its results and those of other inadequate studies (e.g., those showing that southern European immigrants to America tested at Ellis Island performed poorly on English-language intelligence tests) were taken to indicate that feeble-mindedness was inherited. Social problems such as alcoholism, crime, poverty, and slums were interpreted as being caused by intellectually inferior people, and it was concluded that such problems would cease when such individuals were kept from having offspring. Although Goddard did not in principle oppose sterilization to accomplish this end, he thought that it would be unacceptable to society at large and instead opted for institutionalization (Gould, 1998).[1] Nearly one-half of the states in the United States did, however, pass statutes permitting involuntary sterilization of mentally retarded people and, by 1958, about 31,000 people had been legally sterilized (Sarason & Doris, 1969).

The eugenics movement culminated with Adolph Hitler, whose pogrom began with the killing of mentally and physically disabled people. It expanded

---

[1]In fairness to Goddard, we must point out that over time his position changed, and in a 1928 article he concluded: "Feeble-mindedness (the moron) is not incurable [and] the feeble-minded do not generally need to be segregated in institutions" (p. 225). Goddard argued in the same article that "morons" could benefit from training and education, which would enable most of them to live relatively independent lives.

horribly, until some 8 million Jews, Gypsies, disabled and other "undesirable" people were slaughtered in Nazi death camps between 1938 and 1944. This Holocaust in particular, and the eugenics movement in general, clearly and tragically illustrates how legitimate scientific theories can be selectively misconstrued, then used to provide intellectual support for social abuses. The problem in such cases is not with science, but with the people who selectively abuse its findings for their own gain. Hitler's genocide was not the result of Darwin's theory, nor of the shoddy early research suggesting that human behavior was determined by inheritance and impossible to change substantially. Rather, the idea of creating a supreme Aryan race by eliminating "undesirables" provided him with a convenient rationalization for doing away with people likely to cause difficulties for the Third Reich.

Although the eugenics movement was supported by some intellectuals, there was debate from the beginning about the extent to which behavior was determined by inheritance. You may recall from Chapter 1 that John B. Watson argued strongly that environment, not heredity, was the primary determinant of human behavior. He went so far as to assert:

> Give me a dozen healthy infants, well-formed, and my own specified world to bring them up in and I'll guarantee to take any one at random and train him to become any type of specialist I might select—doctor, lawyer, artist, merchant-chief and, yes, even beggarman and thief, regardless of his talents, penchants, tendencies, abilities, vocations, and race of his ancestors. I am going beyond my facts and I admit it, but so have advocates of the contrary and they have been doing it for many thousands of years. (1930, p. 104)

Prominent among the "advocates of the contrary" to whom Watson referred were Galton and other eugenicists. They emphasized inheritance (nature) as the primary determinant of human behavior, whereas Watson placed the environment (nurture) in this role. Even though a great deal of research over the last 70 years has clearly demonstrated the importance of the environment (nurture) in shaping human behavior, well beyond that which Watson could have imagined, some scientists and others continue to speculate about the limits placed on humans by their genes (nature).

The Nature–Nurture Question

Galton coined the phrase **nature–nurture** to distinguish between what a person is born with, or inheritance (nature), and what he or she acquires as a result of experience, or learning (nurture). Although most behaviors of most organisms reflect a combination of both phylogenetic (evolutionary) and ontogenetic (during the lifetime of the individual) causes, some specific actions may not. Therefore, questions about the role of nature versus nurture are meaningful, so long as they are not asked in an either–or manner, but rather in a to-what-extent manner. We begin by asking generally to what extent the different behaviors in humans are related to differences in their genes. In addition, we consider whether there are certain universal traits that make us similar to one another. In order to understand how *behavioral differences* and *behavioral similarities* between individuals could be "conditioned by the differences of their genotypes" (Dobzhansky, 1964, p. 55), that is, inherited, it is first necessary to understand how evolution works.

Although Darwin's theory of evolution by natural selection is now the universally accepted scientific theory of evolution of life on earth, it was neither the first nor the only theory of evolution that had been proposed.

Pre-Darwinian Evolutionary Theories: Lamarck's Theory of Evolution

Many people believe that Charles Darwin was the first to propose that life forms evolve, in the sense of changing across generations such that new species occur. In actuality, evolution in one form or another had been discussed since the time of Aristotle. By the time Darwin left on the *Beagle* in 1831, the idea of the evolution of species was "in the air," as Fancher (1996) put it. By this he meant that the idea of evolution was being discussed by some naturalists and philosophers in Europe, even though most members of the scientific establishment still vigorously embraced the anti-evolutionary notion that all species had been created in fixed and changeless form. What popularity there was for the concept of evolution was an outgrowth of the Enlightenment philosophy that nature was constantly changing and progressing up the ladder of life, the *scala naturae*, toward "nature's crowning perfection, humankind" (Leahey, 1987). The dominant theory of evolution before Darwin, that of the naturalist Jean-Baptiste Lamarck (1744–1829), reflected this philosophy. We present the basic features of Lamarck's theory, and its flaws, in part because many people still hold, erroneously, the concept of Lamarckian evolution.

Lamarck proposed that species were created spontaneously, as in the biblical view of creation, but they were not yet perfectly suited to their environments. According to Lamarck, organisms innately strive toward perfection (an example of the type of inadequate explanation, described in Chapter 2, called teleology), which they achieve by adapting to their environments. As individuals strive to adapt, they use some body parts (e.g., particular muscles) more or less than others, thereby changing the structure of those parts. When these changed organisms mate, their offspring inherit the changes that the parent(s) had acquired. Thus, Lamarck's theory stressed the **inheritance of acquired characteristics.** For example, the long necks of giraffes can be explained according to Lamarckian theory as follows: By attempting to reach leaves high on trees, an ancient generation of short-necked giraffes stretched their necks, making them slightly longer. When those giraffes mated, their offspring were born with slightly elongated necks. This process was repeated over many generations until long-necked giraffes, perfectly suited to eating leaves from tall trees, were the norm. At that point, evolutionary change ceased; perfection for giraffes had been attained. Through similar processes, each and every species on earth allegedly evolved into its present and presumably perfect form.

The fatal flaw in Lamarck's theory of evolution was that its central premise, that characteristics acquired in an individual's lifetime can be passed on to offspring, was shown to be false. They cannot: A woman and her mate can do bench presses until their pectorals bulge like melons, but doing so will have absolutely no effect on the muscularity of their children. Lamarck's theory of how evolution occurred was eventually replaced by Darwin's theory of natural selection.

Natural Selection, Inheritance, and Genes

As already stated, Darwin had been impressed by the extraordinary variety of life he saw on his voyage aboard the *H.M.S. Beagle,* and he proposed his now widely (but not universally; see Sidebar 4-1) accepted theory of evolution

---

Sidebar 4-1
Evolution in the Classroom

Although Darwin's theory of evolution by natural selection is universally accepted by biologists as well as most other scientists, it still faces resistance, mostly by religious fundamentalists. On June 19, 1987, the United States Supreme Court by a 7–2 vote struck down as unconstitutional a Louisiana act requiring its teachers to devote equal time to "creation science" if they taught evolution. Despite this ruling, the Tennessee legislature more recently considered a bill that would permit dismissing teachers who present evolution as a fact rather than a scientific theory of human origin. This is the latest, but unfortunately not the last, case in a long series of battles over the teaching of evolution in public schools. Those battles are instructive in demonstrating the great reluctance with which scientific fact is accepted, especially when it conflicts with traditional belief. And evolution is a scientific fact. Consistent observations by the thousands indicate that, as the well-known paleontologist Stephen Jay Gould (1987–88) affirms:

> The earth is billions of years old and its living creatures are linked by ties of evolutionary descent. Scientists stand accused of promoting dogma by so stating, but do we brand people illiberal when they proclaim that the earth is neither flat nor at the center of the universe? Sci-

ence *has* taught us some things with confidence! Evolution on an ancient earth is as well established as our planet's shape and position. Our continuing struggle to understand how evolution happens (the "theory of evolution") does not cast our documentation of its occurrence—the "fact of evolution"—into doubt. (p. 186; emphasis in original)

Gould's statement underscores an important question in this debate; namely, just what do scientists mean by theory? In these discussions of evolution, religious fundamentalists use the word "theory" as they would the words "guess" or "opinion." What most people don't know, however, is that when the word "theory" is used in science it means something quite different (see Chapter 2). In the natural sciences, a theory is derived from scientific facts. In a loose sense, theory is a way of organizing the facts; a scientific theory begins to take shape when the facts are ordered by scientists according to common features. As Gould implies, evolution is a fact or, rather, many hundreds of facts of geology, archeology, biology, genetics, and so on. Many of the details of *how* evolution occurred, that is, the *theory* of evolution, are still being worked out by scientists. Nonetheless, the evidence for natural selection as the general process is overwhelming.

by natural selection to explain the processes by which that variety came about. That is, Darwin's theory *explained* the so-called mystery of mysteries, the process(es) by which life forms became more varied and complex over time. Like other accepted scientific theories, natural selection provides the greatest understanding using the fewest concepts (parsimony) making it an elegant explanation. But why did Darwin's theory succeed where Lamarck's failed?

Darwin's Theory of Natural Selection

Although natural selection theory was derived independently by both Charles Darwin and Alfred Russell Wallace in the 1850s, it was Darwin's 1859 book, *On The Origin of Species by Means of Natural Selection,* that focused attention on evolution by natural selection and initiated what is now referred to as the Darwinian revolution. In general, **natural selection theory** states that (1) some individuals are more successful in producing offspring because of specific traits they inherited from their parents; (2) individuals born with other traits are less successful and produce fewer offspring; and (3) traits that contribute to reproductive success eventually accumulate in populations.

Natural selection theory is based on three principles: variation, selection, and retention (Donahoe & Palmer, 1994). The theory assumes that all individuals are born (or hatched) different from one another, and those differences (variations) can be passed along from parents to offspring (versus Lamarck's theory, which stated that the differences are acquired during an individual's lifetime and then passed on to offspring). The variations can appear in physical structure or in behavior. Depending on the environments in which animals live, some characteristics (traits) facilitate reproduction, whereas others hinder it. Traits that facilitate reproductive success are "selected for" and are retained across generations, whereas traits that hinder reproductive success are "selected out" and not retained across generations. So long as a particular trait increases reproductive success, that trait will spread through the population and become a defining part of that particular group of individuals, or **species,** which is a group of organisms that reproduce among themselves, but not with organisms outside that group.

Mendel's Principles of Inheritance

Although Darwin's theory explained *why* certain traits became more numerous in populations (species), he himself did not know *how* the traits were inherited (i.e., retained), that is, how they were passed from one generation to the next, or *how* they were translated into the physical characteristics of organisms.

Darwin's theory thus required a persuasive theory of inheritance. In 1866, an Austrian monk, Johann Gregor Mendel (1822–1884), proposed a theory of inheritance based on results from years of breeding experiments with pea plants. Contrary to the prevailing belief that inheritance involved the blending of hereditary material in the blood (a notion accepted by Darwin—remember that science is fallible, but self-correcting), Mendel proposed that hereditary factors are discrete units (particles) transmitted from each parent to the offspring. Each individual inherits two hereditary units, one from each parent, for each physical trait.

Mendel discovered that these hereditary units, which we now call **genes,** could assume slightly different forms (now called alleles). If an offspring inherited different forms of a gene (i.e., is *heterozygotic*), one form, which Mendel called dominant, would always override the other, which he called recessive, to determine the resulting physical trait. In order for the recessive form to determine the physical trait, an individual would have to inherit two copies of it (i.e., be *homozygotic*). For example, with Mendel's pea plants, yellow was dominant over green. Thus, a plant with one green gene and one yellow gene would produce yellow plants even though it possessed a green gene; only plants with two green genes produced green plants.

Although Mendel knew nothing of the molecular basis of genes (see the following discussion), he correctly described the facts of dominance and recessiveness and, relatedly, of heterozygotic and homozygotic genes. Eye color in humans provides another good example of these principles. Each human inherits two genes that determine eye color. Suppose that a person inherits a brown-eye gene (*B*) and a blue-eye gene (*b*). (By convention, the dominant allele is designated by a capital letter, and the recessive allele by a lower-case letter.) In humans, brown eye color is dominant over blue, which is recessive. This means that an individual needs only one brown gene (e.g., *B b*) in order to have brown eyes, but must have two blue genes (*bb*) to have blue eyes. Can you figure out how parents with brown eyes could produce a child with blue eyes? Figure 4-1 shows the possible results of the mating of two parents who are heterozygous for brown eyes.

Mendel's findings suggested for the first time that all of the genes an individual possesses, called its **genotype,** will not always be evident in an individ-

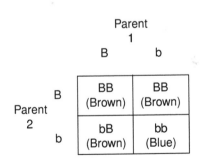

Figure 4-1. The possible outcomes of the mating of two parents who are heterozygous for brown eyes. On average, 75% of the offspring will have the brown genotype, which is dominant in humans, and 25% will have the blue genotype, which is recessive. (From *Psychology: A Behavioral Overview* [p. 80], by A. Poling, H. Schlinger, S. Starin, and E. Blakely, 1990, New York: Plenum Press. Copyright 1990 by Plenum Press. Reprinted with permission.)

ual's physical appearance, called its **phenotype.** In other words, you can't always tell what genes an organism carries by simply looking at the organism; you can't judge a genotype solely by its phenotype. Mendel's findings were consistent with Darwin's observations that offspring differ from their parents and that these differences are inherited. Unfortunately, Mendel's discoveries of the principles of inheritance, that is, how traits are passed from one generation to the next—the principle of retention—were unknown to Darwin and were lost to other scientists until the early 1900s, when they were rediscovered. Also in the early 1900s, more powerful microscopes were developed that enabled scientists to look directly at cells. What they found were **chromosomes** ("colored bodies," so named because they responded so well to the colored dyes used by scientists to make cell contents visible under the microscope).

Mendel's findings and the discovery of chromosomes were important for the concept of natural selection because they provided an answer to the question of how traits are transmitted from an individual to a descendant of that individual. These findings were incorporated into a reasonably comprehensive theory of evolution in the 1930s and 1940s. It encompassed Darwin's theory of evolution by natural selection, Mendel's theory of inheritance, and the observations of the actual genetic material in the cells of organisms (Mayr, 1978). But two questions concerning the basic nature of the hereditary material remained unanswered: (1) How is genetic material copied so that traits can be transmitted from parents to offspring? and (2) How do genes control the development of individual organisms? These questions were finally answered by a chemist, Francis Crick, and a biologist, James D. Watson, and their colleagues, Maurice Wilkens and Rosalind Franklin, with the Nobel prize–winning discovery in 1953 of the molecular structure of DNA.

DNA: The Essence of Life

Scientists now know that chromosomes are simply long strands of **deoxyribonucleic acid (DNA)** and are the physical carriers of genetic information. The DNA molecule contains the genetic information that is the recipe for the production of the proteins that make up all organisms. This discovery proved at the molecular level Darwin's claim that all species are descended from a common ancestor and are, therefore, related. The storage capacity of the DNA molecule is huge: If the *Encyclopaedia Britannica* could be genetically encoded, the DNA in a single human cell could hold all 30 volumes of it three or four times over (Dawkins, 1986). Watson and Crick (1953) discovered that the structure of the DNA molecule is like a **double helix,** that is, two threads, or "backbones," are twisted around each other like a spiral staircase (see Figure 4-2). Each DNA strand consists of a long sequence of molecules. The strands are connected at regular intervals (the rungs of the DNA ladder). Discovering the structure of the DNA molecule was the first step toward discovering its functions.

DNA molecules have two important functions: They make copies of themselves and they carry the instructions (or blueprints) for making organisms.

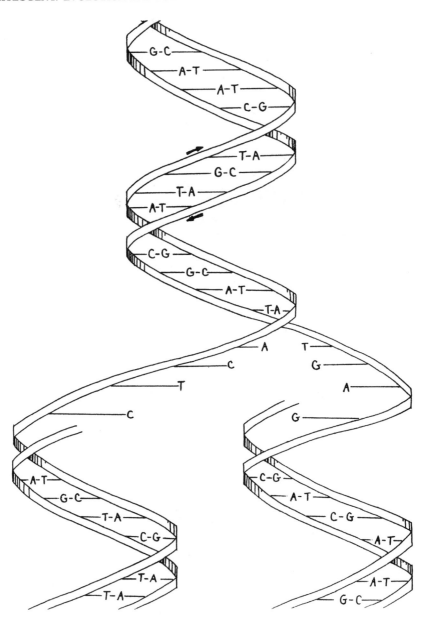

Figure 4-2. The DNA molecule, which looks like a spiral staircase (double helix) with the base pairs forming the steps, is shown here in the beginning stage of self-replication.

During DNA self- replication, the two strands "unzip" and separate, with each strand acting as a template for the construction of a new strand which is identical to the original (see Figure 4-2). This process occurs from birth to death in every cell of all living beings. The precision of DNA self-copying explains why every cell in the body carries the same genetic information and how genes can be transmitted without change over countless generations. For this reason, DNA has been called "the essence of heredity" (Futuyma, 1979) or "the essence of life" (Dworetzky, 1996). Mistakes do occasionally occur during DNA replication; these mistakes slightly change the structure of the molecule and, thus, the meaning of the code. Changes in the structure of the DNA molecule are called **mutations.** Mutations are responsible for much of the variation in traits upon which natural selection acts.

The second function of DNA is to direct the construction of organisms via the genetic code. It does so by making protein molecules, which are the building blocks of living beings. The DNA code is copied in the cell nucleus and then transported out of the nucleus into the cell's cytoplasm, where it is used to make amino acids, which, when grouped together, make protein molecules. Proteins are nothing more than long chains of (100 or more) amino acids. The protein molecules determine the structure and function of cells, for example, whether cells become liver, bone, skin, or brain.

Genes

In all of this talk about DNA replication and protein synthesis, you might be asking, "Where's the gene?" The term *gene* is used very liberally nowadays, almost to the extent of becoming meaningless. What do geneticists mean by "gene"? In a very broad sense, a **gene** is the basic unit of heredity, comprising a unique sequence of amino acids on the DNA molecule which code for the production of a single protein. It is a mistake, however, to assume that there is a one-to-one correspondence between genes and traits; that is, one gene = one trait (e.g., one gene for blue eyes, a second for diabetes, a third for schizophrenia). In actuality, single genes typically affect many different traits and each trait typically reflects the action of many different genes. Also, there are so-called master genes that regulate the activity of other genes. One such master gene, responsible for eye development in fruit flies, was recently discovered by scientists at the University of Basel in Switzerland. By experimentally manipulating the gene, the scientists were able to produce flies with eyes on different parts of their bodies, such as their legs and chest.

Evolution in Action:
The British Peppered Moth

The great diversity of life forms that so impressed Darwin resulted from the accumulation of genetic changes that have continued in populations (evolution of species) because they enhanced the reproductive success of organisms possessing them (natural selection). These genetic changes originated with mutations and have been continuously recombined to produce new sources of variation. We will now consider an example of evolution in action.

The story begins with the industrial revolution in England, and the burning of coal to fuel the fires of factories. Soot from the burning coal blackened the landscape near these industries. As a consequence, the British peppered moth, *Biston betularia,* developed "industrial melanism," or blackening (Kettlewell, 1973). Like most moths, the peppered moth flies at night. During the day it rests on tree trunks and other vertical surfaces. Originally, the common form of the moth was a whitish color with small black marks: On lichen-covered whitish-colored trees, the moth was camouflaged. Colin Patterson (1978) describes what happened to this moth's coloring with the coming of the industrial revolution:

> In all eighteenth- and early nineteenth-century insect collections, the moth had this [i.e., the whitish] coloration. In 1849 a single melanic or black example was caught near Manchester, and by 1900, 98 or 99 per cent of moths collected near Manchester were black. In the 1870s black individuals were still quite uncommon, but in the 1880s they already outnumbered the pale form. In the Manchester district, this change from a pale-colored population of the peppered moth to a 98 per cent dark population took about fifty years, and this period corresponds with the most rapid increase in human population of Manchester, and in the quantity of coal burned there. The same change occurred around other industrial cities, and also in some nearby rural, unpolluted areas. (p. 81)

How did most members of the species change from white to black? First, we may take for granted that, like most organisms, these moths produce more offspring than can possibly survive. The defining difference between the light- and dark-colored moths is the presence in the dark variety of a dominant genetic mutation which makes it black. The primary selective force operating on the moths is that they are eaten by birds. Those moths that stand out against their background are more likely to be seen and eaten than those that do not. The mutation resulting in black moths has presumably arisen spontaneously many times over many hundreds of years. If the mutation is dominant, then all first-generation offspring who inherit the mutant gene will be black. Against normal light-colored trees these moths would be easily seen and probably eaten by birds before they mated. Thus, the mutation would not provide the moths a selective advantage and would not be transmitted to offspring. In this scenario, the nonmutant gene resulting in white-colored moths would continue to predominate. Only when the trees became darker from the burning of coal would the mutation for black color confer a reproductive advantage and be selected. The moths that survived and produced offspring in this particular environment were the darker-colored ones which became common around Manchester.

This example illustrates that natural selection can be envisioned as a creative process that does not require a creator, in that it results in species that are well suited to the ecological niche that they occupy. If, however, that niche changes dramatically, disaster can occur. Consider this:

> Something happened 65 million years ago, at the end of the Cretaceous, something so devastating that it altered the course of life on earth. With seeming abruptness, as geologic time goes, almost half of the genera living throughout the world disappeared, animal life and vegetable, marine and terrestrial, large and small. . . . No species living exclusively on land and weighing more than twenty-five kilograms seem to have survived, and the most conspicuous of the nonsurvivors were the dinosaurs. Although

the fossils of a variety of dinosaurs are found in the uppermost Cretaceous rocks, none has ever been unearthed in the Tertiary layer just above. The dinosaurs had vanished, never to be seen again. Extinctions at the close of the Cretaceous rang down the curtain on the Age of Reptiles. (Wilford, 1985, p. 212)

The cause of this great dying is open to debate. One likely possibility first proposed by the Nobel laureate Luis Alvarez and his son, Walter, is that a sizable extraterrestrial object, perhaps an asteroid, collided with the earth (see Wilford, 1985). The collision spawned earthquakes and tidal waves and hurled into the atmosphere a cloud of dust that darkened the earth. Photosynthesis for the larger more light-dependent plants stopped and temperatures fell. Most species that depended on these plants as a food source were unprepared for this new and hostile environment—they had evolved in a different and more benign world—and did not survive.

Evolution and Behavior

Species-Specific Behavior

As stated in Chapter 1, one consequence of Darwin's theory of evolution by natural selection was that it permitted scientists to begin to view behavior as a biological function. Darwin himself suggested that, in addition to physical characteristics, behavior can aid in an organism's reproductive success. In this section, we discuss behavior, called species-specific behavior, that is similar within a particular species but differs between species.

As the name implies **species-specific behaviors** are behaviors of members of one species that differ from those of another species because each species has different genes (resulting from different evolutionary histories). The study of species-specific behaviors is typically carried out by scientists called ethologists. Ethology has been called the biological study of behavior. But this definition is too broad, because it can be argued that scientific psychologists also study behavior biologically. So how does ethology differ from scientific psychology?

What distinguishes the ethological study of behavior from the psychological study of behavior are the types of behavior studied and the methods used to study them (Slater, 1985). Ethologists characteristically study relatively stereotyped (species-specific) behaviors that distinguish one species from another, and psychologists study behaviors that are thought to reflect general learning processes shared by many species. Ethologists typically study behavior in the animal's natural environment; psychologists often study the behavior of their subjects in controlled laboratory settings. In general, ethologists study the effects of *nature* (or phylogeny) on behavior, and scientific psychologists study the effects of *nurture* (or ontogeny) (Slater, 1985). Complete understanding of the behavior of any animal usually encompasses findings from both ethology and psychology. Just as ethologists must understand something about how learning may contribute to observed behavior, psychologists must understand something about an animal's natural behavioral inclinations, or its inherited behavior.

Inherited Behavior

A trait, whether behavioral or nonbehavioral, is said to be **inherited** if it has a genetic basis different from that of some alternative trait. For example, the sharpness of the canine teeth in lions results from genes that are different from those that produce duller teeth. During the evolution of lions, the genes associated with sharp teeth were selected over those associated with dull ones, probably because sharper teeth more successfully tear the flesh and meat of prey. While physical traits can obviously be inherited, three general types of behavioral relationships can also be inherited: reflexes, fixed-action patterns, and learning capacity. (Learning is discussed in Chapters 5 and 6.) We call them behavioral relationships, not simply behaviors, because they all involve relationships between environmental events and behavior. That is, unlike many inherited physical traits (e.g., sharp teeth), behavioral traits that are inherited cannot always be observed. Instead, they appear under appropriate environmental conditions, as described in the following discussion.

Reflexes

The term "reflex" is often misused as, for example, when we say that a driver reflexively puts his foot on the brakes. A behavior that occurs quickly in response to a stimulus is not necessarily a reflex. In scientific psychology, **reflexes** (also called unconditional reflexes) are *automatic, stereotyped responses to specific stimuli.* Contrary to the popular conception that a reflex is just a response, such as an eyeblink or a knee jerk, a reflex is the *relationship* between a stimulus (S) and a response (R). For example, the patellar (knee-jerk) reflex is not just a leg kick, but rather a leg kick (produced by contraction of the quadriceps muscle) (R) which is *elicited* (caused) by a tap on the patellar tendon (S). The stimulus (tap) is an environmental proximate cause of the response (leg kick) (see Chapter 2).

Another way of saying that reflexes are inherited is to say that they are unlearned. That is, they are due to phylogenetic, not ontogenetic, ultimate causes. The evidence for this is that they appear in similar form in all neurologically healthy members of a species. For example, if each of 50 healthy people places a hand on a hot stove, the odds are close to 100% that the heat will cause hand withdrawal in every one of them. How rapidly this happens will vary across people—there are individual differences even in reflexes—but the stimulus provided by the stove (heat) will elicit the same response (hand withdrawal) in every person. This will occur regardless of whether or not the person has had experience with stoves, or with extreme heat from any other source. Dozens of unconditioned reflexes are evident in humans. A sample of them is provided in Table 4-1. Note that many stimuli elicit a number of different responses.

Further evidence that reflexes are inherited comes from the observation that they are present from birth. In fact, several of them that are present early in life in humans later disappear (see Chapter 10). We may speculate about the origin of reflexes based on their function, just as Darwin did for the behaviors

Table 4-1
Some Unconditioned Reflexes Evident in Humans

Stimulus	Response(s)
Food in mouth	Salivation (glands)
Genital tactile stimulation	Penile erection, vaginal lubrication (smooth muscles, glands)
High temperature	Sweating
Irritation to nasal mucosa	Sneezing (smooth and striped muscles)
Irritation to throat	Coughing (smooth and striped muscles)
Light intensity increase	Pupillary constriction (smooth muscles)
Light intensity decrease	Pupillary dilation (smooth muscles)
Loud sound	Eyelids close, ear drums are pulled inward (striped muscles)
Low temperature	Shivering
Nipple stimulation	Milk release in lactating women (glands)
Painful stimulation of hand or foot	Hand or foot withdrawal (striped muscles)
Sudden and intense stimulation (described as painful or frightening)	Activation syndrome: heart rate and blood pressure increase, release of adrenaline and sugar into bloodstream, cessation of visceral muscle activity, vasoconstriction in periphery, vasodilation in skeletal muscles (smooth muscles, glands)
Tap to knee (patellar tendon)	Leg jerk (striped muscles)

and physical characteristics of various animals he observed. For instance, pulling one's hand away from a hot object prevents tissue damage. Closing one's eyes when an object approaches the face often does the same. And pupillary constriction prevents too much light from entering the eye. All of these reflexes have protective functions.

Fixed Action Patterns

Fixed action patterns are complex patterns of behavior evoked by certain stimuli called **releasers,** or **sign stimuli.** Fixed action patterns are similar to reflexes in that both involve stereotyped responses to specific stimuli that are displayed by all members of the species; that is, they are species-specific. They differ in that reflexes are relatively simple S–R relationships, usually involving very specific stimulus events, like a tap on the patellar tendon, and simple responses, such as contraction of the quadriceps muscle. Fixed action patterns, on the other hand, are more complex S–R relationships, like nest building, courtship, mating, and caring for young. Here, the stimuli that control behavior are complex and often multidimensional, and the responses they control involve many muscles and directed activity.

Consider the following example of two fixed action patterns in the male stickleback (a small fish), each evoked by similar releasers. The entry of a female in breeding condition into the territory of a male that has constructed a nest evokes a zig-zag dance in the male, but the entry of another male evokes a

A California gull (*Lárus califórnicus*) sits on a nest constructed as a result of a complex pattern of species-specific responses.

head-down threat posture. Because female and male sticklebacks look very similar, ethologists wanted to know exactly what stimulus features of the females and males released such different patterns of behavior in the male. In a classic experiment, the ethologist Niko Tindbergen (1951) used different models of males and females and discovered that the swollen belly of a ripe female was the critical stimulus for evoking the zig-zag mating dance, whereas the red coloration on the underside of the male was the critical stimulus evoking the attack posture. Each of these stimuli is a proximate environmental cause of a different species-specific behavior in the male stickleback.

Although we can't be sure, it appears that humans possess no fixed action patterns or, if they do, they have been overridden by human learning (see Liedloff, 1977 for an interesting hypothesis about this). The reason for such a conclusion is that there is a great deal of variability in human behavior related to courtship, mating, and caring for young. Moreover, there is no single stimulus that will evoke in each human a stereotyped (i.e., fixed) pattern of courtship, mating, or parenting. For example, there are substantial differences in how women behave toward their potential mates or their newborn infants.

It is possible that there are some universal behavioral traits in humans that are related to reproductive functions, but their existence is obscured by the great variability in human behavior that is caused by the vastly different social and physical environments that humans experience. The new discipline called evolutionary psychology makes a case for universal behavioral traits in humans, and we will examine that discipline later in this chapter. Before doing so, however, we will explore some of the methods scientists use to study the genetic bases of behavior traits.

Behavior Genetics

Behavior genetics is the study of the relationship between differences in genotype and differences in behavior (phenotype) in a population. Behavior geneticists use three general methods of investigation: crossing experiments, selection experiments, and studies of family resemblance (Brown, 1975). Crossing and selection experiments are used with nonhumans and studies of family resemblance are used with humans.

Crossing Experiments

In **crossing experiments,** organisms that differ with respect to a particular behavior are crossed (mated) while holding environmental factors as constant as possible, and their offspring are then examined. The most convincing evidence for the genetic determination of behavior is obtained by comparing individuals that differ by only a single gene.

One of the most frequently cited examples of a relatively complex behavioral difference resulting from a single gene involves the hygienic behavior of honeybees (Rothenbuhler, 1964). The Van Scoy strain of honeybee is susceptible to a particular type of bacterial infection, whereas the Brown strain is resistant. The Brown strain is resistant because of the cleaning behavior of worker bees, which uncap infected cells and remove the dead larvae, thus preventing the spread of infection. Van Scoy strain workers do not emit these behaviors. Rothenbuhler crossed members of each strain and showed that each behavior pattern (uncapping and removing) was controlled by separate genes (symbolized by U and R) and, moreover, that the genes determining the hygienic behavior were recessive. Therefore, bees homozygous for the recessive allele of each gene (i.e., *uu rr*) would both uncap cells and remove the dead larvae from the hive. Bees that were either heterozygous or homozygous for the dominant form of each gene (i.e., *Uu Rr*, or *UU RR*) would do neither.

In addition to these two groups, Rothenbuhler produced through crossing experiments: (1) Bees with the genotype *(Uu rr)*, which failed to uncap cells with dead larvae, but removed the larvae if Rothenbuhler lifted off the wax cell caps for them; and (2) bees with the genotype *(uu Rr)*, which uncapped the cells but failed to remove dead larvae.

Although studies such as those by Rothenbuhler are informative, few have been conducted, and their interpretation can be very complex. For example, although a single gene can affect behavior, it probably does so only "in a complex developmental process that requires the regulated interaction of dozens or thousands of genes" (Alcock, 1984, p. 36). Thus, in most cases, behavioral traits are **polygenic,** that is, they result from the integrated action of many genes. When single gene effects cannot be determined through crossing experiments, as is almost always the case, other methods must be used.

Selection Experiments

In the typical **selection experiment,** individuals from a genetically varied population are tested for a particular behavioral trait. Males and females with extreme scores are then selectively mated over a number of generations, thereby creating two distinct behavioral lines. Finally, the two lines are compared with randomly mated individuals to discern any significant differences across the three groups (Barnard, 1983). The term *selection* is used because these experiments mirror the process of natural selection, albeit on a much smaller scale. One of the pioneering selection experiments was conducted by Tryon (1940), who attempted to select for maze-running ability in laboratory rats.

Tryon first tested a diverse population of rats for their performance in running a maze. On the basis of the results he divided them into two groups: (1) "maze-bright" rats, which quickly learned to run the maze, and (2) "maze-dull" rats, which slowly learned to run the maze. Tryon then allowed only maze-bright males to breed with maze-bright females and maze-dull females to mate with maze-dull males over several generations. He tested the resulting progeny in the same maze and found that each generation of maze-bright rats ran the maze faster than the preceding generation. Similarly, each generation of maze-dull rats ran the maze more slowly than the preceding generation.

Although there is some question as to what was actually being selected (see L. V. Searle, 1949), Tryon's experiment provided evidence that there were heritable differences related to maze learning among the original population of rats. The selective breeding simply concentrated the genes responsible for these differences in one group and the genes opposing them in the other group. More recently, experimenters have selectively bred strains of mice and rats that consume large amounts of alcohol (e.g., George, 1987, 1990), suggesting that genes could play a part in alcoholism in humans. Other evidence for this possibility comes from studies of family resemblance (below) in humans (e.g., National Institute on Alcohol Abuse and Alcoholism, 1983; Petrakis, 1985). Still, there are many problems in generalizing such research to other species, including humans.

Studies of Family Resemblance

Ethical considerations prevent researchers from conducting crossing or selection experiments with humans, so the most persuasive evidence for heritability of human behavioral characteristics has come from studies of family resemblance. In such studies, a behavioral trait is observed in one individual and his or her biological relatives are observed for the same trait. In principle, if a trait is heritable, then that trait should appear more often in closely related individuals than in individuals who are less closely related. For example, assume that the ability to sing on key is heritable, and that one of a pair of monozygotic (identical) twins is observed to sing on key at a very young age and in the absence of obvious training. We could predict the presence of the ability to sing on key in the individual's biological relatives on the basis of the proportion of genes shared with him or her. Thus, the other identical twin, who shares 100% of the genes, would be expected to do so; the probability of other relatives doing so should decline with the percentage of genetic material shared with the person in whom the trait was initially observed.

The problem with studies of family resemblance is that biological relatives share not only genes, but often environmental histories as well. Hence it is difficult to determine what accounts for any observed consistency in behavior. If, for example, sons of fathers who abuse alcohol are more likely to abuse alcohol than other males, this might mean that (a) genotype contributes to the likelihood of alcohol abuse, (b) exposure to certain environments (growing up in a family where alcohol is abused) increases the likelihood of alcohol abuse, or (c) genotype and environment interact to determine the likelihood of alcohol abuse.

Special circumstances, such as adoption, help researchers to tease apart the contribution of genetic and environmental variables. Adoption reduces the degree to which siblings are exposed to the same environmental variables, making it more probable that any correspondence in observed behavior is the result of genotype. Studies of identical twins reared apart in different environments are especially informative, and are "the only really adequate natural experiment for separating genetic from environmental effects in humans" (Gould, 1981, p. 234). Identical twins reared apart in completely different environments are, however, exceedingly rare. Therefore, other strategies are characteristically used to try to disentangle the role of genetics and environment in controlling human behavior. Consider alcoholism, for example. As Petrakis (1985) notes:

> Separating the effects of environment and heredity is a fundamental problem in studying the genetics of alcoholism, and scientists have used various methods to solve it. One approach to separating these effects is to compare alcoholism rates among identical twins who were separated at an early age, with one brought up in an alcoholic home and the other brought up in a nonalcoholic home. Another is to compare alcoholism rates among identical twins versus fraternal twins. Yet another is to measure the rate of alcoholism among adopted-out children of alcoholics and compare it with the rate in a control group. All such approaches to varying degrees separate the effects of environment and heredity. For example, if separated identical twins tend to become alcoholic regardless of whether one of them is brought up by nonalcoholic adoptive parents, this favors the existence of hereditary factors in their alcoholism, since identical twins have virtually identical genetic makeup. Similarly, genetic factors are indicated if individuals with diverse genetic backgrounds are brought up in the same environment, as in the case of half-siblings, but show different susceptibility to alcoholism. Heredity is also implicated if people born to alcoholic parents, but removed from that environment at an early age through adoption, show a greater than expected rate of alcoholism. (p. 4)

Clearly, many different tactics are used in an attempt to disentangle genetic and environmental contributions to human behavior. The task is a formidable one, and some have argued that it is neither possible nor valuable (see Horgan, 1993 for a critical review of some of the evidence; e.g., Kamin, 1974; Lewontin, Rose, & Kamin, 1984). Nonetheless, there are data to suggest that some behavioral traits, such as intelligence, schizophrenia, and alcoholism, are to some degree heritable. It is worth emphasizing, however, that traits such as intelligence and alcoholism are difficult to define and measure, which complicates any attempt to determine how they are affected by either genotype or environmental variables.

Sociobiology and Evolutionary Psychology[2]

In the past few years, there has been a flood of books and articles offering evolutionary explanations for a variety of human characteristics, including intelligence, morality, mating, sexual preference, aggression, xenophobia, prejudice, and even our tendency to seek out various forms of nature by visiting zoos and national parks. Consider the following headlines:

Cheating Husband? Blame It On His Genes
Is There a Gene for Compassion?
Is Prejudice Hereditary?
A Scientist Weighs Evidence that the X Chromosome May Carry a Gene for
    Gayness.
IQ: Is It Destiny?

Headlines such as these are meant to capture the attention and imagination of readers, and they usually do. More important, readers are led to believe that such claims are supported by scientific evidence. The question for a scientific psychology is whether these claims reflect the results of serious science or just more "pop sociobiology" (Kitcher, 1985).

Sociobiology

The term **sociobiology** was coined by the biologist E. O. Wilson to refer to the systematic study of the biological basis of all social behavior (E. O. Wilson, 1975). In essence, sociobiologists suggest that some patterns of social behavior are inherited because, during the evolution of the species, such behavior was adaptive (i.e., increased reproductive success). They have, for example, proposed that in humans there is a genetic basis for sexual differences in behavior, including "male dominance" (e.g., Barash, 1977); for homosexuality (e.g., E. O. Wilson, 1978); and for altruism (e.g., E. O. Wilson, 1975). An account is offered

---

[2]Much of the material in this section is adapted from two previous articles by Schlinger (1996a, 1996b).

as to how each of these behaviors (phenotypes) might confer adaptive advantage, and hence lead to selection of the genotype responsible for it. For example, dominant males are more likely to get access to females with whom to mate, thus passing on the genes responsible for the dominant behaviors, whereas weaker males get fewer chances to mate.

Recently, the term *evolutionary psychology* has been used to refer to this approach to human nature (e.g., Cosmides & Tooby, 1987; Daly & Wilson, 1988; Symons, 1992; Tooby & Cosmides, 1989; Wright, 1994, 1995). Daly and Wilson (1988) suggest that the phrase **evolutionary psychology** be considered shorthand for theorizing about human psychology using modern evolutionary principles, such as those of natural selection and sexual selection. The range of issues about human nature that evolutionary psychologists have tackled is impressive indeed; it includes romance, love and sex; friendship and enmity; selfishness, self-sacrifice and guilt; social status; racism, xenophobia and war; deception and self-deception; sibling relationships; and parent–child relationships (Wright, 1994).

There have been many critiques of sociobiology (e.g., Futuyma, 1979; Kitcher, 1985) and, more recently, evolutionary psychology (e.g., Horgan, 1995; Schlinger, 1996a, 1996b). There have also been many critiques of the related assertion that human racial groups, such as blacks and whites, differ significantly because of genetic differences (e.g., Kamin, 1974; Lewontin, Rose, Kamin, 1984; Schlinger, 1996a, 1996b). Here we describe only a few criticisms.

One criticism of evolutionary theories of human behavior is related to the concept of adaptation. Evolutionary theories of behavior, whether human or nonhuman, rest on the assumption that an observed behavior (and the genes responsible for it) had some survival value for individuals possessing it. The problem with this assumption is as follows: Although evolution does shape species, including some behavior, it is a mistake to assume that all, or even most, of the characteristics of a species, whether physiological or behavioral, have a genetic basis and also that they somehow enhance the ability to survive and produce offspring. A given characteristic, or trait, may not occur because it has adaptive value, but for at least four other reasons (Futuyma, 1986):

1. The trait is a consequence of the action of the environment or of learning.
2. The trait is a simple consequence of the laws of physics or chemistry.
3. The trait is genetically correlated with another trait that does have adaptive value.
4. The trait is an anachronism. Such traits had adaptive value in the world in which a species evolved, but not in the current environment.

There are several other mechanisms that may account for the occurrence of a trait *without* adaptive value, but the important point is one made clearly by Futuyma (1986): "Adaptation is an onerous concept, and the adaptive value of a trait should be demonstrated rather than assumed, for numerous factors other than adaptation can influence the evolution of a trait" (p. 283).

A related criticism is that evolutionary psychologists, like the sociobiologists before them, rely on casual observation, anecdotes, behavioral comparisons with other species, and correlational studies to support their contention that particular behaviors are inherited (Schlinger, 1996a, 1996b). The following example illustrates the use of behavioral comparisons with other species.

Are We Like Weaverbirds?

African weaverbirds engage in a particularly interesting form of mating ritual. When the male weaverbird spots a female, he displays his nest by hanging upside down and vigorously flapping his wings. Sometimes the female approaches, enters the nest, and "inspects" the nesting materials. As she does so, the male sings from nearby. At any point in this elaborate pattern, the female may leave and perform the same behaviors with another male's nest. If a male's nest is rejected by several females, he will often tear it down and start over. According to Buss (1994), "By exerting a preference for males who can build a superior nest, the female weaverbird solves the problems of protecting and provisioning her future chicks. Her preferences have evolved because they bestowed a reproductive advantage over other weaverbirds who had no preferences and who mated with any males who happened along" (p. 7).

Buss (1994) believes that there are more than superficial comparisons between human courtship behavior and that of African weaverbirds. He writes, "Women, like weaverbirds, prefer men with desirable 'nests' " (p. 7). What he means is that in our own evolutionary history, women's preference for men who could commit to a long-term relationship would have been reproductively advantageous. If a woman chose a man who was "flighty, impulsive, or philandering," she would have to raise her children alone without benefit of the resources and protection of a man. Buss assumes that most women prefer a long-term stable mating relationship and that this preference is directly influenced by genes reflecting an evolutionary history in which such preferences were reproductively advantageous.

Buss's analogies resemble those of earlier sociobiologists concerning sexual behavior in humans (e.g., Barash, 1977) and have the same problems. One problem is that the similarity between human and nonhuman behaviors is superficial and is only suggested *after* it is believed that there may be a common genetic basis for both. In other words, behavioral similarity across species is often in the eyes of the beholder. For instance, in order to make this analogy hold up, Buss and others like him would have to ignore a great deal of other data, such as the 50% divorce rate, the high rates of domestic violence and violence against women in general, unwed mothers, and the fact that men who have been rejected by a couple of women don't usually reconstruct their "personalities" (nests) or their long-term commitment. In fact, they usually continue with their philandering and may insist on abortion in order to avoid unwanted responsibilities, thereby preventing the continuation of their genes. Even if scientists can agree that the behaviors have similar functions for the individuals involved, this does not necessarily mean that the behaviors are controlled in similar ways, that is, genetically. Scientific psychologists must consider more parsimonious explanations of mating strategies before resorting to genetic accounts. Doing so would involve considering the many obvious environmental factors that might control such behavior in women.

Cross-species analogies such as the ones offered by Buss (1994) are intriguing, as they suggest that certain human characteristics that we seem to have in common with other species may be understood as part of our deeper human nature. But we should not permit our fascination to cloud our judgment; we should require scientifically acceptable evidence.

Whether, and how much, human behavior is inherited remains to be answered scientifically. What is unquestionable is that evolution has occurred because of natural selection and that it is responsible not only for species-specific behaviors but also for general learning capacities.

Summary

1. The person most responsible for the shift of interest in psychology toward the study of individual differences was Francis Galton. Galton coined the phrase *nature–nurture* to distinguish between what a person is born with, or inherits (nature), and what he or she acquires as a result of experience or learning (nurture) to explain those individual differences.

2. Darwin's theory of evolution by *natural selection* states that some individuals are more successful in producing offspring because of specific traits they inherited from their parents. This theory was a more parsimonious alternative to Lamarck's theory of evolution through the *inheritance of acquired characteristics*, which states that offspring inherit the changes that the parent(s) had acquired.

3. Mendel's discovery of the principles of inheritance (i.e., dominance, recessiveness, etc.) as a result of his experiments with pea plants provided an explanation for how traits are transmitted from individuals to their descendants.

4. The discovery of the structure of the DNA molecule (the so-called double helix) showed how traits were coded in *genes* (the basic unit of heredity, comprising a unique sequence of amino acids on the DNA molecule which code for the production of a single protein) and at a more basic level how traits (i.e., genes) can be transmitted without change over countless generations.

5. The example of the British peppered moth demonstrates how evolution by natural selection can occur over a relatively short period of time.

6. Having shown how physical traits can evolve due to natural selection, the critical question for psychologists is how differences between individuals can be caused by differences in genes.

7. Species-specific behaviors are behavioral differences between species that arise because each species has different genes (resulting from different evolutionary histories). They are studied by ethologists.

8. There are three types of behavioral relationships that are considered to be inherited: reflexes, fixed action patterns, and learning capacity. Of these, only reflexes and learning capacity are clearly evident in humans.

9. *Behavior geneticists* study the relationship between differences in genotype and differences in behavior (phenotype) in a population in order to discover whether any differences in behaviors are related to differences in genes. They use crossing experiments and selection experiments in nonhuman organisms, such as fruit flies. Studies of family resemblance, in which a behavioral trait is observed in one individual and his or her biological relatives are observed for the same trait, are useful with human subjects.

10. The problem with studies of family resemblance is that biological relatives can share not only genes but environments as well. Hence, it is difficult to determine what accounts for any observed consistency in behavior. In some cases, studying adopted siblings or identical twins reared apart helps researchers to tease apart the contribution of genetic and environmental variables.

11. A specific branch of *sociobiology* (i.e., systematic study of the biological basis of all social behavior) known as *evolutionary psychology* theorizes about human psychology using modern evolutionary principles. These psychologists claim that behavioral differences in areas such as romance, love and sex; friendship and enmity; selfishness, self-sacrifice and guilt; social status; racism, xenophobia and war; deception and self-deception; sibling relationships; and parent–child relationships have a genetic basis. The evidence for such claims is not conclusive.

Study Questions

1. How did Darwin's theory of evolution change our view of human behavior?

2. Who was the person most responsible for the shift of interest in psychology to the study of individual differences?

3. What is eugenics and how is it related to Darwin's theory of natural selection?

4. What was Lamarck's theory of evolution called, what was its basic premise, and how was it shown to be false?

5. What are the three principles on which natural selection theory is based?

6. How were Mendel's findings and the discovery of chromosomes important for the concept of natural selection?

7. How is the DNA molecule structured and how is this related to its (two) functions?

8. Why has DNA been called the essence of heredity or the essence of life?

9. How does the example of the British peppered moth illustrate evolution in action?

10. What are species-specific behaviors and who studies them?

11. What distinguishes the ethological from the psychological study of behavior?

12. What does it mean to say that a trait, behavioral or otherwise, is inherited, and what kinds of behavior are inherited?

13. How are reflexes and fixed action patterns similar? How are they different? Do humans possess both reflexes and fixed action patterns?

14. What are crossing experiments? What are selection experiments? Why can't they be used with humans, and what is the alternative?

15. What are the drawbacks of studies of family resemblance in demonstrating genetically determined behavioral traits?

16. What is sociobiology and evolutionary psychology and what are some criticisms of them?

17. What is the example offered by Buss and what are some problems with it as a scientific explanation?

Ontogeny: Classical Conditioning 5

Chapter 4 described the process of phylogenetic ultimate causation, evolution by natural selection. The other category of ultimate causation—ontogenetic ultimate causation—occurs during the lifetime of individual organisms. Its process, called *learning,* is the selection of behavioral characteristics of organisms as a result of interaction with the environment. Scientific psychologists have found that learning is responsible for many of the similarities and differences in human behavior. This chapter discusses a type of learning called *classical conditioning,* and discusses its importance to humans and other animals.

What Is Learning?

Although the term *learning* is used by different people to mean different things, according to scientific psychologists **learning** refers to relatively permanent changes in relationships between behavior and environmental stimuli due to certain types of experience. There are three important parts to this definition. First, the changes must be long lasting; that is, they must persist for a substantial time after the experience that produces them. Second, the changes are in *relationships* between behavior and environmental events called stimuli. These stimuli are proximate (environmental) causes of the behavior. Third, the changes result from only certain types of experiences, not just any experience. For example, although behavior can be changed relatively permanently by injury, drugs, or disease, all of which are forms of experience, the effects of such agents are not considered to be the result of learning.

Although all animals are capable of learning, no other species learns as readily as *homo sapiens.* Of all the characteristics we humans have acquired through evolution, the ability to learn is perhaps the most important. This ability has enabled us to live successfully from the tropics to the Arctic and to develop sophisticated cultures with social, political, religious, and economic institutions. On a more personal scale, learning accounts for much of what we do each day. The language we speak, the sports we play, even the thoughts we think depend critically on learning. In fact, all of our behavior is fundamentally affected by the experiences scientific psychologists classify as learning.

Learning has long been of interest to psychologists for at least two reasons. First, it is a powerful determinant of behavior. One cannot understand how or why most behavior occurs without understanding learning. Second, understanding learning allows for the development of an effective behavior-change technology. Behavior can be altered greatly through learning and many successful clinical interventions, as well as effective teaching strategies, are based on learning principles.

Pavlov's Discovery of Conditional Reflexes

As described in Chapter 1, Ivan Pavlov was a Russian physiologist. One of his primary interests was the physiology of digestion. To study it, Pavlov developed surgical procedures for laboratory animals that enabled him to collect digestive fluids outside the body. For example, to study salivation, the salivary duct of a dog was directed into a glass tube through an incision cut through the cheek (see Figure 1-1). This procedure did not affect the dog's health, and it allowed Pavlov to quantify salivation with ease.

Much of Pavlov's work concerned the salivary reflex. You will recall from Chapter 4 that reflexes are automatic, stereotyped responses to specific stimuli. In the case of the salivary reflex, the taste of food (the stimulus) elicits salivation (the response). Pavlov quantified the magnitude (i.e., the amount) of the response by measuring drops of saliva; he then determined how the response was affected by variables such as the kind of food presented or a light or sound (see Figure 5-1). He observed, for example, that watery food elicited much less salivation than dry food, and that the amount of saliva elicited by inedible objects placed in the mouth depended on the amount of saliva needed to eject the substance. Sand, for instance, elicited much more salivation than a marble (Chance, 1994).

As Pavlov studied how salivation was affected by the kind of stimulus presented, he observed that dogs with considerable experience in the laboratory often salivated before anything was placed in their mouths, but dogs with little or no laboratory experience did not do so. As Chance (1994) relates, "Pavlov initially assumed that these 'psychic secretions' were caused by the thoughts, memories, or wishes of the animal" (p. 59). (Nowadays, these mental events would be called cognitions.) Given this assumption, it was natural that Pavlov would attempt to understand the secretions by considering the dog's mental state.

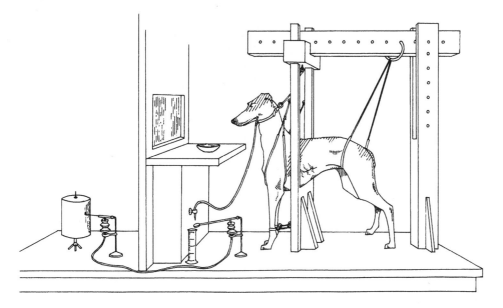

Figure 5-1. A depiction of the conditioning apparatus used by Pavlov to present various stimuli to the subjects and to collect saliva through a tube into a vial, the amount of which could be recorded by a cumulative recorder (see Fig. 1-5). Adapted from Yerkes and Morgulis (1909) based on Pavlov (1927).

There is no direct method by which a person can detect what, if anything, a dog (or for that matter, another human) is wishing, thinking, or remembering. The best that Pavlov could do was to make inferences based on what he would wish, think, or remember if treated as the dog had been. This method is fraught with difficulty, and employing it did not enable Pavlov to make sense of psychic secretions. It was not long before he abandoned the method:

> [In our first experiments] we conscientiously endeavored to explain our results by imagining the subjective state of the animal. But nothing came of this except sterile controversy and individual views that could not be reconciled. And so we could do nothing but conduct the research on a purely objective basis. (Quoted in Cuny, 1965, p. 65)

Having abandoned attempts to understand the dog's mind, Pavlov conducted experiments designed to determine the necessary and sufficient conditions for producing psychic secretions. The essential feature of these experiments was that Pavlov manipulated specified aspects of the environment (as independent variables) and determined how these manipulations affected salivation (as the dependent variable). With this new commitment to objective experimentation, Pavlov also adopted a different terminology that did not make reference to mental states.

As stated in Chapter 1, the work of Pavlov is significant for the development of scientific psychology for several reasons: (1) it relied on strict experimentation using objective variables, (2) it shifted the search for causes of behavior from inside the organism to observable events in the environment, (3) it used nonhuman subjects, and (4) it demonstrated a new form of learning, called classical conditioning. As a result, Pavlov and his associates were able to differentiate two kinds of reflexes, called unconditional and conditional (Pavlov's new term for psychic secretions), and to specify the conditions under which each occurs.

Differences between Unconditional and Conditional Reflexes

Chapter 4 introduced reflexes as inborn, unlearned, stimulus–response relationships. Pavlov termed such reflexes unconditional, because their occurrence was not dependent on (i.e., was not conditional upon) experience during the animal's lifetime. Conditional reflexes,[1] in contrast to unconditional reflexes, did depend critically on specific variables, that is, on a particular kind of experience. This kind of behavior is not present at birth; it depends on learning, and is less permanent than unconditional reflexes.

---

[1]When referring to reflexes and the stimuli and responses of which they are composed, many authors use the terms *conditioned* and *unconditioned* instead of *conditional* and *unconditional*. Either usage is accepted, but the latter appears to be more accurate and a better translation of Pavlov's terms (Gantt, 1966).

As stated in Chapter 4, a reflex is a relationship between two events, a stimulus and a response.[2] This is true of both conditional and unconditional reflexes. Because the stimulus immediately precedes the response (i.e., it is a proximate environmental cause), it is called an **antecedent stimulus.** Using Pavlov's terms, any stimulus that elicits a response in the absence of a special learning history is termed an **unconditional stimulus** (US). The response elicited by the US is termed an **unconditional response** (UR). When we refer to an **unconditional reflex,** we are describing the relationship between a US and a UR. For example, presenting food elicited salivation in Pavlov's dogs, as follows:

$$\text{US (meat powder)} \xrightarrow{\text{elicits}} \text{UR (salivation)}$$

As another example, an air puff directed toward your eye will elicit an eye blink:

$$\text{US (air puff)} \xrightarrow{\text{elicits}} \text{UR (eye blink)}$$

Although the US elicits the UR, this does not mean that their relationship is an invariant one, that is, one in which every US presentation is followed by a response of fixed form and magnitude. Several variables influence unconditional reflexes. Among them are the intensity of the US and the frequency of its presentation, which we discuss below.

Variables that Influence Unconditional Reflexes

Consider this: You're sitting in a boring class, half asleep (not your psychology class, of course). Unknown to you, a construction worker outside the room is about to start a loud circular saw. The saw starts. How does this stimulus affect your behavior? In all likelihood, it causes you to bolt upright and causes your heart to race and your blood pressure to soar (this is the activation response described in Table 4-1). In other words, the sound of the saw, as an antecedent stimulus, elicits startle responses. This is reflexive; the sound of the saw has a similar effect on the behavior of most people in the room. The saw runs for 10 seconds—long enough to cut a two-by-four—then silence. A minute or so later, it starts again. This continues throughout the class. What happens? Eventually, because of its frequent presentation, the sound of the saw fails to elicit these responses. In ordinary language, you get used to it. In the terms of scientific psychology, habituation occurred. **Habituation** refers to the diminished capacity of

---

[2]In scientific psychology, a **stimulus** is any event that affects, or may affect, behavior (the plural form is *stimuli*). In physiological terms, a stimulus affects an organism's sensory receptors (see Chapter 7). In psychology, a **response** is a defined unit of behavior selected for study, whereas in physiology a response is defined in terms of effectors organs, such as muscles or glands.

an unconditional stimulus to elicit an unconditional response as a result of repeated exposures to that stimulus. It is a general phenomenon that is evident across many reflexes.

In an evolutionary sense, habituation is beneficial in that it prevents an organism from wasting time and energy in responding to potentially important but situationally irrelevant stimuli (Fantino & Logan, 1979). For example, an animal drinking at a watering hole will exhibit a startle response to any sudden noise; not doing so may prove fatal if the noise is produced by a predator. If the noise continues, the startle response to it will diminish and the animal will be able to finish drinking. Continued startle responses to the noise in the absence of any obvious danger will waste the animal's energy and prevent it from obtaining enough water. Natural selection has produced both the startle reflex and the change in it due to repeated exposure (habituation).

Because it involves a change in behavior due to experience (i.e., repeated US presentations), habituation may be viewed as a rudimentary form of learning. But is the change a relatively permanent one? This is questionable. Let two hours go without your hearing the circular saw and it will again elicit the startle response. Thus, although habituation may be considered a form of learning, the changes in stimulus–response relationships that define it are not as permanent as are other types of learning experiences.[3] Habituation, by the way, does not involve simple fatigue or satiation. If you have heard the saw 30 times and have stopped responding to it, a dynamite blast (another intense stimulus) will still elicit a startle response. Habituation is stimulus-specific, and does not involve a general waning of responsiveness. (Chapter 7 describes the neurophysiology, or physiological proximate causes, of habituation.)

The Conditioning of Reflexes

Simple unconditional reflexes of the type that have been discussed form the basis of classical conditioning.[4] Classical conditioning as a form of learning provides for a certain flexibility in behavior that goes well beyond that provided by unconditional reflexes. As Pavlov (1927) noted,

> Under natural circumstances the normal animal must respond not only to stimuli which themselves bring immediate benefit or harm, but also to other physical or chemical agencies . . . which in themselves only signal the approach of these stimuli. . . . The essential feature of the highest activity of the central nervous system . . . consists, not in the fact that innumerable signaling stimuli do initiate reflex reactions in the animal, but in the fact that under different conditions these same stimuli may ini-

[3] After a single habituation session of just 10 habituation trials, habituation of the gill-withdrawal reflex in Aplysia (a marine snail) lasts about 2 hours, but several such sessions can produce habituation that lasts for weeks (Carew, Pinsker, & Kandel, 1972).

[4] The term *classical conditioning* was coined by John B. Watson, whereas the term *respondent conditioning* was used by B. F. Skinner. Of course, the term *Pavlovian conditioning* is also often used. These three terms are synonyms and all are acceptable.

tiate quite different reflex actions; and, conversely, the same reactions may be initiated by different stimuli (p. 15, quoted in Fantino & Logan, 1979, p. 60)

The Essence of Classical Conditioning: Stimulus–Stimulus Pairing

The essence of classical conditioning is stimulus–timulus pairing, that is, an arrangement in which some other stimulus reliably and more or less immediately precedes a US. This stimulus is technically termed a **conditional stimulus** (CS). Prior to being paired with the US, the CS is a **neutral stimulus** (NS) in the sense that it does not elicit a response similar to that elicited by the US, although it may control other responses. After being paired with the US, the CS comes to reliably elicit a response that, in most cases, is similar to that elicited by the US. The response elicited by the CS is termed the **conditional response** (CR). Classical conditioning has occurred when a CS comes to elicit a CR reliably. In the language of learning, the experience of pairing the CS with the US has produced a relatively permanent change in the relationship between the CS and CR: the CS now elicits a CR. Figure 5-2 provides a schematic representation of classical conditioning.

Pavlov's work with dogs is the classic example. His basic demonstration of classical coditioning with a tone as the CS, the taste of food powder as the US, salivation elicited by the tone as the CR, and salivation elicited by the food powder as the UR, can be broken down into three steps. First, Pavlov presented the tone alone to verify that it did not already elicit salivation (i.e., that it was indeed neutral with respect to salivation). The second step was to present the tone just before the food was presented. Finally, after several tone–food pairings, the tone was presented alone and elicited salivation in each dog. The tone, previously neutral with respect to salivation, had by virtue of being paired with the food acquired the ability to elicit salivation. This is classical conditioning, and the control of salivation by the tone is an example of a conditional reflex. A

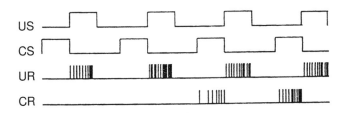

Figure 5-2. Schematic representation of a typical classical conditioning preparation. Note that, from the onset, each time the unconditional stimulus (US) was presented it elicited the unconditional response (UR), but the conditional stimulus (CS) elicited the conditional response (CR) after having been paired with the US on a number of occasions. (From *Psychology: A Behavioral Overview* [p. 131], by A. Poling, H. Schlinger, S. Starin, and E. Blakely, 1990, New York: Plenum Press. Copyright 1990 by Plenum Press. Reprinted with permission.)

conditional reflex is, thus, a learned relationship in which a conditional stimulus comes through classical conditioning to elicit a conditional response. As the preceding example illustrates, three steps are required to demonstrate classical conditioning:

1. The stimulus to be established as a CS is presented several times to demonstrate that it is a neutral stimulus (i.e., it does not elicit a response similar to the UR of interest) prior to being paired with the US.
2. The neutral stimulus (NS) is paired repeatedly with the US, which changes the NS into a CS.
3. The CS is presented without the US to test whether the CS elicits a CR. If so, classical conditioning has occurred.

(For practice, consider how you would establish the sound of the word "car" as a CS controlling an eyeblink response in a young child. Hint: What stimulus normally elicits an eyeblink?)

Higher-Order Conditioning

After an NS has been established as a CS (i.e., acquired eliciting stimulus function through repeated pairings with a US), it can be paired with other neutral stimuli to make them conditional stimuli. This phenomenon is known as **higher-order** or **second-order conditioning.** (The original classical conditioning is the first-order conditioning.). Consider an experiment in which salivation in dogs (CR) is conditioned to the sound of a tone (CS). If a different neutral stimulus, for instance a light, is paired with the tone, the light alone will eventually elicit salivation. This is second-order conditioning. The process could be extended to third-order conditioning by pairing another neutral stimulus, perhaps a touch on the shoulder, with the light. It too might eventually come to elicit salivation. But it probably would not, because third-order conditioning is usually impossible with appetitive USs such as food. Even second-order conditioning is relatively weak, although it can be readily demonstrated (Mackintosh, 1974).

Quantifying Respondent Behaviors

In Pavlov's early accounts, the CR was assumed to be exactly the same as the UR. We know today that this frequently is not so. In many cases, the CR is not a precise equivalent of the UR. For example, the chemical composition of saliva elicited by food differs slightly from that of saliva elicited by a pre-food stimulus (Fantino & Logan, 1979). And, as we discuss below, some CRs, especially those associated with drug use, are the opposite of the UR. Nonetheless, it is typically the case that the responses are similar.

Conditional and unconditional responses are known collectively as **respondent behaviors** (note that respondent conditioning is the same as classical conditioning). Respondent behaviors characteristically are measured along one or more of four dimensions: magnitude, latency, percent occurrence, and duration. Magnitude refers to the amount or force of a response, for example, drops of saliva. Latency refers to the time elapsed between the onset of some stimulus (e.g., the CS) and the occurrence of a response (e.g., the CR). Percent occurrence refers to the relative number (percentage) of CS presentations that elicit the CR. Duration refers to the time elapsed from the onset to the offset of a response.

Which measure researchers use for quantifying respondent behavior largely depends on several factors. One is the nature of the response. For example, it is easier to quantify salivation by measuring its magnitude than by measuring its duration. This is because it is difficult to quantify the duration of a response that does not have a discrete beginning and end.

Respondent behaviors usually, but not always, involve smooth muscles or glands (see Table 4-1). Despite this, it is not possible to determine, on the basis of the type of muscles or glands involved, or topography, whether a particular response is a respondent behavior. To make this determination, one must also be aware of the organism's learning history and the stimuli that elicit the behavior.

Variables that Influence Conditional Reflexes

For any species, a range of stimuli can be established as effective CSs with a given US, but the speed of learning may vary considerably across CSs. In some cases, learning is clearly evident after three or four CS–US pairings; in others, hundreds of pairings are required.

Temporal Relations between Stimuli

With any CS–US pair, learning is influenced by their temporal relation. Figure 5-3 shows five general classical conditioning procedures that have been explored by researchers. *As a rule, learning occurs (i.e., the CS comes to elicit the CR) under all procedures in which the CS occurs shortly before the US.* Such a relation is arranged in **delayed conditioning,** in which the CS begins before the US and ends either when the US begins (a in Figure 5-3) or when the US ends (b in Figure 5-3).[5] **Trace conditioning** (c in Figure 5-3), in which a measurable period of time (called the trace interval) elapses between the end of the CS and the onset of the US, is also effective if the trace interval is short. As a rule, the CS does not come to elicit a CR when the CS and US occur at precisely the same time, which is termed **simultaneous conditioning** (d in Figure 5-3), or when the CS occurs after the US (e in Figure 5-3). The latter relation is termed **backward conditioning.**

---

[5]There is no universally accepted set of terms for describing the various temporal relations that can be arranged between a CS and a US. For example, what we term *delayed conditioning* is sometimes termed *simultaneous conditioning* (a sure misnomer) or *forward pairing*.

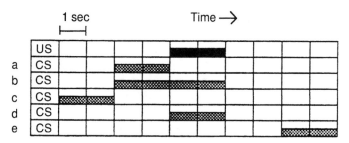

a and b: Delayed conditioning
c: Trace conditioning
d: Simultaneous conditioning
e: Backward conditioning

Figure 5.3. Temporal relations between the CS and US in classical conditioning. (From *Psychology: A Behavioral Overview* [p. 133], by A. Poling, H. Schlinger, S. Starin, and E. Blakely, 1990, New York: Plenum Press. Copyright 1990 by Plenum Press. Reprinted with permission.)

The precise temporal arrangement of CS and US that leads to the most rapid learning depends on many variables, including the nature of the stimuli. With many preparations, including human eyeblink conditioning, a CS presented about 0.5 sec before and overlapping the US is very effective. Regardless of exact temporal parameters, for any learning to occur the CS must be predictive of the US (Rescorla, 1968). This means in essence that the CS must closely precede the US in time, *and* the probability of the US occurring must be higher immediately after CS presentation than at any other time. It is not essential that all CS presentations are followed by the US, nor that all US presentations follow the CS. *The necessary condition for classical conditioning is that the CS and US are correlated in time, so that the probability of the US occurring is greatest after the CS occurs.*

To illustrate the role of the predictive nature of the CS in classical conditioning, consider the following modification of Pavlov's experiment with a tone as the CS and food in mouth as a US. Using a between-subjects design (see Chapter 3), we arrange the following three conditions. In one group of dogs, the CS is presented followed immediately by the US. For a second group of animals, the CS is presented, but the US is never presented. In the third group, the CS sometimes occurs and the US sometimes occurs, but their presentation is random with respect to one another. Figure 5-4 illustrates the experimental arrangement. Thus, the manipulated value of the independent variable is the correlation between the tone and the food. In the first condition they are positively and perfectly correlated; when one occurs, the other always occurs. In the second condition, the two are negatively and perfectly correlated; when one occurs, the other never occurs. And in the third condition, they are explicitly uncorrelated; whether one occurs has nothing to do with whether the other occurs. Our experimental question is "Under which of these conditions will the CS come to elicit a CR (salivation)?"

Group 1: Five-second tone presentations occur on average once each minute. Food is presented immediately after each tone presentation.

Group 2: Five-second tone presentations occur on average once each minute. Food is never presented.

Group 3: Five-second tone presentations occur on average once each minute. Food also is presented on average once each minute, but tone and food presentations are random with respect to one another.

Figure 5-4. Relationships between tone and food presentations for three groups of hungry dogs. Conditioned salivation will be evident only in group one, where there is a predictive relationship between the CS (tone) and US (food).

As dozens of experiments like this have already shown, classical conditioning will occur only in the first group, where the CS always immediately precedes the US. Even though the CS and US are paired together sometimes in the third group, the CS is not at all predictive of the US, so conditioning does not occur. Classical conditioning occurs only when the CS is predictive of the US in a mathematical sense. This does not mean, of course, that the animal is somehow "predicting" that the US will follow the CS, but only that a limited range of relationships between the CS and US is effective. These relationships are "predictive" from the perspective of human observers, not necessarily from the perspective of the experimental subjects. In other words, the subject does not stop and think "food appears only after the tone."

Extinction and Spontaneous Recovery

When classical conditioning does occur, the CS continues to elicit the CR only so long as the CS–US pairing is at least occasionally maintained. If the pairing is ended, either by presenting the CS without the US, or by presenting the two stimuli independent of each other (i.e., in an uncorrelated fashion as described above), the CS–CR relation weakens and eventually ceases to occur. The cessation of responding due to presentation of a CS not paired with a US is termed **classical** (or Pavlovian) **extinction.** If, for instance, Pavlov had stopped giving meat powder (the US) to his dogs after sounding the tone (the CS), salivating to that sound (the CR) eventually would have stopped. Like habituation, respondent extinction serves an organism by preventing it from responding needlessly to once significant but now unimportant stimuli.

Interestingly, if a period of time (e.g., a few hours, a day) passes from the end of one series of extinction trials (CS presentations without the US) to the beginning of a second series of trials, the CS will once again elicit the CR. It is as if the conditional reflex recovers spontaneously. Hence, this phenomenon is known as **spontaneous recovery.** The conditional reflex, however, is not as strong as it was before extinction and if extinction is again carried out, it will proceed more quickly than before.

Stimulus Generalization and Discrimination

After a stimulus is established as a CS, stimuli that are physically similar to the CS may elicit the same CRs, even though these stimuli have never been paired with the US. This phenomenon is termed **stimulus generalization.** Imagine a four-year-old child who has been stung by a wasp. The sting is the US; it is painful and elicits crying and a general activation response (e.g., increased heart rate, increased respiration). The physical characteristics of the wasp (its size, shape, color, pattern of movement, and sound) preceded the US; therefore, they come to serve as a compound CS (a CS with multiple elements): Thereafter, when a wasp approaches, it elicits crying and general arousal in the child. Similar responses are also likely to be elicited by other wasplike insects, such as hornets, or even bees. The likelihood that a given insect or other stimulus will elicit such responses depends on its similarity to the wasp. In general, the greater the similarity between an untrained stimulus and a CS, the greater the likelihood that the untrained stimulus will elicit a response similar to the CR. For example, a common house fly will likely elicit a weaker response than will a bee or a hornet.

The likelihood that untrained stimuli, such as those that are involved in stimulus generalization, will elicit responding can be diminished through **classical discrimination training.** In such training, a CS is repeatedly paired with a US, whereas another stimulus (which differs physically from the CS along a specifiable dimension) is repeatedly presented without such pairing. Consider a discrimination training procedure in which a dog receives food after each presentation of a 7,000 hertz (Hz) tone, but never after presentation of a 12,000 Hz tone. After several pairings, the 7,000 Hz tone will be established as a CS that elicits salivation. In contrast, the 12,000 Hz tone will not elicit salivation. If, however, only the 7,000 Hz tone had been paired with food, presenting the 12,000 Hz tone as a novel stimulus would have elicited some salivation (stimulus generalization), although less than the amount elicited by the training stimulus (i.e., 7,000 Hz tone).

The Importance of Classical Conditioning

We lose interest quickly if we think of reflexes only in the context of salivating dogs and technical terms such as extinction and generalization. We do not need to look too closely, however, to see that reflexes are of critical importance. We cough when our throat is irritated, cry when something enters our eye, sweat when we are hot, blink when an object approaches our eyes. These and a multitude of other unconditional reflexes, which are a product of our phylogenetic history, minimize the adverse effects of potentially harmful environmental variables and help to keep our bodies within working limits. Conditional reflexes often serve similar functions. In some cases, classical conditioning produces remarkable changes in an organism's behavior and physiology, as the following examples illustrate.

Conditioned Taste Aversions

Taste aversion learning provides an interesting example of an adaptive behavior controlled by stimulus–stimulus pairings, although it is more complex than a simple conditional reflex. The phenomenon was first demonstrated in the 1950s by John Garcia and his colleagues. In an early study, Garcia, Kimeldorf, and Koelling (1955) allowed rats to drink saccharin-flavored water (saccharin tastes sweet), then exposed them to gamma radiation, which induced nausea. After a single pairing, the rats preferred tap water alone to saccharin-flavored water, although they had preferred the saccharin-flavored water at the start of the study. Apparently, by virtue of being paired with the radiation, the taste of saccharin-flavored water had acquired nausea-producing characteristics, and was therefore avoided.

Taste aversion learning differs from conventional classical conditioning preparations in three important ways. First, learning typically occurs after only one pairing of the CS and the US. Second, the effective interval between the CS and the US can be minutes or hours in taste aversion learning, but not in most other preparations. In other words, one doesn't have to get sick immediately after eating. Third, taste aversion learning involves operant as well as classical conditioning. In taste aversion learning, animals avoid contact with stimuli paired with nausea and, as discussed in the next chapter, avoidance behavior is considered to be operant. Despite the complexity of taste aversion learning and its differences from typical examples of classical conditioning, it does involve a pairing of stimuli, and is of obvious adaptive value: If an animal eats a food that makes it sick, it is well served not to eat more of the same substance.

One can easily see instances of taste aversion learning in the wild. A fascinating one involves blue jays (Brower & Brower, 1964). Blue jays eat many insects, including butterflies. Despite this, most wild blue jays will not eat monarch butterflies. Beyond being showy and abundant, some monarchs have an interesting characteristic: They are poisonous. Sometimes larval monarchs eat certain kinds of milkweed which are harmless to the larva, but harmful to birds and mammals. Poison from the milkweed is stored in the body of the larva, and is retained as it passes to the butterfly stage. If a blue jay eats a butterfly that has fed on milkweeds, the bird becomes ill and vomits. Subsequently, it avoids all monarchs, even though some are not poisonous.

Humans don't typically eat butterflies, but we aren't immune to taste aversion conditioning. Perhaps you've eaten a new food, then gotten sick to your stomach, and avoided that food since then. If so, you know firsthand the meaning of a learned taste aversion. Taste aversion learning is especially problematic for cancer patients who are treated with radiation or chemotherapy. If patients eat prior to receiving the therapy, they run the risk of having the taste of their food paired with the radiation which produces severe nausea a short time later. This is especially troublesome for these patients because the very treatment meant to help them may produce aversions to the food that provides them necessary nutrition.

To illustrate this problem, consider an experiment conducted by Bernstein (1978) with children who were undergoing chemotherapy to treat cancer. Using a between-subjects design, she divided the children into three groups. Children in the first group were given a novel-flavored ice cream just before their treatment, children in a second group were not given ice cream before their treatment, and children in the third group were given the ice cream without the chemotherapy. Several weeks later the children were given a choice between eating ice cream and playing a game. Only 21% of the children who had the ice cream before chemotherapy chose the ice cream as compared with 73% of the children who had ice cream but no therapy. Knowing about such effects might help doctors and nurses avoid the problem of conditioned taste aversions by being very careful about what cancer patients eat before therapy.

A phenomenon similar to taste aversion learning also causes problems for cancer patients who receive chemotherapy or radiation treatment. The problem is that they become nauseated when they encounter a variety of stimuli associated with the hospital where they receive treatment. Some vomit; others report severe distress. This of course involves classical conditioning: The set of stimuli that constitute the hospital are reliably paired with treatment, which elicits nausea, and these stimuli come, through classical conditioning, to elicit a similar response. For example, the sights and smells of the hospital may all elicit the nausea previously only elicited by the radiation or chemotherapy. In fact, just thinking about going to the hospital may cause them to feel sick. (Thinking is behavior that, like other behavior, generates its own stimuli which can be just as powerful as environmental stimuli such as sights and smells.)

Conditioned Immune and Allergic Responses

Our bodies are constantly beset by potentially harmful microorganisms, called antigens, which include viruses and bacteria. Our immune system protects us from such invaders. It activates "killer cells" that destroy antigens, and also produces antibodies, which attach to antigens and allow killer cells to recognize them. Impaired functioning of the immune system makes people susceptible to a wide variety of opportunistic infections.

Many variables, including antigens (such as the human immunodeficiency virus [HIV]), drugs, age, race, stress, and nutrition (Snyder, 1989), influence how well the immune system functions. For more than 20 years, researchers have known that drug-induced immunosuppression can be classically conditioned (e.g., R. Adler & Cohen, 1975, 1982), and it has recently become apparent that the body's production of both antibodies and killer cells can also be classically conditioned.

A study by R. Adler, Cohen, and Bovbjerg (1982) provides a good example of conditioned immunosuppression. In that study (which used a between-subjects design), rats in the experimental group first drank a novel solution containing saccharin (CS), and then were injected with a drug (cyclophosphamide) (US) that impairs immune function (UR). Rats in a control group did not drink the solution before being injected with the drug. Days later, the level of antibody production induced by exposure to a foreign substance (sheep's blood) was measured in all of the rats. Antibody production was reduced (CR) by exposure to saccharine in animals for which it had previously been paired with cyclophosphamide, but not for control animals exposed to saccharine without such pairing.

Conditioned facilitation of immune function is evident in a study by Gorczynski, Macrae, and Kennedy (1982), who performed skin grafts in mice. Skin grafts (US) automatically led to increased production of certain kinds of killer cells (T-cells) (UR). After the mice experienced skin grafts, exposure to the surgical procedures associated with skin grafts (CS) but with no skin actually grafted increased T-cell production (CR). Such procedures did not affect T-cell production in mice that had not previously received grafts.

A recent study by Bobvjerg and colleagues (1990) underscored the potential treatment implications of classically conditioned immunosuppression. They demonstrated that women receiving chemotherapy for ovarian cancer showed evidence of reduced immune function when they returned to the hospital for treatment. The drugs used in chemotherapy produce immunosuppression (i.e., are USs) and, by virtue of reliably preceding exposure to those drugs, the complex of sights, sounds, and smells comprised by the hospital came to function as CSs. If this analysis is correct, a reasonable strategy to reduce conditioned immunosuppression would be to have patients come to the treatment area on several occasions prior to receiving chemotherapy. This is so because repeatedly presenting a CS before it is paired with a US inhibits conditioning, a phenomenon called **latent inhibition** or the CS-preexposure effect.

How does latent inhibition happen? The answer can be found in terms of the predictive value of the CS as described above. If a CS is repeatedly presented before it is paired with a US, then each instance of its presentation alone in a sense predicts the *absence* of the US. In the example, if cancer patients go to the treatment area on several occasions before they ever receive treatment, then the treatment area, as a CS, will predict the absence of treatment. As a result, when treatment does begin, it will take longer for the treatment area to become a CS for nausea or conditioned immunosuppression.

Conditioned Sexual Arousal

Classical conditioning may play a role even in the stimuli that control sexual arousal. Some stimuli do so automatically as USs. Others may do so by being paired with USs or established CSs. In an interesting nonhuman demonstration of this phenomenon, Farris (1967) showed that the courtship of male Japanese quail could be conditioned easily to the sound of a buzzer. Using a within-subject design, the buzzer (CS), a previously neutral stimulus, was sounded for 10s, after which a female (US) was placed in the male's cage. She remained in the cage until copulation occurred or 1 min elapsed from the start of the CS (buzzer), whichever came first. After a few pairings, the males began to display courting behavior at the sound of a buzzer. Within 32 pairings, the buzzer elicited the full courtship display in every male. This display, which is normally elicited by females, involves a series of behaviors (a fixed action pattern; see Chapter 4) in which (a) the posterior is elevated and the neck is thrust forward, (b) the legs straighten and stiffen so that the body bounces, (c) the bird struts on its toes, (d) the bird emits a subdued, hoarse, vibrating call, and (e) the body feathers are fluffed. Everyday stimuli, such as perfume, or more unusual stimuli, such as leather, whips, or chains, may turn on some humans, but a buzzer sufficed for the quail. Given the right (or wrong!) history, humans might be turned on by a buzzer, too.

Rachman and Hodgson (1968) used procedures similar to those employed by Farris to condition, in male humans, sexual arousal to women's knee-length boots. Subjects were first shown a color slide of the boots (CS), then a slide of an attractive naked woman (US). Sexual arousal was measured by assessing penile erection with a plethysmograph. Initially, the US controlled erection but the CS failed to do so. After a number of pairings, the CS also controlled erection. When the CS was repeatedly presented alone (i.e., extinction was arranged), it eventually failed to elicit arousal. This study suggests that classical conditioning may play a role in the development of sexual fetishes, which are abnormal sexual attachments to inanimate objects, and has implications for how we may treat such problem behaviors. At the very least, this study suggests why each of us has our own sexual turn-ons.

Conditioned Tolerance to Drugs

In the language of drug use, **tolerance** refers to the fact that the effects of a drug diminish as a result of repeated exposure to that drug. A large number of investigations (see Siegel, 1989) have shown that greater tolerance is observed under conditions in whih the drug has been regularly administered in the past. Such an effect is clearly evident in a study by Siegel, Hinson, Krank, and McCully (1982). Using a between-subjects design, the experimenters examined the lethality of a large dose (15 mg/kg) of heroin in three groups of rats.

During the first part of the study, all rats in the two experimental groups received 15 injections of heroin over a 30-day period. Heroin was injected every other day, and the dose was gradually increased from 1 to 8 mg/kg. On days when heroin was not given, rats received an injection of dextrose (a sugar solution). Heroin injections and dextrose injections were given in markedly different environments. Half of the rats received heroin in the colony area; the other half were given the drug in a room with white noise present. On the final day of the study, rats in one of the experimental groups (Same) received 15 mg/kg heroin in the environment in which they historically had received smaller doses, and rats in the other experimental group (Different) received 15 mg/kg heroin in the environment in which dextrose had been given in the past. A group of control rats was also given 15 mg/kg heroin. Half of these rats were given the drug in the colony room, and half in the room with white noise.

Although exposure to heroin alone produced some tolerance to the drug, as evidenced by a lower death rate (64% deaths) in the Different group than in the

Control group (96% deaths), the environment in which the drug was administered strongly affected the degree of tolerance observed. In fact, mortality was twice as great in the group (Different) that received heroin in a novel environment (64%) as in the group (Same) that received the drug in the usual environment (32%).

Such findings cannot be explained in terms of the heroin alone. However, Siegel developed a model that accounts for these findings nicely. He proposed that stimuli paired with drug administration are established as CSs that come to evoke CRs that are opposite in direction to the URs elicited by the drug US. These CRs compensate for (i.e., counteract) the URs elicited by the drug. As the CRs increase in magnitude as a result of repeated CS–US pairings, the magnitude of the observed response to the drug is reduced. Decreases in the observed response with repeated administrations of a drug is by definition tolerance. For example, in humans heroin produces euphoric feelings as a UR, but stimuli that are paired with heroin, such as the sights and sounds of the setting in which the drug is administered, produce dysphoria as a CR. The more the heroin is administered in a particular setting, the greater the feelings of dysphoria in that setting, and the more drug is needed to produce the original feelings of euphoria.

Given the findings of Siegel and colleagues (1982) and others suggesting that tolerance to heroin and other, related drugs (e.g., morphine) is situation-specific, it is reasonable to propose that the likelihood of people suffering problems with heroin overdose would be greater if they took the drug under unusual circumstances. Although this proposition cannot be tested experimentally for obvious ethical reasons, some anecdotal evidence supports it. For instance, Siegel (1984) asked 10 former heroin users who had suffered serious overdoses about the conditions in which the problem occurred. Seven of them reported that the drug was taken in atypical circumstances when the overdose occurred. Siegel (1984, 1989) is careful to emphasize that this observation does not provide *proof* that classical conditioning plays a role in drug overdose by humans. It is, however, consistent with the suggestion.

Explanation of Conditional Reflexes

Scientists conduct research in order to understand the world around them. The beginning of this chapter described how Pavlov struggled to explain his findings. At first, he posited mental events in the dogs to explain salivation to the tone, and even called the learned reflexes "psychical reflexes" to reflect this orientation. Later, however, Pavlov realized that he could explain the findings satisfactorily without speculating about unobservable mental or cognitive events. Nevertheless, people nowadays, including some psychologists, still explain classical conditioning by speaking about mental events. For example, it is not uncommon to hear someone say that Pavlov's dogs salivated to the tone because they "associated" the tone with the food. This explanation sounds logical until one examines it. The verb *to associate* means to combine, join, or unite.

So, technically speaking, it was Pavlov, not the dogs, who joined or united the tone (CS) with the meat powder (US). The implication of this semantic clarification is that we can attribute the salivation at the tone to the experience provided by the dogs' environment—the pairing of the CS and the US—and there is no need to appeal to unseen events. Explanations involving inferred mental or cognitive events are not parsimonious, and they rely on untestable assumptions. In another common but flawed explanation, some people explain the dogs' salivation to the tone by saying that the dogs "expect" the food when they hear the tone. This is a circular explanation if the only evidence for the expectation is the salivation to the tone.

A more scientifically adequate and parsimonious explanation of conditional reflexes is in terms of proximate and ultimate variables. Both the US and the CS are proximate environmental causes of their respective responses (the UR and CR respectively). In both cases we may ask *why* these proximate variables cause the responses. In the case of the unconditional reflex, the US elicits the UR because of the evolutionary history of the species, or ultimate phylogenetic causation. In the case of the conditional reflex, the CS elicits the CR because of particular kinds of experiences called learning, specifically classical conditioning, that occurred in the individual's history, called ultimate ontogenetic causation. Once we account for these variables, there is no need to infer other events, whether or not they are mental.

A great deal more is known about classical conditioning than we have related here. Scientists have, for example, shown that analgesia and allergic responses can be classically conditioned (e.g., Fanselow & Baakes, 1982; Russell, Cummins, Ellman, Callaway, Peeke, 1984). Although classical conditioning appears to be a simple process, many variables affect it. Understanding classical conditioning is fundamental to understanding the behavior of humans and other animals. Some psychologists, most of whom worked in the Soviet Union, have attempted to account fully for human behavior in terms of classical conditioning. Their attempts have been unsuccessful, in large part because another kind of learning, operant conditioning, plays such an important role in human activities. Nonetheless, as the examples presented in this chapter illustrate, classical conditioning can exercise powerful, and perhaps counterintuitive, control over organisms' reactions to particular stimuli. In cases of drug overdose and disease, classical conditioning can even determine life and death.

Summary

1. Scientific psychologists use the term *learning* to refer to relatively permanent changes in relationships between behavior and environmental stimuli due to certain types of experience.

2. One type of experience that produces relatively permanent changes in behavior–environment relationships, called classical (or Pavlovian) conditioning, was discovered by the Russian physiologist Ivan Pavlov, and is significant for the development of scientific psychology for several reasons, including the

fact that it shifted the search for causes of behavior from events inside the organism to events in the environment.

3. Classical conditioning is built upon unconditional reflexes in which any stimulus that elicits a response in the absence of a special learning history, termed an *unconditional stimulus* (US) (e.g., food in mouth) elicits a response, termed an *unconditional response* (UR) (e.g., salivation).

4. Unconditional reflexes can be affected by certain experiences. For example, in *habituation*, repeated exposures (i.e., frequency of presentation) produces a diminished tendency of a US to elicit a UR.

5. The procedure of classical conditioning (the conditioning of reflexes) is stimulus–stimulus pairing in which a stimulus, called a *neutral stimulus* (NS), reliably precedes a US and as a result, becomes a *conditional stimulus* (CS) that elicits a *conditional response* (CR).

6. There are several other variables that can influence conditional reflexes, including the temporal order of the CS–US, classical extinction and spontaneous recovery, and generalization and discrimination.

7. Classical conditioning is important because it sheds light on such human problems as learned taste aversions, conditioned immune and allergic responses, conditioned sexual arousal, conditioned tolerance to drugs, and phobias, among others.

8. The establishment and subsequent modification of conditional reflexes are most parsimoniously explained according to the actual interactions between an individual's behavior and the environment (called classical conditioning), as opposed to mental or cognitive events such as expectations.

Study Questions

1. What is learning and why is it important?

2. Who was Ivan Pavlov and how did he discover classical conditioning?

3. Why is Pavlov's work significant for scientific psychology?

4. How do conditional and unconditional reflexes differ?

5. How do intensity and frequency of presentation affect unconditional reflexes, and how is the term *habituation* used?

6. What is the essence of classical conditioning and how does it produce conditional reflexes?

7. What is higher-order conditioning and how is it different from basic classical conditioning?

8. What are the four ways in which reflexive responses may be quantified (i.e., measured)?

9. What are the four types of temporal relationships that may occur between CSs and USs?

10. What are extinction and spontaneous recovery and under what conditions do they occur?

11. How do stimulus generalization and discrimination occur with conditional reflexes?

12. What are conditioned taste aversions and how are they produced by stimulus–stimulus pairing?

13. How are immune and allergic responses classically conditioned?

14. How is sexual arousal classically conditioned?

15. How can tolerance to drugs that produce physical dependence be classically conditioned?

16. How are conditional reflexes often explained inadequately, and what are adequate scientific explanations?

Ontogeny: Operant Conditioning

6

Chapter 5 described one type of ontogenetic ultimate cause of behavior—classical conditioning. This chapter introduces another ontogenetic ultimate cause—operant conditioning—and the variables that affect it. These variables influence behavior in a wide range of species, especially human beings. We humans are, however, also affected by language, which is a special kind of operant behavior. Chapter 8 examines the role of language in human behavior.

Although survival would be difficult or impossible without them, conditional and unconditional reflexes constitute only a small part of the human repertoire. Most complex and interesting human behavior is determined by operant conditioning. As discussed in Chapter 1, Edward Thorndike contributed, although unknowingly, to the later discovery of operant conditioning by B. F. Skinner. As you may recall, after experimenting with cats in puzzle boxes, Thorndike summarized his findings with the **Law of Effect,** which stated that in a given situation an organism's responses that are closely followed by satisfaction will be more likely to recur in that situation, whereas those that are followed by discomfort will be less likely to recur. In the tradition of Pavlov, Thorndike believed that his Law of Effect rendered mentalistic explanations of behavior unnecessary.

B. F. Skinner, who also found mentalistic explanations unnecessary, expanded on the Law of Effect by systematically examining how the consequences of behavior affect future responding. He coined the term *operant* to emphasize that behavior operates on the environment, changes it in some way (i.e., produces consequences), and is itself altered as a result. All behaviors that produce the same consequence, regardless of their form, are members of the same **operant response class.** For example, there are several ways to turn on a TV. One can push a button on the remote control, one can get up and push the On/Off button on the TV itself, or one can ask someone else to turn it on. Although each of these behaviors is different in form, they all produce the same effect on the environment—the TV goes on—and are, thus, all members of the same response class that we may call "turning on the TV."

An Example of Operant Conditioning

Consider a child, Ann, who is learning to write her name under her father's guidance. Certain movements of the pencil produce something approximating letters, and the father praises the child for producing them. Other movements result in unrecognizable marks; these movements are never praised and sometimes result in mild reprimands (e.g., the father says, "no, not that way"). Under these conditions, the child eventually learns to write her name. She does so because of the consequences of particular movement patterns: Correct movements of the pencil produce one outcome (praise), whereas incorrect movements produce another (reprimands). The child's behavior operates on the environment in the sense of determining what her father says. As a result of the different consequences of particular movement patterns, some are strengthened, others weakened. Finally, a useful pattern emerges.

There is much for little girls to do beyond writing their names, and no reasonable father would want that response to be the primary one in his daughter's repertoire. Therefore, once the child has acquired the response, the father is likely to praise it only under special circumstances, as when someone says, "Ann, please write your name." If, however, the child writes her name at other times, perhaps when her father is talking on the phone or watching television, he either fails to respond to her writing or responds in a way not valued by his daughter: "Not now, Ann, can't you see I'm busy?" Eventually, the girl writes her name only at appropriate times.

The verbal request "please write your name" is considered an antecedent stimulus for the operant response of writing "Ann." The verbal praise delivered by the father is the consequence of that response. Simple operant relationships can be described in terms of three components: An *antecedent stimulus* for a *response* that produces certain *consequences*. Schematically, this is an S–R–S (stimulus–response–stimulus) relationship.

Stimuli produced by a response (i.e., its consequences) can have two effects: The future occurrence of the response under similar circumstances can increase (as did Ann's correct behavior), or it can decrease (as did her incorrect behavior). We use the term reinforcement to refer to the former relation, whereas punishment is used to describe the latter.

Reinforcement

Reinforcement is evident when a response is followed by a change in the environment *(reinforcer)* and is thereby strengthened under similar circumstances. The response-strengthening effects of reinforcement typically involve an increase in the future *rate* (number of responses per unit time) or probability of occurrence of the response, although other changes in behavior (e.g., a decrease in response latency or an increase in response magnitude) may also be indicative of a reinforcement effect. It is important to recognize that, by definition, *reinforcement always strengthens behavior*, although what functions as a reinforcer for one behavior may not do the same for another behavior. It is also important to remember that *reinforcement strengthens behavior under circumstances that are similar to those that were present when reinforcement occurred*. The context in which behavior occurs includes stimuli that comprise the external environment and often includes stimuli located inside the organism.

Positive and Negative Reinforcement

Traditionally, scientific psychologists have classified reinforcers according to whether they involve adding something to the environment (e.g., presenting food), or subtracting something (e.g., turning off a loud noise). When a stimulus strengthens behavior by virtue of being presented following the occurrence of such behavior, the stimulus is termed a **positive reinforcer (S^{R+})** and the procedure is termed **positive reinforcement.** The term *positive* indicates the addition (+) of the consequence. When a stimulus strengthens behavior by virtue of being subtracted (or decreased in intensity) following the occurrence of such behavior, the stimulus is termed a **negative reinforcer (S^{R-})** and the procedure is termed **negative reinforcement** (see Figure 6-1). The term *negative* indicates the subtraction (–) of the consequence.

The distinction between positive and negative reinforcement is simple logically, but in practice it can be hard to tell the two apart. For example, does a person adjust the tuning on a television with a blurry picture to produce a clear image (positive reinforcement), or to terminate a blurry image (negative reinforcement)? Because of such difficulties, and the possibility of confusing negative reinforcement with punishment, there is justification for not differentiating positive and negative reinforcement (see Michael, 1975), although the practice is still common.

The only way to determine whether or not a stimulus functions as a reinforcer is to look at its effect on behavior. If, after arranging for the stimulus to follow a response (whether added or subtracted), the response increases in strength under similar circumstances, the stimulus is called a reinforcer. For example, after rocking a baby for 10 minutes a parent returns the child to its crib. The baby begins to cry. The parent returns and begins to rock the child once more. Has the rocking reinforced (i.e., increased) crying? The only way to tell is to determine whether in the future the child is more likely to cry under similar circumstances, for example, the next night when the parent puts the child to bed.

It is important to recognize that reinforcers are defined in terms of how they affect behavior, not in terms of their subjective effects. Although most reinforcers make us "feel good," this is irrelevant to their definition as reinforcers. Also, humans are typically unaware of the reinforcers that maintain their behavior. Awareness of reinforcers is also not necessary for reinforcement to occur.

	Stimulus is Added	Stimulus is Subtracted
Behavior Increases	Positive Reinforcement (SR+)	Negative Reinforcement (SR–)
Behavior Decreases	Positive Punishment (SP+)	Negative Punishment (SP–)

Figure 6-1. A 2 by 2 matrix showing two types of reinforcers and punishers. Note that reinforcers always strengthen (i.e., increase) responding, whereas punishers always weaken (i.e., decrease) responding.

Conditioned and Unconditioned Reinforcers

A wide variety of environmental changes (i.e., stimuli) can serve as reinforcers. Some stimuli, called **unconditioned reinforcers** (also called primary reinforcers) strengthen behavior in organisms without any particular history of learning, which is to say in most "normal" members of a particular species. Many unconditioned reinforcers are of direct biological significance. Air, food, and water are examples of positive reinforcers that fit into this category. Unconditioned negative reinforcers, which organisms will escape (respond to terminate), or avoid (respond to prevent contact with) include high-intensity stimulation (e.g., loud sounds, bright lights, intense cold or heat) as well as pain.

In contrast to unconditioned reinforcers, **conditioned** (or secondary) **reinforcers** gain their ability to strengthen behavior through learning. Conditioned reinforcers can be established by pairing previously neutral stimuli with unconditioned reinforcers or established conditioned reinforcers in the same way that stimuli are paired in classical conditioning. Perhaps you have trained a dog to perform some behavior. If so, you undoubtedly have made use of a conditioned reinforcer, probably a phrase like "good dog." Early in its puppyhood, and now and again throughout the dog's life, you said "good dog" while you petted him or gave him food. By virtue of being paired with stimuli that are unconditioned reinforcers (petting, food), the sound of the phrase came to function as a conditioned reinforcer. It will strengthen behavior in a dog with a special learning history, which your dog has. Food, in contrast, will strengthen behavior in all healthy dogs if the dog is hungry and the food is presented dependent on the occurrence of a particular response.

The stimuli that serve as conditioned reinforcers can vary greatly across people due to differences in their individual conditioning histories. For example, certain kinds of painful stimulation, such as being struck with a leather belt, will reinforce behavior in certain people. Perhaps such stimulation reliably preceded a powerful unconditioned positive reinforcer, like sexual stimulation. Being struck with a belt did not initially function as a reinforcer, but it eventually came to do so by virtue of its correlation with sexual stimulation. Like other conditioned reinforcers, it will maintain its reinforcing ability only if it continues to be paired at least occasionally with some other reinforcer. Once a conditioned reinforcer is no longer paired with another reinforcer, it loses the capacity to strengthen behavior, just as a CS in classical conditioning loses its capacity to elicit a CR if it is no longer paired with a US.

In humans, some conditioned reinforcers are paired with many other reinforcers. Money is a good example of such a **generalized conditioned reinforcer.** Giving a child a dollar each time she smiled probably would not increase her smiling, but the same operation likely would turn a college freshman into a Cheshire cat. The reason for the disparity of outcome, obviously, is that the freshman, but not the child, has a long history in which money has been paired with (i.e., exchanged for) a great variety of "good things"—positive reinforcers—such as food, compact discs, books, and so on. For almost all people, attention is another powerful and generalized conditioned reinforcer. It may not be reinforcing by itself, but rather because of other things we can get when we have someone's attention. Imagine what other reinforcers you can get from others after first getting their attention.

Delayed Reinforcement

Laboratory studies with nonhumans suggest that the response-strengthening effects of reinforcers diminish rapidly as the delay between the response and the reinforcer increases. Here, consequences delayed by more than a short period—a minute at most—are essentially ineffectual. Because of this, some scientific psychologists stress the importance of immediacy of reinforcement in their definitions of reinforcement.

Long-delayed events appear to be capable of strengthening behavior in humans, although they may do so indirectly. For example, few people would work without pay, even though a paycheck delivered on Friday afternoon probably does not strengthen the responses that occurred throughout the week in the same direct way that food delivered immediately after sitting reinforces the response in a hungry dog. Verbal responses appear to play a critical role in mediating the effects of long-delayed consequences in humans (see Chapter 8), and it may be useful to call these consequences something other than reinforcers (e.g., analogies to reinforcers). At present, however, this convention has not been established.

Superstitious Reinforcement

Environmental events may reinforce responses that precede them even if the response does not actually produce the reinforcer. Reinforcement of this type has been termed *superstitious, adventitious,* or *response-independent.* For instance, a crap shooter who says, "Be there, baby" before rolling the dice is apt to repeat the phrase under similar conditions in the future if the roll is a seven, even though there is no way the verbal statement could affect the outcome of the dice. Try to imagine other examples of superstitious behavior, for example, among athletes, that have no direct relation to the consequences that maintain them.

The Opportunity to Behave as a Reinforcer

Instead of thinking about reinforcers as stimuli, some scientific psychologists have described them as behaviors (the consequences) that only become possible when other behaviors (the operant response) occur. Consider two behaviors that a junior-high student can emit: playing basketball and doing algebra problems. When allowed to do either, much more time is spent playing basketball than doing algebra problems. Arranging conditions so that the student must do algebra problems (the lower probability behavior) before playing basketball (the higher probability behavior) is a good way to increase the time spent in doing algebra problems.

For any two behaviors that occur with different probabilities (here, probability is defined as the amount of time spent engaging in the behavior), the opportunity to engage in the higher probability behavior will reinforce (i.e., increase) the lower probability behavior. Conversely, forcing an organism to engage in the lower probability behavior when a higher probability behavior occurs will punish (i.e., decrease) the higher probability behavior. These two relations constitute the **Premack principle** (Premack, 1959). Perhaps your parents made use of the Premack principle when they made you eat your vegetables before allowing you to have dessert, thus hoping to reinforce eating vegetables. We discuss the use of the Premack principle with punishment later in this chapter.

Reinforcing stimuli often allow an organism to engage in behaviors that otherwise could not occur. For instance, the stimulus food allows for the behavior of eating. One can often predict whether a particular change in the environment (stimulus) will be reinforcing by determining the probability of the response associated with it relative to the probability of the operant response that it follows. All else being equal, a food-deprived rat will spend far more time eating than pressing a bar. Hence it is not surprising that food delivery (which allows for a higher-probability behavior) will reinforce bar pressing (a lower-probability behavior).

Examples of Reinforcement

Table 6-1 provides eight examples of reinforcement. These examples show that operant conditioning can strengthen behaviors that are socially undesirable (Example 7), as well as those that are desirable (Example 5, 6, and 8). Examples 5, 6, and 8 are based on published studies that used procedures similar to those described to help actual participants (K. D. Allen, Loiben, Allen, & Stanley, 1992; Hegel, Ayllon, Vanderplate, & Spiro-Hawkins, 1986; Stock & Milan, 1993).

There are numerous other published demonstrations of significant behavior change induced through the use of reinforcement procedures. In some cases, the effects of such procedures are remarkable. Figure 6-2 shows a case in point. This figure shows the results of a study in which reinforcement procedures were used to treat a middle-aged male who had suffered from severe back pain for more than 15 years (Kallman, Hersen, & O'Toole, 1975). Although no physical problems could be detected, the man was bent forward deeply at the waist, and could not straighten up or move his legs. He had received a variety of treatments, but remained severely distressed and unable to work.

The researchers used social reinforcement to get the patient to walk, and then to stand. Each treatment session involved an initial period of 10 minutes during which the patient talked with a young female assistant. At the end of that period, she asked him to rise from his wheelchair and walk as far as he

Table 6-1
Examples of Reinforcement

Antecedent Situation	Operant Response	Immediate Consequence of Response	Behavioral Effect
1. A musician begins to strum an electric guitar, but the sounds aren't amplified	The musician jiggles a switch near the guitar's pick-up	The music is amplified	In the future, should the music not be amplified, the musician is likely to jiggle the switch
2. A tourist visiting Peru approaches a native, who says "Buenos dias"	The tourist says "Buenos dias"	The Peruvian smiles	There is increased likelihood of the tourist saying "Buenas dias" on approaching other natives in the future
3. A woman is awakened by the cries of her baby, who is in the same bed	The woman begins to sing a soft lullabye	The baby soon stops crying	The future likelihood of the woman singing when the baby cries increases
4. A truckdriver sits with a lighted cigarette	The driver puffs on the cigarette	An amount of nicotine enters the driver's body	The driver is likely to continue smoking
5. An elderly resident of a nursing home is choosing foods at the home's cafeteria	The resident selects a "healthy" food	The person serving food praises the resident's food selection	The elderly resident is more likely to choose "healthy" foods on subsequent occasions
6. A child sits in a dentist's chair, receiving treatment	The child sits still for a specified time	The dentist gives the child a "break" from treatment	The time that the child spends sitting still increases
7. A husband comes home drunk and is confronted by his wife, who complains	The man slaps the woman	The woman runs away	There is an increase in the probability that the man will be abusive under similar circumstances.
8. A severely burned patient is receiving treatment, which requires stretching of the skin over the burned area	The patient stretches for a specified time	The patient does not have to attend scheduled therapy sessions	The time spent in stretching goes up

could. Initially (Phase 1), she verbally praised his efforts to stand (e.g., by saying, "You're standing very well today"). In subsequent phases, she reinforced both standing and walking. Walking increased under these conditions. Walking increased further when the patient started the sessions with a walker (Phase 4B) relative to starting sessions in a wheelchair (Phases 1–3), and when the walker

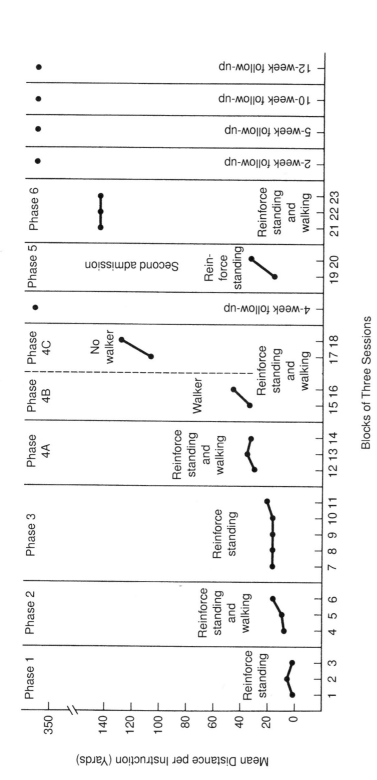

Figure 6-2. Average number of yards walked on request by a man who had suffered from chronic back pain for more than 15 years. Experimental conditions are indicated in the figure. ("The Use of Social Reinforcement in a Case of Conversion Reaction," by W. M. Kallman, M. Hersen, and D. H. O'Toole, 1975, *Behavior Therapy, 6*, p. 411–413. Copyright 1975 by the Association for the Advancement of Behavior Therapy. Adapted with permission.)

was taken away (Phase 4C). After 18 days, the patient was walking normally and was able to leave the hospital.

He continued to walk well at the four-week follow-up, but soon thereafter was readmitted to the hospital, unable to walk. The social reinforcement was again implemented, and was effective (Phase 5 and subsequent phases). During the last phase of treatment (Phase 6), members of the patient's family were taught to reinforce the patient's attempts to stand and to walk, and to ignore his complaints about "drawing over," the term he used to describe his illness. This procedure was used because the researchers determined that, after the initial treatment, the patient's family had reinforced his complaints and other behaviors indicative of illness, but had ignored walking and other behaviors indicative of wellness. The family-implemented treatment was successful and follow-up assessments indicated that the patient was walking normally three months after leaving the hospital for the second time.

This example is important in showing that systematic attempts to change the consequences of particular behaviors can lead to significant improvements in a person's life. It also illustrates that naturally occurring reinforcement (i.e., that arranged by the patient's family before they were trained by the intervention team) can strengthen undesirable behaviors, leading to problems for the behaving person.

Motivational Variables

The reinforcing effectiveness of a given stimulus is not fixed, but depends on several variables. The degree of deprivation and satiation relevant to the reinforcer maintaining behavior, as well as the learning history of the individual, are obvious and strong determinants of the reinforcing effectiveness of a stimulus.

Deprivation is the term used to describe a momentary increase in the reinforcing efficacy of a stimulus as a result of withholding presentations of that stimulus. For example, food is a more effective reinforcer if we have not eaten for a day than if we have just finished a five-course meal. **Satiation** is the term used to describe a momentary reduction in the reinforcing efficacy of a stimulus as a result of repeated presentations of that stimulus.[1] Satiation is common with many unconditioned positive reinforcers (e.g., food, water), but not with all. For example, satiation does not occur when briefly increasing a low tem-

---

[1]Michael (1982) has proposed the term **establishing operation** (EO) as a general label for motivational operations such as deprivation (and satiation) that (1) increase (or decrease) the effectiveness of a particular reinforcer and (2) increase (or decrease) the likelihood of occurrence of behavior that has in the past been followed by that reinforcer. Establishing operations evoke (or suppress) *all* behaviors that have been followed by the relevant consequence. For instance, food deprivation will strengthen not only asking for food, but also looking in places where food has previously been found, going to the store for food, and so on. As noted previously, behaviors that have the same consequences, regardless of their form, are members of the same operant response class. An EO alters the strength of all responses that make up an entire operant response class, not just one particular response.

perature is the reinforcer. Satiation characteristically does not occur with negative reinforcers such as the termination of pain. This is because in order for the termination of pain to function as a reinforcer, pain must be present. But when pain is present, one cannot get too much of its termination.

Satiation also does not characteristically occur with conditioned reinforcers alone, but if the unconditioned positive reinforcer paired with a conditioned reinforcer is presented often enough, satiation may be evident with both the unconditioned and the conditioned reinforcer. Suppose, for example, that a person with food stamps suddenly has access to free food or wins the lottery. Either of these operations will reduce the reinforcing effectiveness of food stamps, and whatever behavior produced them in the past would be suppressed. Finally, satiation rarely occurs with generalized conditioned reinforcers such as money. For example, even if you won a year's supply of all the food you wanted, you would still work for money because you would still need it to buy everything else money buys.

The learning history of the individual is also an important determinant of the reinforcing effectiveness of a particular stimulus. Thus, money is a reinforcer only for persons who have learned of its exchange value. Deprivation (and satiation) and learning history can be considered as antecedent, or setting, variables, in that they precede the response that they affect. When deprivation/satiation and learning history affect behavior, they do so as proximate and ultimate causes, respectively.

Intermittent Reinforcement

Reinforcers need not follow every occurrence of a behavior for the behavior to continue. For example, most of the time the hunting behaviors of a hungry gray fox are not successful in locating a mouse or other food, but the behaviors continue. They continue because they sometimes produce a meal. Our responses, too, are characteristically reinforced intermittently, not continuously. Can you think of anything that you do that is always reinforced? Flipping a switch that turns on a light, perhaps? Interestingly, both appropriate and inappropriate behavior maintained by social reinforcement from other persons is most often intermittently reinforced. For example, parents who reinforce crying and tantruming behavior in their children often say that they hardly ever pay attention to the behavior. Unfortunately, this is actually more problematic than always paying attention to the behavior, because these parents are actually teaching their children to cry more for less, or more infrequent, reinforcement.

Some EOs are rather complex. Consider the reinforcing effects of alcoholic beverages. Under what circumstances does alcohol function as a positive reinforcer for a typical college student who is a moderate drinker? The answer is "in a social setting" such as a bar. Relatively few people drink alcohol when they're alone or having breakfast, even if it's readily available. But many of the same people have a few drinks at evening gatherings with friends. Here, the social environment determines whether or not alcohol is reinforcing.

In the social environment, intermittent reinforcement is the rule, not the exception, and it works best at maintaining operant behavior.

Intermittent reinforcement represents a general type of **schedule of reinforcement**, which is the term scientific psychologists use to refer to relationships among stimuli, responses, and the passage of time that lead to an increase in response strength. Put simply, "schedules of reinforcement are the rules used to present reinforcing stimuli" (Zeiler, 1977, p. 202). Schedules of reinforcement are important for four reasons:

1. *Schedules of reinforcement are ubiquitous.* They operate throughout the natural environment of humans and other animals, even though it is frequently difficult to determine precisely what schedule is in effect at a given time for a particular response class.
2. *Schedules of reinforcement determine the rate and temporal pattern of behavior.* Different schedules generate very different rates and patterns of behavior. Typical behaviors under four simple and well-studied schedules are described in Sidebar 6-1.
3. *Schedules of reinforcement determine resistance to extinction.* Responding always approaches near-zero levels if extinction is arranged for a sufficient period, but the quickness with which it disappears and the pattern of responding during extinction depend on the schedule in effect prior to extinction.
4. *Schedules of reinforcement determine choice.* The time and effort allocated to one particular kind of behavior relative to another (i.e., choice) is determined in part by the schedule in effect for the alternative behaviors.

Sidebar 6-1
Four Simple Schedules of Reinforcement

Fixed-ratio (FR) and variable-ratio (VR) schedules are purely response based. In the former, a reinforcer follows every *n*th response, for instance, every fifth response under an FR 5 schedule. So-called continuous reinforcement is an FR 1 schedule. Under a VR schedule, on average every *n*th response is followed by the reinforcer, although the number of responses required for reinforcement varies irregularly. With protracted exposure, both of these schedules typically engender relatively high rates of responding. Postreinforcement (or pre-ratio) pausing, the cessation of behavior following a reinforcer, is characteristic of performance under FR, but not VR, schedules.

In contrast to FR and VR schedules, fixed-interval (FI) and variable-interval (VI) schedules are both response- and time-based. The FI schedule specifies that the first response emitted after a given period of time has elapsed (e.g., 10 minutes under an FI 10-min schedule) will be reinforced. This interval usually is timed from the delivery of the previous reinforcer. Relatively low overall response rates are typical under FI schedules. In some but not all cases, most responses are emitted toward the end of the interval, a pattern known as "scalloping." Variable-interval schedules specify that the first response emitted after some average period of time has elapsed will be reinforced; this interval varies irregularly around the mean value. These schedules generally evoke moderately high and very steady rates of responding. Resistance to extinction is great after exposure to a VI schedule.

A moment's reflection reveals the presence of simple schedules in everyday life. If, for example, a second-grade student named Amy receives a gold star each time she correctly answers one of 10 addition problems, that response is reinforced under a fixed-ratio 10 (FR 10) schedule. But if the teacher, being busy, delivers stars dependent on the completion of varying numbers of problems that average out at 10, the schedule is a variable-ratio 10 (VR 10). Assuming that stars are effective reinforcers and the student can solve the problems, either the FR 10 or the VR 10 should engender relatively high rates of problem completion.

Now consider a teacher who is both busy and lazy. He checks Amy's performance only at the end of each hour, delivering a star if she completes the problem correctly. This arrangement would constitute a fixed-interval 60-min schedule, and would generate little behavior. Checking at irregular intervals, some short, some long, some of intermediate length, would change the schedule to variable-interval, and substantially increase Amy's rate of problem completion. This is because she could never be certain when the teacher would deliver a star.

Simple schedules can be combined to form complex schedules. The concurrent schedule is an important example of a complex schedule. In **concurrent schedules** reinforcement is arranged simultaneously for two or more response classes. For example, under a concurrent variable-interval 1-min variable-interval 5-min (conc VI 1-min VI 5-min) schedule of food delivery, presses on one lever by a rat would be reinforced under a VI 1-min schedule, whereas presses on another lever would be reinforced under a VI 5-min schedule.

Humans are constantly exposed to concurrent schedules. When such schedules are arranged, we are said to make choices. Consider a typical party. Among the response options are talking to any of a number of people, listening to music, dancing, eating, or drinking. For any person at the party, these responses are not equally likely to occur, and there will be sizable differences across people in the amount of time spent in each. Sue may spend 80% of her time talking to Matt and 5% talking with Jeff, but these proportions may be reversed for Al. Why? There are several possibilities. One is that, by virtue of their histories, the objects and events that function as reinforcers differ for Sue and Al. Matt may talk at great length about chess, which reinforces Sue's listening, but not Al's. Another is that Jeff might arrange different schedules for Al and Sue. Perhaps Jeff compliments Al often, but rarely says anything good to Sue. Obviously, operant contingencies control social behavior (see Chapters 8, 11 & 12). That they do so should be evident in your own life: Who do you first approach at a party attended by your friends, and why do you approach that person? Do the consequences of prior interactions influence your choice?

Reducing Behavior through Operant Extinction

As you might guess, if responses are no longer followed by a reinforcer, the responses eventually stop occurring. The term **operant extinction** refers both to the procedure of failing to reinforce an established operant response *and* the decrease in responding that results. As an example of operant extinction, consider what happens when you try to buy candy from a vending machine that is out of order. The money goes in, and you press the button. Nothing happens. You press again. No candy. Eventually, you stop pressing. But the decline in the response is not necessarily smooth. Several features of responding undergoing extinction may be observed. First, the rate of responding often goes up on initial exposure to extinction—you hammer the button in a phenomenon known as *extinction-induced bursting*. Second, you may also curse or kick the machine, and wiggle the button from side to side, which illustrates both *emotional responding* and an *increase in the variability of behavior* that often occur with extinction.

Another effect of operant extinction is called **resurgence**, which refers to the reappearance of previously extinguished behaviors that once produced the same kind of reinforcer as the behavior currently being extinguished. In a different example, if a parent withholds attention from a child throwing a tantrum, the parent might observe behaviors, such as whining or pouting, that the parent reinforced before the tantruming evolved. These behaviors are all part of the same response class because they have, at one time or another, produced the same consequence—parental attention.

Table 6-2 provides five examples of extinction, each based on an extension of the cases portrayed in Table 6-1. Note that in each case (a) a previously reinforced response is not reinforced and (b) as a result, in the long run the behavior occurs less often.

Example 5 is noteworthy in that extinction involved forcing the person to engage in therapy sessions regardless of whether or not the response that once avoided such sessions (stretching) occurred. Under such conditions, stretching outside therapy sessions would probably fall to low levels, as indicated in Table 6-2. If, however, extinction were arranged in a different way, by not requiring the person to attend therapy sessions regardless of whether or not he stretched outside such sessions, stretching might well have persisted, for the person could not readily detect the changed contingencies (unless they were described to him). That is, during the reinforcement condition he stretched and was not cajoled to attend therapy and the same relation continued during extinction.

Although extinction can be an effective tool for reducing behavior, there are many situations where it is difficult or impossible to arrange, as when the consequences of a particular behavior are automatically reinforcing (e.g., as in masturbation). In addition, because behavior often increases in frequency and intensity when extinction is first arranged, extinction can be difficult to use in some therapeutic settings. For example, suppose we wanted to treat self-injury, say head banging, in a young child, by using extinction. If the behavior was maintained by attention as reinforcement, then we would withhold all attention for the behavior. However, because behavior undergoing extinction initially increases in intensity, we would risk the child seriously hurting himself. With such behaviors, other methods of response suppression may be called for.

Table 6-2
Examples of Extinction

Antecedent Situation	Operant Response	Historical Consequence of Response	Present Consequence	Eventual Behavioral Effect
1. A musician begins to strum an electric guitar, but the sounds aren't amplified	The musician jiggles a switch near the guitar's pick-up	The music was amplified	None; the intensity of music does not change	The musician does not jiggle the switch when amplification fails
2. A tourist visiting Peru approaches a native, who says "Buenos dias"	The tourist says "Buenos dias"	The Peruvians smiled under similar circumstances	None; there is no reaction	The tourist stops greeting natives with "Buenos dias"
3. A woman, sound asleep, is awakened by the cries of her baby, who is in the same bed	The woman begins to sing a soft lullabye	The baby stopped crying under similar circumstances	None; the baby continues to cry	The mother does not sing when her baby cries
4. An elderly resident of a nursing home is choosing foods at the home's cafeteria	The resident selects a "healthy" food	The person serving food praised the resident's food selection	None; no praise follows choices of "healthy" foods	The resident stops choosing healthy foods in the cafeteria
5. A severely burned patient is receiving treatment, which requires stretching of the skin over the burned area	The patient stretches for a specified time	The patient did not have to attend scheduled therapy sessions	None; the patient is required to attend therapy sessions regardless of whether he stretched outside those sessions	The patient stops stretching outside therapy sessions

Discriminative Stimuli and Stimulus Control

It's noon and you're walking along a downtown street. You had breakfast at seven and haven't eaten since. Five hours of deprivation have established food as a powerful reinforcer, and responses that have produced food in the past are at strength. These responses are to a large extent under the control of antecedent stimuli. For example, it is highly unlikely that you'd walk up to the counter in a boutique and say, "I'd like a hamburger, large fries, and a chocolate shake." Change the setting to a fast-food restaurant, however, and the response becomes highly probable. Why? Because in the past the response of asking for food was reinforced in restaurants, but obviously not in boutiques. In technical terms, the sights, sounds, and smells of the restaurant are discriminative stimuli that (as proximate causes) evoke the response of asking for food.

In essence, a **discriminative stimulus (S^D)** evokes a response because in the past that kind of response has been more successful in the presence of that stimulus than in its absence. Discriminative stimuli come to control a particular type of behavior by being present when that behavior is reinforced. Stimuli present when a particular type of behavior is not successful (i.e., is not reinforced) can also influence responding. The term S^{delta} (S^{Δ}) is used to designate such stimuli. An S^{Δ} is a stimulus that (1) suppresses a particular type of behavior (2) because in the past, that type of behavior was extinguished (i.e., not reinforced) in its presence, but reinforced in its absence. Figure 6-3 is a diagram of the relationships between an S^D, a response, and a reinforcing consequence and between an S^{Δ}, a response, and a reinforcing consequence.

When behavior differs in the presence and absence of a stimulus, the behavior is said to be under **stimulus control**. The development and maintenance of stimulus control requires **differential reinforcement,** wherein a response is reinforced in the presence of one stimulus and is extinguished in the presence of one or more other stimuli.[2] These conditions are arranged in **operant discrimination training.** Consider how children are taught to name colors. What we call "color" is determined by the wavelengths of light that an object reflects (see Chapter 7), and we teach children to name colors by reinforcing their voicing of a particular name in the presence of objects that reflect particular wavelengths, but not in the presence of objects that reflect other wavelengths. Humans are capable of detecting wavelengths of approximately 350 to 750 nanometers (nm), and we might teach a child to voice the terms "red," "green," "yellow," and "blue" when presented with objects that reflected wavelengths of 700, 600, 500, and 400 nm, respectively.

What would happen when a child trained in this way was presented with objects that reflected some other wavelength, perhaps 350 nm (which we would call "violet")? In all likelihood, she or he would say that the object was blue. When stimuli that differ along a given dimension (e.g., wavelength) control the same response (e.g., saying "blue"), **stimulus generalization** is evident and the two stimuli, in this example blue and violet, are functionally equivalent, in that they evoke the same response. Figure 6-4 shows a hypothetical graph, called a generalization gradient, showing the number of responses, for example, by a pigeon to different wavelengths (i.e., colors) after being trained to peck only at yellow (580nm).

Humans can, however, detect the difference between wavelengths of 350 and 400 nm (see Chapter 7), and it is possible to train them to respond differently to these wavelengths. In fact, most of us do: Most of us call objects that reflect wavelengths of 350 nm "violet" and those that reflect wavelengths of 400 nm "blue." The social environments of some people, including many artists and fashion designers, force even finer distinctions, giving a different name to each perceptible change in hue. This happens by virtue of a learning history in which making such distinctions was reinforced.

---

[2]The term *differential reinforcement,* which means selective reinforcement, is also used to refer to reinforcing one response in a response class and not reinforcing others in that class. For example, when parents attend to their children only when the children yell for them, but not when their children call out for them in a quieter voice, the parents are differentially reinforcing the yelling.

Figure 6-3. A diagram of the relationship between an S^D, a response, and a reinforcing consequence (S^R), and between an S^Δ, a response, and a reinforcing consequence. Note that the reinforcing consequence follows only when an S^D is present and the response occurs but not when an S^Δ is present and the response occurs.

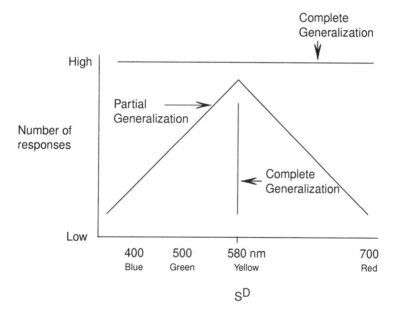

Figure 6-4. Hypothetical generalization gradients showing varying degrees of generalization (i.e., stimulus control). The dimension along which stimuli are varied (nm) determines the perceived color of light. Note that the closer the color to the S^D, the more responding.

People differ dramatically with respect to the discrimination training that they undergo, and as a result, in how they respond to particular stimuli. Consider that many traditional Inuits (Eskimos) respond differently to more than a dozen kinds of snow. Their verbal (and other) responses to snow are controlled by subtle features of frozen precipitation that exercise no control over the behavior of most other North Americans. This reflects a difference in training; young Inuits are reinforced (by their family and others and by the physical environment itself) for responding differently to physically different forms of snow. Most other people do not have such reinforcement histories, and snow exercises only coarse stimulus control over their behavior. That changes if they take up cross-country skiing. In this sport, fine discriminations based on subtle snow characteristics (e.g., age, temperature, compression) are learned due to differential reinforcement—red klister snow (old, crusted snow at relatively warm temperature) simply can't be skied effectively on wax designed for polar green snow (new snow at very low temperature). We learn the discriminations that are relevant to our personal environments.

Obviously, many of these discriminations are based on multiple stimulus dimensions. You recognize your best friend not by virtue of any single physical characteristic (e.g., size, color, form), but on the basis of a unique combination of characteristics. Discriminations also can be conditional. In a **conditional discrimination**, whether a response is reinforced in the presence of one stimulus depends on the presence of a second stimulus. For instance, you're studying in your room, and a friend is in the adjoining room. Your room has a digital clock, your friend's does not. The numbers 8:17 appear on the clock face, but they exercise no control over your behavior until your friend asks, "What time is it?" You respond, "It's eight seventeen." Here, a sequence of two stimuli, the auditory one provided by your friend and the visual one supplied by the clock, controlled your behavior. Your response is conditional upon the presence of not just one, but both stimuli.

Stimulus control plays a critical role in the development of complex human behavior. It is not enough to think about behavior in terms of its consequences. As described in the beginning of this chapter, the consequences of a behavior don't simply increase the frequency of that behavior; they increase it in the presence of circumstances present when reinforcement occurred (under similar circumstances). These circumstances include, but are not limited to, motivational variables and S^Ds. For example, behavior reinforced by food, such as looking for and eating food, will only be observed when the individual has gone without food for a while, *and* when stimuli, such as a place where food has been found and the food itself, are present. As previously described, reinforcement endows both EOs and S^Ds with evocative functions over behavior. In other words, these events become proximate causes (also called antecedent events). Thus, when thinking about behavior, it is necessary to identify the motivational variable, discriminative stimulus, and the reinforcer. As you can see, each of these variables makes understanding any given instance of behavior much more complex.

Developing New Behavior

Shaping

To this point, no mention has been made of how new operant responses are acquired. The fundamental process of operant response acquisition is called the reinforcement of successive approximations, or shaping. **Shaping** is a procedure whereby a given operant response is achieved by reinforcing successively closer approximations to that response. Initially, an existing response that is closest to the desired response is reinforced on a few occasions. After this, a new criterion for reinforcement is adopted. This new criterion demands a response more similar to the desired response than the previously reinforced behavior. Hence, if a parent wants to teach a young child to say "dad," she or he might first reinforce any vocalization. Then, when babbling was occurring at a high rate, the parent would selectively reinforce only "da" sounds, or the nearest observed approximation of that sound. Although it is possible that no response meeting the criterion for reinforcement will occur, this is unlikely. By failing to reinforce general vocalizations, extinction is arranged. You'll recall that the variability of behavior increases in extinction, and this makes it more likely that some da-like sound will be emitted. If, however, this does not occur, prompting (telling the child, "say dad") and modeling the correct response ("dad, dad, dad") probably would serve to evoke the response. Once "da" had been reinforced on several occasions, a final crite-

A rat "dunking" a marble. The target responses were achieved through the process of differentially reinforcing successive approximations, calling shaping.

rion for reinforcement, emitting the "dad" sound, would be adopted and re-inforced.

To help in understanding shaping, imagine that you are the animal trainer at a marine aquarium. Your first job is to train a dolphin to leap completely out of the water and grab a fish. How would you proceed? One possibility would be to hold a fish several feet above the water and wait for the dolphin to leap for it. If this occurred and the animal grabbed the fish, the response should be reinforced and recur. But your wait might be a long one; dolphins don't typically fly through the air pursuing fish. But they do chase and eat fish, and the response of leaping for one could be readily shaped. You might begin by attaching a fish to a rope so that the dolphin could bite off the fish while leaving the rope intact. First, the fish would be placed in the water, and the dolphin would be allowed to eat it. This would occur a few times. Next, the fish would be raised to water level. Once the behavior of grabbing the fish at water level was reliably occurring, the fish would be raised above the surface of the water in one-foot increments, making sure the dolphin was successful at each level before moving on the next. Eventually, it would be flying through the air to delight thousands and to secure your position as master trainer.

Procedures such as the one described of dolphin training are effective in shaping a behavior in a wide variety of animals (see photograph, p. 135). A study by Pryor, Haag, and O'Reilly (1969) demonstrates the effective use of shaping. These researchers worked with a porpoise named Hou that lived at a park in Hawaii. Prior to the intervention, Hou's main "tricks" were leaping and swimming in circles. By failing to reinforce these behaviors, and reinforcing successive approximations to the novel behavior of tail walking, Hou's repertoire was quickly expanded. It was expanded further by shaping, and Hou soon learned to perform somersaults, spins, back flips, and figure eights. When skillfully applied, reinforcement can do wonders.

Not only is shaping used consciously by teachers and trainers to establish new desired behavior, but it can also be responsible for the development of undesired behavior. Consider the following scenario. A parent puts a child to bed and the child softly whimpers. The parent immediately goes back into the room and consoles the child. The child now whimpers every night when put to bed. One night the parents decide to ignore (i.e., extinguish) the whimpering and when the child whimpers they do not go back into the room. The whimpering becomes louder and lasts longer until the parents finally give in and go into the room to console the child. Of course, the parents' behaviors of going into the room and consoling the child are reinforced when the child becomes quiet and falls asleep (negative reinforcement for the parents' behaviors). Unfortunately, the parents are reinforcing the louder whimpering. This process continues over several weeks or months as the whimpering is gradually shaped into loud tantruming and crying. The parents have successfully, but unknowingly, shaped loud crying at bedtime. In such circumstances, the child is viewed as having a problem, and is considered to be spoiled or unruly, but, as you can see, the problem resides in the child's environment, not inside the child.

Chaining

Shaping is a successful device for producing new responses, although other procedures are involved in the development of complex patterns of behavior. One such procedure is **response chaining,** in which a sequence of behaviors must be emitted before the unconditioned reinforcer is delivered. Only the terminal (final) response is followed by an unconditioned reinforcer; prior responses in the sequence simply provide an opportunity for subsequent responses to occur (see photograph, this page). Purchasing soda from a vending machine is a good example of response chaining. A sequence of many different responses is required to produce the drink, including reaching into your pocket or purse for the change, putting it in the machine, and pushing the correct button. Only the final movement of the can to your lips, how-

A rat "jumping hurdles." In addition to shaping, chaining was used by reinforcing the jump over the last hurdle first and then adding additional hurdles.

ever, is followed by the reinforcer that ultimately maintains behavior—a drink of pop.

Reducing Behavior through Punishment: Punishment Procedures Used in Applied Settings

At the beginning of the chapter, we noted that stimuli that follow behavior can have two effects: The future likelihood of occurrence of the response under similar circumstances can increase, which is termed reinforcement, or it can decrease. The term **punishment** is used when a response is followed by a change in the environment *(punisher)* and thereby decreases under similar circumstances. Punishment always *weakens* behavior, whereas reinforcement always *strengthens* it. Although punishment typically is unpleasant, like reinforcement it is defined independently of any subjective feelings concerning it. That being the case, the only way to determine whether a particular stimulus is a punisher is to determine whether presenting that stimulus following a response reduces the future frequency of the response.

Consider a case in which a teacher wants to decrease a child's talking out in class. The teacher decides to say in a stern voice, "Stop that, Dennis!" immediately after each occurrence of the undesired behavior. Is this procedure punishment? It's impossible to tell without further information. Surely it is *intended* as punishment, but it functions as such only if it reduces the rate (or some other dimension) of talking out.

Like reinforcers, punishers can be unconditioned or conditioned, depending on whether their effects depend on a special learning history. Intense stimuli (e.g., loud sounds, bright lights, high temperatures) are likely to function as unconditioned punishers; such stimuli can produce physical damage, and there is obvious survival value in not repeating behaviors that produce or increase exposure to them. Conditioned punishers acquire their ability to weaken behavior through being paired with established punishers, and continue to have this effect only so long as the pairing is maintained. For example, you may establish the verbal stimulus "No" as an effective conditioned punisher for many of your dog's responses by picking up the dog and shaking it while saying "No" when an undesired response occurs. After a few pairings, "No" alone should serve as a punisher.

To retain symmetry with the terms used to describe reinforcement, punishment can be classified as positive or negative, depending on whether it involves adding a stimulus (or increasing its intensity) or subtracting a stimulus (or decreasing its intensity).[3] An example of positive punishment is a reduction in the rate of a college student's touching a television switch due to the delivery of electric shock through that switch. An example of negative punishment is a reduction in the rate of putting money into a broken vending machine due to a loss of money. Figure 6-1 distinguishes positive and negative punishment and makes clear their relation to positive and negative reinforcement.

---

[3]Distinguishing between positive and negative punishers poses the same sorts of problems as distinguishing between positive and negative reinforcers.

Several types of punishment procedures are employed by psychologists in applied settings. **Time-out** *(from positive reinforcement)*, which involves response-dependent institution of a period of time in which one or more positive reinforcers are unavailable, is a form of (negative) punishment commonly used in clinical settings. Making a child go to another room (preferably one that is boring) after cursing at supper is an example of time-out: Because the response of cursing occurred, the child's access to the reinforcers available at supper (e.g., food, interaction with family members) is taken away. Time-out is frequently misused by those who do not understand operant punishment. Fortunately, there are several empirically based rules for the effective use of time-out (see Clark, 1996).

Overcorrection is a clinically useful (positive) punishment procedure that makes use of the Premack principle to decrease responding. In overcorrection procedures, a person is forced to engage in a low-probability behavior each time a higher-probability, and undesired, response occurs. For instance, a teenager may be required to scrub the classroom floor (a low-probability behavior) after spitting on it (a higher-probability behavior).

A final punishment procedure used in applied settings is **response cost,** which involves removing a positive reinforcer that a person has earned whenever misbehavior occurs. An example of this is fining a child $5 each time she or he fights with a sibling. Remember, of course, that this operation, and all others, would be punishment only if it weakened behavior.

Punishment procedures such as these have been widely criticized when used to control human behavior. Such procedures, like any procedure used with human subjects, can be inhumane if poorly conceived. Punishment is nonetheless a part of life and must be considered in attempts to explain behavior. Why, for instance, don't you habitually walk into objects around you? Because running into them in the past has caused pain. Why don't you talk loudly and fidget in church, or strike everyone who displeases you? Same answer: A history of punishing consequences. Adapting to one's environment requires failing to repeat responses that have adverse consequences, as well as repeating responses that have beneficial consequences. Punishment produces the former outcome, reinforcement the latter. Both are everyday parts of our environment and our nervous system.

One way to make sure that punishment procedures are used effectively and humanely is to be well informed about the scientific research on punishment. Laboratory studies have revealed a great deal about the variables that determine the effectiveness of punishment (e.g., Azrin & Holz, 1966). We know, for example, that maximum response suppression occurs when

1. The punisher is delivered immediately after the response.
2. The punisher follows every occurrence of the response. As a rule, and unlike reinforcement, intermittent punishment is less effective than continuous (i.e., FR 1) punishment.
3. The punisher is initially presented at high intensity. Organisms eventually adapt to low-intensity punishers, which lose their ability to suppress responding. If, for example, a parent spanks a child very lightly, the parent may have to increase the intensity of spanking to make the punisher more effective. This may result in the parent having to spank

the child very hard without decreasing the target behavior. A more effective alternative would be to use a more intense spanking for the first occurrence of the behavior. Ironically, this may be more humane than starting off with a mild spanking, although for other reasons, spanking is generally not recommended.

4. An alternative to the punished response is available. Obviously, only responses that have already been reinforced and are occurring at some frequency can be punished. If the response to be punished is the only one that is effective in producing this reinforcer, it will be harder to suppress than if some alternative response which produces the same reinforcer is available. Suppose, for example, that a parent wants to decrease their child's talking back whenever the parent asks the child to do a chore. Obviously, talking back occurs because it is reinforced, that is, it gets something for the child, such as the parent's attention, or getting out of doing the chore. In order for the parent to most effectively reduce talking back, the child must have an alternative response to get the same attention from the parent, such as asking in a more appropriate tone if the chore has to be done right away.

Many attempts to employ punishment are ineffective because they involve weak, delayed, and intermittent punishers and offer no alternative to the punished response. Consider, for example, attempts to reduce illegal drug sales through court-imposed fines and jail sentences. Would you expect them to be effective punishers? Why or why not?

Explaining Operant Behavior

According to Skinner (1978), the very nature of operant behavior encourages the invention of mentalistic explanations. What Skinner meant is that, because any instance of operant behavior is evoked by a variety of variables, including motivational variables and multiple discriminative stimuli, "the behavior seems to start up suddenly . . . as if spontaneously generated" (Skinner, 1978, p. 102). Thus, unlike conditional reflexes, there is often no one obvious evoking stimulus. Elsewhere, Skinner wrote that "operant behavior is the very field of purpose and intention" (1974, p. 55), in the sense that it seems to stretch toward the future (the consequences, although they occurred in the past). For example, it is common to hear someone say that "a dog sat because it knew it would get food" or "in order to get food" (an example of a teleological explanation).

Unlike conditional reflexes, which typically have conspicuous eliciting stimuli, operant behavior has historically been attributed to free will or to such constructs as purpose or intention. You may recall from Chapter 1 that Descartes believed humans were different from nonhumans precisely because humans had free will. B. F. Skinner spent much of his professional life arguing that operant behavior could be explained without reference to mental or cognitive events. The doctrine of parsimony suggests that when explaining behavior, one should adopt the explanation that requires the fewest assumptions. Because operant behavior, by its very nature, is determined by its consequences, it is unnecessary to use concepts such as intention, purpose, or will to explain it.

The Importance of Operant Conditioning

To an even greater extent than classical conditioning, operant conditioning selects behaviors of an organisms and, thus, allows behavior to adapt to its environment. Through operant conditioning, behaviors that produce food, water, sex, a comfortable environment, and a host of other objects and events of obvious biological significance are repeated under similar circumstances. So, too, are responses that prevent or terminate exposure to harmful stimuli. If the environment is static, the same set of responses will persist, but if the environment changes, behavior will also change. The extent to which change occurs varies among species; most human behavior is very sensitive to operant conditioning. It is this sensitivity that accounts for many of the behavioral differences that we observe in people: They have experienced different behavior–environment interactions, and hence have developed different repertoires. Sometimes people ask how two children who were raised in the same family could turn out so differently. Questions like these contain a fundamental fallacy: that two children can have exactly the same environment. It is impossible for any two people, even identical twins raised by the same parents in the same house, to have the same environment if we conceive of environment in terms of the types of moment-to-moment behavior–environment interactions described in this chapter (as well as in Chapter 5).

Operant conditioning provides for behavioral plasticity, but it does not automatically ensure that a person will acquire and emit responses that are deemed desirable by other people or that ensure success in any regard. Some environments foster behaviors that are in the long run harmful to an individual and to society at large. Drug abuse, child abuse, robbery, racism, sexism, and a host of other vexing problems involve troublesome patterns of operant responding that are primarily acquired and maintained due to their short-term consequences. Understanding this is a first step toward the treatment and prevention of these problems.

Unfortunately, adequately understanding human behavior is no easy task. The basic principles of operant (and classical) conditioning are relatively simple, and it is easy to see how these principles apply to the behavior of humans and nonhumans alike in controlled laboratory settings. Applying these principles to the behavior of humans in their natural environment is a more difficult task. Also, practical and ethical considerations make the controlled study of humans difficult. Moreover, within a short time after their birth, humans already have begun to experience a rich and complicated history of behavior–environment interactions (see Chapter 12). By virtue of this history, a given stimulus often has more than one behavioral function, and these functions can change across time or situations. This can make it difficult to determine precisely the variables that control a particular behavior in a given individual. Nonetheless, scientific psychologists know in principle the kinds of variables that do control human learning and, as explained in the balance of this text, can offer plausible if not proven explanations of a very wide range of human activities.

Summary

1. In *operant conditioning*, behavior is controlled primarily by the consequences it produces in the environment.

2. Stimuli produced by a response (i.e., consequences) can have two effects: The future likelihood of occurrence of the response under similar circumstances can increase, a process called *reinforcement*, or it can decrease, a process called *punishment.*

3. *Positive reinforcers* are presented (i.e., added) following behavior, whereas *negative reinforcers* are taken away (i.e., subtracted) following behavior, but both operations increase the future frequency of the behavior under similar circumstances.

4. *Unconditioned reinforcers* can strengthen behavior in organisms without any particular learning history. Other events, called *conditioned reinforcers*, gain their ability to strengthen behavior through learning, specifically by being paired with unconditioned reinforcers.

5. Sometimes the reinforcer for behavior is not an event or a stimulus, but rather the opportunity to engage in another behavior. The *Premack principle* states that for any two behaviors that occur with different probabilities, the opportunity to engage in the higher-probability behavior will reinforce the lower-probability behavior. Conversely, having to engage in the lower-probability behavior will punish the higher-probability behavior.

6. The effectiveness of a given reinforcer varies as a function of several variables, including *motivational variables* (e.g., the amount of food deprivation), the *temporal relations* (the delay between the response and the reinforcer), and the *schedule* according to which the reinforcer is delivered.

7. Operant behavior can be reduced through a procedure called *extinction* in which reinforcers for an already established operant are withheld. The response eventually decreases but frequently other effects occur first. These include an increase in behavioral variability, emotional responding, or aggressive behavior. Sometime earlier forms of the operant class may reappear, a phenomenon called *resurgence*.

8. In the process called *discrimination training*, a response is reinforced in the presence of one stimulus (called a *discriminative stimulus* or S^D) and is extinguished in the presence of one or more other stimuli (called $S^{-\text{deltas}}$). The S^D is then said to evoke the response (and the S^Δ suppresses the response) which is said to be under the stimulus control of the S^D (or S^Δ).

9. In a procedure known as *shaping*, successively closer approximations to a given operant response are reinforced, and new operant behavior can be developed. In a procedure known as *response chaining*, complex patterns of be-

havior can be developed when a sequence of behaviors must be emitted before the unconditioned reinforcer is delivered.

10. Punishment reduces behavior by either presenting (i.e., adding) a stimulus following behavior, called *positive punishment*, or removing (i.e., subtracting) a stimulus following a behavior, known as *negative punishment*.

11. Punishment procedures used with different clinical populations include *time-out* (from positive reinforcement), *overcorrection*, and *response cost*.

12. Just as with classical conditioning, operant behavior is most parsimoniously explained by appealing to the actual interactions between an individual's behavior and the environment, as opposed to mental or cognitive events, such as purpose or intention.

Study Questions

1. What are the two possible effects on responding that consequent stimuli can have?

2. What are the effects of reinforcement on behavior?

3. What are the differences and similarities between positive and negative reinforcers and why is it sometimes difficult to distinguish between the two?

4. What is the only way to determine whether a stimulus functions as a reinforcer?

5. What kinds of objects and events are reinforcing? What is the relationship between conditioned and unconditioned reinforcers?

6. What is the general rule about the delay of reinforcers and their effects on behavior?

7. What is the Premack principle and how can we use it to predict what will function as reinforcement for a particular behavior?

8. What effects do deprivation and satiation have on the effectiveness of reinforcers, and which kinds of reinforcers are not affected by deprivation and satiation?

9. What is intermittent reinforcement and why is it the rule in the social environment?

10. What are schedules of reinforcement and why are they important?

11. How can behavior be reduced through operant extinction and what are the four types of changes that occur in behavior initially undergoing extinction?

12. How is differential reinforcement used in operant discrimination training to establish discriminative stimuli, and what effects do such stimuli have on behavior? How is the phrase *stimulus control* used?

13. How is new behavior established through shaping? How is shaping often used, unknowingly, to condition undesirable behavior?

14. Recalling the two possible effects on responding that consequent stimuli can have, what are the effects of punishment on behavior?

15. What is the distinction between positive and negative punishers as well as conditioned and unconditioned punishers?

16. What are three types of punishment procedures used in applied settings and what are four variables that determine the effectiveness of punishment?

17. Why does knowledge of operant conditioning obviate the need to explain most behavior in terms of mental or cognitive events?

18. Why is operant conditioning important especially for human behavior? How does susceptibility to operant conditioning allow for behavioral adaptability or flexibility?

Neurophysiology and Behavior

7

Chapter 2 introduced the concept of physiological causes of behavior which are classified as proximate causes because they occur immediately before behavior. Physiological psychologists study such causes; their interest is in the bodily activities that are responsible for behavior, especially activities located in the nervous system. **Neurophysiologists,** including physiological psychologists, attempt to answer *how* questions about behavior, for example, How does the brain produce appropriate behavior under certain circumstances? In an effort to understand behavior, scientific psychologists attempt to explain *why* it occurs in terms of general laws, such as the laws of classical and operant conditioning. Neurophysiologists, by contrast, attempt to explain *how* behavior occurs in terms of more elementary, physiological, processes (called reduction[1]) (Carlson, 1995).

The nervous system plays an essential role in behavior and is, therefore, of great interest to psychologists. This chapter describes the general structure and function of the human nervous system and how changes in it are related to behavior. First we outline some historical developments that paved the way for our current understanding of the role of the brain in behavior.

A Brief History of Inquiry into the Brain

The 1980s have been called the decade of the brain because the amount of research and understanding into the role of the human brain dramatically increased during this time. This research has continued into the 1990s and promises to continue full speed ahead into the next century. The importance of the (human) brain wasn't always appreciated by philosophers and psychologists, however. Fancher (1996) tells us that Aristotle, for example, did not think the brain was important, because it was bloodless after death (which to him probably meant that it was devoid of animal spirits), and because he had heard reports of soldiers whose brain surfaces had been exposed by battle wounds who experienced no sensation when their brains were touched. As Fancher writes, "Aristotle found it hard to believe that such a 'bloodless,' 'insensitive,' and generally unimpressive-looking organ could be the seat of the highest human faculties" (p. 73).

In the 1600s, the brain began to be studied more scientifically. For example, the physician Thomas Willis (1621–1675) published the first detailed anatomy

---

[1]The term **reduction** (or reductionism) is used to refer to attempts to explain some phenomena in terms of simpler phenomena. As Carlson (1988) relates, physiological psychologists "may explain the movement of a muscle [which produces behavior] in terms of changes in the members of muscle cells, the entry of particular chemicals, and the interactions among protein molecules within the cells" (p. 11). He goes on to explain that the process of reduction can be taken further, as when a molecular biologist "explains these events in terms of the forces that bind various molecules together and cause various parts of the molecules to be attracted to one another" (p. 11). Different levels of analysis define, in part, different disciplines. There is no one level of analysis (degree of reduction) that best explains a phenomenon, but reductionism becomes nonproductive when it ceases to allow for the prediction and concern of the events to be explained. For example, no matter how much one knows about the forces that bind molecules, that knowledge will not allow for the accurate prediction or control of behavior.

of the brain. The importance of the brain in behavior was first convincingly demonstrated by the German physician and comparative anatomist Franz Josef Gall (1758–1828), who compared the brains and intelligence of different species and showed, in general, that higher mental functions were positively correlated with size of the brain; in other words, the larger the brain the more complex and intelligent the behavior. Unfortunately, Gall is better known for his pseudoscientific theory of phrenology. Phrenology assumed that specific psychological traits such as curiosity, verbal memory, criminality, and benevolence, among many others, were located in specific regions of the brain. If these regions were well developed in a particular individual, they would bulge like well developed muscles, producing bumps on the head. Gall thus believed that one could tell something about the personalities of individuals by measuring the bumps on their head. Like other, more recent pseudoscientific theories, such as facilitated communication (see Chapter 3), alien abduction, repressed memory syndrome, and ESP, to name a few, phrenology was a "pseudoscientific craze" because even though most scientists rejected its scientific merit, it appealed to the general population who, as we know, aren't as selective as scientists about what they believe (Fancher, 1996).

Ironically, although Gall's theory of phrenology has not been supported, his general idea of localization of function in the brain has been. During the next one hundred years, especially after the discovery of electricity by the Italian scientist Galvani, which has been called "the most important discovery of all time" (Bolles, 1993), experiments revealed the structures in the brain underlying many important functions. For example, following Gall, the French scientist Flourens (1794–1867) showed that one structure in the brain (the cerebellum) was responsible for the coordination of muscle movement and another structure (the cerebral cortex) was responsible for general sensory and motor functions. More specific findings about the cortex included the motor strip by the German scientists Gustav Fritsch and Eduard Hitzig, the visual, auditory, and somatosensory areas by the Scottish scientist, David Ferrier, and certain language areas by the French physician Paul Broca and the German neurologist Carl Wernicke.

These and other discoveries are described later in the chapter as well as in Chapter 8. First, we overview the function and structure of the nervous system by answering two questions: (1) What are the primary functions of the nervous system? and (2) What is the general structure of the nervous system that enables those functions?

Two Functions of the Nervous System

What is the nervous system for? What does it do? The answer is simpler than it might appear on first glance. *Ultimately, the primary function of the nervous system is behavior* (Carlson, 1995). The word "ultimately" is important in this context because many researchers, including both psychologists and neuroscientists, are less interested in behavior than in mental or cognitive events (see Chapter 9). Perhaps the most important reason that the primary function of the nervous system must be behavior is that an individual's behavior must "ultimately" make direct contact with the environment in order for that individual to survive, that is, live long enough to pass on genes. Survival in this sense includes behaviors that result in obtaining nourishment, mating, caring for offspring, and avoiding predators. (It is not possible for mental events to make direct contact with the environment.)

As we saw in Chapters 4, 5, and 6, both natural selection and learning, each over different time periods, operate on behaviors that make direct contact with the environment. In this way, the environment selects behavior, both at the phylogenetic level as fixed action patterns and reflexes, and at the ontogenetic level as learned behavior. At the phylogenetic level what is ultimately selected are genes that code for certain neurophysiological structures, and at the ontogenetic level what is selected are connections between neurons. Both make behavior possible.

A second but equally important function of the nervous system is the detection of environmental stimuli. Accurate detection of stimuli makes successful action more likely. Thus, the nervous system is composed of three general types of systems: (1) sensory systems, responsible for detecting, or sensing, environmental stimuli; (2) motor systems, responsible for movement, or behavior; and (3) a central nervous system that coordinates sensory, motor, and other functions. Before we describe how these systems work and interact, we describe the general structure of the nervous system that forms the foundation for these functions.

Structure of the Nervous System: Structural Divisions of the Nervous System

The structure of the nervous system can be viewed at several different levels. For example, one level is that of the individual cell, called a neuron (see below). Another level is that of the brain, which is composed of billions of neurons organized in various ways. Figure 7-1 shows a general schematic of the structure of the nervous system.

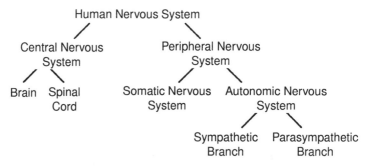

Figure 7-1. Divisions of the human nervous system. (From *Psychology: A Behavioral Overview,* by A. Poling, H. Schlinger, S. Starin, and E. Blakely, 1990, New York: Plenum Press. Copyright 1990 by Plenum Press. Reprinted with permission.)

The two major structural divisions of the nervous system that accomplish its functions are the **central nervous system** (CNS), which consists of the brain and spinal cord, and the **peripheral nervous system** (PNS), which contains all other sensory and motor nerves. Figure 7-2 shows a schematic of the relationship between the central and peripheral nervous systems. As you can see, the nervous system is organized according to its primary functions, that is, getting information from the environment to the brain (sensation; the nerves involved are called **afferent**), doing something with the information (coordination), and then getting the organism to do something about the information (behavior; the nerves involved are called **efferent**). The branch of the PNS that receives information from the sensory organs and controls the skeletal muscles is called the **somatic nervous system,** and the branch that regulates the cardiac muscle and the smooth muscles and glands is called the **autonomic** (meaning self-governing) **nervous system** (ANS). The ANS is further divided into two anatomically separate subdivisions, the sympathetic division, associated with the expenditure of energy, and the **parasympathetic division,** associated with increasing the body's supply of stored energy. Before discussing these divisions further, it is useful to describe **neurons,** the basic structural and functional units in the nervous system.

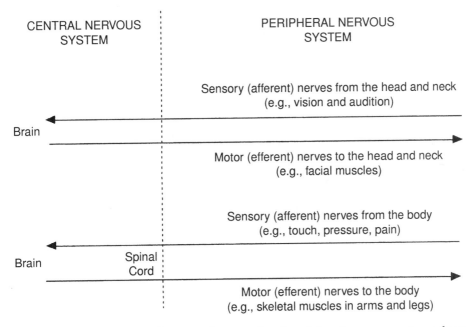

Figure 7-2. The relationship between the central and peripheral nervous systems showing the general direction of afferent nerves, which send sensory information *from* the sensory organs above and below the neck *to* the brain, and efferent nerves, which send motor information *from* the brain *to* muscles and glands above and below the neck.

Neurons

Neurons, the cells of the nervous system, are amazing adaptations. Knowing how neurons function enables scientists to understand how stimuli affect us, how we behave, and how we learn, among other things. Because of their fundamental importance to understanding behavior, they merit more detailed description.

Anatomically, neurons can be divided into four parts (see Figure 7-3): the cell body, the dendrites, the axon, and the terminal buttons. The **cell body** (also known as the *soma,* which is Greek for body) contains the cell's DNA and is primarily responsible for controlling cell maintenance and metabolism. **Dendrites** are branchlike structures that extend from the cell body. They are sensitive to chemicals released by other cells and carry nerve impulses (see below) toward the cell body. The **axon** carries nerve impulses away from the cell body toward the terminal buttons. The **terminal buttons** are located at the end of the axon. They contain **synaptic vesicles** (sacs) which, when stimulated, release chemical substances called **neurotransmitters.** Neurotransmitters alter the activity of other cells.

The terminal buttons of one neuron are in close proximity to (but do not touch) the dendrites and/or cell bodies of adjoining neurons. When two cells are positioned so that they can interact chemically, they are said to be "connected." The terminal buttons of a single neuron typically connect with many other neurons. Likewise, the dendrites and cell body of a given neuron often are connected to the terminal buttons of many other neurons. In this way, neurons affect other neurons with which they are connected and are, thus, said to "communicate" with one another. This arrangement results in billions of possible

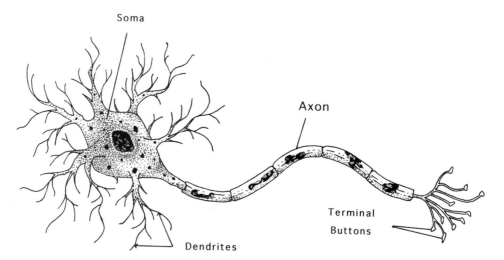

Figure 7-3. Structural features of a typical neuron showing the soma (cell body), dendrites, axon, and terminal buttons.

neuronal "connections" in the nervous system. As you can imagine, there is opportunity for almost endless complexity in the physiological events that cause behavior.

The structure of neurons is directly related to their function which, briefly, is to conduct (or not conduct) nerve impulses.

The Nerve Impulse

In simple terms, the **nerve impulse** is an electrical signal conducted along the neuron. The nerve impulse involves both chemical and electrical processes: It is started chemically by contact with "sending" neurons, but is conducted along the "receiving" neuron electrically. Because mammalian nerve cells are so small, scientific study of the nerve impulse awaited the discovery, in the 1930s, that squid have thick and long nerve cells. These cells can be kept alive outside the body of the squid, which made study of the processes underlying neurotransmission much easier. Much of what is known today about these processes was learned by studying nerve cells from squid.

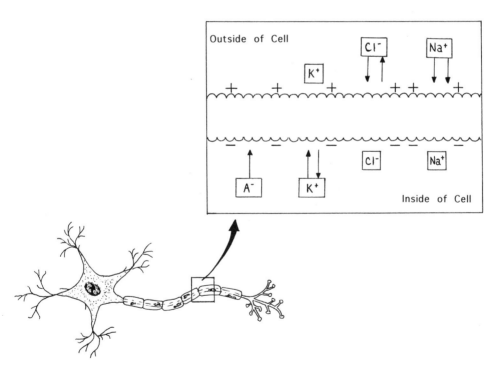

Figure 7-4. The resting state of the inside of a neuron (relative to the outside fluid) showing how the relative concentration of sodium (Na^+), potassium (K^+), and chloride (Cl^-) ions determine the negatively charged resting potential by their movement into or out of the cell.

The easiest way to understand the nerve impulse is to compare it to electricity flowing along a wire. Electricity moves along an electrical wire due to the flow of charged particles (electrons and protons). Similarly, the neural impulse results from the movement of charged particles, particularly molecules of sodium, potassium and chloride, in and out of the cell membrane. These charged particles are called *ions*. Because there are more negatively charged ions inside than outside the cell, the normal (i.e., resting) state of the inside of the neuron is negatively charged or *polarized* with respect to its outside (see Figure 7-4).

Because oppositely charged ions attract, there is the *potential* for movement of these ions through the cell membrane. If the neuron is stimulated either by an electrical charge produced artificially by a researcher, or more naturally by synaptic transmission from another neuron (described below), sodium ions will enter the cell more easily; this entrance causes the electrical potential of the cell to change from negative to positive (because sodium ions are positively charged). The inside of the cell becomes less negative, or depolarized. If depolarization is sufficiently strong, the **threshold of excitation** is reached, and even more positively charged sodium ions begin to enter the neuron.

As sodium ions "rush in," an **action potential** is generated and the neuron "fires." This is the nerve impulse. This wave of electrical activity lasts less than three milliseconds, and passes rapidly, without diminishing, along the axon until it reaches the terminal buttons. After the action potential has ended, the charged ions return to their original positions both inside and outside the cell and the resting potential is restored. If one were able to see a neuron fire with the naked eye, the impulse traveling down the length of the axon would look much like a flame traveling along a fuse.

Synaptic Transmission

As noted, neurons are connected to one another and to other cells (e.g., muscle cells) with which they interact, but this does not occur through direct physical contact. Neurons interact with other cells through a very small fluid-filled gap, known as a **synapse**, between the terminal buttons of one neuron and the dendrites or cell body of adjoining cells (see Figure 7-5). It is estimated that one neuron may share up to 100,000 synapses with other neurons (Zimbardo, 1988) and that the human nervous system may include more than 100 trillion synapses (Hubel, 1979).

Neurons communicate with other cells at the synapse through a chemical process known as **synaptic transmission**. Synaptic transmission begins when a nerve impulse causes the synaptic vesicles in a sending neuron to release *neurotransmitter* substances. Molecules of the neurotransmitter spread out across the synaptic gap and bind with chemical receptors on the membrane of receiving neurons. The type and amount of neurotransmitter and whether there are receptors for that neurotransmitter determine whether or not a nerve impulse will be triggered in the receiving neuron. When it is, the nerve impulse begins on that neuron at the point where the synapse occurs, either on the soma or the den-

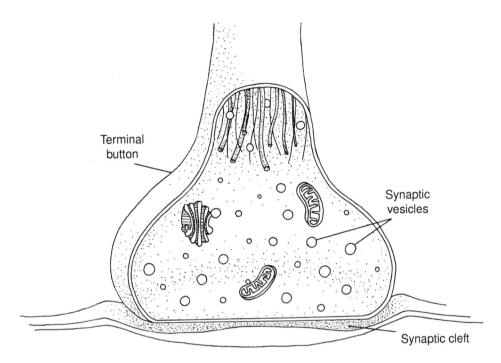

Terminal
button

Synaptic
vesicles

Synaptic cleft

Figure 7-5. A synapse (connection) between the terminal button of a sending neuron and the cell body or dendrite of a receiving neuron. The neurotransmitter substance, which is stored in synaptic vesicles, is released into the fluid-filled space between the two neurons called the synaptic cleft. Adapted from Carlson (1995).

drite, and continues down the axon to the terminal buttons, where a synapse with another neuron exists, and so on.

Neurotransmitter substances are generally classified as excitatory or inhibitory. Both types work by altering the resting potential of receiving neurons. *Excitatory neurotransmitters* depolarize (make less negative) the resting potential of receiving neurons, thus allowing positively charged ions to flow into them. This produces a nerve impulse in these cells. *Inhibitory neurotransmitters* prevent the neural impulse from being conducted in a receiving neuron by polarizing the resting potential of the cells even more, so that a greater than normal amount of excitatory transmitter is required to initiate a nerve impulse. Many excitatory and inhibitory transmitters simultaneously act on a single neuron at any given time. It is the sum of their effects that determines the cell's electrical charge and hence whether or not an action potential is generated.

An Example of Neuronal Communication

Because it may be difficult to digest all of this information about neurons and synaptic transmission, let us put it into a more familiar context. Recall that the patellar reflex is an unconditional reflex (see Chapter 5) in which a tap on the patellar tendon (US) elicits a leg kick (UR), which is produced by contraction of the quadriceps muscle. The patellar reflex is an example of a **monosynaptic reflex,** that is, a reflex involving only one synapse. (Most other reflexes are polysynaptic and involve two or more synapses.)

A tap on the patellar tendon causes the quadriceps muscle to stretch slightly and also produces a nerve impulse in a sensory neuron within the muscle. That nerve impulse travels along the neuron up the leg to the lumbar region of the spinal cord, where it synapses on (i.e., connects with) a motor neuron. When the nerve impulse in the sensory neuron reaches the terminal buttons, it causes them to release a transmitter substance. This substance excites the motor neuron and causes an action potential (nerve impulse). The action potential travels along that neuron back to the quadriceps muscle, where another transmitter substance is released from its terminal buttons. This excitatory transmitter substance causes the muscle to contract and, therefore, the leg to extend. Figure 7-6 depicts the neurons involved in the monosynaptic stretch reflex.

If you consciously tried and succeeded in not moving your leg when the patellar tendon was tapped, this would occur as a result of an inhibitory transmitter substance being released at the synapse with the motor neuron.

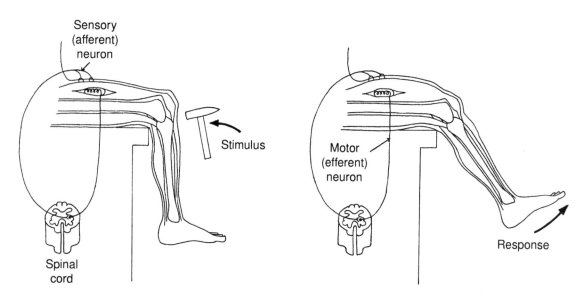

Figure 7-6. The patellar (spinal) reflex showing one synapse (in the spinal cord) between a sensory (afferent) neuron and a motor (efferent) neuron. When the patellar tendon just below the knee cap is tapped, a sensory receptor inside the quadriceps muscle of the leg is stretched, which causes the afferent (sensory) neuron to fire. The sensory neuron synapses with an efferent (motor) neuron in the spinal cord, causing it to fire, which causes the quadriceps muscle to contract and the leg to extend. Adapted from Pinel (1990).

Drugs and Neurotransmission

Researchers have studied at great length the physiological effects of drugs that people use recreationally and medicinally (e.g., Feldman, Meyer, & Quenzer, 1997). Researchers have discovered that some drugs, called **agonists,** facilitate the effects of transmitter substances, and some drugs, called **antagonists,** block the effects of transmitter substances. In short, drugs affect behavior by altering neurotransmission, either by binding directly to receptors of receiving neurons or by altering the production, storage, release, or inactivation of neurotransmitters. For example, drugs like morphine and heroin, called *opioids*, combine with and activate receptors normally occupied by endogenous (i.e., produced within the body) substances in the brain called **endorphins** (*endogenous m orphine*-like substances). Because heroin and morphine mimic the effects of endorphins, they are considered to be agonists.

Other drugs (e.g., naloxone and nalorphine) are classified as opioid antagonists because they block receptors, thus preventing other drugs or endogenous transmitter substances from combining with them. Through this mechanism, antagonists are able to block and reverse the effects of agonists. Therefore, an individual first given naloxone will not be substantially affected by heroin or morphine, and a person who is experiencing the effects of heroin will stop experiencing those effects if injected with naloxone. Naloxone can thus be used to treat heroin or morphine overdose. And an opioid antagonist could be used in treating heroin abuse if a drug were available that worked like naloxone but, unlike it, had long-lasting effects, was orally effective, and did not produce significant adverse reactions. No such drug is available, but when and if scientists develop one, taking it regularly would eliminate the euphoric (and reinforcing) effects of heroin, and use of heroin would eventually cease (through the process of operant extinction).

This example is similar to the use of Antabuse to treat alcohol abuse. A person who consumes alcohol after having taken Antabuse becomes ill, experiencing headache, nausea, vomiting, and breathing difficulties. This occurs because Antabuse interferes with one of the steps of synaptic transmission involving alcohol (Rall, 1990). Specifically, the drug inhibits an enzyme involved in the normal metabolism of alcohol in the liver. Blocking this metabolism produces the unpleasant effects noted. A person taking Antabuse can't take a drink without becoming ill, and this is sufficient in most cases to eliminate drinking.

This example illustrates several learning processes operating simultaneously. For one, the illness may serve as a punisher for drinking alcohol. In addition, the pairing of the taste and the illness may represent a form of taste aversion described in Chapter 5. As a result of both the illness and the taste aversion, avoidance of alcohol is reinforced (negatively). Also, the presence of Antabuse prevents alcohol from serving as a positive reinforcer, which would represent operant extinction. This action lasts for 2 or 3 days after Antabuse is consumed. The obvious problem, however, is that an alcohol abuser can avoid all of these effects by avoiding Antabuse.

Like those of other abused drugs, the neurophysiological actions of cocaine have been explored in detail (Woolverton & Johnson, 1992). Cocaine also produces its behavioral effects by interfering with a step in neurotransmission. This interference results in an increase in the amount of a particular transmitter substance called dopamine available to combine with receptors in receiving neurons, which leads to increased neuronal activity relative to the levels in the absence of cocaine. Many researchers believe that this is the mechanism responsible for the reinforcing effects (and, therefore, the abuse potential) of cocaine. If this is so, then drugs that block dopamine receptors should reduce the reinforcing effects of cocaine and might prove useful in the treatment of cocaine abuse. Following this logic, researchers have examined interactions between cocaine and various substances that affect neurotransmission involving the transmitter substance dopamine, including antipsychotic drugs, (i.e., drugs used to treat schizophrenia), antidepressants, and several experimental drugs that affect particular subtypes of dopamine receptors (Kleber, 1995). The action of these drugs in blocking the neurotransmitter dopamine is shown in stylized form in Figure 7-7. Although treating cocaine abuse with other drugs is not currently possible, prescribing antidepressants appears to be of some value, especially when combined with good behavioral interventions.

As these examples illustrate, neurophysiological studies have allowed scientists to specify how several types of drugs produce their behavioral effects. Results of these studies also suggest strategies for developing useful pharmacological treatments for drug abuse, although few such interventions are currently

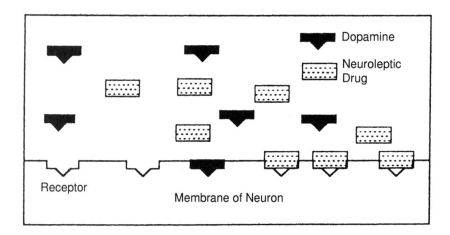

Figure 7-7. A depiction of the action of dopamine and antipsychotic drugs on individual receptors on the membrane of a receiving neuron. Note that the antipsychotic drug blocks the receptor normally occupied by dopamine; as a result, dopaminergic activity is diminished. (From *Psychology: A Behavioral Overview* [p. 124], by A. Poling, H. Schlinger, S. Starin, and E. Blakely, 1990, New York: Plenum Press. Copyright 1990 by Plenum Press. Reprinted with permission.)

available. More and better pharmacological interventions for treating substance abuse are sorely needed, especially in light of the cost and lack of ineffective-ness of the nonpharmacological interventions that are currently used.

Sensation

Behavior must be appropriate to the circumstances in which it occurs. Hence, one of the primary functions of the nervous system is to detect events in the environment. The environment consists of matter and of energy in several forms. To interact effectively with the environment, humans and other animals must be able to detect, that is, to sense, its properties. Humans can detect, and are potentially affected by, energy in electrical, mechanical, chemical, and ra-diant form. These forms of energy are detected through specialized sense or-gans, such as the eyes, ears, and skin.

Located within the sense organs are specialized nerve cells, called **receptor cells,** or **sensory receptors,** whose primary function is to transform energy into neural impulses. In other words, sensory receptors convert environmental en-ergy into the chemical and electrical energy of the nervous system. The process of converting one type of energy into another is known as **transduction.** Recep-tor cells are, therefore, biological transducers.

Many different types of sensory receptors have evolved, and different species are not equally sensitive to particular energy forms. For instance, dogs are sensitive to high-frequency sounds, sharks can detect tiny changes in elec-tric voltage in the water, and some migratory birds can detect changes in the gravitational field. Humans are insensitive to all of these energy forms, but are able to detect a wide range of other energy. In general, "the more diversified an organism's receptors are, the wider the range of environmental stimuli that it can respond to will be and the more varied and flexible its potential for adap-tive behavior" (Schneider & Tarshis, 1975, p.116).

Exteroceptive and Interoceptive Stimuli

Before describing the human sensory systems in more detail, the concept of stimulation must be considered. The term **stimulus** (the plural form is **stimuli**), is used by neurophysiologists to refer to any change in energy that affects the sensory receptors of an organism. When defined in this way, a stimulus does not necessarily affect behavior, but simply provides input into the nervous system.

Energy changes may take place in the external environment (i.e., outside the skin) or in the internal environment (i.e., inside the skin). Therefore, in the present context, the **environment** for a given organism may be defined as all of the stimuli that affect that organism's sensory receptors at a given moment. This means that the environment for a given organism is constantly changing. En-ergy changes in the external environment are known as **exteroceptive stimuli,** whereas energy changes in the internal environment (i.e., inside the body) are known as **interoceptive stimuli.** Exteroceptive stimuli are public stimuli in that they are capable of affecting the receptors of more than one person. The roar of Niagara Falls, the smell of a rose, and the sight of a Picasso painting are all public stimuli. Interoceptive stimuli are private stimuli; they only affect the receptors of the person in whom they occur. Toothaches, muscle cramps, and the feel of hot coffee traveling down one's esophagus are examples of private stimuli. Although private stimuli are more difficult to quantify accurately than public stimuli, they serve the same behavioral functions. In other words, they can function as USs or CSs (see Chapter 5), or as motivational variables, S^Ds, reinforcers, or punishers (see Chapter 6).

A summary of the sensory systems, stimuli, and sensory structures for humans is presented in Table 7-1. Although all of the sensory systems are critical for effective interaction with the environment, the two most important sensory systems for humans are vision and audition.

Vision

Scholars as far back as Aristotle have been interested in the visual sense and the nature of light, the stimulus that affects it. The study of vision was revolutionized by Sir Isaac Newton (Boring, 1950), who made one of the most important breakthroughs in optical research in 1672. In that year, Newton published the results of an experiment in which he directed a beam of white light through a prism, which split the light into all the colors of the rainbow. Newton also projected the colors back through another prism to recreate the white light. He explained these results by suggesting that white light is a mixture of all colors and that colors are produced when white light is differentially refracted. As Murray (1988) noted, Newton also offered a naturalistic, mechanistic account of how we see colors: Different colors produce different kinds of vibrations in the optic

Table 7-1
Sensory Systems in Humans

Sensory System	Stimulus	Sensory Structure
Visual	Electromagnetic radiation 380–760 nm	Eye–retina
Auditory	Sound waves (30–20,000 cps)	Ear–organ of corti (in the cochlea)
Vestibular	Gravity, changes in head rotation, angular acceleration	Semicircular canals; vestibular sacs
Somatosensory (cutaneous touch)	Pressure, vibration (touch)	Skin
Pain	Tissue damage	
Gustatory (taste)	Chemicals	Taste buds
Olfactory (smell)	Chemicals	Olfactory epithelium (at the top of the nasal cavity)

nerve fibers that go to the brain. Newton's explanation was later proven incorrect. (Remember that science is fallible, but self-correcting.)

More than two centuries later, we have a much better understanding of the process of vision. Vision begins when light strikes sensory receptors in the eye. Light is a form of energy, called electromagnetic radiation, consisting of waves or particles (photons) with a specifiable frequency and wavelength. Only wavelengths between approximately 380 nm and 700 nm (a nanometer, or nm, is one billionth of a meter), called the **visible spectrum,** can be detected by the human eye and are called "light" (see Figure 7-8). As also shown in Figure 7-8, other wavelengths of electromagnetic energy exist, and other species are able to detect some of them. Honeybees and certain other insects, for instance, can detect ultraviolet light and some nocturnal predators (e.g., rattlesnakes) detect their prey through infrared radiation.

Light produces its effect on behavior through three components of the visual system: the eyes, certain portions of the brain, and neural pathways that connect them. Much of what we know about the structure and function of the eye and visual perception came from experiments by the brilliant German scientist, Hermann von Helmholtz (1821–1894; Murray, 1988).

The structure of the eye has been likened to that of a camera. Like a camera, the eye admits light through an adjustable diaphragm and focuses images on a sensitive surface by means of a lens. Unlike a camera, however, there is no picture to develop inside the head. This makes the eye far more complicated than

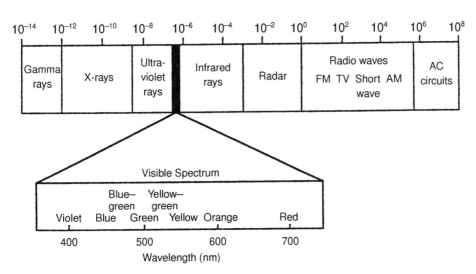

Figure 7-8. The electromagnetic spectrum with wavelengths (from 350 to 700 nm) visible to humans. (From *Psychology: A Behavioral Overview* [p. 99], by A. Poling, H. Schlinger, S. Starin, and E. Blakely, 1990, New York: Plenum Press. Copyright 1990 by Plenum Press. Reprinted with permission.)

any camera. The structure of the human eye is shown in Figure 7-9. When light hits the eye, it passes through several structures (e.g., cornea, pupil, lens) on its way to the retina at the back of the eye, where it eventually stimulates the visual sensory receptors, called **photoreceptors** (rods and cones). These specialized cells transduce the stimulus of light into neural impulses.

When light strikes a photoreceptor, that is, a rod or cone, a chemical and electrical process is begun that ultimately produces an action potential in a specialized cell, which conveys a nerve impulse to the brain via the optic nerve, which exits at the rear of the eye. Upon leaving the eye, neural impulses are carried along the optic nerve through the thalamus (described later) to several regions at the rear of the cerebral cortex (also described later), known collectively as the *primary visual area,* and to other places in the brain. At each of these points, the nerve impulses communicate with (synapse on) other neurons, including motor neurons that affect behavior that scientific psychologists refer to as (visual) perception.

Audition

Audition (or hearing) is also very important to humans, especially because human language is primarily vocal. This makes the auditory system critical in interacting with others. As with vision, scientists have long been interested in

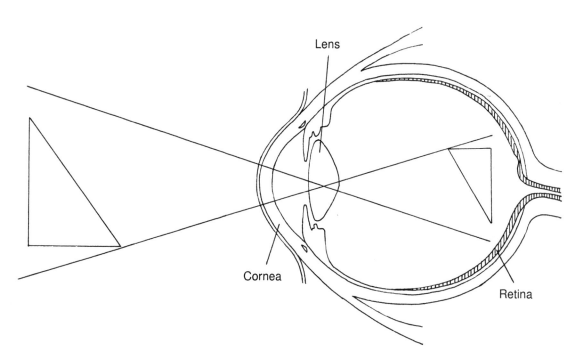

Figure 7-9. Structure of the human eye showing how light from an object (a triangle) is focused through the cornea and lens onto the retina in an inverted image.

the sense of hearing and the properties of sound, the stimulus that affects it. Chapter 1 described some of Galileo's scientific contributions to physics. Galileo also made scientific contributions to physiology and psychology, in particular, in the area of the nature of sound and auditory perception. For example, he showed that the pitch of a sound depended on the frequency of vibration of the object producing the sound. Galileo was the first to suggest that it was the frequency of a plucked string (e.g., of a musical instrument), not its length, that was responsible for its pitch. This discovery had important implications for understanding how the auditory sensory system converts sound into nerve impulses.

Just as photoreceptors in the eye transduce light into neural impulses, **phonoreceptors** in the ear transduce sound waves into neural impulses. The energy to which the ear is sensitive, sound, consists of rhythmic pressure changes in air resulting from the vibration of objects. Vibration of an object, such as the bell in a telephone, or the sound of someone's voice, causes molecules alternately to compress and rarefy (i.e., move together and apart). As the object moves forward, molecules are pressed together (compressed); as it moves backward, they are pulled apart (rarefied). This change in the density of molecules creates a change in air pressure that travels as a wave.

The major structures of the ear are shown in Figure 7-10. Sound first strikes the *pinna* (or auricle), which funnels the sound into the ear canal toward the *tympanic membrane,* also known as the ear drum. Sound waves striking the ear drum cause it to vibrate. Its vibration matches that of the sound waves in frequency and amplitude (loudness). The higher the frequency the higher the pitch and the larger the waves the louder the sound.

Adjacent to the ear drum are the three tiny bones (the malleus, the incus, and the stapes) of the middle ear, called the *ossicles.* You have probably heard

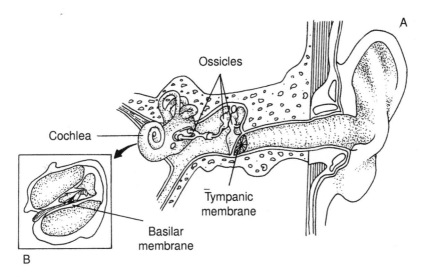

Figure 7-10. Structure of the human ear including the outer and middle ear (A) and (a cross section of) the inner ear (B).

them referred to by their shapes as the hammer, anvil, and stirrup. These bones form a chain running from the ear drum to a membrane (called the oval window) opening into the inner ear. When a sound wave strikes the ear drum, the ear drum vibrates, causing each of the ossicles to move in turn. The stapes presses against the membrane of the oval window, which transmits the vibrations into the fluid-filled inner ear. As Carlson (1995) points out, fluid is normally a very inefficient means for conducting sound, as you probably know from trying to hear while swimming underwater. The chain of ossicles, however, is an extremely efficient means of energy transmission because the baseplate of the stapes makes smaller, but more forceful, movements against the oval window than the ear drum makes against the malleus.

The auditory sensory receptors which transduce the mechanical vibrations caused by sound waves into neural impulses are found in the cochlea, a fluid-filled organ shaped like a snail which lies in the inner ear. When the stapes pushes against the oval window, waves are created in the fluid inside the cochlea. This causes the *basilar membrane,* which runs through the length of the cochlea, to move in wavelike fashion. This motion bends tiny hair cells, the phonoreceptors. The phonoreceptors transform the wavelike motion of the basilar membrane into neural impulses. The nerve impulses leave the ear in bundles of nerve fibers called the auditory nerve. Most of these impulses are ultimately relayed (through the thalamus) to the primary auditory area located in the temporal cortex (described later) and then to other areas, including those that contain motor neurons.

Other Sensory Systems

In addition to vision and audition, humans are able to detect chemical changes that affect receptors in the tongue, called **gustation** (i.e., taste), and in the top of the nasal cavity, called **olfaction** (i.e., smell). Also, changes in the head's orientation and angular acceleration are detected by receptors in the semicircular canals and vestibular sacs of the **vestibular system,** which is responsible for maintaining posture and balance. Finally, changes on the surface of the body and inside it are detected through the **somatosenses** (body senses). These include the *cutaneous senses,* which detect stimuli collectively referred to as touch, such as pressure, vibration, heating and cooling, and pain; *kinesthesia,* which provides information about the position and movement of the body in space through receptors in the muscles, tendons, and joints; and the *organic senses,* which provide information about what is going on in the internal organs, gastrointestinal system, and abdominal and thoracic cavities.

Movement

Along with sensation, movement (i.e., behavior) is the other primary function of the nervous system. This section describes the mechanisms and processes by which the nervous system produces movement.

Although behavior is not easy to define, it can be described, physiologically, in terms of effector action. **Effectors** are cells that form synapses with efferent nerves (from the brain) and, when activated, affect the internal or external environment. Different species have different kinds of effectors. For instance, fireflies have luminescent organs and some eels possess electric organs. Humans can affect the environment in a variety of ways through the use of two kinds of effectors: **muscles** and **glands.**

Muscles

The human body contains two kinds of muscles relevant to behavior, skeletal and smooth muscles. The *skeletal muscles* are usually attached to bones at both ends by tendons. These muscles move the bones relative to each other. When placed under a microscope they have a striped appearance, and for this reason are also referred to as *striped muscles*. The skeletal muscles allow vertebrate animals to operate on their external environments. Whenever you pick up, push, reach, grasp, walk, or talk, you are using skeletal muscles. Not surprisingly, *smooth muscles* have a smooth appearance under the microscope. They generally control movement in internal organs. The movement of smooth muscles is less conspicuous. For example, smooth muscles are responsible for the dilation and constriction of the pupils and the constriction of the esophagus as food is swallowed.

Like neurons, muscle cells are activated by neurotransmitter substances. When a nerve impulse passing down the axon of a motor neuron reaches the terminal buttons, a neurotransmitter is released. This chemical spreads across the synapse (specifically termed the neuromuscular junction, that is, the junction between a nerve cell and a muscle cell) and produces an action potential in the cells making up the muscle. This change causes the muscle to contract.

Glands

Glands are specialized groups of cells which manufacture and secrete chemicals that affect the function of other parts of the body. For example, you have no doubt noticed that your eyes "water" when foreign material gets in them (an unconditional reflex). The watering of the eyes is the result of lachrymal gland secretion. Like muscles, glands are activated by neurotransmitter molecules that are released by efferent neurons. There are many glands in the human body. Some, like the lachrymal gland, possess ducts that carry secretions to the surface of the skin. Such glands are called exocrine glands. Unlike exocrine glands, endocrine glands do not have ducts. They release chemicals called **hormones** directly into the bloodstream.

Perhaps the most influential gland in the endocrine system is the *pituitary gland.* This pea-sized gland is located just below the hypothalamus in the brain (see Figure 7-11), with which it interacts. It produces and releases a relatively large number of hormones that control the action of other endocrine glands. For

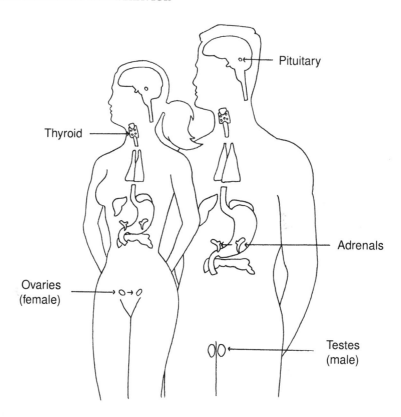

Figure 7-11. Location of the major human endocrine glands.

Table 7-2
Human Endocrine Glands and Their Functions

Gland	Major Functions
Adrenal cortex	Regulates carbohydrate metabolism, salt balance, water balance
Adrenal medulla	Affects sympathetic nervous system and increases carbohydrate metabolism
Anterior pituitary	Affects growth, sexual development, skin pigmentation, thyroid function
Pancreas	Regulates carbohydrate metabolism through the secretion of insulin and glucagon
Parathyroid	Regulates calcium and phosphorous metabolism
Posterior pituitary	Affects absorption of water by the kidney, uterine contraction
Testes and ovaries	Affect secondary sexual characteristics
Thyroid	Affects basal metabolism, indirectly affects growth and nutrition

this reason, it is often referred to as the "master gland." Several other endocrine glands and their functions are listed in Table 7-2. Figure 7-11 shows the location of the major endocrine glands.

Sensation and Perception

Psychologists often distinguish between sensation and perception. The term **sensation** usually refers to the basic effects of stimuli on sensory receptors, in other words the transduction of environmental energy by sensory receptors into nerve impulses. Perception, however, is usually described as a cognitive process:

> ... the process by which animals *gain knowledge* about their environment and about themselves in relation to the environment. It is the beginning of knowing, and so is an essential part of cognition. More specifically, to perceive is to *obtain information* about the world through stimulation. (Gibson & Spelke, 1983, p. 2, emphasis added)

Phrases like "gain knowledge" and "obtain information" are vague and don't really specify what is happening in terms of the functions of the nervous system. Moreover, as explanations of behavior they are often circular and, as you recall from Chapter 2, are therefore inadequate. A better approach is to use the term **perception** to refer to the behavior controlled by sensory stimulation. For example, we say that a child perceives her mother if she reaches out for her, or that you perceive an oncoming car if you swerve your car to miss it.

Several variables determine whether and how a given stimulus affects behavior. Among them are (1) the physical characteristics of the stimulus (for example, how bright or loud it is); (2) the presence of other, potentially competing, stimuli; and (3) the individual's phylogenetic and ontogenetic history with respect to the stimulus.

The Central Nervous System

Sensory (i.e., afferent) and motor (i.e., efferent) nerves are part of the peripheral nervous system (PNS). The system that coordinates sensory and motor functions is the central nervous system (CNS). The CNS includes all neural material within the brain and spinal cord. More than 99% of all neurons are located in the CNS. More than 10 billion neurons, packed at a density of up to 100 million per cubic inch, are found within the CNS.

The Spinal Cord

The spinal cord, which is about the diameter of your little finger, is involved in all sensory and motor functions taking place below the neck. Specifically, its primary functions are (1) to distribute somatosensory nerve fibers (i.e., those carrying information about touch, pressure, pain, etc.) from below the neck to the brain and (2) to distribute motor fibers from the brain to the effectors (muscles and glands) below the neck. Thus, the spinal cord enables the brain and that part of the body below the neck to interact. It is the place where sensory and motor neurons synapse on *interneurons* (those that bridge two other neurons; see Figure 7-12) running to the brain or other parts of the spinal cord, and also is the place where sensory neurons synapse directly on motor neurons to control spinal reflexes.

The **spinal reflex** is among the simplest environment–behavior relations. It occurs when a stimulus elicits a response without the involvement of the brain. For example, the patellar reflex (described previously) involves only sensory and motor neurons. With most spinal reflexes, however, interneurons are interposed between sensory and motor neurons. This allows for more complex forms of behavior. For instance, stepping on a sharp object with the left foot results in reflexive withdrawal of that foot. As this occurs, the opposite leg stiffens, which prevents falling. The latter effect is achieved because interneurons connect the sensory neurons from one leg to the motor neurons of the other leg (see Figure 7-12).

Although the brain is not directly involved in spinal reflexes, it can modulate their occurrence. If instructed not to allow their leg to move as a result of a

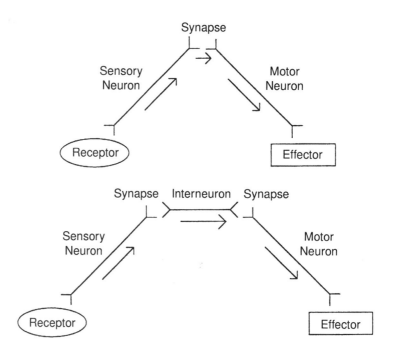

Figure 7-12. Schematic diagram of reflexes that do (bottom panel) and do not (top panel) involve interneurons. (From *Psychology: A Behavioral Overview* [p. 116], by A. Poling, H. Schlinger, S. Starin, and E. Blakely, 1990, New York: Plenum Press. Copyright 1990 by Plenum Press. Reprinted with permission.)

tap to the patellar tendon, most humans can keep the response from occurring. This demonstrates that the brain, while not directly involved in each response, can modulate even simple reflexive behavior. The brain is connected to the PNS through systems of neurons called pathways. The pathways run up (afferent, or sensory) and down (efferent, or motor) the spinal cord. It is through these pathways that the brain receives (afferent) sensory inputs and controls (efferent) motor responses.

The Brain

The human brain weighs only about three pounds, but it contains billions of neurons and trillions of interconnections. Neuroanatomists conventionally divide all mammalian brains into three major divisions: the hindbrain, midbrain, and forebrain. These areas have different functions and developed at different times during the course of evolution. Although most mammals have all three divisions, species differ considerably with respect to the size, complexity, and function of each. Snakes and lizards, for example, do not have well-developed forebrains. They also do not engage in many of the complex behaviors characteristic of humans, who have extremely well-developed forebrains.

Evolutionarily, the **hindbrain** is the oldest and most primitive part of the brain. It connects the spinal cord with the mid- and forebrain and consists of three major subdivisions—the medulla, pons, and cerebellum—which together control activities important for basic survival. In humans, for instance, the medulla is involved in controlling such critical activities as heartbeat, blood pressure, and respiration. The cerebellum controls bodily balance, motor coordination, and locomotion.

The next part of the brain to evolve, the midbrain, is relatively small in humans, but in some species, including snakes and reptiles, it is large and controls much of their behavior. A large and complex structure, termed the reticular formation, occupies the center of the midbrain and controls arousal (activation), sleeping and waking, and many reflexes (e.g., cardiovascular reflexes).

The **forebrain** is the largest part of the human brain and the most recent to evolve. It contains many identifiable structures, including the **thalamus,** which relays most incoming sensory impulses to the cerebral cortex (described later). It also contains the **hypothalamus** (literally, beneath the thalamus), a structure smaller in diameter than a dime, located just below the thalamus.

The Hypothalamus

Although small, the hypothalamus serves functions of heroic proportions. It plays a crucial role in regulating the internal environment of the organism by maintaining proper temperature, fluid balance, and food stores. It performs these functions by controlling the pituitary gland and the autonomic nervous system. The hypothalamus is also involved in controlling the species-specific behaviors sometimes jokingly summarized as the "four Fs": feeding, fighting, fleeing, and mating.

The role of the hypothalamus in controlling all forms of species-specific behavior has been clearly demonstrated. For example, more than 30 years ago Jose Delgado (see Delgado, 1969) implanted electrodes, aimed at the hypothalamus, in the brain of a fighting bull. Then, armed only with a radio transmitter and a cape, he faced the bull in a bullring. When the bull charged, Delgado activated the radio transmitter, delivering electrical stimulation to the electrodes implanted in the bull's brain. The bull came to a complete stop and turned away. Delgado offered this as proof of the role of the hypothalamus in aggressive behavior. There is some controversy as to whether Delgado's electrodes were implanted in the hypothalamus or in motor areas, in which case stimulation might impair locomotion, not aggression. Be that as it may, Delgado's work is an early, and interesting, demonstration of the brain's role in controlling behavior.

More recent research unambiguously shows clear relations between the hypothalamus and other species-specific behavior. For example, sexual behavior in female and male rodents can be elicited by electrical stimulation of parts of the hypothalamus and adjacent areas (Malsbury, 1971; Pfaff & Sakuma, 1979). Of course, such behavior is more naturally caused by sex hormones the release of which is stimulated by the hypothalamus.

The Limbic System

Also located in the forebrain is the limbic system, which includes the hippocampus, the amygdala, and the septal area. The limbic system is closely connected with the hypothalamus and the cortical areas lying above it. The hippocampus is involved in learning and memory. Damage to this area has been linked to memory loss. Also, the hippocampus appears to play a role in movement and spatial organization (Kolb & Whitshaw, 1985). The **amygdala** is also involved in learning and memory. It also plays a role in emotional (e.g., aggressive, fearful) and stress-related behavior. The septal area appears to be involved in emotional behavior of another kind. Stimulation to parts of the septal area produce what have been described as pleasurable sensations. In an early demonstration of this phenomenon, J. Olds and Milner (1954) implanted electrodes in the septal area of rats. By pressing a lever in an operant conditioning chamber, the rats could self-administer electrical current to their septal area. They did so repeatedly, pressing the lever thousands of time per hour, often to the point of exhaustion. When the septal area of humans is electrically stimulated, they report experiencing sensations similar to those preceding orgasm.

The Cerebrum

In humans, the **cerebrum** is extensively developed. It is the outermost and largest portion of the brain and consists of a right and left hemisphere. The hemispheres are connected to each other by several bundles of nerve fibers; the largest and most important is the **corpus callosum.** The cerebrum is covered by a layer of neurons, approximately 2 millimeters thick, called the **cerebral cortex** (cortex means *bark*). The cerebral cortex of humans, which if smoothed and flattened would be about the size of a double sheet of newsprint, consists of more than 10 billion neurons and trillions of interconnections. Some species, such as snakes, have no cortex at all; the cortex of other species is small and relatively smooth, whereas in humans it is large and wrinkled. This wrinkling has the effect of dramatically increasing surface area. The convoluted nature of the cortex coupled with the vast numbers of neuronal interconnections affords humans the capacity to perform many complex activities.

Most sensory fibers eventually terminate in the cerebral cortex. And all behavior, except the spinal reflexes, is controlled by specific areas in the cortex. The cortex is crucially involved in many complex behaviors including learning, memory, thinking, and emotion. Because of its importance to all human functioning, we will consider the structure of the cerebral cortex in more detail.

Cerebral Structure and Function

As noted above, the cerebral cortex is typically divided into the left and right hemispheres. The hemispheres are structurally symmetrical, and each can be divided into four *lobes:* the *frontal, parietal, temporal,* and *occipital.* Figure 7-13 shows the location of these lobes. Within each lobe, specific areas of the cerebral cortex have been shown to be associated with specific functions, a phenomenon known as localization of function. An early theory of localization, that of phrenology developed by Gall, was described at the beginning of this chapter. We also described how, during the past one hundred years, the major areas of the cerebral cortex have been identified, among them the motor, somatosensory, visual, auditory, and association areas (see Figure 7-14).

Located at the rear of the frontal lobe is the motor strip of the cortex. This area controls the more than 600 skeletal muscles found in the human body. Electrical stimulation at specific points in the motor area produces movement of specific body parts. In all cases, the movement occurs on the side of the body *opposite* the hemisphere to which stimulation was applied. Thus, the right side of the brain controls movement on the left, and vice versa. Interestingly, areas of the body capable of the finest movement (e.g., the fingers, vocal apparatus), regardless of size, are controlled by the greatest quantity of neural material in the motor strip.

The *somatosensory* (body-sense) area of the cortex, which is involved in the sensations of pain, temperature, touch, and body position, is located along a strip of the parietal lobe adjacent to the motor strip. Stimulation of neurons in the somatosensory area produces specific sensations. Humans report experiencing pain, heat, cold, touch, or changes of body position when certain somatosensory neurons are stimulated. As in the motor area, the somatosensory area receives input from the opposite side of the body (e.g., input from the left hand stimulates the somatosensory area in the right hemisphere).

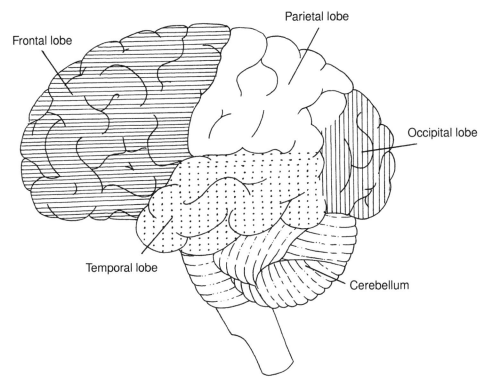

Figure 7-13. Location of the four lobes of the human cerebral cortex and the cerebellum.

As its name implies, the *visual area* receives input from photoreceptors. As described previously, this area is located at the rear of the occipital lobes. Each visual area receives stimulation from both eyes. Stimulation from the left visual field of both eyes is transmitted to the right hemisphere and stimulation from the right visual field of both eyes is transmitted to the left hemisphere. The primary visual cortex of each hemisphere contains a "map" of half the other eye's visual field. As David Hubel and Torsten Wiesel (see Hubel & Wiesel, 1979) have shown in their Nobel prize–winning work, neurons in the visual cortex respond not only to light but to specific features of the visual world, such as line orientation and movement, retinal disparity, and color, among others. These researchers also showed that a disproportionate number of neurons in the primary visual cortex receive input from the fovea, the area of the retina that contains the greatest proportion of cones and, consequently, the area where the most acute vision occurs.

The *auditory area* is located in the temporal lobe. The auditory area in each hemisphere receives stimulation from both ears but primarily from the one on the opposite side. Moreover, just as with the visual cortex described above, the auditory cortex is organized according to specific features of the auditory world, namely, the frequencies of different sounds.

The areas just described constitute only one-quarter of the total area of the cortex; the remaining three-quarters is devoted to processes other than those involved in direct sensory and motor functions. The *association areas* play a role in the many higher-level activities engaged in by humans, including complex learning. Evidence of involvement of the association areas in these activities comes primarily from humans who have sustained injury (e.g., tumors, stroke) to certain parts of the cortex. In these individuals, an injury to one part of the cortex disrupts only certain processes, leaving others intact. By testing many different individuals with damage to known areas, the areas responsible for specific functions can be mapped (see Sidebar 7-1).

Hemispheric Specialization

We have noted that the two hemispheres are essentially symmetrical anatomically. This is not so, however, with respect to function. Some functions

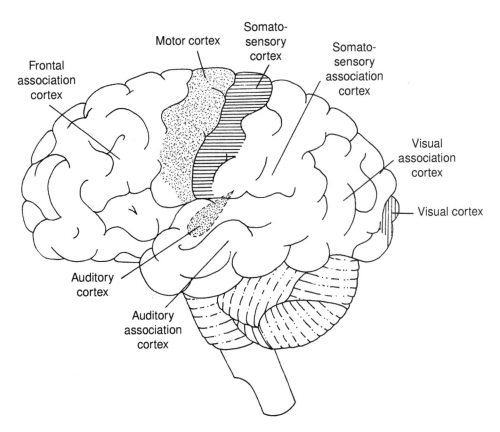

Figure 7-14. Location of the primary motor, visual, auditory, somatosensory, and association cortexes.

Sidebar 7-1
Visual Agnosias

The term **agnosia** refers to the inability of an individual to identify or recognize an object by means of a particular sensory modality. People with visual agnosias are often unable to recognize objects visually even though they can recognize them by touch or sound. For example, if you show a screwdriver to a person with a visual agnosia and ask what it is, he will be unable to tell you. If you permit him or her to hold and touch it, however, he will be able to say it is a screwdriver. Some people suffer from a more specific form of visual agnosia called **prosopagnosia.** Such individuals are unable to say who a familiar face belongs to even though they can say they are looking at a face and can say who the person is after hearing their voice. Interestingly, people with visual agnosias usually have no problems seeing. The problems occur because of damage to certain areas of the visual association cortex, where visual neurons synapse with neurons conveying other information (Damasio, 1985; Meadows, 1974).

How can we best understand such deficits? Have individuals with visual agnosias lost their memories for particular objects or faces? Obviously, individuals with visual agnosias have lost memories, in particular, memories of the names of objects when they see them. But their memories of the names of objects when they feel or hear them are intact, because the individuals are still able to say the names of objects when they hear them or touch them.

We can better understand this apparent dilemma if we view memories simply as interconnections between sensory and motor neurons that have been established by operant conditioning. Consider how a child acquires the name for an object or a face. Initially, saying the name to the sight and (separately) to the sound or touch of the object is reinforced. (Some objects, like the moon in the sky, produce only visual stimulation; thus, we would expect the neural patterns underlying the name "moon" to involve only sensory nerves in the visual cortex. Of course, there are many other neural connections involving the name "moon," for example, those to the auditory question, "What is the biggest or brightest object in the night sky?") For objects that can stimulate three sensory modalities (e.g., vision, audition, and touch), a child learns through operant conditioning to name the stimulus given sensory input through each modality. Responses other than naming also are acquired, as when a child learns to point to the object when asked to do so, to classify it with other similar objects, and to talk about it in words other than just its name. All of these stimulus–response relationships are separately established, whether by direct operant conditioning or more indirectly by instruction or modeling.

Presumably, each of these separately acquired behavioral relations is mediated by different neural pathways. When the stimulus is visual, the pathways extend from the retina to the primary visual cortex in the occipital lobe of the cortex and then to adjacent areas of the visual association cortex. When brain damage occurs to specific parts of the visual association cortex, only pathways that mediate visual control over behavior are disrupted. This explains why individuals with prosopagnosia are not able to give the name of a person whose face they see, but can give the name when they hear the person's voice. These are two separate and separately acquired stimulus–response relationships, controlled by different groups of neurons. The person has not lost the memory (i.e., the neural connections) for the face per se, but they have lost the memory for the name of the face when they see it. Their memory for the name of the face when they hear the person's voice remains intact. That is, stimulus control of the naming response is lost when the stimulus is visual, but not when it is auditory. This analysis of prosopagnosias suggests that many memories are specific to learned relationships between specific stimuli and behavior.

---

are lateralized; that is, they are controlled primarily by one side of the brain (Springer & Deutsch, 1984). Much evidence for lateralization of function comes from humans who have sustained some injury to one hemisphere. Injury to a specific area of one hemisphere often produces quite different effects than does injury to the identical area in the other hemisphere. For instance, in right-handed individuals, injury to the left hemisphere may interfere with language abilities, whereas similar injury to the right hemisphere leaves language intact (but produces other problems). Such findings led researchers to classify the left hemisphere as dominant over the right hemisphere. This was because of the belief that the right hemisphere was simply a left hemisphere without language capabilities.

More recently, however, evidence has indicated that both hemispheres perform specialized functions. Much of this evidence comes from patients with *split* brains. The split brain results from a procedure in which the corpus callosum (the

---

Sidebar 7-2
Hemispheric Asymmetry and Risky Choices*

Several studies have shown that when a person pays attention to stimuli to his or her right, there is increased activity in the left cerebral hemisphere. Similarly, attending to stimuli on the left increases activity in the right hemisphere. This activity is measured by electrical activity (De Toffol, Autret, Gaymard, & Degiovanni, 1992) and by blood flow (Malamed & Larsen, 1977). If one hemisphere of the brain is activated by attending to stimuli on the side of the opposite hemisphere, this improves performance in activities associated with the activated hemisphere. For example, attending to stimuli on the right side improves verbal tasks associated with the left cerebral hemisphere, and attending to stimuli on the left side improves spatial performance associated with the right hemisphere (Lempert & Kinsbourne, 1982; Walker, Wade, & Waldman, 1982).

After examining people who received frontal lobe surgery for brain tumors, L. Miller and Milner (1985) reported that patients who became more dependent on their left cerebral hemisphere took more risks than they did prior to surgery. Those who had to rely on their right hemisphere, in contrast, became more cautious. To determine whether this hemispheric asymmetry in risk taking was a general phenomenon, Drake (1985) asked students to respond to choice dilemmas that they heard through either their right or left ear. An example of such a dilemma is a case where a man has a limp and is offered an operation that could either improve or worsen walking ability. The student's task is to recommend to the man the lowest probability of success from the operation that would be acceptable. Here, the lower the accept-

able probability of success, the greater the risk to the patient. Drake found students recommended substantially higher acceptable risk levels when the message was played into the right ear (activating the left hemisphere) than into the left ear.

Other research seems to support such hemispheric differences. For example, several studies have linked left hemispheric activity in right-handers with positive emotions (e.g., Davidson, 1992). And positive emotions have been shown to lower estimates of the likelihood of negative or unpleasant events (Johnson & Tversky, 1983). Furthermore, attention toward the right side produces more positive evaluations of music (McFarland & Kennison, 1986) and of pictures (Merckelbach & van Oppen, 1989). Thus, a given decision may appear to be less risky and more attractive when we have a positive mood, and our mood can become more positive when we activate the left hemisphere by orienting our attention toward the right. Doing so also increases reported optimism and personal control and reduces feelings of helpless, which may further contribute to a willingness to take risks (Drake & Seligman, 1989).

Given the foregoing information and what else you know about the variables that control behavior, does it make sense to stand to a friend's right if you wish to reduce a false sense of optimism in that person, or to convince him or her to take fewer risks? Should you be at the left if your advice is to take more risks, such as joining a club, seeking out new friends, or signing up for a hard class? Think about it.

*Much of this material was provided by Roger Drake, whom we thank.

neurological bridge connecting one hemisphere to the other) is surgically severed. This is sometimes performed in patients with severe forms of epilepsy that cannot be managed by other treatments. By severing the corpus callosum, seizure activity cannot spread from one hemisphere to the other. Although usually successful in reducing seizures, the split brain procedure leaves the patient with functionally separate hemispheres.

It is now known that the right hemisphere plays a role in detecting a pattern as a whole rather than as its constituent parts. The right hemisphere is also involved in spatial organization, solving simple (two-digit) addition problems, and emotion and impulsiveness. Moreover, the right side of the brain underlies some language capabilities, although the left side controls most language-related activities (i.e., those that involve words or numbers). In addition, the left hemisphere has been implicated in controlling fine motor skills in left-handed persons; the right side controls them in right-handers. Finally, analytical skills and high-level mathematical skills, probably because they are verbal, are primarily under the control of the left side of the brain. It is even possible that the two hemispheres differ with respect to how risk is assessed when they are activated (see Sidebar 7-2.)

Neuroscience and Learning

This chapter has described two crucial functions of the nervous system—detecting stimuli and producing behavior—and the various structures that are responsible for those functions. It is impossible to provide more than a cursory overview of the nervous system and its relation to behavior. Because of the importance of both classical and operant conditioning for human behavior, this chapter ends with a brief consideration of the research that has begun to uncover the neurophysiological processes involved in both types of conditioning.

The Neurophysiology of Habituation and Classical Conditioning

Findings from the study of the neurophysiological processes underlying habituation and classical conditioning confirm the general laws discovered at the behavioral level and described in Chapter 5. Eric Kandel and his colleagues (e.g., Carew, Hawkins, & Kandel, 1983; Kandel & Hawkins, 1992; Kandel & Schwartz, 1982) have studied habituation and classical conditioning using the gill-withdrawal reflex of the marine snail *Aplysia*. This animal is easy to study because its central nervous system contains only about 20,000 nerve cells. The gill, which is used to extract oxygen from sea water, is protected by a sheet of tissue called the mantle shelf, which ends in a fleshy spout called a siphon that expels sea water and waste. These structures normally extend out from the body as the animal moves about. If either the mantle shelf or the siphon is touched (US), however, the entire organ withdraws (UR). This is the gill-withdrawal reflex.

Habituation of the gill-withdrawal reflex is achieved by briefly squirting the siphon or mantle with a mild jet of water. Just 10–15 presentations can produce a short-term decrease in the withdrawal response. Habituation of the withdrawal reflex can also be produced at the neurophysiological level by applying an electrical charge directly to the sensory neuron of the mantle or siphon sufficient to cause an action potential. The mantle shelf and siphon contain sensory neurons that synapse on motor neurons for the gill. Repeated applications of the electrical charge to the sensory neuron results in smaller and smaller contractions of the muscle controlling gill withdrawal. Kandel and his colleagues discovered that the less frequent firing of the motor neuron was caused by smaller amounts of the neurotransmitter substance being released by the sensory neuron into the synapse with the motor neuron (Castellucci & Kandel, 1974; see Figure 7-15). Results like these show *how* (i.e., the proximate neurophysiological causes) a general psychological phenomenon, in this case, habituation, works at the neurophysiological level. But Kandel and his colleagues

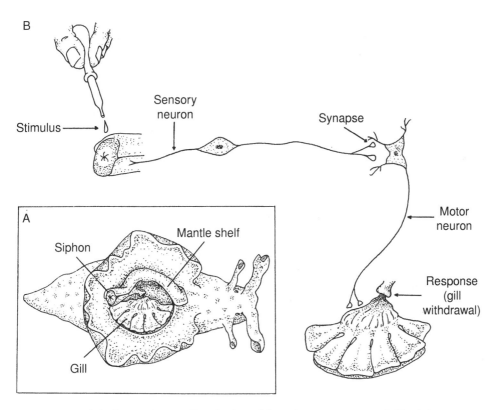

Figure 7-15. (A) The marine snail Aplysia and its primary structures (gill, siphon, mantle shelf) involved in the gill-withdrawal reflex, and (B) the synapse between a sensory neuron of the siphon stimulated by a squirt of water (US) and a motor neuron which produces the gill withdrawal (UR). Adapted from Pinel (1990).

have gone one step further to show how an actual learning process—classical conditioning—works at the neurophysiological level.

In studies on classical conditioning of the gill-withdrawal reflex, the CS was a brief touch to the siphon with a nylon bristle, and the US was a weak electrical shock to the tail which elicits gill withdrawal as a UR. After as few as 15 pairings of the CS and US, presentation of the CS alone elicited gill withdrawal as a CR. But how does this work at the level of neurons?

Kandel and his colleagues discovered that a mild electric shock (US) to the tail stimulates certain so-called modulatory neurons. These modulatory neurons synapse on sensory neurons from both the siphon and mantle and increase the release of a particular transmitter substance from their terminal buttons. Classical conditioning occurs when these modulatory neurons cause the sensory neurons to increase their release of neurotransmitter substance if those sensory neurons had just fired in response to a CS, for example, a brief touch to the siphon with a nylon bristle. The researchers discovered that the sensory neurons released more neurotransmitter substance in response to the CS if they had just been stimulated by the US (the electric shock), just as the behavioral facts of classical conditioning would suggest.

The importance of these findings is that they show *how* the processes of habituation and classical conditioning occur at the neurophysiological level. Pavlov and those who followed him discovered the ultimate and proximate environmental causes of conditioned reflexes; Kandel and his colleagues have begun to discover some of the proximate physiological causes.

The Neurophysiology of Reinforcement

Discoveries of the neural bases of operant conditioning may be said to have begun with J. Olds and Milner's (1954) finding (described earlier) that electrical brain stimulation, especially in certain neural pathways, could function as a powerful reinforcer for behavior. Since then researchers have discovered, among other things, that the best location in the brain for producing reinforcing electrical brain stimulation is a bundle of axons that carries neural impulses from the midbrain to the forebrain (M. E. Olds & Forbes, 1981), and that the primary neurotransmitter substance involved in the reinforcement of operant behavior is dopamine (Hoebel, 1988).

In part, these discoveries were confirmed by studies showing that drugs that block dopamine receptors (dopamine antagonists), such as those used to treat schizophrenia, reduce the effects of natural reinforcers such as food, the effects of reinforcing electrical brain stimulation, and the effects of conditioned reinforcers (e.g., Franklin & McCoy, 1979; Gallistel & Karras, 1984; Spyraki, Fibiger, & Philips, 1982a). Conversely, drugs that increase the activity of dopamine in the synapse (dopamine agonists), such as amphetamine or cocaine, function as powerful reinforcers when injected into the bloodstream, or directly into the brain contingent on behavior (e.g., Gallistel & Karras, 1984; G. F. Guerin, Goeders, Dworkin, & Smith, 1984; Hoebel et al., 1983; Koob & Bloom, 1988; Spyraki, Fibiger, & Philips, 1982b).

Taken together, these findings begin to answer the question of *how* the process of reinforcement works. That is, it works by increasing activity in certain areas of the brain in which the neurotransmitter is dopamine. Although this explanation is incomplete (i.e., not sufficiently detailed) and some data are inconsistent with it (Feldman et al., 1997), it is a useful hypothesis for guiding researchers' attempts to develop pharmacological treatments for cocaine abuse (as explained earlier). But researchers have gone even further and have shown that individual neurons can be operantly conditioned in a manner similar to the conditioning of behavior.

Operant Conditioning of Individual Neurons

The first demonstration of the operant conditioning of individual neurons occurred in the 1960s (e.g., see J. Olds, 1965). More recently, researchers (e.g., Belluzzi & Stein, 1983; Stein & Belluzzi, 1985) have improved on those early studies. Specifically, modern researchers have delivered a reinforcing stimulus—a microinjection of dopamine—directly to a cell in the hippocampus (previously described) dependent on a burst of cellular activity (firing). The results showed that

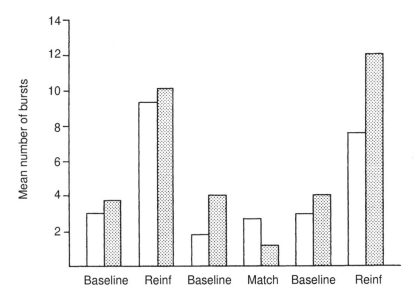

Figure 7-16. Results from the operant conditioning of individual neurons using microinjections of dopamine and cocaine as reinforcement. The graph summarizes eight experiments with dopamine (nonshaded areas) and eleven experiments with cocaine (shaded areas). In the match condition, the reinforcer was delivered the same number of times as in the reinforcement condition, but not contingent on the neuron firing. Data from Stein and Belluzzi (1988).

the frequency of bursts and the overall firing rate of the neuron increased during reinforcement compared to all baseline conditions. The researchers repeated the experiment using micro-injections of cocaine as the reinforcer, with essentially the same results (see Figure 7-16). The experimenters also found that, just as at the behavioral level, the activity of the neuron immediately before the administration of the neurotransmitter reinforcer was the best predictor of future activity of the cell. For example, if dopamine was made dependent on cellular activity, firing rate increased, but if dopamine was made dependent on cellular inactivity, firing rate decreased (Stein & Belluzzi, 1988).

The work of Stein and Belluzzi, among others, suggests that the individual neuron may be the basic unit for positive reinforcement in the brain (Stein & Belluzzi, 1988). If so, such a finding would provide strong neurophysical verification of reinforcement and would go some way toward clarifying the proximate physiological causes of operant behavior and showing *how* reinforcement produces the changes in behavior described in Chapter 6.

Summary

1. Neurophysiology is the study of the physiology of the nervous system, and it answers questions about the proximate physiological causes of behavior. For example, how is behavior caused at the neurophysiological level?

2. Ultimately, the primary function of the nervous system is behavior, but a second and equally important function of the nervous system is sensation, that is, detecting environmental stimuli. The three systems involved are (1) sensory systems that are responsible for detecting (i.e., sensing) environmental stimuli, (2) motor systems that are responsible for movement (i.e., behavior), and (3) a central nervous system that coordinates sensory, motor, and other functions.

3. The two major divisions of the nervous system are the *central nervous system* (CNS), which consists of the brain and spinal cord, and the *peripheral nervous system* (PNS), which contains all other sensory and motor nerves. The PNS is further divided into the *somatic nervous system*, which receives information from the sensory organs and controls the skeletal muscles, and the *autonomic nervous system*, which regulates the cardiac muscle, the smooth muscles, and the glands.

4. The basic structural and functional unit of the nervous system is the *neuron*, the structure of which consists of a cell body, dendrites, an axon, and terminal buttons. The terminal buttons contain the synaptic vesicles that, when stimulated, release chemical substances called *neurotransmitters*, which affect adjoining neurons.

5. The nerve impulse, also called an action potential, is a chemically initiated electric signal that is conducted along neurons.

6. The environment consists of energy (called *stimuli*) in several forms which are detected by receptor cells, or sensory receptors, located within the sense organs and whose main function is to transform (i.e., transduce) energy into neural impulses.

7. The sensory systems possessed by humans include vision, audition, gustation (taste), olfaction (smell), and somatosenses (body senses, such as touch and kinesthesia).

8. Movement is produced through effector cells which include skeletal and smooth muscles and glands.

9. *Sensation* refers to the basic effects of stimuli on sensory receptors, or the transduction of environmental energy by sensory receptors into nerve impulses. *Perception* refers to the behavior controlled by sensory stimulation.

10. The CNS includes all neural material within the brain and spinal cord. The brain is divided into the hindbrain, midbrain, and forebrain, each of which evolved at different times and mediates different functions.

11. The forebrain is the largest and the most recent part to evolve. It contains the *thalamus,* where most incoming sensory impulses are relayed to the cerebral cortex, and the *hypothalamus,* which plays a crucial role in regulating the internal environment of the organism by controlling the pituitary gland and the autonomic nervous system. The hypothalamus is also responsible for species-specific behaviors.

12. Also part of the forebrain is the cerebrum, which is covered by a thin layer of neurons called the *cerebral cortex* where all sensory fibers eventually terminate. All behavior, including learning, memory, thinking, and emotion, is generated in the cerebrum. The cerebral cortex is typically divided into the left and right hemispheres, and these are further divided into the frontal, parietal, temporal, and occipital lobes (regions), each of which is associated with specific functions such as motor, somatosensory, auditory, visual, and association functions.

13. Recent research has uncovered the neurophysiological processes (i.e., the proximate physiological causes) involved in both classical and operant conditioning and has begun to show how the general laws of behavior discovered by scientific psychologists work at the neurophysiological level.

Study Questions

1. What are the two primary functions of the nervous system?

2. What are the primary structural divisions of the nervous system? What do the central nervous system and peripheral nervous system consist of?

3. What are the four structural parts of the neuron and how does each contribute to its function?

4. How do nerve impulses occur, both chemically and electrically, and how are they like electricity flowing along a wire? What is the threshold of excitation and the action potential?

5. What is synaptic transmission and how does it occur? How are neurotransmitter substances involved?

6. How does the monosynaptic stretch reflex illustrate neuronal communication?

7. What is the relationship between drugs and neurotransmitter substances? What are agonists and antagonists?

8. What are (sensory) receptor cells and what is their function (i.e., transduction)?

9. How do neurophysiologists use the term "stimulus" and what is the difference between exteroceptive and interoceptive stimuli?

10. What form of energy is light and how does it produce its effects on behavior?

11. What form of energy is sound and how does it produce its effects on behavior?

12. What is the relationship between effector cells and movement and what are the two types of effectors in humans?

13. What is the relationship between sensation and perception?

14. What are the two divisions of the central nervous system and the functions of each?

15. What are the three general divisions of the brain and specifically the function of the structures in the forebrain, especially the hypothalamus?

16. What are the lobes of the cerebral cortex and the general functions of each, including the motor strip, somatosensory, visual, and auditory areas, and the association areas?

17. What is hemispheric specialization and how do split-brain patients illustrate it?

18. What is the importance of findings on the neurophysiological processes underlying habituation, classical conditioning, and operant conditioning, and what is their relationship to the general psychological laws they explain?

Applications of Scientific Psychology

Language

8

Psychologists and philosophers have long been interested in human language and, by extension, human cognition. You may recall from Chapter 1 that although Descartes believed that the bodily processes of both humans and nonhumans could be understood according to natural physical laws, he believed that human reason could not be understood in the same way. Descartes attempted to solve this dilemma by proposing a nonphysical rational soul (mind) in humans that was responsible for their ability to reason. To understand reason, then, one must first understand the rational mind. What evidence is there for such a mind? Descartes's evidence for a nonphysical and unobservable rational mind is apparent in his famous words: *Cognito ergo sum* ("I think, therefore, I am"). Because Descartes assumed that human language was a direct reflection of the rational mind, we can modify his saying as follows: "Because I talk to my self, I know I exist." Either way, we may conclude that for Descartes, language and awareness (i.e., consciousness) were intimately related (as we discuss in Chapter 9). Psychology inherited this Cartesian philosophical tradition, especially with respect to the study of human language and such phenomena as consciousness.

This chapter discusses language according to the scientific perspective presented in previous chapters. Two assumptions underlie this perspective. The first is that language is behavior, and scientific psychologists call it *verbal behavior* to emphasize this point. Second, verbal behavior is determined by the same general variables as other behavior, namely, phylogenetic and ontogenetic causes.

Is Human Language Unique?

For a variety of reasons, including Descartes's legacy of dualism, psychologists and philosophers have long assumed that human language is unique. It is true that verbal behavior, whether it is vocal speech or writing, is different in form from other behavior.[1] However, although behaviors may look different, they don't necessarily have different causes or functions. For example, if you are thirsty, you can get a drink of water yourself or you can ask someone to get it for you. Both behaviors are caused proximately (i.e., evoked) by a motivational variable, water deprivation, and by current discriminative stimuli, such as the presence of a faucet or, in the case of asking, someone who can get the water for you. Also, both behaviors produce the same reinforcing consequence, getting the water to drink. Even though we would classify one response as nonverbal and the other as verbal, both have the same function, namely, they produce water. And both are controlled by similar variables (motivational variables, discriminative stimuli, reinforcing consequences). Whether verbal behavior is really a special kind of behavior requiring a special kind of expla-

---

[1]Interestingly, the form of sign language, especially finger spelling, is much like that of nonverbal behavior, although it can be represented by a set of symbols, making it seem more similar to talking and writing.

nation is ultimately an empirical question, that is, one that should be answered scientifically, not philosophically. But how is one to do this?

One way to begin to show that verbal behavior is not truly a special kind of behavior is to demonstrate it in nonhuman animals. In fact, if we assume that verbal behavior is fundamentally different from nonverbal behavior, then we would expect only humans to possess it. Following from Descartes, many philosophers, including some modern linguists, believe that nonhumans are incapable of human language. But recent research on teaching American Sign Language (ASL) to chimpanzees and gorillas (see Sidebar 8-1), the so-called "ape-language" projects, shows this to be a questionable assumption. Critics of these attempts claim that the apes' sign language is constantly cued by their human trainers and, thus, does not possess the creative component that characterizes human language. In short,

---

Sidebar 8-1
Language in Apes

Philosophers have long discussed the possibility of teaching language to apes. For example, the French philosopher Julien Offray de La Mettrie (1709–1751) suggested that apes might be taught language and thereby transformed into "little gentlemen" (Leahey, 1987). In one of the first documented efforts, researchers attempted to teach a chimpanzee named Viki to talk (Hayes, 1952). After six years of training Viki could say only three or four words. Viki would be no "little lady." We now know that the Hayeses failed with Viki because chimpanzees lack the vocal apparatus that humans possess that physically permits speech. Real progress came when researchers taught apes American Sign Language (Ameslan or ASL), which is used extensively by hearing-impaired people.

In one project, Beatrice T. and R. Allen Gardner acquired a 10-month-old chimpanzee named Washoe. The Gardners were primarily interested in showing that chimpanzees could acquire a human language, given the appropriate medium (i.e., ASL), and then comparing the language skills of the chimpanzee with those of children (R. A. Gardner & Gardner, 1978). Washoe lived in a home environment similar to that enjoyed by a normal human child. Washoe lived in separate quarters, but most of her day was spent interacting with human caretakers. The ASL was used for all interactions.

After approximately four years of training, Washoe acquired a 132-sign vocabulary. She learned to ask for rewards and describe features of the environment, and also showed generalization of both skills. For example, Washoe would sign "dog" when she saw a breed of dog she had never seen before, or a picture of a dog. Moreover, in some instances the resulting sign was a novel combination of two previously separate signs. When shown a duck, for which Washoe had not learned a sign, she made the signs for "water" and "bird." Other sequences emerged such as "open-drink" (for water faucet), "listen dog" (at the sound of barking), and "more tickle" (for Washoe's companion to resume tickling her).

Did Washoe acquire language? The question is moot, and depends critically on how language is defined and, consequently, how an organism must behave to demonstrate it. Washoe's behavior is remarkable in its own right, regardless of how we label it. Since project Washoe, several other language projects have been undertaken with great apes including chimpanzees and gorillas. Some have focused on ASL (e.g., F. Patterson & Linden, 1981; Terrace, 1979); others have used symbols on a computer panel (e.g., Rumbaugh, 1977). Although there is still debate among philosophers about whether the apes exhibited "true language," there is no question that the ape language projects have succeeded in demonstrating that, given the appropriate experiences (namely, operant conditioning and discrimination training), our nearest relatives will behave more like us.

critics have charged that the apes simply lack the cognitive capacity to acquire real language. For the present we will ignore the fact that human verbal behavior is also constantly cued by the people with whom we interact, and turn to the question of whether true language is creative and whether it requires certain cognitive capacities.

For Descartes, human language was innate, creative, voluntary, and expressed rational thought, but nonhuman vocal signals communicated only primitive bodily states like hunger or fear (Leahey, 1987). The Cartesian view of language as a vehicle for the expression of internal events, such as thoughts, ideas, needs, wants, or reasons, has persisted to the present both in ordinary conceptions and in much of psychology. This approach has caused problems, in large part because these internal events are not directly observable themselves, but are inferred from the very verbal behavior that is said to express them.

Theories of Language

Most attempts to understand language have focused largely on its structure and have continued the Cartesian tradition of assuming unobservable, cognitive mechanisms responsible for that structure. The linguist Noam Chomsky is well known for his structural approach to language. In the tradition of Descartes, Chomsky has argued steadfastly that language is a creative, innate reflection of the rational human mind. Thus, Chomsky's approach assumes that much can be learned about the mind by discovering the structure and rules of language (grammar).

Chomsky's Structural Theory of Language

In the 1950s and 1960s, Chomsky (1957, 1965) developed a theory of language that emphasized innate factors. He suggested that (a) humans are born with an innate (cognitive) capacity to acquire language, and (b) children only need brief exposure to the language of others to develop language.

Chomsky's argument is that the essential feature of human language is a universal grammar that has evolved in the human species according to the principles of natural selection, and is, therefore, represented somehow in the human brain. One line of evidence for such a universal grammar is that all languages possess similar grammatical forms, such as nouns, verbs, and modifiers. According to Chomsky, every sentence can be analyzed grammatically on two levels. One is the deep structure—so called because it is said to exist in the brain—that provides the basic meaning of a sentence. "The house fell down; the house was old" is an example of what a deep structure might be like (Wardhaugh, 1977, p. 118). Deep structures are formed according to certain grammatical rules. Such rules dictate that any sentence must have at least a noun and a verb; the noun may be accompanied by other words such as adjectives or articles, and the verb by adverbs, prepositional phrases, and so on. Thus, "The man hit the ball" includes a noun phrase ("the man") and a verb phrase ("hit the ball"). The noun phrase consists of a noun and an article, and the verb phrase consists of a verb ("hit") and a noun phrase ("the ball").

The second level of sentence analysis is the surface structure, or the actual form of a spoken sentence. A surface structure "expresses" the meaning embedded in its corresponding deep structure. Thus, the deep structure "The house fell down; the house was old" might be spoken as "The old house fell down." How does the deep structure become a surface structure? A deep structure is changed into a surface structure according to certain transformation rules and operations. They serve to create different sentence types, reorder words, select the correct verb form, and so on (Owens, 1984). According to Chomsky, these rules allow a person to produce sentences from deep structures even though the actual sentences themselves have never been heard or spoken before. Because these transformational rules act like a generator to produce different sentences, Chomsky called this the generative, or creative, aspect of human language.

Chomsky's View of Language Development

Following Chomsky's suggestion that innate factors play the critical role in acquiring language, he claimed that each child is "pre-wired" with a Language Acquisition Device (LAD) (see Figure 8-1), which contains a collection of basic rules of grammar common to all languages. When the child is exposed to the language of others, hypotheses are formulated based on these universal rules that apply to the child's native language. These rules are then used to transform deep structures into appropriate surface structures. Reynolds and Flagg (1977) suggest that the LAD (or the child) initially "constructs sweeping rules of broad utility. Through later feedback from the environment and increased exposure to language, the LAD/child becomes more accurate and finely tuned" (p. 333).

Evaluation of Chomsky's Theory

Although Chomsky's theory, or variations of it, has been widely accepted, it has not gone without criticism. For example, Palmer (1986) challenges Chomsky's contention that a universal grammar has evolved in the human species.

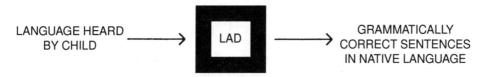

Figure 8-1. The language acquisition device (LAD) hypothesized by Chomsky. (From *Psychology: A Behavioral Overview* [p. 159], by A. Poling, H. Schlinger, S. Starin, and E. Blakely, 1990, New York: Plenum Press. Copyright 1990 by Plenum Press. Reprinted with permission.)

Palmer points out Chomsky's own admission that the laws responsible for the evolution of these principles "are quite unknown." Also, Chomsky offers no information about specific structures in the brain or the relationship between them and a language structure, thus violating the logical support criterion of scientific theories (see Chapter 2). In short, Palmer criticizes Chomsky for claiming that a language-specific structure has evolved, and then either ignoring or dismissing the very evolutionary principles (see Chapter 4) that would be necessary to explain *how* such a structure evolved. Palmer (1986) noted:

> Chomsky has been able to formulate precisely his theoretical ideas because they have remained abstract, but useful theories cannot remain abstract forever. If there is no way to use them to predict, control, or describe actual events, then they are empty. (p. 56)

Others have noted problems with Chomsky's concept of the LAD. For example, Owens (1984) has said that it is too simplified and provides an inadequate explanation of language. Moreover, Owens pointed out that simply assuming that language ability is innate does nothing to help us understand the actual process of language development.

Obviously, the LAD represents an example of *reification* in that it is an abstraction that is treated as if it were a real thing (see Chapter 2). As such, it provides a fundamentally inadequate explanation of language. There is no *direct* evidence that deep structures exist. They are not physical entities that can be measured. Moreover, the role of innate rules in language is at present untestable. Although being able to state the rules of grammar may help, humans have been speaking appropriately (i.e., formulating good sentences) without being able to describe such rules long before grammatical rules were ever described in the first place (Skinner, 1974). It might be argued that in such cases rules are somehow used "unconsciously," but this hypothesis is also untestable and hence meaningless.

There are also explanations for the presence of universal grammatical structures in all human languages that are more parsimonious than positing innate grammatical rules. For instance, the environment contains persons, places, and things, otherwise called nouns. Moreover, the persons, and sometimes the things, act. Verbs describe actions. Thus, all languages contain nouns and verbs because all humans talk about the same things, namely, other persons and things in the environment and their actions. In other words, language contains universals because the environment in which people live has universal features.

What about linguists' contention that language is creative? Essentially the claim is that we rarely ever speak the same sentence twice. This is used as evidence for an inherited generative grammar that spits out sentences that differ in such things as word order or use of certain words, even though their meaning may be the same. However, it can be argued that nonverbal behavior is also creative; that is, it never occurs the same way twice even though the meaning (read "function") may be the same. For example, when you get in your car and start it, do you ever do it exactly the same way? Obviously not. Even though the function is always the same—that is, the car starts, which permits you to drive somewhere—the behaviors are always at least slightly different. In this sense, all behavior is creative. Thus, it appears that verbal behavior may not be different from nonverbal behavior, at least in terms of creativity or novelty. Even if verbal behavior is especially creative, Chomsky's theory does not represent the most parsimonious explanation.

Structural approaches to language, like Chomsky's, emphasize topics such as *syntax* (grammar), *phonetics* (the study of the constituent sounds of words), and *semantics* (the study of word meaning). Research and theorizing in these areas has revealed much about what patterns of language characteristically occur and the grammatical and syntactical rules that describe those patterns. Very little has been revealed about *why* certain patterns develop, that is, about the actual processes that produce the complex behaviors described by the term *language* or, more simply, why a person says what she or he says in a given circumstance. Such questions are better answered by a functional analysis, which treats language as behavior and searches for its causes in the interaction of empirical variables. A scientific interpretation of verbal behavior is such an analysis.

A Functional Analysis of Language

Fully aware of problems associated with a structural approach to language, Leonard Bloomfield, in his 1933 book, *Language,* argued that the facts of language are observable phenomena—behavior—that can be studied profitably without inferring mental factors. Bloomfield also emphasized that the verbal behavior of the speaker results from interacting with other people, and, thus, the meaning of any utterance is to be found in the circumstances in which it occurs, not inside the speaker. This is, by definition, a functional analysis. In 1957, B. F. Skinner dramatically extended a functional analysis of language with his book *Verbal Behavior,* in which he considered language as operant behavior, that is, as behavior determined by its consequences.

Skinner (e.g., 1957) and many other scientific psychologists (e.g., Salzinger, 1978) treat language first of all as *behavior* to be explained by appealing to environmental influences in concert with physiological and genetic variables. From this perspective, language does not exist apart from behavior (i.e., speaking, writing, listening, reading, signing), and it is not a reflection of cognitive phenomena such as ideas, concepts or thoughts. Instead, it is simply a class of behavior that is determined by the same kinds of variables as nonverbal behavior. For these reasons, Skinner uses the term *verbal behavior* to refer to what is commonly termed language. One unique feature of **verbal behavior** is that it is reinforced through the mediation of other persons who are taught (though not formally) to reinforce such behavior (Skinner, 1957). Verbal behavior is like nonverbal operant behavior in that it is acquired and maintained as a result of its effects on the environment. The specific environment for verbal behavior is a social one composed of other people. Whereas the effects of nonverbal operant behavior on the environment are direct (e.g., when you push on a door it opens), the effects of verbal behavior on the environment are indirect (e.g., the door opens but only when you ask someone to open it); that is, the effects, or reinforcers, are mediated by other people.

The foregoing discussion demonstrates that verbal behavior is first and foremost social behavior; it exists primarily because of its effects on listeners, collectively called the verbal community. Listeners perform two general functions with respect to the acquisition of verbal behavior. First, they condition verbal behavior in new speakers (i.e., children). And, second, they teach new speakers to become listeners, that is, to be able to condition verbal behavior in others. In this way, a verbal community and its linguistic conventions are passed from generation to generation.

The Meaning of Verbal Behavior

Much has been written about the meaning of language. Traditional approaches assume that the meaning of an utterance is inside the speaker, in his or her mind, for example. Accordingly, if we want to understand what a speaker means when he or she says something, we must understand what is going on in his or her mind at the time, a difficult task, to be sure. How then can scientific psychologists begin to understand the meaning of verbal behavior? They do so through a functional analysis.

Verbal behavior, like nonverbal behavior, exists because of its *function* for a speaker. One characteristic of verbal behavior that may distinguish it from nonverbal behavior is that a given form of verbal behavior (e.g., saying a word) can have several different functions depending on the circumstances in which it occurs. For example, suppose you hear someone say "fire." What does it mean? The answer depends on its function for the individual who spoke it in a given situation, that is, on why it was spoken. For example, it has a different function if it was shouted by an army officer to his squad than if it was uttered by a child standing in front of a burning log. If it is someone's reply to the question, "What did early humans discover by rubbing two sticks together?" then "fire" again has a different function. The meaning of the response "fire" cannot be revealed solely by its form or by the way it sounds. Instead, its meaning depends on why the speaker said it, in other words, the proximate and ultimate variables that caused it to occur. *The "meaning" of a word is, thus, its function in a social environment.*

Multiple Causation

It is important to point out that any given verbal response, whether a single word or a combination of words (e. g., a sentence), usually has multiple functions simultaneously and is under the proximate control of more than one antecedent stimulus. This means that verbal behavior is not simply a linear sequence of stimuli and responses. For example, the response "fire," by a child to the question, "What is that?" by a parent is determined not only by the presence of a fire but also by the question of the parent (a conditional discrimination [see Chapter 6]). Moreover, the child's response is influenced by his or her past experience with the parent, for instance, whether the parent has always praised correct answers and chided incorrect answers. As you can see, it is difficult to know all of the variables affecting a response. Identifying the proximate and ultimate variables responsible for verbal behavior is the goal of a scientific analysis.

The Development of Speech

Vocal Babbling

Verbal behavior, like nonverbal behavior, arises through the interplay of maturation (see Chapter 10) and learning, primarily operant conditioning. Consider babbling. Evidence suggests that all children begin babbling at about the same age. Even deaf children with deaf parents babble, despite the fact that neither they nor their parents can hear the sounds produced (Lenneberg, Rebelsky, & Nichols, 1965). The fact that babbling occurs at approximately the same age in all children suggests that innate (maturational) factors play a role in speech development.

The shaping of babbling into functional verbal behavior, however, depends on operant conditioning, which involves environmental variables. The plausibility of such an interpretation is illustrated by research showing that social consequences can increase the frequency of vocalizations in infants. For example, Rheingold, Gewirtz, and Ross (1959) reported that the vocalizations of 3-month-old infants increased when they were followed by experimenter smiles, "tsk" sounds, and light touches to the infant's abdomen. Whitehurst (1972) showed that 2-year-old children learned two-word sequences (of the adjective-noun form) through a combination of imitation and reinforcement. Studies have also shown that proper use of syntax can be trained, and just as important, that the new skills transfer to the child's everyday environment (e.g., Hester & Hendrickson, 1977).

Automatic Reinforcement

If the continuation and refinement of babbling is largely due to reinforcement, it is not unreasonable to ask what the reinforcement is. The answer may surprise you. Here's a hint. You now know that reinforcement usually follows behavior immediately. So, what is the most immediate consequence of babbling, or of any vocal utterance for that matter? It is the natural result of the behavior, in this case, the sound that is produced. It is a mistake, therefore, to assume that the reinforcement for babbling, and indeed, verbal behavior in general, comes solely from others in the form of praise or approval. In fact, one of the most powerful, yet subtle, forms of reinforcement for verbal behavior, as well as much nonverbal behavior, is automatic reinforcement. According to

Vaughan and Michael (1982), **automatic reinforcement** is reinforcement that is "a natural result of behavior when it operates upon the behaver's own body or the surrounding world" (p. 219). In short, automatic reinforcers do not require direct mediation by other persons. For example, what is the reinforcement for pushing a button that turns a TV on? Or what is the reinforcement for reaching to pick up a pencil? In both cases, the reinforcement is the natural result of the behavior itself; in the first example, the TV comes on, and in the second example, you are able to pick up the pencil. In both cases the behavior operates on the surrounding world. This sounds almost too simple until you imagine what would happen to both behaviors if these consequences did not occur, that is, pushing a button did not cause the TV to go on and reaching for and grasping a pencil did not permit you to pick it up.

Now let's consider the role of automatic reinforcement in the development of babbling. There are two general steps in the process by which automatic conditioned reinforcers shape babbling (Schlinger, 1995). First, from birth, or even before, the infant constantly hears the phonological sounds of the language community. These sounds are heard when the infant is feeding, being held and caressed, and being played with, and also at times when the infant is not directly interacting with others. The effect of the constant correlation of these sounds with other stimulus events establishes the sounds as conditioned reinforcers (see Chapter 6). The second step is the shaping of the infant's own sound-making into the phonological sounds of the language community that he or she has been hearing for months. When the infant makes sounds that resemble those that he or she has heard, the frequency of those sounds increases. Other sounds that do not match what the infant has heard decrease in frequency. It follows that the closer the match between what the infant has heard and what the infant produces, the stronger the reinforcing effect. In the present case, babbling operates upon the behaver's own body in that the infant immediately hears what he or she has uttered. Automatic reinforcement also explains how children learn to speak with the accent or dialect of their parents, not to mention the actual sounds of the parents' voices (Vaughan & Michael, 1982).

Interestingly, children of deaf parents, who themselves are native speakers of American Sign Language, apparently exhibit a kind of "manual babbling" as early as five months of age (see Bates, O'Connell, & Shore, 1987). Like vocal babbling, over time this manual behavior becomes more like the environmental input of the specific language community (i.e., it looks more like actual signing). Presumably, this process is guided by automatic reinforcement, although in this case, it would consist of the visual match between the infant's hand movements and those he or she has seen produced by the parents.

There is much experimental support for the claim that environmental variables, acting through operant conditioning, play a critical role in the acquisition and development of vocal speech. This development can be divided into prespeech and speech, each including several periods. Prespeech development consists of maturational changes in vocal behavior and ends at about one year of age, when formal words (sometimes called "true language") are emitted. Language scholars (e.g., Eisenson, Auer, & Irwin, 1963) have described several periods of such prespeech development. Table 8-1 shows the periods of prespeech development in terms of approximate ages and relevant behaviors.

As with prespeech development, psychologists and linguists have traditionally described the development of speech in terms of stages. But in the case of speech, the stages are defined by the length of the utterance or, more specifically, the number of words involved. You may recognize this as a structural approach because what is important is the number of words and their ordering, rather than their function or why they are spoken. Structural analyses of verbal behavior, which frequently include normative data (e.g., the average ages at which particular behaviors are first observed), do have merit. For example, it is informative to know the average sequence of development of words and sentences in a given community and the average ages they occur. Parents, teachers, and pediatricians can use such knowledge to help predict the age at which certain behaviors should be observed in a particular child. If they are not observed by that age, then the child is carefully watched to make sure there are no developmental problems. Although structural approaches are useful in predicting

Table 8-1
Periods of Pre-Speech Development

Period of Development	Approximate Age	Behaviors
Undifferentiated crying	Birth	Reflexive crying elicited by a variety of stimuli including sudden loud noises, strong odors and tastes, discomfort from hunger or pain, and loss of support
Differentiated crying	Begins in the first few weeks after birth	Operant crying producing many different reinforcers (e.g., food, termination of pain)
Cooing	1 Month	Quasi-vowel sounds like "ooh" and "aah"
Babbling	3–4 months	Consonantal sounds that approximate those that occur in speech
Lallation	6 months	Consonant-vowel (CV) sequences (e.g., "mamama" or "dahdahdah")
Echolalia	9–10 months	Imitation (echoing) sound made by others which are important for later language development in that these sounds are elements of the more sophisticated language exhibited by adults

Based on Eisenson, Auer, and Irwin, (1963).

when on average certain forms of behavior are likely to be seen, such approaches cannot reveal the processes (i.e., causes) responsible for the behavior.

Single Word Utterances

The first single word utterances occur at about 10 to 13 months of age. They are often nouns (Vetter, 1963), and consist of a single consonant-vowel (CV) unit, or a series of such units (CVCV). The first vowel voiced is usually the soft *a* sound of "father." For this reason, the first word uttered is often "dada," "papa," or "mama."

Although single words are characteristically involved in asking for or naming objects in the environment, some researchers suggest that they sometimes have more complex meanings for the child (de Villiers & de Villiers, 1978). Such words are called **holophrases.** For example, "papa" may mean that the child wants her father, or perhaps that some object in the environment belongs to her father. However, we don't need to infer unobservable processes to explain holophrases because they can be more parsimoniously explained according to principles of operant conditioning. According to Schlinger:

> When a child points to a pair of shoes and says, "Daddy," what are we to make of it? Rather than asking what the child really means, or what the deep structure of this one-word utterance is, it is more scientific to ask about the controlling variables of the response. The response "Daddy" evoked by a pair of (daddy's) shoes has become a . . . verbal response evoked by a nonverbal object because of social reinforcement. When a mother talks to a language-learning child we wouldn't be too surprised to hear her point to the shoes and say something like, "Are those daddy's shoes?" or "Those are daddy's shoes." The child immediately says, "Daddy?" (an example of imitation) and the mother says, "Yes, daddy's shoes." The next time the child sees the shoes, she says "Daddy," and the mother says, "That's right, daddy's shoes." (1995, p. 170)

Multiword Combinations

At 18 to 24 months of age, children begin to utter two-word combinations that consist of nouns, verbs, and adjectives (Stroufe & Cooper, 1988). Words are included that are essential in inferring the meaning of the sentence. An infant's response "want milk" is roughly equivalent to (i.e., has the same meaning as) an adult's "I want some milk, please," and her response "where block?" is equivalent to your "where is my block?" Because the economy of words resembles a telegraphed message, these two-word combinations are termed **telegraphic speech.** Two-word combinations are used in a variety of situations. R. Brown (1973) reported a number of two-word utterances that, in addition to naming or asking for objects, indicated possession ("Mommy car"), specified a location ("Mommy home"), or declared nonexistence ("Dog away"). The most parsimonious explanation of telegraphic speech is that, in most cases, these words are all that are necessary for reinforcement in the form of some reaction from the parents (Schlinger, 1995). Of course, parents ultimately require more words and, indeed, sentences from their children.

The Role of the Environment in the Development of Verbal Behavior

For theorists who stress innate factors in language development (e.g., Chomsky), the environment is important only as the source of acquired sounds. Language develops automatically, but the specific sounds acquired depend on what the child hears. This is one explanation of why Chinese children grow up speaking Chinese and French children grow up speaking French. By contrast, a functional approach views the environment as having a far more active role in the acquisition of language, a view that is supported by considerable research. For example, it is clear that parents (and others) constantly reinforce verbal behavior in language-learning children (e.g., Hart & Risley, 1995; Moerk, 1990), although not necessarily consciously. Parents also speak very differently to language-learning children than to other people (de Villiers & de Villiers, 1978; Hoff-Ginsburg & Shatz, 1982). In particular, the utterances of adults to young children are short, syntactically and semantically simple, well formed, and repetitive (Brown & Bellugi, 1964). Interestingly, a mother's utterances become even shorter when her child begins to emit words (Lord, 1975, cited in de Villiers & de Villiers, 1978; Phillips, 1973). As a rule, adults' utterances to language-learning children are clearly pronounced, with distinct pauses between them and an exaggerated singsong intonation (de Villiers & de Villiers, 1978). This may partially explain why infants' babbling frequently has such an intonation. The sound of this singsong intonation becomes a conditioned reinforcer and the infant reproduction of it either by babbling or in early simple sentences is automatically reinforced.

The Physiology of Speech

The Vocal Apparatus

Verbal behavior is not limited to vocal behavior (speech), but producing and responding to speech is the dominant form of human interaction. Speech is produced by a portion of the human anatomy collectively called the **vocal apparatus,** which includes the lips, mouth, tongue, nasal cavity, pharynx, larynx, and diaphragm (see Figure 8-2). To produce a sound, air expelled from the lungs contacts the larynx. As a result, the vocal folds of the larynx vibrate to form short puffs of air into a tone. This tone is further modified in the vocal tract, which includes the pharynx, mouth, and nasal cavity.

The pharynx serves as a combined opening for the windpipe (which goes to the lungs) and the gullet (which goes to the stomach), and is also the anchor

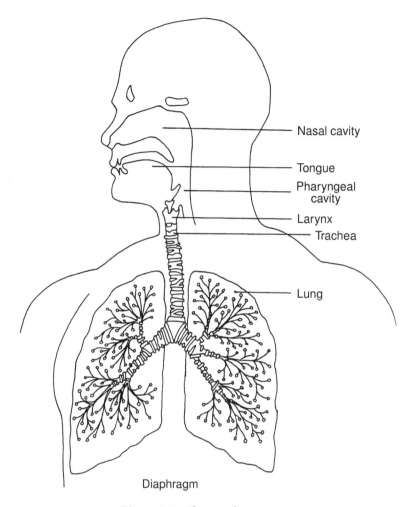

Figure 8-2. The vocal apparatus.

for the base of the tongue.[2] During speech, the muscles in the walls of the pharynx and the base of the tongue move continuously, constantly varying the dimensions of the pharynx and the sound produced. The actions of the pharynx are like those of a pipe organ with numerous pipes of different lengths and di-

---

[2]Comparisons of human adults with monkeys, apes, and human infants demonstrate the importance of the human pharynx (see Figure 8-2). Monkeys and apes have a limited ability to vocalize. Although they can vary the shape of their mouths, there is almost no movement of their pharynx. Human infants' ability to vocalize is limited by an undeveloped pharynx in which the larynx sits high in the throat, permitting the infant to swallow and breathe at the same time without choking. By the time infants reach the babbling state at about three months, the base of the tongue and the larynx have begun to descend into the throat, and, therefore, enlarge the pharyngeal region. It is only then that human infants are able to make speech sounds like those of adults (Campbell, 1985).

ameters, each making a particular tone (Campbell, 1985). To produce some sounds, such as *m* and *n*, the nasal cavity is closed off from or opened to the vocal tract; the mouth (including the tongue, lips, and jaw), too, can be manipulated to produce a variety of sounds.

The Brain

All behavior is most proximately caused by changes in the brain, and verbal behavior is no exception. By the early 1900s, scientists had identified several regions of the brain that were implicated in language production and comprehension. Much of this information was obtained through studying people with brain injury. Since then other methods have also been developed to study brain function (e.g., electrical brain stimulation).

Paul Broca, a French scientist of the mid-1800s, demonstrated that certain areas of the brain were associated with language. He discovered that damage to an area on the left side of the frontal lobe, now called **Broca's area** (see Figure 8-3), produced speech disorders such as **aphasia** (an impairment of language production or comprehension). The speech of persons with damage to Broca's area (e.g., from stroke) is slow and laborious and often without articles, adverbs, and adjectives. For this reason, the speech is often described as telegraphic; the words used tend to be in the correct order and have clear meaning, but speech is reduced to its rudiments. Hence, the request "I would please like to have some milk," may instead be "want milk." Broca found that damage to the left side of the brain produced aphasia, but damage to the corresponding part of the right side did not. For some functions, including the production of verbal behavior, one side of the brain is vastly more important than the other (see Chapter 7).

A German scientist, Carl Wernicke, identified another type of aphasia, and in so doing linked language to another area of the brain. **Wernicke's aphasia** results from damage to a localized region in the left cortex. This region, called **Wernicke's area** (see Figure 8-3), is located between the primary auditory cortex and a structure called the angular gyrus, which probably mediates between the visual and auditory centers of the brain (Geschwind, 1979). Those afflicted with Wernicke's aphasia do not comprehend what they hear. Although speech is grammatically correct in patients with Wernicke's aphasia, it is meaningless or inappropriate for current circumstances because what they hear is meaningless.

Damage to the angular gyrus results in another type of aphasia, called anomic aphasia. In this disorder, language comprehension and production are intact, but nouns are often omitted, substituted, or paraphrased (Beaumont, 1983). In some cases, damage to the angular gyrus "functionally disconnects" the systems involved in auditory and written language. This results patients' speaking and understanding speech, but having trouble with written language. Such disorders suggest that speaking and writing are repertoires that are acquired separately even though they are connected in persons who can both speak and write. This evidence argues against language as a unitary ability that people either possess or do not possess.

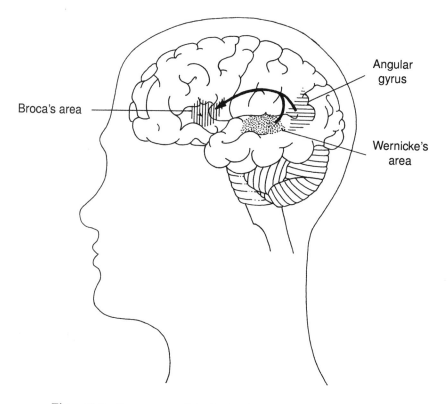

Figure 8-3. Some areas of the brain that are involved in speech.

From the study of aphasia, scientists concluded that Broca's area, Wernicke's area, and the angular gyrus, among other areas of the cortex, must be important in the production and comprehension of normal speech. Carl Wernicke was the first to propose a theoretical model of the brain's role in language production that is still accepted today. According to this model, an utterance (actually a neural transmission) arises in Wernicke's area; from there it moves to Broca's area, which determines its vocal structure; and finally, the adjacent area of the motor cortex is stimulated, activating the appropriate muscles of the mouth, lips, larynx, and pharynx. Though this model clarifies the proximate physiological causes of verbal behavior, it does not consider how or why language develops, in other words, the phylogenetic and ontogenetic causes. That is why neuroscientists interested in human language must be aware of the work of scientific psychologists.

The Relationship between Verbal and Nonverbal Behavior

Despite the fact that verbal behavior possesses some features that distinguish it from nonverbal behavior (see below), both verbal and nonverbal behavior are operant in the sense that they operate on the environment to generate consequences which then determine the future frequency of the behavior under similar circumstances. Nevertheless, most of us assume that there is often perfect correspondence between the verbal and nonverbal behavior in a given individual. For example, if someone tells you that she is not racist, then you expect her to behave in ways that are consistent with that statement. At a simpler level, if a friend tells you that he will call you on Tuesday, then you expect him to call. We are often surprised and disappointed when our friend doesn't call, saying, "I don't understand; he said he would call." Common sense suggests that there is reasonably good correspondence between what a person says he will do and what he actually does because the two are somehow related. Psychologists have traditionally studied this relation in terms of the relationship between attitude and behavior.

Attitudes and Behavior

Historically, the question "How do attitudes affect behavior?" has been of considerable interest to many psychologists. The question seems to be reasonable, but problems lurk beneath its innocent veneer. One problem is that such questions assume that attitudes have a real existence apart from behavior (a problem of reification). According to Bandura (1969), attitudes, like other cognitive tendencies, are inferred from overt behavior, for example, self-ratings or self-descriptions. If an attitude is inferred from one form of overt behavior and used to explain another form of behavior, then, according to Bandura, we are creating arbitrary distinctions between different types of response—one we call attitude and another we don't. For Bandura, then, the question of whether attitudes determine overt behavior is a "pseudo-issue," and might be more meaningfully conceptualized as a problem of the correlation between response systems, which can be either high or not depending upon the response systems' respective contingencies of reinforcement. Bandura (1969) concludes:

> The differentiation between attitudes and overt actions disappears completely when the former are primarily inferred from nonverbal behavior. For example, a person who displays antagonistic responses or actively avoids members of a given ethnic group is believed to have a negative attitude, whereas he is assumed to possess a positive attitude if he exhibits approving amicable reactions. In such circumstances, the issue of whether attitudes influence behavior reduces to the meaningless question of whether a particular response pattern determines itself! (pp. 597–598)

Bandura makes a number of important points. One is that attitudes are always inferred on the basis of overt behavior, characteristically verbal self-reports; they are never observed directly. For example, a subject is asked to report how he or she might respond in a given situation. The answers are taken to indicate an underlying attitude. The self-report is then compared with how the subject actually behaves in the situation of interest (i.e., whether the two correspond). If there is correspondence, the attitude is assumed to cause the overt behavior. If not, no causal status is assigned.

This research strategy is exemplified in a study by LaPiere (1934). In his study, a Chinese couple visited more than 200 motels and restaurants throughout the United States. Even though there was considerable prejudice against Asians in the 1920s, only one facility refused service to the couple. When these same motels and restaurants were sent a questionnaire asking whether or not they would serve the couple, 92% of the respondents said that they would not. Although this study might be construed as evaluating whether attitudes toward Asians controlled overt behavior, it actually examined the correspondence between saying and doing: Was overt behavior toward Asians correlated with, and hence predictable on the basis of, verbal behavior concerning them?

From the scientific perspective presented in this book, saying and doing represent separate responses that are shaped and maintained by different experiences and do not necessarily affect one another. Given this, it is not surprising that both research and common experience suggest that there is not necessarily a high degree of correspondence between saying and doing (e.g., Bandura, 1969). The entire field of social psychology underwent dramatic changes in the 1960s when researchers found that only a small proportion of behavior could be reliably predicted from self-reports. Once this was apparent, attention by scientific psychologists turned to discovering the variables that determined the correspondence between verbal and nonverbal behavior.

The Correspondence between Saying and Doing

An attitude can be considered as a subject's verbal report of her or his tendency to behave in a particular way with respect to some person, place or thing. Several variables are known to affect the degree of correspondence between saying and doing, or, in the terms favored by many social psychologists, between attitudes and behavior.

One general variable that affects correspondence is the amount of experience in the situation of interest. In general, verbal responses by individuals with direct experience in a given situation are more likely to reflect behavior in that situation than are verbal responses by individuals without such experience. Imagine two people who say "I don't like watching professional football." One grew up on Long Island and has seen dozens of Jets and Giants games. The other grew up in Sioux Falls, and has never seen a game; her attitude (verbal statement) reflects variables other than actual exposure to professional football. That being the case, it is likely (although not assured) that she would, if given the option, be more likely than the New Yorker to attend a game and to enjoy it (i.e., laugh, cheer).

As you might anticipate, the probability that correspondence will occur can be increased by providing reinforcement when what is done is consistent with what is said. Such a relation was demonstrated by Isreal and Brown (1977), who asked a group of children to state which play activity they intended to engage in at a later time (e.g., "I am going to play with dinosaurs"). First, the children received a snack for making such statements. As a result, the number of children who promised to play with a particular toy increased, but the number of children who actually played with the toy did not. The experimenters then provided snacks for correspondence—that is, each child received a snack when she or he promised to play with a toy and then played with it at the appropriate time. Under this condition, correspondence increased.

Although the relation is imperfect, it is abundantly clear that verbal behavior sometimes allows us to predict other behavior. This does not, however, mean that the verbal behavior *causes* the other behavior in any simple sense. Each reflects in large part the conditioning history of the individual, and must be explained in terms of that history. Our attitudes, like the rest of our behavior, are learned. Thus, they can be changed by changing the environment.

The Importance of Verbal Behavior

Although we can only speculate about the phylogenetic (i.e., evolutionary) functions of verbal behavior in humans, its ontogenetic functions are more obvious. As noted, verbal behavior is first and foremost social behavior and it exists primarily because of its social functions, that is, its effects on listeners. To appreciate this fully, imagine what your life would be like if all of a sudden you had no more verbal interactions with others. Imagine how difficult life would be if you were unable to tell a doctor your symptoms, your teacher could not explain a difficult concept, your friend could not give you directions to an important destination, or, more simply, if you could not get things by asking for them.

From these few examples, you can see that verbal behavior may be classified according to two general functions: asking for things ("Please give me that pencil") and describing the environment for others ("The book is on the table in the bedroom"). The advantages for the speaker are obvious: Many important reinforcers, including information about the world, can be obtained as a function of language. Language also has important functions for the listener, and it is these important characteristics that we will now discuss.

Instructions and Rules

People frequently describe relationships observed in the environment. The relationships described may involve only stimuli ("When the stove is *red,* it is very *hot*"), antecedent stimuli and responses ("When the timer sounds, take the cake out of the oven"), or antecedent stimuli, responses, and consequent stimuli ("When you hear the song by Pearl Jam, be the tenth caller, and you will win $1000"). Skinner called these descriptions of relations among stimuli and responses **rules** (Skinner, 1969).[3] For Skinner, rules involve a speaker's behavior

---

[3]The term *instruction* is reserved only for the discriminative effect of verbal stimuli on behavior, such as when a parent instructs a child, "Pick up your toys." The instruction "Pick up your toys" is an S^D in that it evokes the behavior of picking up toys because in the past such behavior has been reinforced after that instruction has been stated. The term *rule* is reserved for verbal stimuli with different effects, namely, that the functions of other stimuli are altered as a result. For example, a teacher says to his students, "When the bell rings, please go inside." The ringing of the bell will now evoke the behavior of going inside; its S^D-like function was established by the teacher's rule (Schlinger & Blakely, 1987; Blakely & Schlinger, 1987).

(i.e., they are spoken or written and can be observed and measured); thus, they constitute a physical stimulus (usually auditory) for a listener. Contrast these rules with those inferred by Chomsky (e.g., transformational rules possessed by a hypothetical LAD), which cannot be directly observed or measured.

The important characteristic of rules is that listeners can learn from them (i.e., their behavior is altered). For example, a person can acquire new behavior, with very little effort, through rules such as, "Turn the computer on by pushing the green button," "To get to Main Street, turn left on Maple," or "If you touch that wire, you will get shocked." Without the rules, the listener would have to learn the behaviors through direct exposure to the environment (imagine how difficult it would be if you had to find Main Street without rules, or if you always had to learn to avoid potentially painful situations by first directly experiencing the pain). In a sense, rules mimic the effects of conditioning, both classical and operant, by producing novel behavior–environment relations. Hence, rules may be called analogs of classical and operant conditioning (Alessi, 1992). In other words, behavior acquired as a result of exposure to rules also could be acquired directly through classical and operant conditioning.

Rules and the Function of Stimuli

One effect of conditioning is to change the function of stimuli. In classical conditioning, for instance, pairing an NS with a US changes the function of the NS, which is then called a CS. Through a similar type of conditioning, stimuli which initially do not function as conditioned reinforcers come to do so by virtue of being paired with unconditioned reinforcers. And discriminative stimuli acquire their evocative function over operant behavior because the behavior produced certain consequences only when those stimuli were present. These are all examples of stimulus functions being altered through direct conditioning.

A related type of conditioning history makes it possible for the functions of stimuli to be changed indirectly, either through hearing rules or through observing the behavior of someone else. In the latter, observing someone else's behavior substitutes for a direct conditioning history in that it instantaneously changes the behavioral function of stimuli. This type of learning, called *social learning* or *observational learning,* is described in Sidebar 8-2. As with observational learning, rules also substitute for conditioning histories. As an example of such an effect, assume that you are the subject in an experiment. You sit facing a panel with a green light, a red light, a counter that can be incremented and decremented, and a lever. The experimenter comes in and tells you: "You can only earn points by pressing the lever when the green light is on. You will lose points for pressing at any other time. When the session ends, you will receive a dollar for each point on the counter."

These instructions identify relations among antecedent stimuli, responses, and consequences. In most people, they would control behavior by (1) establishing point gain as a reinforcer, (2) establishing point loss as a punisher, and (3) establishing the green light as a stimulus that evokes lever pressing. The experimenter's instructions in this case serve as function-altering stimuli, that is,

Sidebar 8-2
Observational Learning

Some psychologists, Albert Bandura (e.g., 1977) and other social-learning theorists among them, consider one person's imitation of another's behavior to involve a special kind of learning. They term it **observational learning.** Observational learning has three important features:

1. Learning occurs in one trial. A person need observe a model only once to behave as he or she behaved.

2. The observer may emit the modeled response long after observing it, and in the absence of the model.

3. Behavior by a model that leads to a positive outcome is more likely than other behavior to be emitted by an observer. "Vicarious reinforcement" is assumed to be responsible for this phenomenon.

Although some social-learning theorists assume that observational learning cannot be accounted for in terms of operant and respondent conditioning principles, this is not the case (Deguchi, 1984). Observational learning appears to involve a complex operant history in which a person initially is reinforced for imitating a model's actions. You've undoubtedly seen parents attempting to get their child to behave as they do (say "Mama," shake the rattle). They typically succeed, and generalized imitation, that is, being able to imitate behavior for which the individual has never before received reinforcement, develops in most people as operant behavior. Observational learning begins to have the same effect as learning by rules; that is, seeing another person's behavior in a given situation alters the observer such that that situation will evoke the behavior in them. Such learning often serves a person well, for it provides a rapid means of behavior change. For example, suppose you just received your bank card in the mail and you don't know how to use such a card to get money from a bank machine. There are at least three ways you can learn how to use your card to get money from a machine. One way is to go to a bank machine and try all sorts of behaviors. Chances are it will take a very long time to get money this way. Another method is to have someone give you instructions, or rules, for the behavior. A third, and perhaps quicker, way is simply to go to a bank machine and watch someone else get money. Although you may describe their behavior to yourself as you observe, and then repeat it back to yourself as you try, it is also likely that you can now engage in some of the behavior "automatically," that is, without stating any rules to yourself. Observing the other person's behavior in that situation has enabled you to do the same behavior under the same circumstances. Of course, if the new behavior of operating the bank machine is successful, that is, if it produces money, then it will be more likely to occur in the future under similar circumstances. In other words, it is reinforced. As with rules, learning by observation is a rapid way to acquire new behavior–environment relationships.

stimuli that alter the ability of other stimuli to control behavior. They do so, of course, because the person whose behavior they control has a special history with respect to verbal statements and the reinforcing consequences of behaving in accordance with them.

Rules are stimuli that can produce a wide range of behavioral effects. How they do so becomes easier to understand if one remembers, first, that rules are contingency-specifying stimuli. That is, they are verbal statements that spell out relationships (contingencies) among stimuli and responses. Second, rules are function-altering stimuli (Blakely & Schlinger, 1987; Schlinger & Blakely, 1987); that is, verbal statements that alter the behavioral functions of other stimuli.

Of course, rules are not always effective. Whether or not a particular rule alters the behavioral functions of stimuli for a given individual depends in large part on her or his prior experience with respect to the rule-giver and the accuracy of similar rules provided in the past. We learn through operant conditioning to follow rules or to refrain from following them. For instance, a parent says to a child, "Don't touch the stove; it's hot and you'll get burned." Contrary to the rule, the child touches the stove and gets burned. As a result of the correspondence between real and described contingencies, the future likelihood of rule following increases. If, however, the child touches the stove but does not get burned, the future likelihood of rule following decreases. Can you think of rules that are not effective because they do not correspond to real-world contingencies?

Self-Generated Rules

Rules can be provided by others or formulated by the individual whose behavior they are to control. Assume that you are in an airport in a foreign country, which we'll call Xanadu, and are hungry. There is a vending machine that's getting lots of use by other travelers, and you have a pocketful of Xanadu change. The only problem is that you can't read Xanadu, and the machine has no pictures, just labels in Xanadu script. You can't tell what kind of food is available, or what it costs. One way to learn is simply by trying (i.e., exposure to contingencies): Go to the machine, then put in money and push buttons until something happens. Eventually, if you had enough time and money, appropriate behavior would emerge—you'd learn how to obtained a desired food. This would occur with less effort if a person skilled in the English and Xanadu languages came along and said, "You can get rice soup, plain tofu, and chicken feet from that machine. Each costs five cellops (a Xanadu coin which she shows you). Push the top button for soup, the middle for tofu, and the bottom for feet." No problem. Go for the feet.

Unfortunately, there aren't many people conversant in English and Xanadu. That being the case, your best bet would be to watch other travelers operate the machine and, on the basis of your observations, formulate your own rule. You see that everyone inserts a particular kind of coin (which you call a little round one), and the food they receive depends on the button they push. Hence you generate the rule, "To get soup, put in a little round coin, then push the top button," and behave accordingly. Of course, it is also possible that as a result of simply observing everyone else's behavior, you are able to do the same thing without necessarily stating rules and, if this were the case, it would illustrate observational learning (see Sidebar 8-2).

Advantages of Learning as a Function of Rules

Rule-governed behavior occurs when an individual's behavior is affected by verbal instructions describing environmental relations that person has not directly contacted. (Behavior that is affected by directly contacting environmental relations is termed **contingency-governed.**) For example, a motorcyclist's friend may say, "Don't ride in the rain; the road gets slick and it's darned easy to wipe out." This rule describes relations among an antecedent stimulus (the presence of rain) a response (riding a cycle), and a probable outcome of that response (an accident). If the biker refrains from riding in the rain—and whether this occurs depends largely on the biker's prior experience with respect to the rule giver and the accuracy of similar rules provided in the past—the behavior is rule-governed. Rule-governed behavior is of crucial importance to humans, because it (a) provides for very rapid behavior change and (b) enables us to behave effectively without requiring direct exposure to environmental events that might prove harmful or ineffectual.

Rule-governed and contingency-governed behaviors are not necessarily identical; a person whose behavior is controlled by exposure to a verbal description of a response–outcome relation (e.g., "If you eat yellow snow, you'll get sick") may not behave in exactly the same manner as a person who actually has been exposed to that relation (e.g., someone who ate yellow snow and got sick). Moreover, rules can be faulty (e.g., speakers can lie), fostering behaviors inappropriate for the situation at hand. "All Irish setters are mean and to be avoided" is an example of such a rule.

The ability to state and be affected by rules is a unique characteristic made possible by verbal behavior. For example, rules are important in transmitting information across generations. The lessons of life are passed down from father to son, grandmother to granddaughter, tradesman to apprentice. Without rules, each new generation would have to relearn old lessons. Some rules describe facts about nature, as when scientists report the results of experiments (e.g., "Compound A combined with compound B will produce compound C"). Others describe the social environment (e.g., "To get along with Mr. Higgins, you have to ask about his garden").

Among other functions, rules can increase the effectiveness of delayed consequences. For example, the consequences of poor study habits, low grades, are often too delayed to improve study behavior. Low grades can, however, be made more effective as behavioral consequences by rules such as "Your low grades are a result of insufficient attention to the study guides." Drug abuse can often lead to serious problems with social relations and job functioning, but these consequences are delayed and, more often than not, do not decrease drug taking. But rules that describe these consequences can be effective: "If you want to keep your job and your family you must stop taking drugs."

It is important to remember that although producing and being affected by rules occurs as verbal behavior, it is also operant behavior, acquired through a complex interaction with the social and natural environment. But what about so-called higher-level processes such as memory and consciousness? Can they also be explained scientifically? In the next chapter we will find out.

Summary

1. Whether human language really is a special kind of behavior requiring a special kind of explanation, as many psychologists and philosophers have long assumed, is ultimately an empirical, that is, a scientific, question.

2. The theory of language proposed by the linguist Noam Chomsky is the most recent Cartesian view in which language is seen as a creative, innate reflection of the rational human mind. Thus, to understand language, one must understand the rational mind that produces it, and for Chomsky this means understanding the rules of grammar that he believes all humans inherit and which determine the form of language.

3. Chomsky believes that the rules of grammar are somehow coded in a language acquisition device (LAD) that spits out grammatical sentences in children after only brief exposure to the language of their parents. However, critics have pointed out that the LAD is a hypothetical construct, that is, a nonphysical entity inferred from observed behavior and, as such, it provides a fundamentally inadequate explanation of language.

4. An alternative to a Cartesian approach to language is the functional approach taken by Bloomfield and Skinner in which language—verbal behavior—is viewed as observable behavior that can be studied profitably without inferring mental factors; that is, verbal behavior of a speaker results from interacting with other people, and the meaning of any utterance is to be found in the circumstances in which it occurs, not inside the speaker.

5. Skinner defined *verbal behavior* as behavior reinforced through the mediation of other persons (i. e., listeners collectively called the verbal community) who are trained (although not formally) to mediate and reinforce such behavior.

6. The development of verbal (vocal) behavior occurs through a series of changes in sounds that arise through the interplay of maturation and learning beginning with prespeech development, such as babbling, which is seen in all infants, even deaf infants. The learning continues only if reinforcing stimulation follows, and proceeds through the development of single words and then multiword combinations.

7. Despite the popularity of hypotheses of inherited language acquisition and production, a wealth of empirically based research demonstrates the important role of the environment.

8. Speech is produced by a part of the human anatomy collectively called the *vocal apparatus,* which includes the lips, mouth, tongue, nasal cavity, pharynx, larynx, and diaphragm, and proximate physiological mechanisms located in the brain, such as Broca's and Wernicke's areas. Damage to these language areas of the brain results in disorders of speech called *aphasias.*

9. Although common sense may suggest that a person's *attitude,* as observed in verbal self-reports, determines how he or she will behave with respect to that attitude, research has shown the correspondence to be very low. If attitudes are conceptualized as other types of (verbal) response, subject to the same variables as other responses, then the question about the relationship between attitudes and behavior is whether or not they are correlated. Either way, the verbal behavior said to indicate attitude is operant behavior and, therefore, subject to the same variables as other behavior.

10. Verbal behavior is important because of its inherent social functions, which may be classified as either asking others for things or describing the en-

vironment for others. The latter function occurs in forms called *rules* (or instructions), which are descriptions of relations between stimuli or between stimuli and behavior that mimic the effects of classical and operant conditioning in their effect on the behavior of listeners.

Study Questions

1. Is human language unique, and, if so, what does this imply about nonhumans?

2. What is Chomsky's basic argument about human language and how does it represent a Cartesian approach?

3. How does language develop in children according to Chomsky and what is the role of the LAD?

4. What are the main problems with Chomsky's theory of language, including those dealing with the LAD as a hypothetical construct, and how do the construct and the theory in general represent an inadequate explanation of language behavior?

5. What are the general features of functional approaches to language and what questions about language can such approaches answer?

6. What is Skinner's general approach to verbal behavior? How is verbal behavior similar to and different from nonverbal behavior and what is the role of the environment?

7. What is the relationship between the meaning and the function of verbal behavior?

8. What is babbling and how can the onset and continuation of babbling be explained in terms of reinforcement, especially automatic reinforcement?

9. How is manual babbling like vocal babbling?

10. How can such utterances as holophrases and telegraphic speech be parsimoniously explained in terms of environmental variables?

11. What are some of the ways that the environment influences the development of verbal behavior?

12. What does the vocal apparatus consist of?

13. What are some important language areas of the brain and what are the consequences of damage to those areas on an individual's verbal behavior?

14. What is the relationship between attitudes and verbal behavior and what determines the correspondence between attitudes and other behavior?

15. Why is verbal behavior important? What are its two general functions?

16. What is the important characteristic of rules? How are rules function altering? What are some advantages of learning as a function of rules?

Cognition

9

This chapter examines an approach to the understanding of behavior called cognitive psychology. Three related subject areas that are of interest to cognitive psychologists—memory, mental imagery, and consciousness—are overviewed, and some typical experiments are summarized. Where appropriate, the cognitive approach is evaluated according to the characteristics of science discussed in Chapter 2 and alternative explanations are presented.

Cognitive versus Behavioral Approaches to Psychology

According to many cognitive psychologists, a scientific revolution occurred in psychology sometime in the years immediately following World War II (e.g., Baars, 1986; H. Gardner, 1985). In that revolution, cognitive psychology is said to have replaced behaviorism as the dominant paradigm in psychology. What is a paradigm? Scientists who employ the same conceptual framework and share a body of assumptions, methods, and values adhere to the same **paradigm.** Thomas Kuhn (e.g., 1970) popularized the use of paradigm in this sense, and he suggested that science proceeds not in a smooth progression but rather in a series of rather dramatic *paradigm shifts,* or revolutions. In a paradigm shift, one way of examining and explaining a part of the world is usurped by another. The usurper is usually a paradigm that in some sense better accounts for observations than the one it replaces.

Astronomy provides a clear example of a paradigm shift. As explained in Chapter 1, the Ptolemaic (earth-centered) system was replaced by the Copernican (sun-centered) system. This paradigm shift, however, could hardly be called revolutionary, if by that one means abrupt, since it took place over about 200 years. If the term *revolutionary* is used to mean a dramatic change from one world view to another, then there was indeed a Copernican revolution. The same may be said about a Darwinian revolution in biology. Psychology, however, is a different story. The cognitive revolution was proclaimed mostly by cognitive psychologists, and it could be argued equally that the rejection of commonsense mentalistic (i.e., cognitive) explanations of human behavior by scientific psychologists beginning with Pavlov, Thorndike, Watson, and Skinner represented the real revolution in psychology. For modern-day scientific psychologists, decades of experimentation finally permitted behavior to be explained objectively, that is, without having to make guesses about unobservable entities and processes in the mind.

It may be most accurate to consider the field of contemporary psychology as encompassed by two general and competing paradigms, the *behavioral* (or behavioristic) and the *cognitive.* These paradigms differ in that

> . . . the behavioristic paradigm emphasizes objective descriptions of environmental events, operational definitions, and controlled experiments while the cognitive paradigm emphasizes internal information processing and programming. . . . These contrasting paradigms lead to different questions and to different ways of designing and

conducting investigations. Furthermore, even if psychologists who adhere to these divergent paradigms obtain similar data—which is highly unlikely since they will conduct quite different studies—their paradigms will lead to divergent interpretations of the data. (Barber, 1976, p. 8)

Regardless of whether or not a cognitive revolution ever occurred, it is clear that over the last 50 years or so cognitive psychology has become the most popular approach to the study not only of human behavior, but, interestingly, of nonhuman behavior as well. Broadly speaking, **cognitive psychology** is the study of observable behavior in order to infer unobservable processes, such as representations and memories, as explanations. Because this is how most people already think about behavior, cognitive psychology is the psychology of common sense and, therefore, it is hardly new (Baars, 1986). One result of this approach is that cognitive psychologists are more interested in the unobservable processes than in behavior itself. Sometimes cognitive processes are viewed as dependent variables and at other times they are viewed as independent variables and, thus, as causes of the very behavior said to reflect them.

In contrast, the scientific approach presented in this book (closer to the behavioral view) studies observable behavior, but not as a reflection of inferred structures or processes. Scientific psychologists are interested in all of the objective variables of which behavior is a function, but especially ontogenetic causes of behavior, such as classical and operant conditioning. B. F. Skinner explained that cognitive psychologists also study these relations, but they "seldom deal with them directly" (1978, p. 97). Instead, cognitive psychologists invent internal substitutes for both the causes and the effects.

Consider the following example. Suppose we show subjects a list of word pairs and then at a later time we ask them to recall one member of the pair when we present the other member. Although the dependent variable is the recall, that is, what the subjects actually say, cognitive psychologists would say that what is really being studied is something called associative, or long-term, memory. The difference is subtle. The actual recall of one word given the other is an instance of verbal behavior (see Chapter 8) and is measured directly. The long-term memory is a cognitive process and presumably takes place at another level altogether, that is, in the mind. The only evidence for the long-term memory, however, is what the subject says in recall, in other words, the observed behavior.

Cognitive psychologists may then actually attribute the recall to the long-term memory, for example, by saying that a subject has good recall *because* she has a good long-term memory. You should recognize this as a circular explanation (Chapter 2). Because cognitive psychologists never observe the long-term memory directly, we may question the scientific validity of the concept. Scientific psychologists, in contrast, would want to know what objective independent variables determine the probability and accuracy of the recall. Thus, they might compare the effects of different training procedures on such behavior.

Cognitive Psychology, Computers, and the Information-Processing Metaphor

The term *cognition* literally means to become acquainted with or, more simply, *to know*. As it is used in modern psychology, the term **cognition** refers to the cognitive or mental processes by which one acquires knowledge of the world. Thus, acquiring knowledge about the environment, and the processes by which we acquire such knowledge, is the subject matter for cognitive psychologists. Since these processes are internal, and unobservable, cognitive psychologists must observe what they can, namely, behavior, and then try to make some guesses about the internal processes responsible for it. Consequently, it is not uncommon to hear cognitive psychologists talking about such commonsense concepts as memories, representations, knowledge, and other presumably mental events. For cognitive psychologists, these are the mechanisms through which we know our world.

We may ask, "What justifies cognitive psychology returning to a common-sense approach to the understanding of behavior?" After all, we don't see physicists returning to a Ptolemaic view of the universe or to the belief that was prevalent in the late 1800s that a substance called the "ether" was present everywhere, even in empty space, and that explained the constant speed of light. Nor do we see physicians embracing the long-held view that malaria spreads through "bad air" (malaria literally means "bad air") from its source in poisonous marsh gas, or that yellow fever originates in sewage and the putrefaction of dead animals and also spreads through the air (Snelson, 1995). What is different about psychology?

According to Gardner (1985), World War II stimulated several different technological advances in fields such as mathematics and engineering. Perhaps most important for cognitive psychology were the development of calculating machines that later came to be called computers, and anti-aircraft devices and missiles that required feedback systems that permitted in-flight adjustments so that the projectile accurately hit the target. Why were these two developments important for the development of modern cognitive psychology? Very simply, they were viewed as analogies to human functioning. For example, human memory was likened to computers as an information-processing system and human behavior in general was seen to be purposive and goal directed just like the anti-aircraft guns and guided missiles. Even the possibility that machines and humans are similarly intelligent has been considered, as illustrated in Sidebar 9-1, which considers "Artificial Intelligence."

Modern cognitive psychology is based on the metaphor (or analogy) of humans as information processors. Thus, as one might expect from a discipline that relies almost totally on inferred processes, much of the description of human psychology is based on analogies with other systems that are better understood, like the computer. A well-known cognitive psychologist, John Anderson (1985), offers the following analogy to clarify the information-processing metaphor:

Sidebar 9-1
Artificial Intelligence

As computers grew more sophisticated and capable of more complex functioning, it became clear that they could perform tasks that resembled the types of human functioning that we describe with the word *intelligence*. Thus, the term **artificial intelligence** (AI) was coined. As research in AI expanded, different views of it emerged. According to the so-called strong view, AI "seeks to produce, on a computer, a pattern of output that would be considered intelligent if displayed by a human being" (Gardner, 1985, p. 11). In this view an "appropriately programmed computer really is a mind in the sense that computers given the right programs can literally be said to understand and have other cognitive states" (J. Searle, 1984).

The strong view of AI evolved during different phases of research in AI from 1957 to 1977, as described by Dreyfus (1979). For example, Phase I, from 1957 until 1962, was characterized by programs in so-called cognitive simulation such as language translation, problem solving, and pattern recognition. Examples of fairly successful programs in cognitive simulation included the Logic Theorist, devised by Newell, Shaw, and Simon, which successfully proved 38 of 52 mathematical theorems, and the General Problem Solver (GPS), which was capable of solving theorems, playing chess, and solving complex logical problems. Phase II, from 1962 to 1967, was characterized by programs that could simulate English language understanding with "understanding" narrowly defined to mean that with a limited subset of English words as input, the computer would respond with a limited subset of appropriate English words as output (Crossman, 1985). Phase III, from 1967 to 1972, was characterized by so-called microworlds, or computer programs with greatly restricted domains. Perhaps the best-known example was Terry Winograd's (1975) program SHRDLU, which allowed a person to "engage in a dialogue with the computer" by using simple English commands which caused a simulated robot arm to manipulate a set of variously shaped blocks. Phase IV, from 1972 to 1977, was characterized by so-called "expert systems." A well-known example is MYCIN, a program for diagnosing blood and meningitis infections, which did a respectable job of simulating the expertise of a medical practitioner.

Although computer programs succeeded at performing more and more complex functions that would be considered signs of intelligence if carried out by a human, the real question was whether the computer output was functionally the same as that of humans. Critics such as Hubert Dreyfus claimed that AI programs were merely engineering tricks and would be successful only so long as they were limited to their very restricted domains. In other words, they are not generalizable. Dreyfus also argued that AI has failed in its goals because its workers have based their efforts on fundamentally incorrect assumptions. One such assumption is that the brain and the digital computer are functionally similar in that they both process information digitally and serially.

Dreyfus argued that AI will continue to fail so long as workers in the field ignore some important differences between computers and humans, namely, that humans have bodies that sense the environment and act upon the environment and, most important, that a body has needs and that much if not all human behavior, like the behavior of all animals, involves the drive to survive. Essentially, much of AI has ignored the functional aspects of an organism's adaptive behavior and, instead, has stressed a logical structural approach that has no scientific support (Dreyfus, 1979). The point to be made is that the essence of human intelligence and adaptability is not an ability to manipulate symbols or representations, as cognitive scientists believe, but rather the modifiability of behavior by contact with the environment.

---

*The material in this section is taken from Schlinger (1992).

Suppose we followed a letter . . . through the postal system. First, the letter would be put in a mailbox; the mailbox would be emptied and the contents brought to a central station. The letter would be sorted according to region, and the letters for a particular region shipped off to their destination. There they would be sorted again as to area within the postal district. Letters having the same destination would be given to a carrier, and the carrier would deliver the letter to the correct address. Now, just as we traced the letter through the postal system, let us follow this question as it is processed through the human mind:

Where does your grandmother live?

First, you must identify each word and retrieve its meaning. Then you must determine the meaning of this configuration of words, that is, understand the question being asked. Next, you must search your memory for the correct answer. Upon finding the answer in memory, you have to formulate a plan for generating the answer in words, and then transform the plan into the actual answer:

She lives in San Francisco. (p. 11)

According to Anderson (1985), the most important feature of an **information-processing analysis** is that it involves tracing a sequence of mental operations and their products (the information) in the performance of a cognitive task.

Before we continue, let us briefly demonstrate how a scientific psychologist might interpret the previous example. The question, "Where does your grandmother live?" as a discriminative stimulus (S^D), evokes the response, "She lives in San Francisco." It does so because in the past saying "My grandmother lives in San Francisco" (or another member of the same response class) in response to that question was reinforced. For a different person, the answer "My grandmother lives in Dallas" would have been reinforced. We can accurately predict the response to the question to the extent that we know certain things about the individual's history with respect to such questions.

The scientific analysis focuses on observed relations between behavior and environment and does not infer such unobservable activities as identifying and retrieving meaning, searching memory, and formulating and transforming plans for the answer. From the scientific perspective presented in this book, the only evidence for all of these presumed activities is simply the answer to the question, "Where does your grandmother live?" Nothing else is observed. Of course, one day neuroscientists may be able to trace the nerve impulses in the brain that are generated by the question and that ultimately produce the response. But the resulting description will be in terms of measurable neurophysiological events, not information processing, and will supplement, not replace, a scientific psychological analysis.

Although not explicitly stated, the above example illustrates, among other things, the phenomenon called memory. Cognitive psychologists would frame the issue as follows: When you hear the question, "Where does your grandmother live?" you must remember the answer. Two important questions for cognitive and scientific psychologists alike are "How can we explain the fact that the question produces the answer?" and "What factors determine whether the answer is correct (i.e., the person remembered the answer) or incorrect (i.e., the person forgot the answer)?"

Memory

Past events obviously influence current behavior. Your grandmother, for example, may say, "I remember my granddad's old horse, Jasper, a big bay," then go on to tell a series of stories about it. Here, her experiences with an animal now long dead play the major role in determining what she says. How and why does this occur? In asking these questions, we enter the realm of memory. Unfortunately, like most commonsense words borrowed from everyday language, the term memory has no precise scientific definition.

Some Memory Phenomena

Psychologists who are interested in memory typically study the ability to recall words, syllables, facts, or events, and ask questions such as "What word followed 'apple' in the list?" or "What were the first and last words in the list?" In other words, they are interested in what might be called *verbal memory*. A series of famous studies employing this tactic was conducted in the late 19th century by Herman Ebbinghaus. Using himself as the only subject, Ebbinghaus identified a number of important phenomena that still provide the empirical bases of many theories of memory. He first devised thousands of nonsense syllables, each of which consisted of a consonant-vowel-consonant combination (e.g., DAZ, WIC). Such nonsense syllables were used so that the results would not be affected by previous familiarity with words. The basic procedure in most of his experiments was to form a list of nonsense syllables (e.g., 13 nonsense syllables), and then learn to say them in the correct order by going through the list over and over until he could recall all the syllables perfectly. The number of times that he went through the list was noted. At a later time, Ebbinghaus relearned the list, and compared the number of repetitions required for mastery with the number required for mastery on initial exposure. Data were usually expressed as a percent savings measure computed by dividing the difference in the repetitions by the initial repetitions. If learning the list required 50 repetitions, and the relearning required 40, then the percent savings would be ([50 − 40] / 50) × 100, or 20%. In this example, very little was remembered.

What did Ebbinghaus discover? One important finding was that as the length of a list increased, the number of repetitions required for mastery of the entire list also increased, as did the number of repetitions per syllable. Moreover, when Ebbinghaus varied the amount of time between the initial learning and the relearning of the list, he found that a large portion of the list was forgotten after 20 minutes. Thereafter, less and less was forgotten, even after a full month. He also reported an overlearning phenomenon: After the list was recited perfectly, additional repetitions improved recall at a later date.

Many other memory phenomena have been discovered since Ebbinghaus performed his studies. For example, Glanzer and Cunitz (1966) demonstrated serial position effects. Subjects were given a series of words, and then asked to recall as many as possible in any order. The results showed that the subjects were generally able to recall words at the beginning of the list, a primacy effect, and words at the end of list, a recency effect, better than those in the middle of the list.

Other research has shown that learning different material can interfere with recall. **Retroactive interference** occurs when learning new material interferes with recalling previously learned material. For example, learning Spanish grammar in second period might interfere with recalling an English lesson learned in first period. In **proactive interference,** previously learned material interferes with recall of newly learned material. For instance, if Jane learns a French lesson in first period, this material may inhibit recall of a Latin lesson learned in second period. The research designs for studying retroactive and proactive interference are presented in Figure 9-1.

In both proactive and retroactive interference, the degree of interference often depends on the nature of the task. Kroll, Parks, Parkinson, Bieber, and Johnson (1970) gave subjects a letter to remember, which was either presented visually or spoken aloud. The subjects then recited aloud a list of other letters and, after 10 or 25 seconds, were asked to recall the original letter. The results showed that there was more interference, or poorer recall, when the memory letter and interference task were in the same sensory modality, termed in-tramodal interference, than when they were in different sensory modalities, called intermodal interference. Of course, simply demonstrating these memory phenomena and giving them names in no way explains how or why they occur. That task is left up to theories of memory. Currently, the most popular theory of memory is the cognitive information-processing theory.

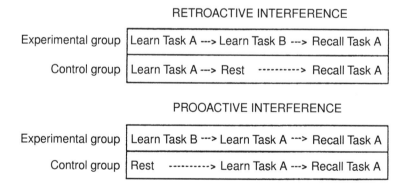

Figure 9-1. Experimental designs for studying retroactive and proactive interference. (From *Psychology: A Behavioral Overview* [p. 177], by A. Poling, H. Schlinger, S. Starin, and E. Blakely, 1990, New York: Plenum Press. Copyright 1990 by Plenum Press. Reprinted with permission.)

A Cognitive Theory of Memory

A unique feature of the cognitive approach to memory is concerned with *representations* of stimuli over time. Consider our example of grandmother and the horse. It is obvious that her experiences with the horse altered her in some way, so that she could talk about it years later. In a sense, some representation of the horse persisted through time. Clearly, there is no little horse in granny's head; the initial stimuli—the sights and sounds of the horse—were somehow transformed. One assumes the horse became an *engram,* which is a term coined to label "a persistent protoplasmic alteration hypothesized to occur on stimulation of living neural tissue and to account for memory" (*The American Heritage Dictionary of the English Language,* 1984).

No one has ever found an engram, although physiological psychologists continue to explore the correlation between neurophysiological events and learning (see Chapter 8). Cognitive psychologists do not work at this level of analysis, however. Instead, they liken what goes on in the human body to what goes on in some other, better understood, system. As noted previously, the current favorite is the computer, which is the basis of the information-processing model of memory. To the extent that the study of memory cannot be separated from the general study of what is called information processing (Cohen & Gelber, 1975), it is possible to view it as the very essence of modern cognitive psychology.

The Information-Processing Model

Psychologists have historically conceived of memory metaphorically. For example, memory has been compared to a muscle (it could be strengthened through frequent use), to a system of writing or recording, to electrical pathways, and to a library in which memories are stored, classified in a hierarchical fashion, referenced, and then retrieved just as books would be (Hunt, 1982). The most popular recent model, that of **information processing,** reflects current technology and was first suggested by Atkinson and Shiffrin (1968).

The information-processing model attempts to explain memory by referring to mechanisms similar to those of computers. This model posits structural *components,* which are analogous to the hardware (e.g., a central processing unit) of a computer because they are assumed to be permanent, built-in components, and *control processes,* which are analogous to the software of a computer (Howard, 1983). The structural components (e.g., permanent memory stores, temporary sensory registers) "contain" representations of stimuli, and the control processes (e.g., storage and retrieval processes) govern the form and movement of these representations—the flow of information—within the system (see Figure 9-2).

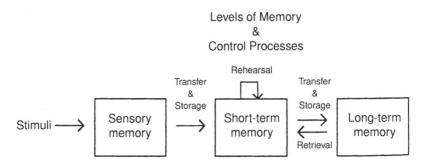

Figure 9-2. A depiction of the information-processing model of memory, including the three levels of memory and the various control processes. (From *Psychology: A Behavioral Overview* [p. 178], by A. Poling, H. Schlinger, S. Starin, and E. Blakely, 1990, New York: Plenum Press. Copyright 1990 by Plenum Press. Reprinted with permission.)

Structural Components

Information-processing theory assumes that there are three distinct kinds of memory systems, or structural components: sensory memory (also called the sensory registers), working memory (also called short-term memory), and long-term memory. Moreover, each can be described in terms of three characteristics: its storage capacity, the form of the representation in each, and the cause of forgetting from each.

All stimuli first enter **sensory memory** (SM), a temporary store with a rather large capacity. Stimuli in SM exist in the same form as in the environment; for example, a visual image of a visual stimulus or an echo of an auditory stimulus exist in SM. Only a portion of the stimuli in SM are processed further; most are not and are forgotten in a second or less. The cause of forgetting is usually through decay (i.e., passage of time), although displacement by a new stimulus representation also occurs.[1]

Suppose you were shown a visual array containing 3 rows of 4 letters each (12 letters in all; see Figure 9-3) for a duration of 50 ms and then asked to report how many of the letters you actually remembered seeing. How many do you think you could recall? Studies like this have previously shown that subjects could report only approximately 4 items out of a 12-item array. Interestingly, however, most subjects claim to be able to perceive more letters than they could actually report. What do they mean by this?

---

[1]Some theoreticians (e.g., Palmer, 1991) argue that time itself cannot cause forgetting, because time is not a real event itself, but rather a way humans have invented to measure other real events, such as the rotation of the earth (the rising and setting of the sun). Forgetting is caused by other events, such as interference from other related behavior. Saying that memory "decays" is just another way of saying that we really don't know what causes the forgetting.

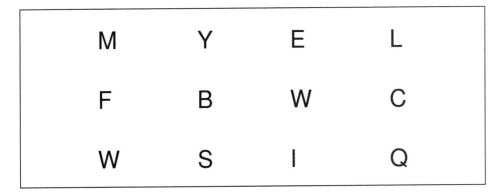

Figure 9-3. A visual array like those used in experiments on sensory memory.

Sperling (1960) designed an experiment to test how much can be seen in a single brief exposure. He presented subjects with a very brief (50 ms) visual array with either 9 or 12 letters contained in 3 rows of either 3 or 4 letters each. Immediately after the array disappeared, subjects were presented with a cue, for example, either a high-, medium-, or low-frequency tone, that specified which of the three rows they were to report, for example, either the top, middle, or bottom row. In addition, Sperling presented the cues at different delays, up to 1 s after the array had been terminated. The results showed that subjects were able to recall most of the letters in the cued row. Sperling's *partial report procedure* confirmed claims by subjects in earlier studies that they could perceive more than they could actually report. In addition, Sperling showed that the accuracy of the recall was related to the length of delay: The shorter the delay, the better the recall, which seemed to indicate that the duration of sensory memory is indeed very short.

The next system, **working memory,** also called **short-term memory** (STM), presumably holds information with which the person is in immediate contact. The form of the stimuli in STM is an encoded, or transformed, version of those first entered into SM. For example, a written word may be stored in terms of its sound. Short-term memory also differs from SM in that the capacity is limited to between five and nine individual bits of information (G. A. Miller, 1956). Forgetting usually results from displacement of old items by new ones, although some forgetting may be caused by decay (see footnote on page 218). Material typically resides in STM for 15 to 30 seconds, depending on whether rehearsal is permitted.

According to cognitive psychologists, information in STM can be encoded by rehearsing the information. Consider what happens when you look up a telephone number. As long as the amount of information is not greater than the capacity of the memory system, and you can repeat (i.e., rehearse) the number, you will increase your chances of remembering it (Howard, 1983). But how long would you remember the number if you were prevented from rehearsing it? Two researchers, L. R. Peterson and M. J. Peterson (1959), attempted to answer this question. Subjects in the experiment first heard three consonants and after a period of time (called a retention interval) they were asked to recall the letters. When subjects could rehearse the consonants, their recall was perfect. On some occasions, the researchers had the subjects perform a distracter task during the retention interval. The task involved repeating a three-digit number once and then counting backwards from it by threes. Obviously, the purpose of the distracter task was to prevent rehearsal of the consonants. As you might expect, the results showed that the accuracy of recall of the three consonants was almost perfect with a 0-s retention interval, but dropped to about 10% with an interval of only 18 s. These results, and those of many similar studies, show that in the absence of rehearsal, forgetting from STM occurs in a few seconds.

The third memory system is **long-term memory** (LTM). Information in LTM exists as an encoded version of STM information. The meanings of words, as well as important additional information, are stored in LTM. Thus, for the word *peach*, information pertaining to its meaning, appearance, taste, and smell is also stored. The capacity of LTM is unlimited, and forgetting results from interference or from some difficulty in a control process, like retrieval. Unlike SM and STM, LTM can hold material for many years. Some researchers believe that there are different divisions of LTM. Winograd (1975), for example, suggested that we have *declarative memory* (names, dates, events) and *procedural memory* (information about how to execute tasks, perform skills).

Control Processes

Control processes orchestrate the flow of information through the three levels of memory. In *encoding,* information is transformed into a memory code for subsequent storage in STM or LTM. One encoding process is *pattern recognition* (Klatzky, 1980), in which information in SM is transformed into a meaningful form for subsequent storage in STM (e.g., the visual image of the letter "A" might be given its appropriate name). Once in STM, further encoding can occur to enable storage in LTM. For example, a sequence of words may be encoded according to their meaning.

When material is encoded, it is ready for *storage.* Storage in STM usually involves rehearsal. For example, you can keep a seven-digit number in STM as long as you continue to repeat it. If the number of digits is increased to 12, then even rehearsal will not keep the information in STM. However, some of the individual bits may be grouped into units. Thus, instead of trying to remember 12 individual numbers, one might remember 4 "chunks" of 3 numbers each. This grouping of individual bits into units is called *chunking.*

Some material in STM is transferred to and stored in LTM. This can be accomplished through rehearsal, wherein material is repeated over and over. *Mnemonic devices,* which are rules that aid in recall (e.g., "30 days hath September . . ." or "*i* before *e* except after *c*"), are often developed to enhance storage in LTM. Interestingly, particularly meaningful or important information (i.e., "flashbulb memories") may be stored in LTM with little rehearsal. For instance, many people can provide detailed accounts of their activities and whereabouts when they learned that the space shuttle *Challenger* had exploded, when John F. Kennedy was assassinated, or when they were married.

When material is stored in LTM, it can be extracted through *retrieval*. It is thought that many strategies are used for retrieval. One such strategy is using retrieval cues. If Robert is unable to remember a friend's last name, he might repeat the first name a few times in the hope that the last will be remembered. Another strategy involves imagery—retrieval of the score of yesterday's football game might involve imagining what you were doing when you heard the score. We will return to the issue of mental imagery shortly, but first let us briefly evaluate the information-processing model of memory and demonstrate how scientific psychologists would generally approach the issue.

Evaluation of the Information-Processing Model

The information-processing model of memory is popular, but its adequacy as an explanation of memory is difficult for scientists to evaluate. The task is made easier if we ask a simple question: Are structural components and control processes real?

Computers have real memory stores in the form of disks, cards, and chips. Moreover, information can be compiled and translated ("encoded") for use by the computer, and such information can be stored on and retrieved from its memory stores. These systems are real and their operation can be observed. In humans, however, such systems cannot be observed and have no physical existence. We humans are not factory-equipped with memory cards, encoders, or internal drives. Physiological activities underlie all that we do, including what is termed remembering and forgetting, but these activities resemble computer processes only by analogy. Analogical models are not completely useless (see Chapter 2), but they neither describe physiology nor provide an adequate explanation of behavior. Scientific psychologists are still left with the task of adequately accounting for the processes (both ontogenetic and phylogenetic) responsible for observed behavior. With this in mind (so to speak), how would scientific psychologists address the area of memory, which seems to deal inherently with cognitive events and processes?

Memory: A Natural Science Perspective

In many (but not all) cases, what is termed memory is closely related to, if not identical with, learning. Consider the following example of operant conditioning. During World War II, B. F. Skinner trained pigeons to guide a missile by reinforcing accurate pecking at a plexiglass disk upon which an aerial target was projected. Three pigeons were placed in the nosecone of the missile. Skinner used three pigeons so that a majority of two would always be required to guide the missile toward a given location. The department of defense never actually made use of Skinner's pigeon guidance system. But, several years afterwards, and with no subsequent training of any sort, Skinner removed the pigeons from their home cages and placed them back into the original training apparatus. What do you think they did? Interestingly, the pigeons behaved almost exactly as they had several years earlier during training. In the language of memory, we can say that the pigeons "remembered" what to do. In other words, there was very little forgetting, which suggests, among other things, that the passage of time itself (decay) does not produce much forgetting (Palmer, 1991).

Instead of saying that the pigeons remembered what to do, it would be equally informative to say that they had learned what to do. In fact, as you recall, learning is defined as a relatively permanent change in behavior–environment relations because of certain types of experiences. In this example, the training apparatus (as an S^D) evoked pecking because in the past such behavior produced food in that circumstance. To take this one step further, suppose we teach a little girl to say "My grandmother lives in San Francisco" (R) to the question (S^D), "Where does your grandmother live?" by praising each correct answer (S^{R+}). We could say that the child remembers the answer when asked the question. But is this saying anything more than that she has learned how to respond to the question?

In scientific approaches to what is commonly called memory, the object of inquiry is the persistence of behavior, usually verbal behavior, over time. Consider a child who memorizes a math fact. On Monday, Tyler learns to say "9" when the teacher says "What is 3 times 3?" To test Tyler's recall, the teacher on Tuesday again asks "What is 3 times 3?" and Tyler excitedly says "9." The teacher exclaims "Very good, you *remembered.*" The important thing here is that the behavior learned on Monday persisted over time—Tyler was, 24 hours later, able to say "9" when asked "What is 3 times 3?" At the level of real observation, *to remember* is to emit a particular behavior appropriate to a set of circumstances (S^Ds), despite the passage of time. Likewise, *to forget* is to be unable to emit a behavior that is appropriate to a circumstance (e.g., "He forgot his manners," "She forgot the answer to question #4").

The variables that determine persistence of behavior over time (or the lack thereof) have been examined at length. For example, scientific psychologists have shown that operant conditioning (e.g., reinforcement) and the verbal operations that mimic them (e.g., rules) produce long-lasting changes in behavior (see Chapters 6 and 8). Moreover, they have offered simpler accounts for memory phenomena in terms of established laws (Palmer, 1991). And neurophysiologists are beginning to understand how operant learning affects synapses in the brain at the level of proximate physiological causes of behavior (see Chapter 7). Together, these two disciplines are probably sufficient to understand much of what is spoken of as memory.

Imagery

Not only does imagery facilitate memory, as described above, but imagery is an interesting phenomenon in its own right. Let us, therefore, look at how some cognitive psychologists have studied it and how scientific psychologists interpret it.

Like most other cognitive concepts, imagery seems to be implicitly understood by everyone. If a person is asked to imagine his mother, he believes that he can "see" her fairly well. But what exactly is he seeing? There is certainly no picture in his head. So what is mental imagery? A simple answer is that the image of an event contains some of the same features as the actual event. But how is that possible if there is no real stimulus? And how do we experience the image? All cognitive psychologists can tell us is that "experiencing an image is similar, subjectively, to experiencing the original object" (Howard, 1983, p. 224). But we experience real objects with our sensory systems (sensation) and our reactions to them (perception). How do we experience an image, that is, something that is not really there? Or is it?

Obviously, there are substantial difficulties in trying to understand scientifically concepts such as mental imagery. To provide an idea of how researchers attempt to do so, we consider in the following section some experiments by Roger Shepard and his colleagues (e.g., L. A. Cooper & Shepard, 1973; Metzler & Shepard, 1974; hepard & Metzler, 1971). These studies are among the most influential research on mental imagery (Anderson, 1985; Dennett, 1991).

In the first of a series of studies, Shepard and Metzler (1971) showed human subjects pictures of pairs of identical three-dimensional figures, one of which was rotated up to 180° (see Figure 9-4), and then asked the subjects to say whether the rotated figure was the same as the nonrotated one. The results showed that the latency of subjects' reports (the time it took them to answer) was linearly related to the degree of rotation. That is, the more the figure was rotated the longer it took the subjects to say whether it was the same as the unrotated figure.

In another study, L. A. Cooper and Shepard (1973) used letter stimuli such as those in Figure 9-5. Notice that the six items on the top are normal Rs that have been rotated different degrees from upright, whereas the six items on the bottom are backward Rs that have been rotated the same number of degrees from upright. Subjects were presented with one of the stimuli and then asked whether it was a normal or backward R. As you can see, the results, which are shown in Figure 9-6, show that the time it took subjects to judge a letter as being normal was a function of its deviation from the 180° R.

When asked by the researchers, the subjects reported that they had to rotate the figure mentally before deciding about its identity. Thus, the researchers attributed the relation between latency of response and degrees of rotation to the mental images, called "mental rotation," subjectively reported by the subjects. One way of trying to understand the results of these studies is to replicate them with nonhumans. Hollard and Delius (1982) replicated the Shepard and Metzler (1971) study with pigeons and showed that, although pigeons learned to

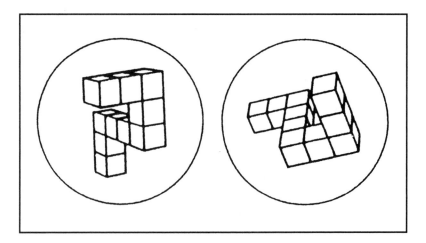

Figure 9-4. An example of the stimuli used in the study on mental rotation by Shepard and Metzler (1971), here rotated by a difference of 80°. Adapted from Metzler & Shepard (1974).

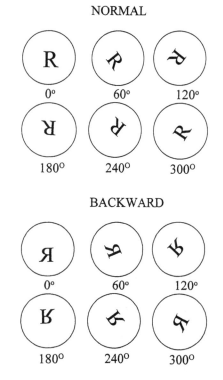

Figure 9-5. Normal and backward versions of one stimulus used in the study on mental rotation by Cooper and Shepard (1973). Adapted from Anderson (1985).

match rotated figures as accurately as humans, there was no relation between reaction time and correct responding. These results seem to support Shepard and Metzler's (1971) conclusion that humans mentally rotate an image in order to judge its identity to the sample.

Is inferring mental imagery, however, the most parsimonious explanation of the studies by Shepard and his colleagues? Some psychologists (e.g., Catania, 1992; Chance, 1994) believe it is not. Chance (1994) notes that the graphic representation of the L. A. Cooper and Shepard (1973) data (see Figure 9-6) looks remarkably like the generalization gradients produced when novel stimuli that differ from an established S^D are presented (see Figure 6-4). In general, the closer a novel stimulus is to an established S^D with respect to the dimension of concern (e.g., orientation), the greater the probability that the novel stimulus will control the same behavior evoked by the S^D. If we understand the processes responsible for generalization, then we may understand mental rotation as an instance of it. Moreover, Chance notes that simply naming the phenomenon mental rotation in no way explains it; this is a nominal fallacy as described in Chapter 2.

Catania (1992) cautions that if we treat the mental image as a thing then we will be misled into using it to explain behavior. You should recognize this as an example of the inadequate explanation called reification (see Chapter 2). Instead, Catania suggests that we should recast our description in terms of what the subject *does* (i.e., her or his behavior) rather than what the subject presumably *has* (i.e., an image). For Catania, the time it takes to rotate both real and imagined objects are similar because what the observer does when seeing an object and what the observer does when imagining it are presumably very similar; in other

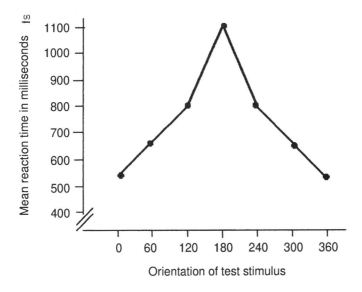

Figure 9-6. Results from the Cooper and Shepard (1973) study showing mean reaction time for judging whether a letter was normal as a function of its orientation.

words, the subject engages in the same behavior, but in the absence of the stimulus. As Catania (1992) states: "Imagining is visual behavior in the absence of the visual stimulus" (p. 334). This accounts for the fact that seeing in the absence of the object is not very good compared with seeing the actual object.

Catania's analysis allows for the existence of unobservable (covert) behavior (we may call it mental or cognitive), which then enables scientific psychologists to understand and explain it according to the same principles as public behavior, that is, in terms of reinforcement and stimulus control (see Chapter 6). In fact, some cognitive psychologists appear to say the same thing. For example, Anderson (1985) writes that "when people operate on mental images they appear to go through a process analogous to actually operating on a physical object" (p. 83). The problem for a scientific psychology is to accurately and parsimoniously describe these processes. Describing them as behaviors rather than as cognitions at least meets the criteria for a scientific approach set forth in Chapter 2.

Consciousness

Consciousness, perhaps more than any other human characteristic, has mystified philosophers and psychologists. As Hunt (1982) describes it, the concept of consciousness "has proven as elusive as a drop of mercury under one's finger. . ." (p. 353), meaning that it is a very difficult concept to understand. This is evident in the number of books on the subject. One recent computer search in a college library database alone revealed almost 300 books on the topic! So much has been written on consciousness that it is hard to know how to address the topic, even if discussion is limited to contributions by psychologists. We try only to introduce some of the issues that consciousness raises, and then to interpret consciousness as self-awareness.

The following quote by Julian Jaynes (1976) nicely conveys how many people feel about consciousness:

> O, what a world of unseen visions and heard silences, this insubstantial country of the mind! What ineffable essences, these touchless rememberings and unshowable reveries! And the privacy of it all! A secret theater of speechless monologue and prevenient counsel, an invisible mansion of all moods, musings, and mysteries, an infinite resort of disappointments and discoveries. A whole kingdom where each of us reigns reclusively alone, questioning what we will, commanding what we can. A hidden hermitage where we may study out the troubled book of what we have done and yet may do. An introcosm that is more myself than anything I can find in a mirror. This consciousness that is myself of selves, that is everything, and yet nothing at all—what is it?
> And where did it come from?
> And why? (p. 1)

Jaynes's statement implies several things about what we call consciousness, but above all underscores its privacy. This feature, more than any other, renders consciousness so difficult to study.

Rather than asking what consciousness is, perhaps a better question, according to Jaynes (1976), would be "What is it not?" According to Jaynes, it is not the same as reacting to stimuli, such as orienting responses. It is not involved in much of what we call perception. It is not involved in the performance of many skills, for example, playing the piano or playing basketball and, in fact, can interfere with their execution if, for example, one tries to be aware of performing the skill during the performance. Jaynes goes even further to say that consciousness is not necessary when speaking, writing, listening, and reading. Nor is it necessary for much of what we call thinking, or for learning through either classical or operant conditioning.

Finally, Jaynes says that consciousness "has no location except an imaginary one" which leaves us with the question of whether consciousness exists at all. Rather than debating the existence of something so private, we will take another approach in this section; namely, we will look at what behaviors occur when we use the word consciousness. Although this approach may not get at everything we mean by the word consciousness, it can nevertheless address some important issues. But first, let us look briefly at the history of the study of consciousness in psychology.

The study of consciousness has long occupied an important place in psychology. In fact, Wilhelm Wundt, who founded experimental psychology as an independent discipline in the 1860s (see Sidebar 9-2), was interested in consciousness in a restricted sense. For him, consciousness consisted of an individual's sensory experience at a given moment. Given this orientation, much of the research conducted by Wundt and his immediate successors (e.g., Titchener and the Gestalt psychologists) entailed manipulating the stimuli to which subjects were exposed and then recording their reports of the resulting sensory experience. For example, the experimenter might present a 4-row by 4-column array of randomly chosen letters for a brief period (e.g., 0.1 s), then immediately ask the subject to recall as many letters as possible. (You may recognize this as a forerunner to the studies by Sperling mentioned previously.) Presumably, this would reveal "conscious content," the sensations, perceptions, and ideas that are included in consciousness.

Even if Wundt or Titchener's approach had been successful, much of what is meant by the word consciousness is still left unexplained. We, therefore, address the role of verbal behavior in the development of the behavior we call consciousness.

Consciousness and Verbal Behavior

Due in part to the criticisms of early behaviorists (e.g., J. B. Watson), the term consciousness fell into some disrepute through the mid part of the present century, but it has undergone a revival in popularity fostered by cognitive psychologists and philosophers. Psychologists use *consciousness* and *conscious* in a variety of ways. In humans, the terms are usually used to refer to (a) the verbal description of stimuli impinging on sensory receptors or (b) the verbal description of our own behavior or internal states. (The issue of consciousness in nonhumans is complex and will not be addressed here. Griffin [1981] and

Sidebar 9-2
Wilhelm Wundt and the Founding of an Experimental Psychology

Wilhelm Wundt (1832–1920) may fairly be considered the founder of psychology as a formal academic discipline. He founded the first psychological laboratory, edited the first psychology journal, and initiated psychology as a science (D. P. Schultz, 1975). Wundt investigated sensation and perception, attention, feeling, and association, areas that continue to be important to psychologists today. He approached these topics from a perspective that later came to be known as *structuralism*. Structuralism was one of two major schools of thought in the early days of psychology. Like most other early psychologists, Wundt was concerned with the nature of the mind. For him, the appropriate goal of psychology was to discern mental structures and processes.

Using a method of self-observation called *introspection,* Wundt and other structuralists, among them Edward Titchener (1867-1927), investigated private activities such as sensations, images, and feelings. The term introspection comes from the Latin *introspicere,* meaning "to look into." In the vernacular of today, introspection refers to self-examination, the contemplation of one's own feelings and thoughts. Introspection is commonly considered as a means of accessing mental activity, which is revealed to others in verbal statements. A friend asks, for example, "What are you thinking about?" You introspect briefly, then reply, "I was thinking about how to study for my biology final next Friday." Your friend has no way of knowing whether this is

true—you may have been thinking about how you'd like to be left alone—or of determining what is responsible for the thoughts you reported.Nonetheless, the report may be of some practical value: It may, for instance, suggest that you are more likely to study Thursday evening than to go dancing.

The introspective techniques used by Wundt, Titchener, and other early psychologists were far more tightly structured than the example above. These techniques employed well-trained subjects who were taught to use a limited range of words to describe their conscious response to specific items, perhaps a word or a color, presented under tightly controlled conditions. These refinements were intended to make the techniques less subjective and more scientific. To some extent they did so, but introspection was still widely criticized for several reasons (Schultz, 1975). Perhaps the most telling cricitism was that introspective reports are not reliable.

Contemporary psychologists do not deny that people "talk to themselves" or that they can report their internal states. They do, however, recognize that introspection does not provide a useful window on the mind. The objectives of structuralism were three (Schultz, 1975): "(1) to analyze the conscious processes into their basic elements, (2) to discover how these elements are connected, and (3) to determine their laws of connection" (p. 61). These objectives were not attained, and structuralism died with Titchener in 1927.

Rollin [1986] overview this topic.) Although the verbal description of stimuli interested many early psychologists, including Wundt and Titchener, it is consciousness in the sense of self-awareness that interests most contemporary psychologists and that will be considered here.

When we say that we are conscious of our surroundings, our behavior, or our feelings, we are reporting the fact that we can talk about them (i.e., our verbal behavior is under their discriminative control). Consider a woman who is looking at the wall of a museum on which 10 paintings are hanging. Light is reflected from each painting to her eyes, and affects the rods and cones (visual receptors) located there. Thus, she senses the paintings. Is she conscious of the small abstract painting at the lower left of the display? In other words, does she perceive it? It's impossible to tell from this description. If, however, she said, "I'm looking at that weird little blue abstract," there would be no ambiguity: She is obviously conscious of it and perceives it in the sense that it determines some behavior on her part. In this case, the woman not only reports that she is looking at the abstract, but describes it as well. As Skinner (1974) put it, we are conscious of a visual stimulus when we "see" that we are seeing it. In this case, to "see" is a metaphor for the fact that we talk to ourselves or to others about it.

Self-Awareness

When we refer to **self-awareness**, we usually mean that we are able to describe verbally (i.e., are conscious of) our own behavior, or stimuli that originate within our body. But how do we become self-aware? The following quotation from Helen Keller (1908; cited in Dennett, 1991) reveals that becoming self-aware, or conscious, is a process that involves learning:

> Before my teacher came to me, I did not know that I am. I lived in a world that was no-world. I cannot hope to describe adequately that unconscious, yet conscious time of nothingness. . . . Since I had no power of thought, I did not compare one mental state with another. (p. 227)

People are taught to be aware of their overt behavior (responses that other people can easily detect) as they are taught to be aware of other objects and events, that is, through discrimination training. From the time children can first describe objects in the external environment, they are asked to describe their own behavior. A parent might, for example, ask "Gina, what are you doing, *crawling?*"(with heavy emphasis on the *crawling*) as the child crawls across the floor. In the beginning, Gina cannot know the answer, "crawling." If, however, the child has learned to imitate or echo words, she is likely to say "crawling." When this occurs, the parent says something like, "Good, you're crawling," which reinforces Gina's response "crawling" the next time (a) the parent asks "what are you doing?" and (b) Gina is crawling at the time. Note that in this example the verbal response, "crawling," is jointly controlled by Gina's behavior and the parent's question, both of which serve as S^Ds (i.e., a conditional discrimination).

Through protracted training of this sort, we eventually learn to describe in great detail our actions and the environment in which they occur. Of course, the behaviors and environmental variables that are characteristically described and the words that we use in their descriptions are determined by the verbal community. A child reared by parents with little interest in birds and no training in recognizing bird species will not describe a small gray and black bird in the same fashion as will a child reared by ornithologists. The two sets of parents are different verbal communities, and they condition different patterns of verbal behavior. The ornithologists' child will learn to call the bird a chickadee, because only that response is reinforced. Similarly, the other child may learn to call it a little snowbird, because that response is adequate to secure reinforcement in her world.

People's descriptions of their own overt behavior and of objects and events in the external environment are also consistent within a verbal community, in large part because members of this community can check the relations described and respond appropriately. For example, a parent is unlikely to reinforce a child's response of "I'm walking," when the child is crawling, or to reinforce the response of saying "table" in the presence of a chair. In both cases, the parent can directly check the accuracy of the child's response. With private events this is not so easy.

Awareness of Private Events

In addition to public events, we also learn to describe **private events**—stimuli and responses that occur inside the body. As Skinner (1953) noted, "Strangely enough, it is the community which teaches the individual to 'know himself' " (p. 261). In other words, just as we are taught by others to know, or be conscious of, our overt behavior, we are also taught by others to know our private events. This is strange because the verbal community has very limited access to our private events. The main difference between learning to describe public and private events is that other people can't directly check to see whether the private events are actually occurring. If, for example, a child says that he has a stomachache and pleads that he can't go to school, how can a parent tell if this is true? At one level, it is impossible. Only the child knows how he feels. You can, however, search for public events that might reasonably occur in conjunction with a stomachache.

Some private events, including stomachaches, may have associated **collateral responses** (Skinner, 1945). These are overt (public) changes in behavior that occur in conjunction with a private event. A child with a stomachache may, for instance, rub his stomach, vomit, fail to eat, or grimace. Experience teaches and the verbal community recognizes that these responses regularly, but not inevitably, occur in conjunction with a stomachache. In such cases, a parent asks, "David, how do you feel?" Just as with questions about overt behavior, in the beginning David doesn't know, so the parent adds, "Does your stomach hurt?" and David imitates "stomach hurt," whereupon the parent says "Yes, your stomach hurts" and proceeds to attend to him. The parent makes a reasonable guess about David's private events based on other responses he makes and then teaches David to describe those private events.

Public accompaniments (public nonbehavioral events) may also occur in conjunction with private events. A warm and swollen stomach is likely to be correlated with a stomachache, as is having suffered an injury to the stomach, and parents may use these public accompaniments in teaching children to describe (i.e., become aware of) their private events. Thus, how the verbal community responds to a description of some private events depends to some extent on whether the description is supported by collateral responses and public accompaniment. Many private events, however, are not highly correlated with directly observable events. In such cases, it is difficult or impossible to teach people to describe them accurately.

Because private events cannot be observed, we frequently don't know how we feel when someone asks. We are probably not even very conscious or aware of our overt behavior or its causes much of the time. One purpose of psychotherapy is to teach patients to describe accurately (i.e., be aware of) their overt behavior and its possible causes, as well as to be aware of private events, that is, feelings.

To summarize, awareness of internal events (self-awareness) is taught in the same fashion as awareness of external events, by reinforcing descriptive verbal behavior in the presence of particular stimuli. The only difference between describing behavioral and nonbehavioral events is in the nature of what is described. The only difference between describing external and internal events is their accessibility to the community that teaches us to describe them.

The Role of Consciousness in Learning

Everyday experience suggests that a great deal of human behavior occurs without our being conscious of it. You are, for example, now breathing. What happens if someone asks you, "Please breathe faster"? As you respond to the request, you become aware of your breathing. It is tempting to assert that, in the absence of the request, "Please breathe faster," your breathing was unconsciously controlled, whereas conscious control was manifested after hearing the request. In a sense, that is true. In one situation your rate of breathing was not affected by a statement that you could verbally describe; in another it was. Using "conscious control" and "unconscious control" to distinguish these situations is consistent with the ordinary commonsense vocabulary, and poses no real problem. But doing so in no sense explains breathing, and it tempts one to propose (reified) entities, perhaps a "conscious mind" and an "unconscious mind," that cannot be legitimate scientific explanations.

Positing such entities certainly has precedent in the history of psychology and philosophy. The notion that behavior is conjointly controlled by the conscious and unconscious was made popular by Freud, and continues to be widespread today. For example, in a popular book on cognitive science, Morton Hunt (1982) writes:

> We identify ourselves with the conscious mind, whose thoughts we are aware of and can more or less control, but it is the unconscious, the unruly, mystifying and often alien other self within us, that is responsible both for our everyday habitual acts and for our rare creative solutions to problems. The most common and least common of our mental products come from the part of ourselves that we scarcely know. (p. 273)

Beyond the major issue that the conscious and unconscious mind are inferred from the behaviors they are assumed to control, such an analysis leaves unanswered the question "What determines the action of the conscious and unconscious mind?"

Like Freud and contemporary cognitive psychologists, scientific psychologists recognize that most behavior in humans is unconscious in the sense that the behaver is unaware of (i.e., cannot verbally describe) its causes. But a scientific explanation of this phenomenon does not rest on unobservable and hypothetical entities. For Skinner and many other scientific psychologists, "conscious" behavior is characteristically rule-governed, whereas "unconscious" behavior is contingency-governed. As discussed in Chapter 8, contingency-governed behavior is controlled by direct exposure to operant contingencies of reinforcement (or punishment), whereas rule-governed behavior is controlled by descriptions of such contingencies. Contingency-governed behavior is no more the result of a hypothetical entity called the conscious mind than rule-governed behavior is a result of a conscious mind. Both can be fully explained in terms of lawful behavior–environment interactions.

Interestingly, some cognitive psychologists contend that contingency-governed behavior does not occur in adult humans. Their position, evident in the following quotation from Brewer (1974), is that all adult learning requires awareness:

> In human beings, classical conditioning and operant conditioning work according to behaviorist theory in very young children, in the mentally retarded, and normal people who are asleep. In these cases, consciousness and the internal representation of the world outside are undeveloped or turned off; when that is so, people do behave according to stimulus–response theory. (p. 73)

The falsity of this position is twofold. First, there is no "internal representation of the world" to turn off. Second, several experiments have shown that learning can occur (through both operant and respondent conditioning) without the subjects being aware of what they are to learn. Carter (1973), for example, told college students that they could earn points for pressing a key, but actually delivered points dependent on blinks of their right eye. This relation yielded a high rate of eye-blinking, which fell to near-zero levels when blinking no longer produced points. Key pressing, which never produced points, occurred throughout the study.

This is not to say that awareness of the contingencies is never a factor in learning. Parton and DeNike (1966) gave children a task involving marbles, and found that learning occurred only in the children who were able to state the contingencies. Moreover, those children who gave incorrect accounts of the contingencies behaved in accordance with their false hypotheses. This and other experiments show that awareness, when defined as statements about contingencies in the world, can strongly influence behavior. Such statements interact with other variables to determine behavior in a given situation.

Conclusion

This chapter has discussed cognitive approaches to memory, mental imagery, and consciousness (three topics of great historical importance in psychology). These phenomena are also important in drawing distinctions between cognitive and behavioral approaches to psychology. In general, cognitive explanations of the phenomena presented in this chapter appeal to hypothetical entities; for example, recall is a function of retrieval from long-term memory and overt behavior is determined by a conscious mind. Behavioral interpretations reject the relevance of hypothetical entities, and emphasize instead (1) the behaviors that lead us to use the terms memory, imagery, and consciousness, and (2) the empirical variables that determine these behaviors.

The scientific perspective leads to an emphasis on phenomena that are somewhat different from those of concern to other psychologists. The phenomena of interest to scientific psychologists are primarily interactions between behavior and environmental, and, to a lesser extent, genetic and physiological, variables. These variables, working together in ways that are often difficult to study and always difficult to understand, control the complex behaviors encompassed by the terms memory, imagery, and consciousness.

Summary

1. The two general and competing paradigms in psychology are cognitive psychology, which studies observable behavior in order to infer unobservable processes, such as representations and memories, as explanations, and behavioral psychology, which studies observable behavior as a function not of inferred structures or processes but of objective variables.

2. The term *cognition* refers to the cognitive or mental processes by which one acquires knowledge of the world. The current popularity of the information-processing metaphor of cognitive psychology began in the aftermath of World War II as a direct result of technological innovations in computers and missile guidance systems.

3. The modern theme in the study of memory began in the late 19th century with Herman Ebbinghaus's studies of lists of nonsense syllables, which together with more recent studies have described such phenomena as overlearning, serial position effects, primacy and recency effects, and retroactive and proactive interference.

4. The recent cognitive theory of memory rests on comparing human memory with the information processing of computers. This model, which attempts to explain memory by referring to mechanisms similar to those of computers, includes (a) structural components, which are analogous to the hardware and include *sensory memory, working memory* (also called short-term memory), and *long-term memory;* and (b) control processes, which are analogous to the software of a computer and include encoding, in which information is transformed into a memory code for subsequent storage in STM or LTM, storage, which is accomplished through rehearsal wherein material is repeated over and over, and retrieval.

5. The information-processing model makes a complex set of phenomena—called memory—easier to understand by comparing it with more familiar things such as the computer, but critics have argued that structural components and control processes in the human mind are not real and in no way resemble those physiological structures and processes that are real.

6. In contrast, memory from a scientific perspective is closely related to, if not identical with, learning in which behavior–environment relationships

persist over time. The evidence is that S^D s will continue to evoke behavior that has in the past produced reinforcing consequences.

7. Cognitive psychologists have also studied mental imagery which, because it is inaccessible, can be described only by saying that we experience the image subjectively in ways that are similar to experiencing the object objectively. A more parsimonious explanation of studies of mental imagery suggests that even though it is unobservable, mental imagery is something that subjects do and not something subjects have.

8. Experimental psychology was originally defined by Wundt and Titchener as the study of individual consciousness and although that definition has changed the subject of consciousness still mystifies psychologists and philosophers alike.

9. One way of thinking about consciousness is that it involves verbal behavior, so that when we say we are conscious of our surroundings or of our behavior and feelings (termed self-awareness), we are reporting the fact that we can talk about them. Of course we learn to talk about these things as language-learning children through discrimination training and later through modeling and rules.

10. Although consciousness is not necessary for learning (e.g., classical or operant conditioning), some aspects of awareness can facilitate learning.

Study Questions

1. What is a paradigm in science and what are the two dominant paradigms in psychology?

2. How do cognitive psychologists approach the study of behavior and what are the main differences between the cognitive and behavioral approaches?

3. What does the term *cognition* actually mean?

4. What is the information-processing metaphor and what is the most important feature of an information-processing analysis?

5. Who was Ebbinghaus and what were some of the memory phenomena he studied as well as some that were later described?

6. What is the information-processing model of memory, including the three types of memory systems (structural components) and the different types of control processes?

7. What are some problems with the information-processing model of memory?

8. What is the general scientific approach to the study of memory in terms of what memory is and how it is to be explained?

9. What is mental imagery and how did Shepard and his colleagues study it?

10. What are some problems with a cognitive explanation of mental rotation and what is a more parsimonious explanation?

11. Why has consciousness been so difficult to study, especially scientifically?

12. How is consciousness, in the sense of awareness, related to verbal behavior?

13. What does it mean to say that we are self-aware (or conscious of ourselves) and how do we learn such self-awareness?

14. What are private events and how do we learn to become aware of them?

15. What is the role of consciousness in learning?

Human Evolutionary and Prenatal Development

10

"We are what we are because of history, both our ancestors' history and the history of our own lives" (Carlson, 1984, p. 6). This is another way of saying that our phenotype (physical appearance and behavior) is determined jointly by characteristics that we inherit from our ancestors (phylogeny) and from our unique individual histories (ontogeny). We can trace the beginning of each individual's history to conception, when a single sperm fertilizes an ovum. At that precise moment, the fertilized ovum contains all the genetic information needed to form an adult human being, given extensive environmental influences. This "genetic heritage" represents the accumulation of approximately 3.5 billion of years of evolution by natural selection. This chapter overviews some important phylogenetic developments related to the evolution of the human species (*Homo sapiens*), including how humans are similar to other mammals and more specifically the primates to whom we are closely related. Then it describes the ontogenetic developmental changes that begin to occur from conception through birth.

Human Evolutionary (Phylogenetic) Development

The Evolution of Life on Earth

As stated in Chapters 1 and 4, the essence of evolution is descent from common ancestors. This implies that all life forms traced backward eventually converge. For example,

> if we go back about 20 million years, we ourselves are connected to all other apes. Likewise, about 150 million years ago our lineage converges with those of all other mammals. And finally, if we go back a half billion years, all vertebrates are seen to have sprung from a single common ancestor. (Trivers, 1985, p. 10)

The historical connectedness of various animals is often represented pictorially by the kind of diagram shown in Figure 10-1, which depicts the evolution of our own species, *Homo sapiens*. In this figure, time is represented along the vertical axis and offshoots from a lineage along the horizontal axis. Because species become differentiated and branch off from one another over time, the diagram resembles a tree. (A **species** is a group of actually or potentially interbreeding organisms, which do not interbreed with other organisms outside of the species.) Sometimes the earlier species still exist alongside the more recent species, but more often than not they become extinct. For example, chimpanzees and gorillas are the closest living relatives of modern humans; all three species evolved (i.e., branched off) from a common ancestor that is now extinct.[1] In becoming extinct it shared a fate common to most of the species that

---

[1]It is often said that humans evolved from monkeys or apes. But the fact that monkeys and apes are still around shows this to be faulty reasoning. It is more accurate to say that monkeys, apes, and humans all evolved from a common ancestor.

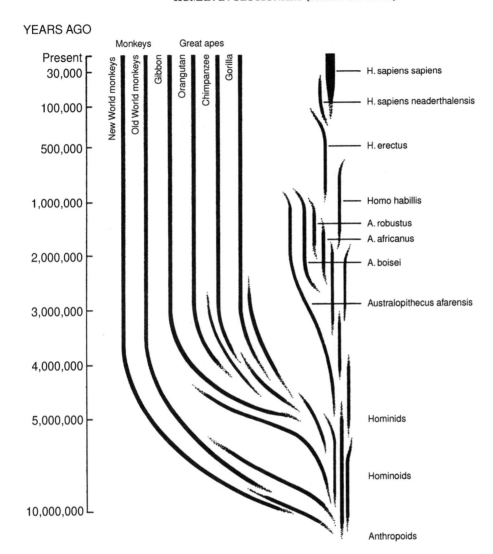

Figure 10-1. The anthropoid evolutionary tree beginning about 10 million years ago and leading up to present-day anthropoids, including *Homo sapiens*. Shown is the evolutionary branching of monkeys from hominoids (approximately 10 million years ago) and of apes from hominids (approximately 5 million years ago). There is debate about the specific ancestors of modern humans. Adapted from Washburn (1960).

have occupied earth. In fact, although scientists estimate that two million species exist today, this represents only about 1% of those that have ever lived. This means that approximately two billion species have existed since life on earth began.

We humans are connected not only to all other life on the planet, but to all matter in the universe (see Sidebar 10-1). In order to trace human evolutionary history on the planet, we would have to go back to the beginning of life on earth approximately 3.5 billion years ago (Dickerson, 1978). Scientists speculate that the first organic material in the form of amino acids was created in the oceans when gases in the atmosphere of the primeval earth were subjected to ultraviolet radiation from the sun. These early amino acids then combined in an "organic soup" to form complex molecules. The most important event in evolution, and without which there would be no evolution, was the formation of a special molecule that could replicate itself (Dawkins, 1976). This self-replicating molecule was the ancestor of DNA.

Once genetic material could replicate, life was off and running, progressing from single- to multicelled organisms (about 1.5 billion years ago), aquatic oxygen-breathing animals (about 1 billion years ago), amphibians (500 million years ago), reptiles (400 million years ago), mammals (100 million years ago), and primates (50 million years ago) (see Table 10-1).

The Evolution of Primates

The earliest mammals were small ratlike insectivores that moved about on the ground. Some of these small creatures began climbing into the trees of the immense forests that covered much of the world. Presumably, they did so because of the fierce competition on the ground and the plentiful supply of fruits, seeds, and insects in the trees. These were the earliest primates, the *prosimians* (pre-

---

Sidebar 10-1
Cosmic Custodians[1]

We are custodians of the stars. The calcium in our bones, the iron in our blood, the oxygen that gives us life were all forged in stellar furnaces. And someday, they'll return to the stars. Our bodies contain about two dozen chemical elements in all. The simplest is hydrogen. All the hydrogen in the universe was created in the Big Bang, about 10 to 15 billion years ago. Hydrogen is the fundamental building block of all the other elements. The nuclear furnaces that power the stars "fuse" together hydrogen atoms to create helium—the second-lightest element. Stars like our Sun eventually use up their hydrogen and helium, and create two heavier elements: carbon and oxygen. And heavier stars create still-heav-ier elements. When stars die, some or all of their material is expelled into space. So the carbon, oxygen, and heavier elements in our bodies are recycled star-stuff: elements that were created in other stars, then incorporated into Earth when it formed four-and-a-half billion years ago. When WE die, our elements are absorbed back into the earth. And when our Sun dies, it will expand to many times its former size, consuming Earth in the process. It will vaporize our planet, releasing its chemical elements back into space. Eventually, some of these elements—including those that form our bodies today —will be incorporated into new stars, new planets—and perhaps new living beings.

---

[1]Written by Damond Beningfield and adapted from a presentation by Tom Barnes. Copyright 1996, The University of Texas McDonald Observatory. Reproduced with permission.

Table 10-1
The Evolution of Life

Number of Years Ago	Evolutionary Event
4.5 billion	Formation of the earth
4.25 billion	Formation of the oceans and continents
3.6 billion	Primitive one-celled organisms that obtain energy through fermentation
3 billion	Sulfur bacteria that use hydrogen sulfide to conduct photosynthesis
	Single-celled organisms that use water in photosynthesis instead of sulfur (the ancestors of the blue-green algae and green plants)
2 billion	Oxygen atmosphere
1.6 billion	Bacteria that use nonsulfur photosynthesis and oxygen in respiration (These bacteria could extract 19 times more energy from food than could the first primitive bacteria.)
1.3 billion	Cells with nuclei
1 billion	Multicelled organisms; plant and animal kingdoms divide
500 million	Many marine animals, corals, clams, and fish
300 million	Amphibians, ferns, spiders, insects, and first reptiles
150 million	Dinosaurs and reptiles
	First birds evolve from smaller dinosaurs
	Modern insects (bees, moths, flies)
70 million	Dinosaurs extinct
	Marsupials and primitive mammals
	Flowering plants, deciduous trees, giant redwoods
50 million	Modern birds, the early horse (only 1 foot high), the ancestors of the cat, dog, elephant, camel and other mammals
	Seed-bearing plants and small primates
1.5 million	*Homo erectus*
100,000	*Homo sapiens neanderthalensis*
100,000	*Homo sapiens sapiens* (modern humans)

monkeys). For 30 million years, the early prosimians were extremely successful in the tropical forests of the world. They subsequently evolved into many specialized populations (species), leading eventually to the present array of prosimians (e.g., lemurs and lorises) and *anthropoids,* the monkeys, apes, and humans.

According to Campbell (1985), life in the forest provided an environment that selected many of the unique characteristics found in today's monkeys, apes, and humans (see Table 10-2). As you might expect, important changes occurred in those body parts that made direct contact with the world, that is, the limbs and extremities. Hind legs, which were used for jumping through the trees and clinging to branches, became longer; claws on the front paws, which were unnecessary for moving about in the trees, disappeared; and the paws transformed into grasping organs with longer and more flexible, padded digits.

These innovations greatly improved the ability of these "new-model animals" to move rapidly in trees, to grasp branches, and to catch fast-moving prey, like insects and lizards. These developments were accompanied by changes in the sensory systems of the prosimians. They developed upright posture and

Table 10-2
Major Characteristics of Primates

A. Characteristics relating to motor adaptations
  1. Retention of ancestral mammalian limb structure, with five digits on hands and feet, and free mobility of limbs
  2. Evolution of mobile, grasping digits, with sensitive friction pads (palmar surfaces with friction skin), and nails replacing claws
  3. Retention of tail as an organ of balance (except in apes and a few monkeys) and as a grasping "limb" in some New World monkeys
  4. Evolution of erect posture in many groups with extensive head rotation
  5. Evolution of nervous system to give precise and rapid control of musculature
B. Characteristics relating to sensory adaptations
  1. Enlargement of the eyes, increasing amount of light and detail received
  2. Evolution of retina to increase sensitivity to low levels of illumination and to different frequencies (that is, to color)
  3. Eyes that look forward with overlapping visual fields that give stereoscopic vision
  4. Enclosure of eyes in a bony orbit
  5. Reduction in olfactory apparatus, especially the snout
C. Dental characteristics
  1. Simple cusp patterns in molar teeth
  2. In most groups 32 or 36 teeth; all the *Anthropoidea* have 32 teeth
D. General characteristics
  1. Lengthened period of maturation, of infant dependency, and of gestation, compared with most mammals; relatively long life span
  2. Low reproductive rate, especially among *Hominoidea*
  3. Relatively large and complex brain, especially those parts involved with vision, tactile inputs, muscle coordination and control, memory, and learning

rotating heads, which together with their new lifestyle of leaping, clinging, and catching, made their reliance on seeing more important than their reliance on smelling. As the retinas of the eyes became more sensitive to low levels of illumination and able to differentiate colors, the eyes became larger, thus increasing the amount of light and detail received. The eyes moved gradually to the front of the head and vision became binocular (two-eyed: vision from one eye overlaps that from the other) and stereoscopic (depth-perceiving). At the same time, the head also began to change: the snout became shorter and the skull rounder. At this point, many of the characteristics were similar to those belonging to present-day monkeys, apes, and humans (Campbell, 1985; see Table 10-2).

After the early primates took to the trees, they began to increase in size, their arms grew longer, and they became more dexterous. These early populations then began to spread out in the forest and to eat novel foods. Some of these primates, the monkeys, became quadrupeds, running along on all fours. Others, whose arms became still longer, moved about by reaching, climbing, hanging, and swinging; these were the apes (Campbell, 1985).[2]

---

[2]It is a common mistake to call the great apes, that is, the orangutans, chimpanzees, and gorillas, "monkeys." Technically, they are apes, not monkeys. Apes, monkeys, and humans are all primates.

An African gorilla.

Despite the obvious differences between monkeys, apes, and humans, there are many similarities that attest to our common evolutionary lineage. For example, the sensory system of all the monkeys, apes, and humans has remained virtually unchanged for perhaps 15 million years: we see, hear, smell, taste, and touch very much as monkeys and apes do. Still, monkeys, apes, and humans differ in important ways. Monkeys are quadrupeds, while the apes have evolved short, wide, shallow trunks and long arms that swing and rotate at the shoulders. These anatomical changes evolved as the apes became more successful at horizontal arm-over-arm locomotion (brachiation). The African apes, the chimpanzee and gorilla, unlike the gibbon and orangutan, adapted to terrestrial quadrupedalism; that is, they walk on the ground on the soles of their feet and the knuckles of their hands (see photograph, p. 243). Human ancestors took a different route than did the African apes—to terrestrial bipedalism—which is walking upright on the ground (Campbell, 1985).

Hominid Evolutionary Development

Hominids are primates of the family *Hominidae,* of which *Homo sapiens* is the sole surviving species. Our immediate ancestors were of this family. Although there is controversy about the specifics of hominid evolution, the earliest hominids probably emerged from the trees of the great forests of Africa and moved into the savanna about 4 to 6 million years ago. Once there, many of the important features that distinguish humans from apes began to evolve. Early developments included bipedalism, changes in the structure of the teeth from large to small canines, and improvements in manual dexterity, all of which probably resulted from a change in diet as well as from an increase in tool use. These developments were paralleled by an increase in brain size which, along with hunting and scavenging, was a relatively late development. For example, although *Australopithecus afarensis,* an early hominid that lived approximately 3.5 million years ago (see Figure 10-1), was completely bipedal, it had a brain no bigger than that of a chimpanzee (Campbell, 1985).

The changes in the pelvis that were necessary precursors of upright bipedalism predated changes in the size of the human brain. As the brain became larger, the female's pelvis underwent further modifications as a sort of "compromise—not compact enough for the most efficient walking but large enough for the birth of large-brained infants" (Campbell, 1985, p. 234). Another part of the solution to the small-pelvis, large-brain problem was for the female to give birth at an earlier stage in infant development, before the infant's head got too big. Compared to other primates, human infants enter the world at a much earlier stage of development. For example, at birth, the human brain is 25% of its eventual size. Chimpanzee and baboon brains are much further developed at birth, being 45% and 75%, respectively, of their eventual sizes (Campbell, 1985). Because they are born relatively early in development, humans require a much longer period of parental care than do other primates. Human social groups, in particular the nuclear family (consisting of a mother, father, and their children), provide a mechanism through which such care can be provided, and the tendency of humans to form nuclear family units, with characteristic male and female roles, may be an evolved characteristic. Other important evolved characteristics of humans are pronounced sexual dimorphism (males are generally bigger, stronger, and faster than females) and the loss of a well-defined period in females, called estrus, during which the female is sexually receptive. It is, however, difficult to determine how exactly these characteristics affect the behavior of individuals.

The Concept of Development

Because human infants are born fairly early in development, especially that of the central nervous system, many important changes in physiology and behavior must occur during the time when human adults care for their young. This means that the environment has significant influence on infant development. Psychologists who study these changes are interested in ontogenetic development. As used by many psychologists, **development** refers simply to change related in an orderly fashion to time. Such a definition has led, not surprisingly, to the encouragment of normative theories in which children's ages are correlated with developmental changes in physical and behavioral traits. Normative data, which are derived from correlational research (see Chapter 3), tell us when on average a particular behavior, such as reaching and grasping or walking, is likely to appear.

Normative approaches only describe *what* behavior occurs (e.g., walking) and *when* on average it is most likely to be observed (e.g., around 12 months of age); they do not explain *how* or *why* the behavior occurs. When pressed with the question of how behavioral development occurs, many psychologists infer some underlying hypothetical biological or cognitive structure that changes. Once such structures are assumed, some psychologists invent stages of development through which those structures presumably progress in an orderly fashion.

One problem with this approach is that the unobserved structures and processes and the developmental stages said to describe them become reified (see Chapter 2). In other words, some psychologists talk as if those structures are real entities when, in fact, they have never been observed. A second and related problem is that once behavioral change is reified into unobserved entities, it becomes easier to fall into the trap of circular reasoning. For example, probably the most famous developmental psychologist, Jean Piaget (discussed in Chapter 11), theorized that infants possess cognitive structures, called *schemas,* that determine an infant's behavior in a given situation. Schemas supposedly change in an orderly fashion over time as a result of biological maturation and the infant's interaction with the environment. One schema has been called a thumb-sucking schema. Giving it a name leads us to think of the schema as a tangible entity located somewhere inside infants (reification) that causes them to suck their thumbs. Of course, if the only evidence for the thumb-sucking schema is the actual behavior of sucking the thumb, then saying this is circular reasoning. In actuality, the term *schema* is just a label for certain ways of acting on the world (Lamb & Bornstein, 1987), or organized patterns of behavior (Ginsburg & Opper, 1988).

The easiest way to solve the problems inherent in normative definitions of development is to refine the definition. First we could slightly alter the definition to read "change *in behavior* related in an orderly fashion to time." This alteration would have the advantage of shifting the emphasis from invented time-related variables to "the *processes* that produce, facilitate, or retard change" (Horowitz, 1987, p. 159, emphasis added), that is, to the genetic, physiological, and environmental variables that influence behavior.

In most instances, normative data provide clues about environmental changes rather than about underlying genetic or biological changes. For any systematic change in a child's behavior over time, we should look at how the interactions between the child's behavior and the environment have changed over that period. This is why some scientists consider development in terms of "*progressive* changes in interactions between the behavior of individuals and the events in their environment" (Bijou & Baer, 1978, p. 2, emphasis added). This is how the term *development* will be used in this chapter.

Before continuing, however, let us explain the inclusion of the term *progressive* in the definition of behavioral development. Berndt (1992) has pointed out that not all changes in behavior may be considered to be developmental because such a definition would be far too inclusive. He has suggested, after Lerner, that "developmental changes are [1] systematic rather than haphazard and [2] successive rather than independent of earlier conditions" (1992, p. 5).

The use of "progressive" in our definition is meant to take these two features into account.

The Beginnings of Ontogenetic Development

Prenatal Development

Prenatal development is usually described in terms of three time periods: the periods of the ovum, the embryo, and the fetus. In the *period of the ovum* (or germinal period), a **zygote** is formed in one of the mother's fallopian tubes through the union of a sperm (from the father) and an ovum (from the mother). The sperm and ovum both contain 23 single chromosomes, and the zygote therefore has 46 chromosomes. The single-celled zygote immediately begins an approximately two-week trip down the fallopian tube toward the uterus. Along the way, the zygote begins to divide and redivide (via mitosis), each time producing new cells with a copy of the original 23 pairs of chromosomes. Sometimes, two ova are available in the fallopian tubes and both unite with a sperm, resulting in fraternal (or dizygotic) twins. Fraternal twins have different genetic makeups. On other occasions, a single zygote splits into two separate units, producing identical (or monozygotic) twins who have the same genetic makeup.

When the zygote finally reaches the uterus it attaches to the uterine wall via tendril-like extensions. At this time, the **embryonic period** of prenatal development commences and the woman is technically considered to be pregnant.[3] The tiny cell mass, called an *embryo,* is no bigger than a drop of water. During the next six weeks it differentiates into three layers: (1) the ectoderm, or outer layer, which later differentiates into the hair, nails, outer skin, sensory cells, and nervous system; (2) the mesoderm, or middle layer, which will develop into the muscles, skeleton, excretory and circulatory systems, and the inner skin; and (3) the endoderm, or inner layer, which develops into the gastrointestinal track, trachea, bronchia, glands, and vital organs.

The embryo's three life-support systems, the amniotic sac, placenta, and umbilical cord, form after implantation in the uterus. The *amniotic sac,* in which the embryo floats, contains fluid that serves as a protective buffer against phys-

---

[3]During the first two weeks after conception and before implanation, the woman is not technically pregnant and hence, a pregnancy test will not detect a pregnancy. Implantation of the zygote on the uterine wall and, thus, pregnancy, is not inevitable. Implantation can be prevented either naturally, for example, if there is genetic damage to the zygote, or through the use of an intrauterine device (IUD) or the drug RU-486. In such instances, the term *abortion* is not correctly used, because a pregnancy is being prevented rather than aborted. After implantation, spontaneous abortions (i.e., miscarriages) may occur, wherein the embryo becomes detached from the uterine wall and is expelled. It has been estimated that approximately 1 out of 3 pregnancies end in spontaneous abortion (Grobstein, 1988). The majority of aborted embryos have severe genetic or chromosomal disorders. It is not surprising that a mechanism, spontaneous miscarriage, has evolved to eliminate such embryos early in pregnancy.

ical shock and temperature changes. The tendrils that attach the embryo to the uterine wall grow into a semipermeable membrane, called the *placenta,* through which nutrients pass to and waste products pass from the developing infant. Semipermeable membranes are so called because some molecules (e.g., oxygen, carbon dioxide, nutrients), but not all, can cross them. Nutrients and wastes travel to and from the embryo through blood vessels in the *umbilical cord.*

The **fetal period** begins between the sixth and the eighth week when, among other things, the first bone cells appear. The embryologist Clifford Grobstein (1988) has suggested, however, that a more logical starting point for the fetal period is when movement of the fetus first occurs. Such movement is spontaneous, that is, reflexive. By the time this period begins, 95% of the major body parts have been differentiated; thus, the bulk of the changes that occur in the fetal stage involve growth and refinement of these parts. Kicking, swallowing, and head turning begin to occur, although such movements typically are not detected by the mother until the fourth or fifth month. Fingers, toes, eyebrows, and eyelashes form in the fetal stage. There are significant increases in body length early in this period, and substantial increases in body weight near the time of birth.

Effects of the External Environment on Prenatal Development

It may seem odd at first to think that the external environment can have any effect on the developing individual, especially when it is apparently completely protected from the outside world. Nevertheless, the developing individual is vulnerable to damage from environmental agents which can affect it in the same way that nutrients do, that is, by way of the mother through the umbilical cord and placenta.

Agents that cause abnormal prenatal development are called **teratogens**. Known teratogens include cigarette smoke, alcohol and other drugs (both illegal and prescription), some maternal diseases (e.g., rubella, or German measles), irradiation, and temperature extremes. The effects of a particular teratogen often depend on the developmental stage of the infant (see Figure 10-2). In general, vulnerability to teratogens is greater during the embryonic period (i.e., during the first trimester of pregnancy), because most of the major organs and systems develop during this stage of prenatal development.

The effects of the drug thalidomide provide tragic documentation of the sensitivity of the embryo to environmental agents. Thalidomide, developed by a German company, was introduced in 1958 as a safe and effective agent for reducing nausea and inducing sleep. The drug was given to thousands of pregnant women in Europe, Australia, and Japan, but not in the United States. It soon became apparent that thalidomide caused severe malformations in some children. The deformities included eye defects, cleft palate, depressed nose bridge, small external ears, fusing of the fingers and toes, dislocated hips, and malformations of the digestive tract and heart. A characteristic deformity was

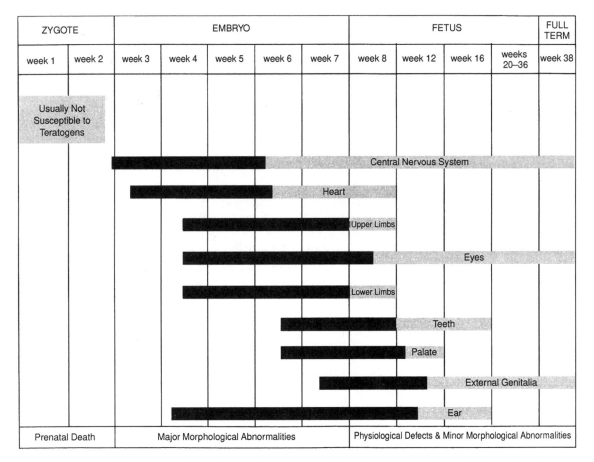

Figure 10-2. Critical periods in prenatal development and sensitivity to teratogens. Adapted from Moore (1989).

phocomelia, a condition characterized by missing limbs, with hands and feet attached directly to the torso. In all, about 8,000 babies in 20 countries were afflicted. As is typically the case with a teratogen, the damage was most severe when the drug was taken during embryonic development.

It might appear that only extremely toxic agents can produce developmental abnormalities. That is not the case. A variety of widely used drugs can harm the developing individual. For example, the incidence of miscarriage, prematurity, low birth weight, and sudden infant death syndrome is higher for mothers who smoke cigarettes and drink alcohol than for those who do not. Alcoholic mothers have about a 1-in-3 chance of giving birth to an infant with **fetal alcohol syndrome,** in which the infants have facial, heart, and limb defects, and are likely to be mentally retarded and hyperactive. Even moderate drinking or occasional binges can cause damage to the developing infant (Council Report, 1983).

Inherited Abnormalities

A wide range of inherited abnormalities can interfere with development. Examples of such abnormalities are phenylketonuria, Down syndrome, and various sex-linked disorders.

Phenylketonuria (PKU) is a genetic disorder caused by a single recessive gene. PKU is caused by the inaction or absence of the enzyme phenylalanine hydroxylase, which converts the amino acid phenylalanine (found in most protein sources) into the amino acid tyrosine. In this disorder, phenylalanine levels in the blood increase and phenylpyruvic acid accumulates in the urine. Although PKU infants appear normal at birth, they show increasing signs of mental retardation, irritability, poor coordination, and convulsions as phenylpyruvic acid builds up in the body. Phenylketonuria illustrates the effects that a single gene can have. Mendelian genetics predicts that if two people who carry a recessive allele for PKU (i.e., are heterozygous for the trait) produce a child, there is a 1-in-4 chance that it will homozygous for PKU and actually have the disorder (see Figure 10-3).

Fortunately, infants can be tested prior to or at birth for PKU, and most states require such testing. If an infant tests positive for the disorder, he or she can be treated with a diet that limits the amount of phenylalanine. If such a diet is continued through middle childhood, much of the damage caused by PKU can be averted.

Down syndrome, also called trisomy 21, is a chromosome (versus a genetic) disorder that occurs when there is an extra 21st chromosome. Children with Down syndrome have upward slanting eyelids, small (epicanthal) folds of skin over the inner corners of the eyes, and thick protruding tongues. In addition, they have a higher than average incidence of hearing problems, respiratory infection, heart problems, and leukemia. Perhaps the most striking feature of Down syndrome is the presence of mental retardation, which ranges from moderate to severe (see Chapter 13).

	P	p
P	PP Normal Child	Pp Carrier
p	pP Carrier	pp PKU Child

Figure 10-3. Genetic transmission of phenylketonuria in the children of two heterozygous parents. (P is the dominant gene; p is the recessive gene.)

Sex-linked disorders result from problems with the 23rd pair of chromosomes, the so-called sex chromosomes. Twenty-two of the 23 pairs of chromosomes are possessed equally by males and females. The 23rd chromosome differs for males and females. Females have two X chromosomes (XX), and males possess one X and one Y chromosome (XY) (see Figure 10-4). Because the mother is XX, her sex cells produce only X chromosomes. In contrast, the father is XY, therefore, his sex cells produce an approximately equal number of X and Y chromosomes. Because the father can contribute either an X or a Y chromosome, he determines the sex of the zygote.

The X chromosome is about five times longer than the Y chromosome and hence carries more genes. Because the X chromosome carries more genes than the Y chromosome, some genes on the X chromosome have no counterpart on the Y chromosome. A recessive trait on the X chromosome may be expressed in the phenotype if there is no equivalent dominant allele on the Y chromosome to counteract it. Characteristics that result from this circumstance are called *sex-linked,* or X-linked. They are not a problem unless the recessive trait codes for developmental defects. There are unfortunately many such X-linked characteristics, among them hemophilia and color blindness.

In addition to sex-linked characteristics, there can be deviations in the number of sex chromosomes. These result in individuals with problems in sex-

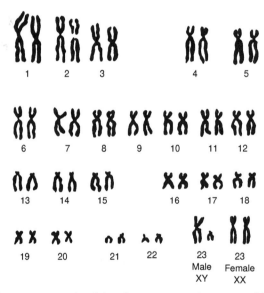

Figure 10-4. A photomicrograph of the chromosomes in a normal human male and female. The first 22 pairs of chromosomes are similar for both sexes, but the 23rd pair in the female contains two X chromosomes whereas the 23rd pair in the male contains an X and a Y chromosome. (From *Psychology: A Concise Introduction,* [2nd ed., p. 43], by T. E. Pettijohn, 1989, Guilford, CT: Dushkin. Copyright 1989 by the Dushkin Publishing Group, Inc. Reprinted with permission.)

Table 10-3
Summary of Chromosomal Anomalies

	Type of Anomaly	Incidence of Live Births	Symptoms
Autosomal anomalies			
Edward's syndrome	Trisomy-18	1 in 5,000	Early death; many congenital problems
D-trisomy	Trisomy-13	1 in 6,000	Early death; many congenital problems
Cri du chat	Deletion of part of short arm of chromosome 4 or 5	1 in 10,000	High-pitched monotonous cry; severe retardation
Down's syndrome	Trisomy-21; 5% involve 15/21 translocation	1 in 700	Congenital problems; retardation
Sex chromosomal anomalies Turner's syndrome	XO or XX-XO mosaics	1 in 2,500	Some physical stigmata and hormonal problems; specific spatial deficit
Females with extra X chromosomes	XXX XXXX XXXXX	1 in 1,000	For trisomy X, no distinctive physical stigmata; perhaps some retardation
Klinefelter's males	XXY XXXY XXXXY XXYY XXYY	2 in 1,000	For XXY, sexual development problems; tall; perhaps some retardation
Males with extra Y chromosomes	XYYY XYYY XYYYY	1 in 1,000	Tall; perhaps some retardation

ual differentiation. Table 10-3 provides a summary of sex-linked chromosomal abnormalities.

Birth and Postnatal Development

Birth represents a drastic change in that the developing individual goes immediately from an existence in which it depends entirely upon the mother for respiration, digestion, thermal regulation, and protection to an independent existence in which circulatory relations with the mother are terminated and autonomous respiration begins (Bijou, 1979). But the **neonate** (the term applied to infants during the first two weeks of life) is ready for the change. It inherits (1) sensory structures (receptors) that enable it to detect the stimuli that define its environment, (2) motor structures (effectors) with which it acts on that environment and moves about in space, and (3) a central nervous system that coordinates and organizes the sensory input and motor output (see Chapter 7). The basic development of these structures follows a plan determined by the individual's genes. But it is a plan that can only be fully realized with extensive input from the environment.

From the time of birth, interactions with the environment, which includes other people, alter an individual's behavior, increasing its diversity and complexity until the remarkable behavioral repertoire characteristic of the adult human is evident. Scientific psychologists refer to this process as **psychological (or behavioral) development,** which, as described previously, is defined as progressive changes over time in behavior–environment interactions (Bijou & Baer, 1978).

Behavioral development results from the interaction of maturational and environmental factors. The term **maturation** is used to refer to a genetically determined plan of biological development that is relatively independent of experience (i.e., environment) (Dworetzky, 1996). The word "relatively" is included because it is extremely difficult to separate completely the effects of the environment from those of maturation. The best way to characterize the relationship between maturation and experience is to say that maturation sets limits on the effects of the environment on behavior (Baldwin & Baldwin, 1988). For example, successful reaching and grasping depend on a sufficiently developed central nervous system and musculature system. However, as discussed in the next chapter, evidence indicates that reaching and grasping can be speeded up considerably by providing a more reactive environment, that is, one in which reaching and grasping produces immediate reinforcing consequences (e.g., White, 1967).

The infant comes into the world largely helpless in terms of organized behavior; it exhibits uncoordinated motor movements and little else. Such behavior has not yet come under the control of environmental stimuli. In fact, most stimuli have no meaning for the neonate; that is, they affect sensory receptors, but do not influence behavior either as antecedent or consequent stimuli (see Chapters 5 and 6). Although neonates are almost completely helpless, they are not passive. Immediately after birth they are able to respond in specific ways to specific stimuli. These inherited (organized) stimulus–response relations are known as **unconditioned** (or unlearned) **reflexes.**

Infant Reflexes

As described in Chapters 4 and 5, **reflexes** are automatic, stereotyped responses to specific stimuli. The fact that many reflexes are present in all neurologically healthy neonates is good evidence that those reflexes are inherited. Most of them appear to have had adaptive value; for example, the rooting reflex, in which a touch on an infant's cheek causes its head to turn in that direction, may have helped the infant's ancestors to find the nipple when nursing.

The neonate is a veritable reflex machine. Its behavior resembles the actions of a complex pinball machine in which pushing different buttons produces different outcomes. For example, a touch on the palm will cause an infant's fingers to close (palmar or grasp reflex), a stroke up and down the sole of the foot will cause the toes to fan out (Babinski reflex), a sudden loud noise will elicit crying and related autonomic responses such as increased heart rate (startle reflex), and a sudden loss of balance will cause the arms and legs to extend and then be pulled back (Moro reflex). Table 10-4 lists the major reflexes found in newborns and their developmental course. It is important to recognize that the eliciting stimulus for some reflexes may be internal, and therefore hard to observe, but it is nonetheless present.

Table 10-4
Major Newborn Reflexes

Name	Eliciting Stimulus	Response	Developmental Course	Significance
Blink	Light flash	Closing of both eyelids	Permanent	Protection of eyes to strong stimuli
Biceps reflex	Tap on the tendon of the biceps muscle	Short contraction of the biceps muscle	In the first few days it is brisker than in later days	Absent in depressed infants or in cases of congenital muscular disease
Knee jerk or patellar tendon reflex	Tap on the tendon below the patella or kneecap	Quick extension or kick of the knee	More pronounced in the first 2 days than later	Absent or difficult to obtain in depressed infants with muscular disease; exaggerated in hyperexcitable infants
Babinski reflex	Gentle stroking of the side of the infant's foot from heel to toes	Dorsal flexion of the big toe; extension of the other toes	Usually disappears near the end of the first year; replaced by plantar flexion of big toe as in the normal adult	Absent in defects of the lower spine
Withdrawl reflex	Pinprick is applied to the sole of the infant's foot	Leg flexion	Constantly present during the first 10 days, present but less intense later	Absent with sciatic nerve damage
Plantar or toe grasp	Pressure is applied with finger against the balls of the infant's feet	Plantar flexion of all toes	Disappears between 8 and 12 months	Absent in defects of the lower spinal cord
Palmar or automatic hand grasp	Rod or finger is pressed against the infant's palm	Infant grasps the object	Disappears at 3 to 4 months; increases during the first month and then gradually declines; replaced by voluntary grasp between 4 and 5 months	Response is weak or absent in depressed babies; sucking movement facilitates grasping
Moro reflex	(1) Sudden loud sound or jarring (for example, bang on the examination table); or (2) head drop—head is dropped a few inches; or (3) baby drop—baby is suspended horizontally, and examiner lowers hands rapidly about 6 inches and stops abruptly	Arms are thrown out in extension and then brought toward each other in a convulsive manner; hands are fanned out at first and then clenched tightly; spine and lower extremities extend	Disappears in 6 to 7 months	Absent or constantly weak Moro indicates series disturbance of the central nervous system

(continued)

Table 10-4
(Continued)

Name	Eliciting Stimulus	Response	Developmental Course	Significance
Stepping	Baby is supported in upright position; examinaer moves the infant forward and tilts it slightly to one side	Rhythmic stepping movements	Independent walking develops by about 15 months	Absent in depressed infants
Rooting response	Cheek of infant is stimulated by light pressure of the finger	Baby turns head toward finger, opens mouth, and tries to suck finger	Disappears at approximately 3 to 4 months	Absent in depressed infants; appears in adults only in severe cerebral palsy diseases
Sucking response	Index finger is inserted about 3 to 4 centimeters into the mouth	Rhythmical sucking	Sucking is often less intensive and less regular during the first 3 to 4 days	Poor sucking (weak, slow, and short periods) is found in apathetic babies; maternal medication during childbirth may depress sucking
Babkin or palmar-mental reflex	Pressure is applied on both of baby's palm when it is lying on its back	Mouth opens, eyes close, and head returns to middle	Disappears in 3 to 4 months	General depression of central nervous system inhibits this response

Neurological Development

As indicated earlier in this chapter, human infants are developmentally more immature at birth than other primates. The human brain at birth is only about 25% of its eventual size. This means, among other things, that 75% of the development of the human brain occurs while the individual is in contact with the external environment. Given this, two important questions are: (1) How do changes in the developing brain influence behavior? and (2) How does contact with the environment influence brain growth?

Neurological development, which includes changes in the shape and size of the brain, density of synaptic connections, and speed of transmission among the neurons, is certainly necessary for behavioral development. If we consider that by adulthood there are approximately 1 trillion neurons with each neuron participating in 100 to 1,000 synaptic contacts with other neurons (Lerner, 1984), then we can begin to appreciate not only the complexity of the central nervous system, but also the difficulty inherent in trying to understand how it mediates behavior.

Until recently, it has been extremely difficult to observe developmental changes in the brain. A device called the PET (position emission tomography) scanner now makes the task easier. During a PET scan, the patient is injected with a radioactive chemical, 2-deoxyglucose (2-DG), which resembles the glucose that normally fuels the brain. This chemical is absorbed into cells that are metabolically active (i.e., using energy) but, unlike glucose, it is not metabolized. Rather, it accumulates within cells, from which it eventually dissipates. After an injection of 2-DG, the patient's head is placed in the scanner and X-ray beams are passed through. The PET scanner detects which areas of the brain have absorbed the 2-DG (i.e., are using energy) and produces a picture that displays those areas (Carlson, 1995).

Pictures from PET scans have shown that in newborns the deeper (subcortical) brain structures (e.g., thalamus, hypothalamus) are more active than the cerebral cortex. The cerebral cortex, which is associated with sensory and motor control, learning, memory, and speech, shows activity only in the areas that mediate sensation and physical movement; most of the cerebral cortex shows low metabolism (energy use). As the infant grows older, activity in the association areas of the cerebral cortex increases and more of the brain becomes active. Many scientists interpret the correlational data provided by the PET scan as supporting the view that brain growth precedes, and is necessary for, behavioral development (e.g., Chugani & Phelps, 1986). But another hypothesis is possible: experience may be responsible for modifications in the brain that mediate behavioral relations (as proximate causes). If infants have not had the experiences necessary to modify the structure of their cerebral cortexes, then scientists would not observe much activity there with a PET scan.

Brain growth obviously influences behavior, but early experience can also have a profound affect on brain size, biochemistry, and the structure of neurons (Greenough & Green, 1981). For example, Rosenzweig (1966) showed that rats' cerebral cortex increased in weight as a result of exposing them to an enriched environment (consisting of "toys" such as ladders, wheels, boxes, and platforms), daily 30-minute exploratory sessions, and formal maze training at 25–30 days of age. In addition, Rosenzweig and Bennet (1970) showed that the activity of two enzymes important in synaptic transmission of nerve impulses also increased as a function of the enriched environment. The branches that develop from the neuron, called dendrites, also increased, expanding the number of synapses per neuron, and contributing to the increase in brain size. All of this may lead to smarter rats, that is, rats that learn faster and more efficiently. These effects on brain weight and biochemistry have also been demonstrated with older animals, indicating that the brain may be sensitive to environmental factors throughout life, although sensitivity may diminish as the organism ages (Greenough & Green, 1981).

The implications for human infants are obvious. Infants exposed to a stimulating reactive environment, that is, to an environment in which behavior produces a rich variety of reinforcing consequences, may be better learners than infants reared in homogeneous, restrictive, and unreactive environments. If, however, an infant is neglected or otherwise unstimulated, we may be able to overcome at least some of the damage through intensive remedial training. It is unclear at present how much plasticity is possible in the human brain.

Maximizing it, and consequently maximizing the behavioral repertoire, is the challenge that faces parents, teachers, and therapists.

We are now in a better position to answer the questions posed at the beginning of this section: How do changes in the developing brain influence behavior? and How does contact with the environment influence brain growth? As a rule, neurological growth is necessary, but not sufficient, for behavioral development. Conversely, interaction with the environment is generally necessary, but not sufficient, for healthy neurological development. Deficiencies in either will retard the other.

Summary

1. The genetic heritage located in the nucleus of the fertilized ovum represents the accumulation of hundreds of millions of years of evolution by natural selection, that is, the phylogenetic development of the human species.

2. Scientists suggest that the beginning of life on earth occurred about 3.5 billion years ago when amino acids were accidentally formed and then combined to form special complex molecules, now called DNA, that had the property of self-replication. The earliest self-replicating molecules were subjected to the force of natural selection and over very long time periods began to diversify into more and more complex and independent groups of self-replicating molecules (called *species*).

3. After the mass extinction of dinosaurs about 70 million years ago, natural selection began to operate more conspicuously on small mammals that were already present such that they began to diversify and multiply (i.e., evolve).

4. The small mammals that moved into the trees were the earliest primates, called *prosimians* (pre-monkeys), from which sprang the present array of prosimians (e.g., lemurs and lorises) and *anthropoids,* the monkeys, apes, and humans, whose characteristics, selected by the contingencies of living in the forest, included those found in today's monkeys, apes, and humans, such as longer hind legs and grasping padded digits, upright posture, rotating heads, larger, more sensitive eyes, and binocular vision.

5. African apes and humans diverged (evolved apart) based on how they walked on the ground: African apes walk on all four legs and humans on two. Human evolution took off on its own approximately 4–6 million years ago when the earliest hominids emerged from the trees of the great forests of Africa and moved into the savanna where further structural developments occurred, such as bipedalism; changes in the structure of the teeth from large to smaller canines; improvements in manual dexterity; and an increase in brain size, all of which probably resulted from a change in diet as well as from an increase in tool use.

6. Two other important characteristics of early hominids that evolved after moving into the grasslands were (1) the nuclear family, consisting of a father, mother, and children, and (2) the different roles of males and females that resulted in part from changes in the female's pelvis which, among other things, affected and was affected by the size and shape of the infant's brain.

7. Psychologists define the term *development* as progressive changes in interactions between the behavior of individuals and the events in their environment.

8. The three periods of prenatal development are the period of the ovum, in which a *zygote* is formed in one of the mother's fallopian tubes through the union of a sperm and an ovum; the period of the embryo, which begins when the zygote attaches to the uterine wall; and the period of the fetus, which begins at about the eighth week, or when primitive reflexive movement of the fetus first occurs.

9. The embryo and fetus are vulnerable to damage from environmental agents, called *teratogens* (e.g., alcohol and other drugs, certain maternal diseases, irradiation, and temperature extremes), which can affect it through the umbilical cord and placenta.

10. A range of inherited abnormalities (e.g., genetic disorders such as phenylketonuria and chromosome disorders such as Down syndrome) can also interfere with development.

11. From the time of birth, an individual's psychological (or behavioral) development results from the interaction of maturational and environmental factors.

12. Although the neonate (newborn) comes into the world largely helpless in terms of organized behavior, it is not completely passive; it does possess inherited automatic, stereotyped responses to specific stimuli (stimulus–response relations) known as *reflexes,* many of which are temporary and disappear within the first year of life.

13. Because human infants are developmentally more immature at birth than other primates (approximately 75% of the development of the human brain occurs after birth) much of the development of the human brain is affected by experiences, many of which produce learning.

Study Questions

1. How do scientists think that life on the earth began and what are the major events of this evolutionary timetable?

2. What are some of the characteristics that distinguish the primates, including monkeys, apes, and humans?

3. How are monkeys, apes, and humans both similar to and different from one another?

4. In what ways did early hominids change (develop) into modern humans and how were these changes selected?

5. How is the term *development* defined in terms of progressive changes in behavior?

6. Why is it preferable to talk about "time periods" instead of "stages of development"?

7. What are the three periods of prenatal development and what are their major distinguishing features?

8. What are teratogens and when are they most likely to produce their effects?

9. What are some examples of genetic abnormalities and how do they affect the developing individual?

10. What is behavioral development and how is it influenced by both maturation and experience?

11. What is the best way to characterize the neonate?

12. What are some of the reflexes that infants possess at birth?

13. What are the two questions one can ask about the relationship between brain and behavior and how they affect one another?

Development through Early Childhood

11

Much of the material in this chapter is taken from Schlinger (1995).

Chapter 10 began with a quote, "We are what we are because of history, both our ancestors' history and the history of our own lives" (Carlson, 1984, p. 6), and went on to consider our ancestral history. It also summarized important events characteristic of the history of all humans from conception to birth. This chapter describes some of the major developmental changes that occur from birth onward, including motor development, perceptual development, cognitive development, and social-emotional development, with a special focus on how behavior–environment interactions change through early childhood.

The Development of Motor Behavior

When developmental psychologists speak of the development of motor behavior, they are referring to changes in behaviors such as sitting, crawling, standing, walking, reaching, and grasping. These behaviors are obviously important because it is through them that humans interact with their environment. Many developmental psychologists seem interested primarily in the normative aspects of motor development. In this context, **normative** changes are changes in behavior that are correlated with changes in age. An interest in normative aspects of development leads to different questions than does an interest in functional aspects of development. The following are examples of questions generated by normative concerns: "What course does the infant's motor development follow? How soon can an infant reach and grasp? How early do infants crawl and walk?" (Hetherington & Parke, 1986, p. 202).

These questions are all about *when, on average*, certain changes occur in infants. They are important questions because motor development is indeed influenced by maturational variables. But answers to such questions only tell us *what* develops and *when* on average it does so, not *how* or *why* development occurs. The alternative to a normative approach is to study the functional aspects of motor development. The questions generated by a functional approach emphasize the variables that cause developmental changes. In addition to generating basic scientific knowledge, a functional approach to motor development may offer practical benefits. It could, for example, benefit therapists in helping children who for unknown reasons display delayed motor development, or who are recovering from injury that results in loss of motor behavior.

Motor development (like most behavioral development) occurs as a result of the interaction between maturing biological structures and the antecedent and postcedent stimuli for relevant behaviors (Bijou, 1979). Although mature biological structures (e.g., nerves, muscles, and bones) are necessary for all motor development, understanding the effects of interaction with the environment may provide some clue as to how early the biological structures develop. For example, White and his associates showed that institutionalized infants whose crib environments were enriched in various ways displayed visually guided reaching approximately 45 days before similar infants who had no enrichment (White, 1967; White & Held, 1966; White, Castle, & Held, 1964). Thus it appears that interactions with a stimulating and reactive environment may speed the development or function of biological structures involved in motor behavior. You may recall from the previous chapter that Rosenzweig and his associates demonstrated that enriched environments were related to changes in brain structure and chemistry in rats.

Motor development can be classified according to whether it involves postural/locomotive behavior or prehensile behavior. *Postural/locomotive* behavior controls the body, arms, and legs and includes behavior that gets an individual into an upright position, as well as behavior that directly produces movement. *Prehension,* or manual control, involves using the hands to manipulate the environment and includes such behaviors as reaching and grasping.

Locomotion

As Gallahue (1989), among others, has noted, the infant is in a constant struggle against gravity to achieve and maintain an upright posture. Because postural/locomotive behaviors result in the infant rising and moving around, they oppose gravitational force. Keogh and Sugden (1985) describe the early development of postural control in terms of three progressions: head control, sitting, and standing.

Postural behavior begins with the infant pushing its chest up from the prone position. Although initial attempts to rise may be reflexive, they operate on and are changed by the environment. Perhaps the most important consequence of such attempts is an increase in the range of visual stimuli; in other words, the infant can see more. As discussed in the next section, changing visual stimuli can function as reinforcement for behavior that produces such changes.

The next major step in the development of mobility comes when the infant is able to sit on its own, which occurs between 4 and 10 months of age. One immediate effect of sitting up is to increase the range of visual stimuli further; the child can now see things on the horizontal plane. True locomotion occurs when the infant begins to crawl. It is at this point that stimuli previously out of reach become accessible. Finally, to both the delight and horror of many parents, walking appears at about 10 to 19 months of age. More than any other type of locomotion, walking increases dramatically that part of the environment that is accessible to the infant, and decreases the amount of time required to access it. These are powerful consequences that reinforce the behavior that produces them.

Table 11-1 shows the normative stages of development of postural control and locomotion. Although various aspects of behavioral development in children have been averaged and plotted normatively, we must not misinterpret these data. Although they reveal something about the development of underlying biological structures, they also probably reveal something about environmental variables, both nonsocial and cultural. For example, Dworetzky (1996) points out that children today typically walk a few months earlier than the 15 months indicated by Shirley (1933). He says that the generally earlier development

might be due to parents who are eager to see their children walk. Such parents might encourage their children to try just as soon as they are able. On the other hand, parents during the 1930s, who often had larger families, might have been considerably less excited by the first steps of their fourth, fifth, and sixth children and so have encouraged them less. (p. 107)

Dworetzky (1996) emphasizes that general training practices may have changed over time, resulting in earlier walking on average. Surely, the time at which a particular child walks is determined in part by the antecedent and consequent stimuli related to the behavior. Of course, there is certainly an age younger than which children are incapable of walking because they do not have the muscle or bone mass either to stand upright or to move their bodies.

Several studies have, nevertheless, shown that early training can facilitate walking in infants. For instance, researchers have taken advantage of the neonate's unlearned walking reflex to facilitate nonreflexive walking. If a neonate is held by the hands in an upright position with the soles of the feet barely touching the ground, the infant will walk forward in the direction led. The walking reflex is transitory and usually disappears at about 3 months. Zelazo, Zelazo, and Kolb (1972), however, showed that if infants are made to practice reflexive walking during four 3-minute sessions each day, the walking reflex lasts longer than usual and normal nonreflexive walking begins much sooner. Moreover, infants 6 to 10 months of age who are placed in walkers (i.e., devices that support infants on wheels such that their feet just touch the ground) have their behavior of propelling the walker reinforced by most of the same events that reinforcing actual walking (e.g., contact with stimulating objects and people). They appear precocious and resemble walking infants more than their nonlocomoting peers (Gustafson, 1984).

Eventually, the differences between infants exposed to walkers and those not exposed disappear as the latter begin to walk and contact the same environmental events. Practice and exposure to walkers may well lead to walking at a relatively early age, but it is unclear whether the child derives any real long-term benefit from these practices. Although the practical significance of their findings is limited, studies such as those discussed above are important because they show that by maximizing the effectiveness of environmental variables, it may be possible to lower the average age associated with various behavioral accomplishments. This outcome emphasizes that human development is not sim-

Table 11-1
Normative Development of Postural Control and Locomotion

Average Age	Behavior
1 month	Raises chin up
2 months	Raises chest up
4 months	Rolls back to stomach
6 months	Sits without support
7 months	Crawls, creeps
8 months	Stands holding onto furniture
9 months	Walks holding onto furniture
12 months	Walks alone
16 months	Walks upstairs and downstairs with help

ply a fixed progression through genetically hard-wired stages, but is instead the result of complex interactions between environmental and genetic variables.

Prehension

Soon after birth, the newborn's arms move reflexively. These are uncoordinated movements that have not yet had any effect on the external environment. In infants as young as 2 months, the infant's mother and other "attractive" objects evoke stretching of the arms and legs (Brazelton, 1982). Eventually, these arm movements will affect some aspect of the environment. They might, for example, cause a mobile hanging above the crib to move. Typically, any behavior, such as reaching and swatting, that produces such an effect will be strengthened (i.e., reinforced).

Prehension skills (grasping) begin to develop at about 16 weeks. By the end of the first year, the child is able to make a neat pincer grasp of small objects (see Figure 11-2). Although grasping requires a minimal level of muscle and bone strength and brain development, the behavior is controlled in large part by interactions with the environment. The reinforcement for grasping may not be obvious until we consider its immediate effects on the environment. The most

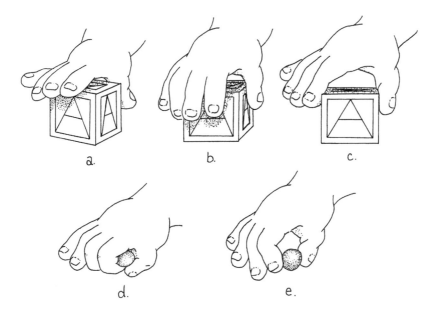

Figure 11-1. Shows some of the major milestones in the development of prehension skills (grasping). Prehension skills begin to develop at about 16 weeks, when the infant can push a block with an open hand (a). At approximately 28 weeks, the infant can grasp a block with the entire hand (b). At about 36 weeks, the infant can make a scissors grasp of small objects (d), and by the end of the first year, the infant can grasp a block with the forefinger and thumb (c) and make a neat pincer grasp (using thumb and forefinger) of small objects (e).

immediate and strongest effect is that the infant successfully manipulates and moves objects. The resulting tactile and proprioceptive stimulation and visual feedback act as reinforcers. These reinforcers have been termed **ecological reinforcers** because they result from the successful manipulation of the natural environment (Bijou, 1979). Because ecological reinforcers are effective in almost all infants from birth, they can be classified as unconditioned reinforcers.

The development of other kinds of body management is more subtle. For example, an uncomfortable position evokes behaviors that historically have produced a more comfortable one; the more comfortable position reinforces the behaviors that produced it. The "discomfort" and "comfort" consist of interoceptive and exteroceptive stimuli that are altered by the infant's moving. How could we test such an analysis?

Consider a theoretical experiment. Suppose an infant is placed in an uncomfortable position. She will be moved to a new position if and when she pushes a large button. Will she learn to push the button? What do you think? Or, as a test of the notion of ecological reinforcement, would an infant learn to kick its leg with a string tied to its ankle if doing so produced a moving mobile? Carolyn Rovee-Collier and her colleagues have conducted experiments to answer these questions, and the answer to each is a resounding "yes" (e.g., Rovee & Fagen, 1976; C. Rovee-Collier, Griesler, & Earley, 1985; C. K. Rovee-Collier, Morrongiello, Aron, & Kupersmidt, 1978). In a related vein, J. S. Watson and Ramey (1972) showed that infants would learn to press their heads against their pillow if it caused a mobile suspended above them to move. Similarly, Kalnins and Bruner (1973) showed that infants would suck a nonnutritive nipple if doing so caused a blurry visual image projected on a screen in front of them to become focused. These and other studies underscore the critical importance of operant conditioning in gross motor development.

Gross motor development represents the beginning of the general shaping of the infant's behavior to fit the environment. The more opportunities the infant has to interact with different aspects of the environment, the faster motor development proceeds. The previously mentioned experiments offer general support for this position (Watson & Ramey, 1972; White, 1967; White & Held, 1966; White, Castle, & Held, 1964).

The Development of Visual Perceptual Behavior

According to Gallahue (1989), learning how to interact with the environment is a perceptual as well as a motor process. In other words, moving around in the world requires sensory as well as motor capabilities. Recall from Chapter 8 that the two major functions of the nervous system are movement and the detection of energy changes called stimuli. Recall also from that chapter that **perception** is evident when stimuli affect not only sensory receptors but also behavior. From a scientific psychological perspective, perception is not a mental or cognitive process, but is simply behavior under particular types of stimulus control (e.g., Knapp, 1987; Nevin, 1973; Schoenfeld & Cumming, 1963). The development of visual perception refers to progressive changes in interactions between behavior and visual stimuli; in other words, the change from simpler to more complex instances of visual stimulus control.

If researchers want to assess the sensory capabilities of verbal humans, they simply manipulate stimuli and ask the subjects whether they can detect (e.g., see, hear, or smell) the relevant environmental change. Such methods cannot be used with infants. (The word *infant* comes from the Latin for *without speech*.) With infants, researchers must examine nonverbal behavior in order to measure stimulus control. As described by Dworetzky (1996), the three most common methods employed for this purpose are (1) the single-stimulus procedure, in which a single stimulus is presented and the infant's reactions (e.g., eye movements, vocalization, reaching) are measured; (2) the preference method, in which two stimuli are presented and the amount of behavior directed to both stimuli is measured; and (3) the habituation method, in which a stimulus that elicits a response (e.g., sucking, heart rate changes, or visual fixation) is presented until responding diminishes. A second stimulus is then presented to see if responding recurs. Because vision is especially important for humans, the infant's visual abilities are considered in the remainder of this section.

Basic Visual Abilities of Infants

By measuring changes in reflexive sucking rates and heart rates as objects are passed through the infant's visual field, researchers have determined that the infant's visual system is sensitive to movement as early as 2 or 3 days after birth (Finlay & Ivinkis, 1984; Haith, 1966). But visual acuity is not good early in life, being about 20/150 in very young infants (Dayton et al., 1964). This means that the infant sees an object at 20 feet with the clarity of a visually normal adult at 150 feet.

This determination resulted from measuring a reflex in the newborn called **optokinetic nystagmus,** a kind of reflexive focusing wherein lateral movement of the eyes is elicited by passing a series of fine vertical stripes past the infant's eyes. The black lines are gradually made finer until the reflex is no longer elicited. By 1 to 3 months, focused (vs. nonfocused) visual stimuli will function as reinforcement for behaviors that produce the focusing, as the previously mentioned experiment by Kalnins and Bruner (1973) demonstrated.

One dimension of visual behavior that is measurable and also appears to be sensitive to various environmental manipulations is the amount of time an infant's eyes look at an object, called *fixation time.* Two techniques have been developed to study fixation time. One involves the preference method described previously. In this technique, the infant lies on its back a few inches beneath a screen on which various stimuli are placed (e.g., Fantz, 1961). The experimenter can observe the infant through a small window in the top of the apparatus. Usually, two different stimuli are placed side by side and the experimenter measures the amount of time the infant spends looking at each. Researchers have found that fixation time is greatest to visual stimuli that are complex and elicit eye movements (Carlson, 1986; Kagan, 1970). Infants will, for example, spend more time looking at (a) patterns with a high degree of black-and-white contrast (e.g., checkerboard) than solid colors (Fantz, 1961), and (b) moving or intermittent lights than continuous light sources (Haith, 1966).

The general finding that infants orient toward stimuli that provide considerable visual stimulation has been reproduced using a variant of the single-stimulus method and a technologically more sophisticated technique (Haith, 1969, 1976; Salapatek, 1975). In this technique, a harmless spot of infrared light is projected onto the infant's eyes. A television camera, specially designed to be sensitive to infrared light, records the spot and superimposes on it an image of the display at which the infant is looking. This allows a precise determination of which parts of the stimulus array the eyes are scanning. Salapatek (1975) reported that 1-month-old infants spend more time looking at the edge of a figure than at its inside. By 2 months, however, infants scan across the border and look at the interior.

When human faces are the stimuli, infants look first at the areas of greatest contrast, for example, the hairline, and then the features of the face that move, such as the eyes and mouth. This pattern is understandable: Seeing movement of someone's eyes and mouth reinforces looking at those facial features. Cognitive psychologists might say that the eyes and mouth communicate important information to the infant. But all this means is that eye and mouth movements (probably as discriminative stimuli) evoke looking by the infant, which is then followed by important consequences, such as being talked to or touched.

Perception of Depth

Humans perceive depth primarily through stereoscopic (binocular) cues, which occur because each eye receives a slightly different picture when we look at an object. As indicated in Chapter 10, the use of stereoscopic cues became possible through evolution. Once eyes were located in front of the head, rather than on the side, our ancestors attained far greater ability to react to distances. Being able to react accurately to distances was critical for early primates.

Developmental psychologists have explored the age at which infants are able to react to depth (distance) cues. To test this, Gibson and Walk (1960) devised an apparatus called the *visual cliff* (see Figure 11-2). The visual cliff consists of two sides covered by a glass surface. On one side (the shallow side) is a checkerboard-patterned platform directly beneath the glass; on the other side (the deep side) is a similar pattern, but it is located a considerable distance below the glass.

When placed on the visual cliff, newborn chicks, kittens, and baby mountain goats did not venture over to the deep end. This suggests that in these species the ability to react to depth cues is innate in the sense of requiring little interaction with the environment. Human infants generally showed the same tendency. But it is difficult to compare humans and nonhumans on this task because nonhumans are able to move on their own soon after birth, and can be tested then. Human infants do not begin to self-propel until about 6 months of age. By that time, they have had ample opportunity to learn about depth cues.

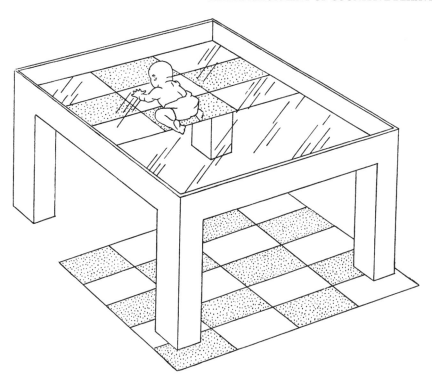

Figure 11-2. A diagram of the visual cliff apparatus used by Gibson and Walk (1960). Adapted from Dworetzky (1996).

To determine whether depth perception in humans is innate, investigators obviously had to find a dependent variable that was sensitive to depth cues and could also be measured before infants became mobile.

Campos and his colleagues decided to measure infants' heart rates on the visual cliff. Interestingly, they found that when infants as young as 1.5 months were placed on the deep side, their heart rates decreased (Campos, Langer, & Krowitz, 1970). Only when infants were able to crawl did they show heart rate increases, which can be interpreted as a fear response. Because any consistent change in heart rate can be interpreted as a reaction to depth cues, the heart-rate decreases found in Campos and colleagues' (1970) study showed that young (e.g., 1-month-old) infants detect and react to depth cues, although they have not yet learned to fear heights. The heart-rate increases found in older infants suggest that by the time infants become mobile they have learned to fear high places.

The Development of Cognitive Behavior

According to Hetherington and Parke (1986), "**Cognition** refers to mental activity and behavior through which knowledge of the world is attained and processed, including learning, perception, memory and thinking" (see Chapter 9,

p. 212). Consequently, "The study of cognitive development is concerned with describing and understanding the ways in which children's intellectual abilities and their knowledge of the world . . . change throughout the course of development" (p. 337). Although a number of theories of cognitive development have been advanced, the most popular one and the only one we will consider is that of Jean Piaget (1896–1980).

Piaget's Theory of Cognitive Development

Piaget, who was initially trained as a biologist, became interested in the development of intelligence in children while doing mental testing on children in Alfred Binet's Paris laboratory.[1] Unlike his colleagues who were interested in children's ability to answer questions correctly, Piaget was interested in the similarity of *incorrect* answers by children of the same age and in how those answers differed from those given by children of different ages. To Piaget, these consistencies seemed to reveal a developmental sequence of thinking processes. His goal was to understand these processes; he wanted to understand not just *what* children think or know, but more important, *how* they think and acquire knowledge. Piaget's strategy was to construct "thinking" problems and then observe children as they solved the problems. His subjects consisted primarily of his own children, although he later extended his observations to other children.

As a biologist, Piaget understood that humans, like other animals, adapt to their environment. Piaget's theory of cognitive development (e.g., Piaget, 1952) attempted to explain how the child adapts to the world around it. In short, Piaget argued that a child adapts to its environment through the use of innate cognitive processes that produce modifications in cognitive structures and, consequently, in behavior.

Cognitive Structures and Processes

For Piaget, cognitive structures develop through a fixed series of stages and become ever more complex, allowing for more effective adaptation to the environment. (The only evidence for their existence is regular patterns of behavior that become more complex as the child grows older and interacts more with the environment.) The infant's organizing structure is called a *schema* (Piaget's preferred term), although we will use the term scheme.

Schemes are different mental activities that are used by children to organize and to respond to experiences. Although it is tempting to view schemes as actual structures in the brain, Hetherington and Parke (1986) suggest that they are "an interrelated and organized group of memories, thoughts, actions, and strategies that the child uses in an attempt to understand the world" (p. 341), where "understand" refers to adapting. The child's interactions with its environment alter the cognitive structures (schemes), which typically become more

---

[1]Alfred Binet developed the first modern standardized intelligence test.

complex as a result of experience with the environment and of biological maturation. Increasingly complex cognitive structures allow for more complex ways of adapting to the environment.

In very young infants, schemes consist of nonlearned sensorimotor relations such as reflexes. Infants are said to possess various reflexive schemes, for example, a sucking scheme, a kicking scheme, and a grasping scheme, which are manifested in organized sensorimotor activities (stimulus–response relations). Consider the following description of a thumb-sucking scheme (Ginsburg & Opper, 1988):

> If we examine the infant's behavior in detail, we will see that no two acts of thumb-sucking performed by one child are precisely the same. On one occasion the activity starts when the thumb is 10 inches from the mouth, on another when it is 11 inches away. At one time the thumb travels in almost a straight line to the mouth; at another time its trajectory is quite irregular. In short, if we describe behavior in sufficient detail, we find that there are no two identical actions. There is no one act of thumb-sucking, but many; in fact there are as many as the number of times the child brings the thumb to the mouth. (pp. 20–21)

This example illustrates that it is behavior, or more accurately, "certain features common to a wide variety of acts which differ in detail" (Ginsburg & Opper, 1988, p. 21), not some unobservable entity, that must be understood. What is the common feature that defines the behaviors we call thumb sucking? It is simply getting the thumb into the mouth. As explained in Chapter 10, inventing a scheme to explain such behavior is a problem because doing so leads to reification and circular explanation. Clearly, thumb sucking is operant behavior: Getting the thumb in the mouth is the reinforcer for all the behaviors that, although they may differ slightly, produce that outcome.

As the infant's interactions with the environment expand, his or her schemes (behavioral patterns) are quickly modified and new cognitive structures (behaviors) emerge. According to Piaget, these new cognitive structures, called **operations,** are internalized, symbolically represented schemes—the "mental equivalents of behavioral schemata"—which can be viewed as a set of rules, or plans, of problem solving and classification (Hetherington & Parke, 1986, p. 341). The cognitive development of children involves a gradual shift from schemes to operations. But how does this shift occur? And how does experience contribute to cognitive development?

According to Piaget, intellectual or cognitive development—the modification of cognitive structures—involves two innate methods of processing environmental experience: organization and adaptation. Organization refers to the infant's tendency to integrate and coordinate behaviors and mental events into more complex systems. For example, an infant first possesses looking, reaching, and touching schemes that are independent of one another. As development proceeds, these schemes become organized into a higher-order system of coordinated actions that can function as an independent unit: a looking-reaching-touching unit.

Adaptation refers to the tendency of humans to change as the result of experience and involves two processes, assimilation and accommodation. In **assimilation,** new experiences are interpreted in terms of existing knowledge (cognitive structures). Therefore, behavior in the new circumstance is similar to that in similar circumstances in the past. If, however, this resultant behavior is unsuccessful in the new situations, cognitive structures are altered, and behavior changes: Piaget called this accommodation. Accommodation and assimilation work together to adapt behavior to a changing environment.

Ginsburg and Opper (1988) offer the following example of assimilation and accommodation. In this example, an infant is given a rattle for the first time. First the infant assimilates the rattle into existing cognitive structures:

> In the past the infant has already grasped things; for him grasping is a well-formed structure of behavior. When he sees the rattle for the first time, he tries to deal with the novel object by incorporating it into a habitual pattern of behavior. In a sense, he tries to transform the novel object to something with which he is familiar, namely, a thing to be grasped. We can say, therefore, that he assimilates the object into his framework and thereby assigns the object a "meaning." (p. 19)

When assimilation is not entirely adequate, the infant must accommodate his behavior to the environment:

> The infant tries to grasp the rattle. To do this successfully he must accommodate in more ways than are immediately apparent. First, he must accommodate his visual activities to perceive the rattle correctly, for example, by locating it in space. Then he must reach out, adjusting his arm movements to the distance between himself and the rattle. In grasping the rattle, he must mold his fingers to its shape; in lifting the rattle he must accommodate his muscular exertion to its weight. (p. 19)

Piaget's conception of the interaction of individuals with the environment shares some similarities with that of scientific psychologists. First, they both assume an active child. Second, they both assume that the child's behavior constantly conforms to the environment. The major difference lies in the processes proposed to account for that behavioral adaptation. In Piaget's approach, it is the child who does the adapting (either by assimilating or accommodating). A more scientifically adequate view is that it is the selective action of the consequences of the child's behavior that gradually shapes the behavior.

An analysis of Piaget's concept of assimilation based on principles of learning introduced in Chapter 6 is simply stated: stimuli similar to those that were present when behavior was successful in the past will evoke that behavior in the future; this is stimulus control. If the behavior is no longer successful in producing the same consequences (extinction), its variability increases, as does the probability that small variations will produce the effective behavioral consequence and, thus, come under the control of the present stimuli.

From a scientific perspective, the processes of assimilation and accommodation are relatively straightforward. Let us return to the example presented above. As a discriminative stimulus (S^D), the sight of the rattle evokes behavior, for example, reaching and grasping, that historically has been successful in contacting objects. If the rattle is presented at some distance, then reaching farther is necessary before grasping can take place, so the specific form of the grasp may have to be different from previous forms. There is inherent variability in behavior; some of the variations in reaching and grasping are successful and some are not. In a very short time, the successful variations prevail; they have been reinforced by the feel and perhaps the sound of the rattle that follows them (ecological reinforcers).

Periods of Cognitive Development

Piaget viewed cognitive development in terms of progressive changes in cognitive structures. Because Piaget assumed that these changes in children's intellectual development are qualitative and are correlated with changes in age, he classified them according to a series of stages. All children go through the same stages in the same order, but not necessarily at exactly the same rate. The four main stages of cognitive development described by Piaget (the sensorimotor period, the preoperational period, the concrete operational period, and the formal operational period) are summarized in Table 11-2.

Evaluation of Piaget's Theory

Piaget's theory is based on accurate observations of behavior: The stages that he described generally capture the changes in behavior that occur as a child ages. Moreover, his explanations of cognitive development are widely accepted. But Piaget's theory is scientifically unsatisfactory primarily because the cognitive structures and processes on which the theory rests are hypothetical enti-

Table 11-2
Piagetian Stages of Cognitive Development[a]

1. Sensorimotor stage (birth to 2 years)	Children begin to distinguish between themselves and the rest of the world. Behavior gradually becomes more intentional. They begin to acquire object permanence, and to learn that actions have consequences (cause and effect).
2. Preoperational stage (2–7 years)	Children develop the ability to perform mental actions (e.g., imagination, memory). They begin to use symbols (e.g., language) to represent the external world internally. They are egocentric—they cannot put themselves in someone else's place and they see everything only from their own point of view. They tend to focus on one aspect or dimension of an object and ignore all others, and cannot mentally retrace steps to reach a conclusion (irreversibility).
3. Concrete operational stage (7–11 years)	Children have the ability to cognitively operate only on concrete objects, that is, those that can be experienced, although such objects need not be physically present. Children learn to retrace thoughts, and to correct themselves. They can consider two or more aspects of a situation at a time. They are able to look at a problem in different ways and see other people's points of view. They develop concepts of conservation, for example, number, volume, mass.
4. Formal operational stage (12 years and up)	Children (adolescents) can think in abstract terms; and can formulate and test hypotheses through logic. They can think through various solutions to a problem or possible consequences of an action. They are no longer tied to concrete testing of ideas in external world—they can test them internally through logic. Adolescents can "think about thinking"; they can contemplate their own thoughts.

[a]Adapted from Piaget and Inhelder (1969)

Sidebar 11-1
Conservation: Cognitive Process or Learned Behavior?

According to Piagetians, perhaps the single most important intellectual achievement of children in the concrete operational period is that of conservation. **Conservation** refers to the fact that a person can respond to an object as unchanged despite transformations of that object. Consider the following test. Two glasses of water that are the same size, shape, height, and width are filled with equal amounts of water. Then the contents of one glass are poured into a taller, narrower glass. If a person says that the amount of water in the tall, narrow glass is the same as that in the short, wide glass, conservation (of volume) is evident. According to Piaget, not until a child reaches the concrete operational stage (at about 7 years of age) will she be able to say that the amounts are the same (see Figure 11-3). In another typical Piagetian test for conservation, a child is presented with two equal-sized lumps of clay and when asked if they are the same size, will report that they are. If the experimenter then stretches one of the lumps into an elongated form and asks the child if they are still the same size, the preoperational child will report that they are not. Only the concrete operational child will answer correctly. Piaget's explanation for the preoperational child's lack of conservation in both of the above examples was that the child lacked the necessary cognitive structures.

There are several dimensions along which objects can change, including position, shape, space, and volume. And there are several tests that can be used to judge conservation when these dimensions are altered. Cognitive developmental psychologists have determined that the average age at which children demonstrate conservation varies for different stimulus characteristics: Conservation of number usually occurs by about six years of age, conservation of mass by seven, and weight around nine.

But must we wait for hypothetical cognitive structures to "develop" before a child can behave appropriately in these circumstances? Can a child under seven years of age be taught conservation skills? And, why don't children under seven typi-

cally conserve? These questions have been partially answered by several studies demonstrating that conservation can be accelerated simply by arranging the environment to facilitate learning (e. g., Gelman, 1969; Sigel, Roeper, & Hooper, 1966). Moreover, Gelman (1969) suggests that the reason that many children fail tests of conservation is simply that they are not attending to the cue that the experimenters deem critical. Consider the liquid conservation test (described above). In that test, "the stimulus complex of each glass with water can be thought of as a multidimensional pattern with at least six attributes; these being size, shape, height, width, water level, and actual amount of water" (p. 168). Gelman reminds us that the child is likely to react to relations and dimensions other than those specified by the experimenter (E).

> From the E's point of view only one cue is relevant, i.e., related to the solution of the conservation problem, and this is amount of water. All others are irrelevant. However, from the viewpoint of a young S (subject) all cues are potentially relevant to his definition of amount. When he is asked to judge amount, he may do so on the basis of any or all cues in the complex. (p. 169)

If the subject is attending to an irrelevant cue, such as the height of the water level, conservation will not occur. In her study, Gelman (1969) used a discrimination training procedure with a large number of conservation problems containing many stimuli that differed along several dimensions except for one common one. The subjects (children whose median age was 5 years 4 months) were asked questions about the stimuli (e. g., "Do these have the same or different amounts of clay?"). When the children gave correct responses to the common element they were told, "Yes, that is right," and were given a prize. When incorrect answers were given, they were told, "No, that is not right." The results showed clearly that children who were given explicit discrimination training learned to conserve with much greater accuracy than control subjects.

ties. They have no physical status and cannot be observed directly. As discussed in Chapter 2, behavior cannot be explained adequately in terms of such hypothetical entities. Although Piaget's theory has some predictive validity, that is, it may be able to predict when, on average, certain behaviors may be ob-

Figure 11-3. Conservation of volume. One of two glasses that contain an equal amount of water (A), is poured into a taller, narrower glass (B), and a child is asked which of the two contains more water.

served, it affords no control over the subject matter. For example, Piaget's system cannot account for individual differences between children of the same age or between children of different ages except by assuming differences in unobservable cognitive structures. Appealing to changes in cognitive structures as explanations of behavior without the ability to observe, measure, and control those changes makes such explanations circular: The only evidence for the explanations is the behavioral changes they attempt to explain. In addition, stage theories such as Piaget's tempt the nominal fallacy. Assigning a label to a child on the basis of age and behavior does not explain anything, but this is not obvious at first glance.

A further problem with Piaget's theory is that studies have shown that development is not a simple maturational process, as Piaget assumed it to be. These studies involved attempting to teach intellectual skills to children who, according to Piaget, would be too young to learn them. With relatively simple and explicit training, children can acquire behaviors assumed to be indicative of particular cognitive structures well before the time that the structures supposedly develop (e.g., Gelman, 1969; J. S. Watson & Ramey, 1972). Sidebar 11-1 discusses the early training of conservation.

The Development of Social-Emotional Behavior

Many species, *Homo sapiens* among them, are social in the sense that the behavior of individual members of a group is affected by, and in turn affects, the behavior of other members of that group. The ways in which we interact with other members of our culture are determined in large part by our early interactions with parents or other caretakers. As discussed in Chapter 10, the prolonged period of childhood dependency in humans allows the child to acquire a rich repertoire of social relations.

Social behavior occurs when an individual's actions are determined by stimuli arising from other persons. These stimuli are called *social stimuli*. **Social environment** is the term used to describe all of the social stimuli that affect the behavior of an individual at a given time. Social stimuli do not differ from other stimuli in their dimensions; they affect visual, auditory, olfactory, and tactile receptors. Social stimuli also do not differ in function from other stimuli; they have eliciting, reinforcing, punishing, discriminative, and motivational functions (F. S. Keller & Schoenfeld, 1950). Social stimuli are unique only in that they arise from the behavior of other people. The actual behavior determined by social stimuli is likely to vary somewhat from person to person but, in general, it will be fairly consistent within a culture.

Because emotional behaviors are often social as well, developmental psychologists generally analyze them together as social-emotional development. Consider the following example. As her grandparents look on, a one-year-old girl is sitting in a stroller gnawing on a plastic rattle. The rattle slips from her grasp and falls to the floor. A rapid sequence of events ensues: She reaches for the rattle, can't get it, turns red in the face, screams and cries, and flails her arms. Grandmother laughs, saying, "She's mad as a hornet." Grandfather retrieves the rattle, wipes it off, and returns it to the baby. This terminates the screaming and crying; the rattle goes back in the mouth, to be sucked with accompanying grins and coos. "That's one happy kid," the old man observes. The terms, "mad" and "happy," refer to what are commonly called emotions. In this instance, however, the emotional behaviors—crying and smiling—also have social functions in that they affect the behavior of the grandparents, whose behavior in turn affects the infant's future emotional behavior under similar circumstances.

Social-emotional development usually denotes the development of *attachment behaviors* in both infants and caregivers, although the emphasis is usually on the behavior of infants.

The Development of Attachment Behaviors

Social-emotional behavior begins very early in life and contributes to what is called *attachment.* Just as most researchers in the field of cognitive development followed Jean Piaget, most modern researchers in the area of social-emotional development have followed the lead of John Bowlby. According to Bowlby, people (or other animals) who are attached will interact often, exhibit behaviors that result in proximity to each other, and protest upon separation. Thus, the term **attachment** is used to describe special kinds of parent–child interactions, specifically those that indicate that the child seeks to be close to and in other ways prefers the parent over other people. Although both parents and children display attachment behaviors, we focus largely on those of the children. Many behaviors of the infant are indicative of attachment. Among the most important are crying, cuddling, and smiling. In general, these behaviors follow a similar progression in development. Early in life, the infant's behavior is nonselectively evoked by a variety of social stimuli. Next, social stimuli associated with familiar people come to exercise discriminative control over behavior. Finally, specific attachment behaviors appear; the infant behaves in ways that increase contact with specific persons (e.g., the parents) and may protest (e.g., cry) when they depart.

Just as Piaget felt that the earliest signs of cognitive development were seen in infant reflexes, which then became more coordinated after interaction with the environment, Bowlby believed that the earliest signs of attachment were seen in the same reflexes. And, like Piaget, Bowlby believed that these attachment behaviors become more directed and complex after interaction with the social environment. We illustrate with the example of crying.

Crying typically has multiple causes. From birth, crying can be elicited as an unconditional reflex by diverse stimuli including sudden loud sounds, bright lights, loss of support, and objects or events associated with discomfort (e.g., food deprivation, pain, or cold). This latter form of crying, perhaps more than any other, is related to attachment.

Crying initially is elicited by stimuli associated with hunger or discomfort, but it quickly comes under the control of the social environment. In fact, evolutionarily speaking, crying exists only because it affects other humans: Infants who cried when hungry or in discomfort were more likely to be attended to by parents than those who did not. Thus, crying is described as an emotional and social response. Some psychologists, including Bowlby, have even argued that adults are genetically predisposed to react to an infant's crying. Adults who responded to crying ensured that their children survived and transmitted their genes to future generations. Thus, crying has obvious communicative value (Lester & Zeskind, 1982).

Although crying begins as part of unconditional reflexes, it soon becomes both classically and operantly conditioned. Operant conditioning is especially important for the development of attachment. Not only does the parent's reaction strengthen the infant's crying under certain circumstances, the cessation of the infant's crying also strengthens the parent's behavior that produced it. Although Bell and Ainsworth (1972) suggested in a widely cited article that maternal responding to infant crying actually reduces the frequency and duration of future crying, other psychologists have pointed out flaws both in the researchers' methodology and conclusions (e.g., Gewirtz, 1977; Gewirtz & Boyd, 1977). They suggest that parents may inadvertently increase their child's crying "when nothing is wrong" by attending to (reinforcing) it.

Theories of Attachment

Several theories of attachment have been popular. An early learning theory asserted that by virtue of being associated with food and the reduction of hunger, the mother acquires conditioned reinforcing properties (e.g., Sears, Maccoby, &

Levin, 1957). Consequently, behavior that results in contact with the mother will be reinforced by that contact. In short, the child becomes attached to the mother because she fills a biological need for food. A variety of findings logically contradict the notion that attachment is based solely on the mother meeting the biological needs of the child. First, infants display attachment behavior in situations in which they have not received food. Second, attachment behaviors continue after biological needs have been met. Third, as shown in a famous series of studies by Harry Harlow (e.g., Harlow, 1958; Harlow & Suomi, 1970; Harlow & Zimmerman, 1959), attachment behaviors may be directed toward individuals and objects that never provide nourishment (see photograph on this page).

To test the hypothesis that attachment depends on the mother meeting the biological needs of the infant, Harlow separated infant rhesus monkeys from their mothers at an early age and placed them in a room with two surrogate (substitute) "mothers." The mothers were identical except that one was constructed of wire mesh and the other was covered with soft terry cloth (see photograph, p. 278).

An infant rhesus monkey clinging to a cloth surrogate mother with researcher Harry Harlow. Photo courtesy of Roger Ulrich. (From *Psychology: A Behavioral Overview* [p. 209], by A. Poling, H. Schlinger, S. Starin, and E. Blakely, 1990, New York: Plenum Press. Copyright 1990 by Plenum Press. Reprinted with permission.)

Both were heated and had in the center of the chest a nipple that the infants could suckle. In one experiment, the infants were allowed to feed on the wire mother but not on the cloth mother. The dependent variable was the amount of time the infants spent clinging to each mother. Results showed quite clearly that, except for feeding time, the infants spent a majority of their time clinging to the cloth mother (see Figure 11-4). From these and other results, Harlow concluded that even though the infants received all of their nourishment from the wire mother,

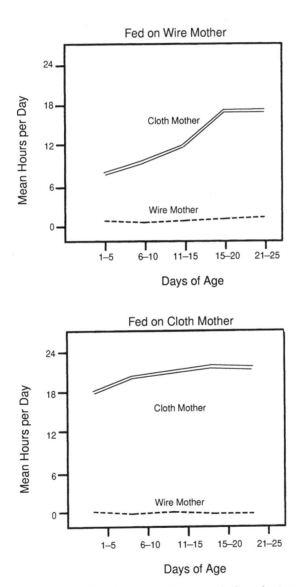

Figure 11-4. Time spent by infant rhesus monkeys on cloth and wire mother surrogates. Adapted from Harlow (1958).

they developed attachment behavior only to the cloth mother. Attachment did not appear to result from food delivery.

Harlow clearly showed that feeding is not the only important variable in the development of attachment in rhesus monkeys. Whether this finding generalizes to humans is unclear, for infant rhesus monkeys differ from infant humans in many ways (e.g., monkeys are mobile, have the upper-body strength to cling, and have more fully developed brains). Regardless of the generality of Harlow's findings, few contemporary theoreticians hold to the old view that feeding is the ultimate source of attachment.

Interpretation of Harlow's findings presents two serious problems. First, even Harlow (1967) has admitted that feeding is important in attachment behavior, although it is by no means the only important variable. Second, Harlow and Zimmerman's (1959) study has a potentially serious flaw: The two surrogate mothers were not identical (see photograph this page); the cloth-covered mother had a realistic head, whereas the wire mesh mother had an unrealistic head. Why is this important? Because Harlow and his colleagues showed that infant monkeys learned to press a lever if the consequence was the sight of the cloth surrogate or a real monkey, but not if the consequence was the sight of the wire mother (see Harlow, 1967 for a description). For a control group raised with no mothers at all,

The two surrogate mothers used by Harlow and his colleagues. Photo courtesy of the Harlow Primate Laboratory.

however, the rate of lever pressing was higher when they could see a real monkey as opposed to either surrogate. These findings suggest that some visual characteristics of real monkeys function as reinforcement without any prior exposure to real monkeys. Given this, infant monkeys might cling initially to a cloth surrogate mother, but not to a wire surrogate mother, because the former resembled a real monkey.

In attempting to explain attachment in general, it may be profitable to combine an ethological analysis with a scientific psychological one. Ethological analysis suggests that infants and mothers are genetically predisposed to behave in certain ways with respect to each other. For example, infants will smile, cry, and suck under specific circumstances, and the stimuli arising from these behaviors will control specific behaviors in the mother. Such reciprocal mother–child interactions historically facilitated survival, so the genotype that permitted them became prominent. It is important to understand that this genotype does not lead to the inheritance of specific behaviors but, rather, a tendency to acquire, or learn, certain behavioral relations (Bowlby, 1969).

Imprinting and Sensitive Periods[2]

An early proponent of the ethological view of attachment was Konrad Lorenz. By 1940, researchers had shown that newly hatched chicks, ducklings, and goslings will follow the first moving object they see, which is usually their mother. Because all healthy hatchlings were observed to do this, it appeared that the "following" response was innate. Lorenz provided a dramatic demonstration of innate following by ensuring that he was the first moving object seen by newly hatched ducklings and goslings. Thereafter, they followed him everywhere just as they normally would their mothers. Lorenz called this phenomenon **imprinting,** and he soon discovered that it occurred only during a **sensitive** (or critical) **period** lasting for about two days from the time of hatching. The possible survival value of imprinting is obvious: The first moving object a hatchling sees is likely to be its mother, and following her may provide increased access to food or safety from predators. Precocial birds (those able to move about from birth) with a genotype that favors following may on that basis be more apt to survive and procreate than those without it. Hence, this genotype has become predominant.

Although imprinting is rigidly controlled by innate factors (Fantino & Logan, 1979), there is good evidence that the actual behavior of following a mov-

---

[2]Although the terms are sometimes used as approximate synonyms, sensitive, optimal, and critical periods are distinguished by ethologists (see Fantino & Logan, 1979). A sensitive period is one in which an individual is exceptionally susceptible to the effects of a particular experience; such periods often can be defined only loosely. An optimal period is that portion of a sensitive period in which a particular experience produces the greatest effect. For example, the strongest imprinting in ducks is produced when the moving stimulus is presented 13 to 16 hours after hatching (Hess, 1958). A critical period is evident if (1) susceptibility to an experience is limited to a very brief period of time, and (2) absence of the experience during this time produces permanent behavioral abnormality.

ing object is learned. This was first demonstrated in a clever experiment conducted by Neil Peterson (1960). Peterson arranged conditions so that a yellow cylinder (10 by 20 cm) was the first moving object seen by Black and Peking ducklings. He then allowed the ducklings to view the cylinder if they pecked a plexiglass disc. Pecking occurred reliably so that the sight of the imprinted object could be called a positive reinforcer. There are two points of interest in this demonstration. First, imprinting established the imprinted object as a powerful reinforcer. Second, the imprinted object served to reinforce a response—pecking a stationary object—other than, and in fact incompatible with, following. This suggests that "following" behavior is not inherited directly in imprinting. What is inherited is the capacity to be reinforced by the sight of, or proximity to, the imprinted object. In precocial birds, "following" is the behavior most likely to achieve this.

A similar analysis might be extended to Harlow's findings with infant monkeys. Monkeys probably do not directly inherit clinging behavior, but rather the tendency to be reinforced by warmth, softness, or even the sight of another monkey. In rhesus monkeys, clinging is the behavior most likely to achieve these outcomes. This surmise could be tested by selecting some arbitrary response, such as button pushing, and assessing the reinforcing functions of these stimulus dimensions.

As already mentioned, Harlow arranged such an experiment and showed that infant monkeys pressed much more when they could see either the cloth surrogate or the other infant monkey, which indicates that the sight of both was reinforcing. Other work by Harlow indicated that visual, tactile, or thermal contact with the surrogate mother reinforced running toward and clinging to her. The question remains as to why those events function as reinforcers and whether the same events function as reinforcers for human infants.

Bowlby (e.g., 1973) has suggested that human infants have a predisposition to learn behaviors that maximize contact with the mother, and that mothers are predisposed to be affected by infants' behaviors, including smiling, crying, and looking. The stimuli arising from these infant behaviors may be eliciting, motivational, or reinforcing, depending on their temporal relationship to and effect on behaviors in the mother. After extensive interactions between the mother and child, the mother acquires conditioned reinforcing functions such that the child will continue to behave in ways that bring her closer. Although the association with food may be important, it is not the sole basis of conditioned reinforcement.

Studies of imprinting are important in revealing the existence of sensitive periods for the acquisition of certain behaviors, and in showing that organisms inherit the capacity to be reinforced by ecologically relevant stimuli. They are also noteworthy in revealing that early experiences can have delayed, enduring, and counterintuitive effects. All of these outcomes are evident in research on cross-fostering, in which young birds of one species are raised by and imprinted on foster parents of another species. If, for example, mallard ducks are reared by another species, the males at sexual maturity attempt to mate with females of the species that reared them, not with female mallards. Female mallards, in contrast, typically mate with male mallards, regardless of how the females were reared (F. Schultz, 1971). In this case, the effects of imprinting are (1) delayed by several months, (2) persistent across years even with exposure to appropriate mates, (3) evident in responses (sexual behavior) that are not an obvious part of imprinting, and (4) different for males and females.

Although imprinting as we have discussed it occurs only in birds, it is clear that the early experiences of primates, including humans, powerfully influence subsequent behavior–environment interactions. One way in which they do so is by narrowing the range of stimuli with reinforcing properties.

Summary

1. The development of motor behaviors, such as sitting, crawling, standing, walking, reaching, and grasping is important because it is through them that humans act upon and interact with their environment. Although many developmental psychologists are interested primarily in the normative aspects of motor development, an alternative is to study the functional aspects of motor development, that is, the actual variables that cause developmental changes. Such variables include the interaction between maturing biological structures (proximate physiological causes) and the antecedent and consequent stimuli (proximate and ultimate environmental causes) for relevant behaviors.

2. Motor development is classified according to whether it involves postural/locomotive behaviors (those which control the body, arms, and legs) and prehensile behaviors (those abilities of the hands to manipulate the environment such as reaching and grasping).

3. The development of visual-perceptual behavior refers to progressive changes in interactions between behavior and visual stimuli, and researchers have developed several ways to overcome the lack of language in infants in order to assess such development, including the single-stimulus procedure, and the preference and habituation methods.

4. Researchers have studied the age at which infants are able to react to depth (distance) cues, otherwise called *depth perception*, with a device called the *visual cliff*, and have discovered that newborns' heart rates change when moved over the "deep" side of the cliff, indicating that depth cues do affect their behavior.

5. Some researchers are interested in *cognitive development*, which consists of such activities as memory and thinking. The most prominent cognitive developmental psychologist, Jean Piaget, hypothesized that such development in children progresses through a series of four general but relatively fixed maturational stages through general processes of *assimilation*, in which new experiences are interpreted in terms of existing knowledge, and *accommodation*, where cognitive structures are altered.

6. Although Piaget's theory is based on accurate observations of behavior, the cognitive structures and processes on which the theory rests cannot be observed and are, thus, hypothetical entities which lead to inadequate explana-

tions of the observed behavior such as nominal fallacy, reification, and circular explanation.

7. Social behavior is behavior that is determined by stimuli from other persons called *social stimuli.* Because most emotional behaviors (e.g., crying, smiling) are often social as well, developmental psychologists generally analyze them together in terms of social-emotional development.

8. Researchers interested in the development of social behavior study what is called *attachment behaviors,* that is, special kinds of parent–child interactions in which the child seeks to be close to and in other ways prefers the parent over other people. The most prominent developmental psychologist interested in attachment was John Bowlby.

9. One of the best-known series of studies was conducted by Harry Harlow and his colleagues who studied the role of contact comfort on attachment behavior (e.g., clinging) in rhesus monkeys, using surrogate mothers.

10. Researchers have also studied a phenomenon called *imprinting,* which in the present context refers to the following behavior of precocial animals, especially birds such as ducks and geese who, as newly hatched infants, will follow the first moving object they see, but only during a sensitive period. Although imprinting is rigidly controlled by innate factors, there is good evidence that the actual behavior of following a moving object is learned.

Study Questions

1. What is meant by motor development and how is it described in normative terms?

2. How is the infant in a constant struggle against the force of gravity, what behaviors develop that oppose it, and how are they learned?

3. How can early training facilitate walking in infants?

4. What are the possible reinforcers for prehensile behaviors, especially ecological reinforcers?

5. What are some specific types of ecological reinforcers for infant behavior?

6. How is perception better described as something we do rather than something we have?

7. What are the three methods researchers use to assess the perceptual capacities of infants?

8. What are some of the basic visual capacities of the infant?

9. What is the visual cliff and how have researchers used it to assess depth perception in infants?

10. What does the study of cognitive development entail and who was its most famous investigator?

11. What type of cognitive structure do infants possess according to Piaget and how is it more parsimoniously viewed from a scientific perspective?

12. What are assimilation and accommodation, including an example, and how can the same facts be explained more scientifically?

13. What are the four major stages of cognitive development according to Piaget?

14. What are the pros and cons of Piaget's theory of cognitive development?

15. How is the term "attachment" used, how did Bowlby view it, and how does the example of crying illustrate it?

16. What did Harlow do with rhesus monkeys and what importance did the results have for humans and for theories of attachment?

17. What is imprinting, including examples, and how does a theory that incorporates both ethological (phylogenetic ultimate) and psychological (ontogenetic ultimate) causes explain imprinting as well as Harlow's results?

Individual Differences: Intelligence, Personality, and Social Behavior

12

Chapter 11 discussed the development of behavior through childhood. By the time a person enters primary school, there are obvious similarities in how she or he behaves under particular circumstances. Each of us also behaves in ways both similar to and different from other individuals. Any attempt to understand behavior must account for these similarities and differences. Psychologists are referring to these behavioral similarities and differences when they use terms such as *intelligence, personality,* and *social behavior.* For example, when we say that someone has an aggressive personality, we are saying that under certain circumstances this person will predictably behave aggressively. Other individuals, however, may or may not behave aggressively under those same circumstances. The topics of intelligence, personality, and social behavior have long interested psychologists, and we consider them in this chapter, including how scientific psychology would approach the same topics.

Intelligence

The term *intelligence* is used in many different ways. The word comes from the Latin *intellegere,* meaning to perceive or understand, from the roots *inter,* meaning between or among, and *legere,* meaning to gather, pick, or choose. (Notice that these roots do not refer to inferred mental or cognitive processes but, rather, to behavior—gathering, picking, and choosing.) As characteristically used today, **intelligence** refers to the ability of an individual to learn, to remember information and use it appropriately, to solve problems, to acquire and use language, to exercise good judgment, to find similarities and differences, and generally to behave in ways that are deemed appropriate by the culture. As you read on, it is important to remember that intelligence is not a thing (to assume that it is a thing is to commit the error of reification) and, thus, it cannot explain behavior.

Intelligence is typically measured through the use of standardized tests. The first such test was developed in France by Alfred Binet. Binet, whose initial test appeared in 1904, had one practical goal: to devise an instrument appropriate for detecting schoolchildren likely to need special services (e.g., mentally retarded children). With the help of his student Theophile Simon, Binet published three versions of the scale before his death in 1911. In each version, the child was required to perform a series of short tasks, each related to everyday problems. As Stephen Jay Gould (1981) explained:

> Binet decided to assign an age level to each task, defined as the youngest age at which a child of normal intelligence would be able to complete the task successfully. A child began the Binet test with tasks for the youngest age and proceeded in sequence until he could no longer complete the tasks. The age associated with the last tasks he could perform became his "mental age," and his general intellectual level was calculated by subtracting this mental age from his true chronological age. Children whose mental ages were sufficiently behind their chronological ages could then be identified for special educational programs. . . . In 1912 the German psychologist W. Stern argued that mental age should be divided by chronological age, not subtracted from it, and the intelligence *quotient,* or IQ, was born. (pp. 149–150; emphasis in origial)

Gould further noted that Binet insisted on three cardinal principles for using his tests:

1. The scores are a practical device; they do not buttress any theory of intellect. They do not define anything innate or permanent. We may not designate what they measure as "intelligence" or any other reified entity.
2. The scale is a rough, empirical guide for identifying mildly retarded and learning-disabled children who need special help. It is not a device for ranking children.
3. Whatever the cause of difficulty in children identified for help, emphasis shall be placed upon improvement through special training. Low scores shall not be used to mark children as innately incapable. (p. 150)

Unfortunately, the history of the intelligence testing movement, especially in the United States, shows that all three of these principles have been repeatedly violated, resulting in untold harm being caused for countless individuals.

The first useful version of Binet and Simon's test, called the Binet-Simon Scale, was published in 1905. This test was translated into English and revised as the Stanford-Binet scale. These tests were the first of what eventually became dozens of intelligence tests (e.g., Flanagan, Genshaft, & Harrison, 1997). The Wechsler scales, the intelligence tests most often used by psychologists today (Wilson & Reschly, 1996), were designed to provide a measure of "global intelligence" (Wechsler, 1991), but they also provide scores in several subtest areas.

Like most modern intelligence tests, the Wechsler scales do not calculate intelligence by comparing mental age to chronological age. Although the formula for calculating IQ, that is, mental age/chronological age) × 100, was popular for many years, an individual's knowledge and abilities (which determine "mental age") do not increase progressively over time. For example, a person who is 60 years of age will not do twice as well as he or she did at 30. In fact, performance is apt to be similar, or somewhat poorer, at the older age. Today, instead of expressing IQ as a ratio of mental age to chronological age, most scales yield a **deviation IQ,** which expresses a given person's score in relation to scores earned by other people of the same age. These individuals are the group of individuals who are actually tested during standardization of the test. Their scores constitute the norm against which the score of an individual is compared.

As with several other intelligence scales, the reliability of the Wechsler Adult Intelligence Scale–Revised (WAIS-R) is rather good. That is, a person's scores tend to be similar if she or he takes the test on multiple occasions. But are intelligence tests really useful?

Intelligence tests are useful primarily as devices for predicting success in school (Reschly & Grimes, 1995). The primary value of being able to predict academic success is to provide special services for individuals with special needs or talents. Recall that this was the purpose for which Binet developed the first intelligence test. Other purposes, such as screening applicants for jobs, are more controversial. There is ongoing debate concerning the extent to which intelligence tests measure innate ability, as opposed to learned information, and concerning how many kinds of intelligence exist (Flanagan et al., 1997) (see Sidebar 12-1). Also, cultural bias has been a problem with many tests, although steps have been taken to correct this problem (Helms, 1997). Cultural, racial, and socioeconomic variables appear to influence nearly all aspects of human behavior, including performance on standardized tests (Grubb & Dozier, 1989; Willis, 1989). Historically, intelligence tests have emphasized behaviors that are most readily acquired in White American middle to upper-class environments. Such emphasis obscures innate ability and penalizes people from other cultures. Given this, and the limited predictive value of intelligence tests, a warning first stated by Reschly in 1979 remains appropriate:

Sidebar 12-1
How Many Kinds of Intelligence Are There?

The British psychologist and statistician Charles Spearman discovered that scores on different tests of intelligence were positively correlated with each other and then postulated a common underlying factor, or cause of behavior, which he called *g* for *general intelligence.* In the past several years, however, other theories of intelligence have been offered in which intelligence is seen not as a single general trait but, rather, as a number of different traits or capacities. For example, Howard Gardner, in his book *Frames of Mind: The Theory of Multiple Intelligences* (1983), has postulated no fewer than six intelligences, including linguistic and musical intelligence, logical-mathematical and spatial intelligence, and bodily-kinesthetic and personal intelligence. One of the obvious innovations in Gardner's theory is his inclusion of intelligences not exclusively related to academic success. In fact, a recent trend in the study of intelligence is to expand the concept of intelligence to include capabilities or skills explicitly not related to success in school and, thus, not assessable by conventional IQ tests. Toward that end, some psychologists (e.g., Neisser, 1976; Sternberg, Wagner, Williams, and Horvath, 1995) have distinguished between academic and practical intelligence. Academic intelligence enables one to perform well on school-related tasks and can be assessed by conventional standardized intelligence tests, whereas practical intelligence, known by the ordinary term common-sense, enables one to perform well in the real world.

More recently, in his book *Emotional Intelligence: Why It Can Matter More Than IQ* (1995), Daniel Goleman moves even further away from the conventional and narrow conception of intelligence as a "genetic given that cannot be changed by life experience" (p. xi). Goleman believes a challenging question needs to be answered: "What *can* we change that will help our children fare better in life?" (pp. xi–xii; emphasis in original). For Goleman, the answer lies in the abilities he calls "emotional intelligence," which include, among other capabilities, "self-control, zeal and persistence, and the ability to motivate oneself" (p. xii). Goleman believes that addressing emotional intelligence is not only a practical issue, but a moral one as well. He suggests that parents should better prepare children for life by placing more emphasis on their emotional education.

Because intelligence is not a thing that can be observed independently of the behavior said to reflect it, we may not appropriately ask how many different kinds of intelligence there are. In fact, psychologists cannot even agree on a definition of intelligence. For example, when Sternberg and Detterman (1986) asked two dozen prominent theorists to define intelligence, they got two dozen different definitions. From the perspective of scientific psychology, a more important and potentially useful approach is to look at the behaviors that psychologists and others label intelligence, and try to explain those behaviors according to genetic, physiological, and environmental variables.

IQ tests measure only a portion of the competencies involved with human intelligence. The IQ results are best seen as estimates of likely performance in school and reflections of the degree to which children have mastered the middle class cultural symbols and broad culturally rooted facts, concepts, and problem solving strategies. This information is useful but limited. IQ tests do not reflect innate genetic capacity and the scores are not fixed. Some persons do exhibit significant increases or decreases in their measured intellectual abilities. (p. 224)

Having asked about the usefulness of intelligence tests, we may go one step further and ask if the concept of intelligence itself is useful. After all, in the last century or so, most theories of intelligence were based on the assumption that intelligence is an inherited quality that we all possess in varying degrees and that is relatively fixed. And because proponents of such theories have succeeded in persuading those with political power that standardized intelligence tests reliably measure this fixed quality, these tests have been used to make important decisions about vast numbers of individuals including immigrants, U.S. soldiers in World War I, normal schoolchildren, and the developmentally disabled. Hence, it is important to determine whether or not the concept of intelligence is useful.

We may say that the concept of intelligence is useful, but only as a term to describe behaviors in certain contexts, not to describe people. Intelligence is not a thing that causes behavior; it is an abstraction (i.e., a descriptive term). To further assume that someone's intelligence explains his or her behavior is an example of a scientifically inadequate explanation. A person's behavior is described as intelligent only to the degree that it is exhibited in certain contexts (e.g., in school), and that is the extent of it. If we want to understand behavior that we call *intelligent,* then we need to look at the variables known to influence behavior, such as genes, physiology, and particularly environment. Because people have different genotypes, different learning histories, and, hence, different physiologies, they differ in how they behave, including how readily they learn and remember.

Personality

As with "intelligence," psychologists have had difficulty defining "personality." Sixty years ago, there were more than 50 definitions of the term (Allport, 1937), and no consensus has yet been reached. In fact, Hjelle and Ziegler (1992) suggest that "there may be as many different definitions of the concept of personality as there are psychologists who have tried to define it" (p. 3). In general, when psychologists study **personality**, they are attempting to identify and explain consistencies in behavior across time and situations. As you will see, all attempts to study personality follow from the same basic flaw: the assumption that personality is a thing (which is to commit the error of reification) that each of us possesses and that somehow determines our behavior.

An early attempt to understand consistencies in behavior was made by the famous Greek physician Hippocrates. Hippocrates (c. 460–377 B.C.E.) proposed that body fluids determined general behavior patterns. According to him, the body contains four humors, or fluids: yellow bile, black bile, phlegm, and blood. Behavior was thought to result from the relative quantities of these substances.

For example, those who possessed an abundance of yellow bile were aggressive, excitable, and impulsive; Hippocrates termed these individuals *choleric*.

Like many personality theories to follow, Hippocrates's model accounted for psychopathology (pathological or maladaptive styles of behavior), as well as for differences in the behavior of well-adapted people. It also suggested a strategy for treating psychopathology: Drain the excessive fluid responsible for the undesired behavior. Not unsurprisingly, Hippocrates's model didn't stand the test of time or science.

We may laugh at Hippocrates's theory today, but there is about as much support for it as for many better-known theories of personality, such as Freud's psychoanalytic model. The following section overviews some theories of personality that have been popular over the years. They are of historical importance as organized attempts to explain human behavior. They are of general cultural importance because they have influenced the language used to describe and explain behavior. Have you ever said "____ has a big ego" or "____ is introverted"? If so, you have borrowed terms from a personality theorist.

Freud and Psychoanalysis

Sigmund Freud (1856–1939) was a physician whose work with hysteric patients formed the basis for psychoanalysis. Hysteria is a condition in which the patient acts as though some sensory or motor function is lost when it actually is not. For example, an individual with hysterical paralysis may report not being able to move her arm (most of Freud's patients were female). On the basis of his clinical interactions with patients, Freud fashioned an elaborate theory to explain these symptoms. Over time, the theory was extended to explain the behavior of normal individuals. Freud and his colleagues developed both a set of clinical procedures (e.g., dream analysis, free association) and a theory of personality, and the term **psychoanalysis** is used to refer to both.

In essence, Freud (e.g., 1933, 1938) proposed that human behavior is motivated by instincts. These instincts generate energy which, if not released through behavior, produces tension. The kind of behavior that occurs in response to a particular kind of tension (e.g., that arising from unfulfilled sexual needs) depends on the interaction of three structures: the id, the superego, and the ego. According to Freud, the id is primitive and demands immediate gratification of all needs. The superego requires that the ego choose socially acceptable activity to gratify the needs. The ego mediates between the demands of the id and those of the superego, and decides how needs can be met in the real world. For example, as a result of a gradual increase in sexual energy (from the id), a person (ego) must find a generally socially acceptable way of releasing that energy (superego) and then, on a more practical level, whether such activity is possible in the immediate environment. As you can imagine, such a situation has the potential for producing much sexual tension, or anxiety. Freud did not observe the id, superego, and ego directly, and he could not do so, for they are not physical entities. But he inferred their existence on the basis of how people behave. In other words, he named the behaviors.

Freud believed that anxiety, which primarily arises from conflicts among the demands of the id, the superego, and the external world, warns the ego of impending danger. *Defensive reactions* allow the ego temporarily to reduce conflict and the anxiety associated with it. For example, one defense mechanism, *repression,* involving unconsciously eliminating threatening material from awareness and being unable to recall it on demand, is an especially important defensive reaction. Thus, a person with a great deal of ungratified sexual tension may report that he has not thought about sex for a long time and has no interest in it. A stated goal of psychoanalytic therapy is to bring repressed conflicts to conscious awareness so they can be realized and confronted.

Sexual desires and activities were especially important in Freud's theory, and he proposed that personality developed in a series of stages, during which the anatomical focus of sexual urges (i.e. the *erogenous zones*) shifts. The stages (and the approximate years of age associated with them) are the oral stage (first year), the anal stage (1 to 2 years), the phallic stage (2 to 5 years), the latency stage (6 to 12 years), and the genital stage (12 years and older). Specific experiences that occur during each stage determine a person's subsequent personality and adjustment. Problems can arise at each stage, as when a person becomes fixated. In *fixation,* the focus of pleasure remains at an early erogenous zone, and personality development ceases. For example, from the psychoanalytic perspective, adults who smoke and abuse alcohol may be fixated at the oral stage.

Although not very effective, psychoanalytic therapy remains popular on the east and west coasts of the United States. Certain intellectuals, especially those in the arts and the entertainment industry, continue to make use of psychoanalytic lingo and procedures. For instance, parodies of free association and dream analysis, in which a nonjudgmental clinician listens to a patient talk about dreams and events from the past, are common in books and movies alike. Adding a gray beard to the therapist, sexual problems to the patient's complaints, and a leather couch to the office sets the stage for comedy.

Levity aside, Freud's observations of human behavior were astute, and his attempts to develop effective clinical interventions are noteworthy. Nonetheless, his theory lacks empirical support, and the structures supposedly responsible for behavioral consistencies (id, ego, and superego) are not real structures in the brain. And, despite the fact that they are frequently described as if they were acting like people—the id "seeks gratification," the ego "represses desire," and the superego "demands perfection," they are not homunculi (little people) that control the actions of the body. They are reifications and, as discussed in Chapter 2, reifications cannot provide adequate explanations of behavior.

Reactions to Freud: Adler and Jung

Freud's ideas generated vigorous discussion. Some who were initially intrigued by his theory came eventually to criticize it on various grounds, and to develop their own theories of personality. This section summarizes the views of two such individuals: Alfred Adler and Carl Jung.

Adler and Individual Psychology

Alfred Adler (1870–1937) appears to have been something of a follower of Freud from 1902 until 1911. Over time, Adler came to believe that Freud overemphasized the importance of sexuality as a determinant of behavior and underestimated the importance of the ego defenses. Eventually, Adler (e.g., 1924) developed a theory of personality, termed **individual psychology,** that had little in common with psychoanalysis (Phares, 1984).

Adler emphasized the role of society in determining how people behave. He believed that humans *strive for superiority* or control of their environment. They do so, in part, because as children they develop feelings of inferiority as a result of not being able to control the world around them. In striving for superiority, people set goals for themselves and decide upon *lifestyles* that enable them to accomplish those goals. Some lifestyles are adaptive, others are pathological. Adler believed that *birth order, parental neglect,* and *parental pampering* influenced the lifestyle selected by an individual.

No matter the lifestyle chosen, obstacles in the path toward achieving superiority are inevitable. Adler believed that problems occurred in three general areas: (1) family and other social interactions, (2) school and work, and (3) sex and marriage. Well-adjusted individuals respond to problems in any of these areas with courage, common sense, and concern for the welfare of others as well as for themselves.

Of course, other, less desirable reactions are also possible. For example, a person who has been pampered by parents (i.e., received excessive attention and protection) is apt to develop an *inferiority complex,* in which she or he has exaggerated and pathological feelings of weakness and believes that it is impossible to overcome difficulties through personal effort. When confronted with an obstacle to attaining a goal, such a person is apt to be depressed, demanding, and ineffective. In this case, and in dealing with most other problems, the primary goal of Adlerian psychotherapy would be to reduce feelings of inferiority. As Adler himself put it, "The important thing [in therapy] is to decrease the patient's feeling of inferiority. . . . The method of individual psychology—we have no hesitation in confessing it—begins and ends with the problem of inferiority" (1929, p. 45).

Adler's individual psychology was not especially well developed, and it has had less influence on literature and the everyday culture than has Freud's psychoanalysis. Nonetheless, Adlerian terms such as "inferiority complex," "lifestyle," and "feelings of inferiority" are part of the vernacular, and Adler's view that social interactions are a powerful determinant of human behavior continues to be widely accepted.

Jung and Analytical Psychology

Carl Jung (1875–1961) was a colleague and friend of Freud. But Jung soon found fault with many of Freud's notions, including the importance that Freud assigned to the Oedipus complex. Freud proposed that during the phallic stage, sexual attraction to the parent of the opposite sex develops in both boys (the *Oedipus complex*) and girls (the *Electra complex*). As a result, a difficult stage in the child's life begins in which there is intense resentment of the parent of the same sex. These complexes are resolved only after much effort, if at all. Ewen (1988) notes that "Jung's skepticism about the Oedipus complex may have been due in part to a mother who was a 'kindly, fat old woman' troubled by marital difficulties [reference omitted], an influence different from that of Freud's beautiful, young doting mother" (p. 82). This point is worth making because it emphasizes that theories of personality are influenced by the unique personal experiences of those who formulate them. Personality theorists, like all scholars and scientists, are products of the cultures in which they live and of the unique experiences they have, and this is reflected in their theories. The difference is that most personality theories are not scientific theories and are, thus, not self-correcting in the face of scientific data. In the absence of supporting scientific data, most personality theories must be taken on faith alone.

Jung was not a scientist in the conventional sense, and his view of behavior, like Freud's, was influenced by his knowledge of archaeology, mythology, religion, and Eastern and Western philosophy. In essence, Jung proposed (e.g., Jung, 1928) that the personality is determined by three structures: the ego, the personal unconscious, and the collective unconscious. This *ego* is roughly equivalent to what is called the mind in everyday terms. It contains thoughts, feelings, and memories of which we are aware. The *personal unconscious* contains material that can easily be brought to awareness. The *collective unconscious* is, in Jung's terms, the "deposit of ancestral experience from untold millions of years, the echo of prehistoric world events to which each century adds an infinitesimally small amount of variance and differentiation" (p. 162). Although the contents of the ego and personal unconscious differ from person to person, the contents of the collective unconscious are similar for everyone.

Jung called the contents of the collective unconscious *archetypes,* which are "universal, collective, primordial images" (Phares, 1984, p. 104). Archetypes are determined by the universal experiences of ancestral humans, and they influence how people react to current circumstances. Anima, animus, and shadow are examples of Jungian archetypes. The *anima* represents feminine qualities present in men, the *animus* represents masculine qualities present in women, and the *shadow* represents the sinister and animalistic side of all people. Adler proposed that adjustment requires balancing all archetypes (and, in fact, all aspects of the psyche), so that the person can achieve unity and harmony. For Adler, personality could reflect two ego orientations (introversion and extroversion) and four psychological functions (thinking, feeling, sensing, and intuiting). Thus, eight general personality types are possible. For example, an introvert-intuitive type would focus on her or his inner world, whereas an extrovert-thinking person would focus on obtaining practical facts about the external world (Hjelle & Zigler, 1992).

Although the terms *introvert* and *extrovert* are familiar to most people, and analytical psychology has exerted some influence on intellectuals in recent years, logical and empirical support for Jung's theory is lacking. In fact, because many of his notions are mystical and vague, they are essentially untestable.

Moreover, analytical psychology has not fostered effective strategies for dealing with behavioral problems.

Rogers and Phenomenological Psychology

Carl Rogers's (1902–1987) approach to explaining human behavior, termed **phenomenological** (or **humanistic**) **psychology,** was developed, in part, as a reaction to Skinnerian behaviorism, not to Freudian psychoanalysis. For Rogers (e.g., 1951), humans are inherently good and their lives are characterized by choices, creativity, and growth. People strive for personal fulfillment, and if their choices are not overly restricted, they obtain that goal.

Rogers believed that the *actualizing tendency* is the primary motivator of behavior. This tendency promotes behavior that results in physiological maintenance, growth, maturation, and fulfillment of potentials. Thus, we ensure our physical well-being through eating, drinking, and avoiding injury. We also seek new experiences and learn new skills to grow, enhance our lives, and move toward "self-government, self-regulation, and autonomy, and away from . . . control by external forces" (1951, p. 488). Those experiences that are *perceived* to be self-actualizing, regardless of their physical nature, are actively sought out. For phenomenologists such as Rogers, the only reality that is important to understanding why an individual behaves is the subjective reality that he or she experiences.

The self is an especially important part of subjective reality. Each person has a unique self-concept that develops, in part, as a consequence of certain kinds of interactions with others. Rogers stressed that children must initially be given unconditional positive regard if they are to develop a positive self-concept. From childhood on, people regularly compare their self-concept with how they actually behave. If there is congruity, the person obtains self-regard and feels good. If there is incongruity, however, the person feels threatened and anxious. Two defenses, *denial* and *distortion,* are used to reduce incongruity. In denial, the experience that is inconsistent with the self-concept is denied, and the

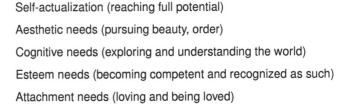

Maslow's Hierarchy of Needs

Self-actualization (reaching full potential)

Aesthetic needs (pursuing beauty, order)

Cognitive needs (exploring and understanding the world)

Esteem needs (becoming competent and recognized as such)

Attachment needs (loving and being loved)

Safety needs (securing a safe and comfortable environment)

Physiological needs (obtaining food, water, oxygen, etc.)

More basic needs ↓

Figure 12-1. Maslow's hierarchy of needs. Maslow proposed that every person ultimately aspired to be self-actualized, but before this could occur, several more basic needs had to satisfied.

self-concept is retained. In distortion, the experience is misrepresented (i.e., distorted). Psychopathology develops when denial and distortion become commonplace. For Rogers, the goal of therapy is eliminating perceived incongruity between experience and the self. This **person-** (or client) **centered therapy,** based on establishing warm and nurturing client–therapist relations, has been widely employed to treat a variety of problems, with variable success (e.g., Levant & Schlein, 1984).

Although self-actualization was for Rogers the cornerstone of a healthy personality, Abraham Maslow (1908–1970), another influential humanistic psychologist, proposed that self-actualization is possible only if other, more basic needs are met. Maslow's hierarchy of needs (1970) is depicted in Figure 12-1.

Bandura and Social Learning Theory

In a sense, any person who develops general ideas about why humans behave as they do is concerned with personality. So, for example, it could be said that B. F. Skinner developed a theory of personality, insofar as he proposed that a combination of environmental, genetic, and physiological variables determine how people behave. He especially emphasized the importance of those environmental variables that contribute to operant conditioning, in particular, the consequences of behavior. Unlike the other personality theorists described in this chapter, Skinner did not propose an enduring structure of personality, nor use personality to explain observed behavior. For him, behavior is consistent across situations only to the extent that the variables that control behavior are consistent across situations, and inferred entities such as personality are irrelevant.

Albert Bandura (1925–), like Skinner, recognizes that consequences play an important role in determining how people behave. But in Bandura's view (e.g., 1977, 1986), called **social learning theory,** both the actual consequences of behavior and an individual's beliefs about the consequences of behavior, termed *expectancies,* determine behavior. He proposed that personality is the result of the interaction between behavior, personal variables such as expectancies, and environmental variables including the actual consequences of behavior. Figure 12-2 depicts this process, which Bandura calls *reciprocal determinism.*

A person's beliefs about the probable consequences of his or her actions are given an especially important role in Bandura's theory. He proposes that information about probable consequences can arise through direct personal experience or

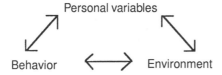

Figure 12-2. Reciprocal determinism as construed by Bandura. Arrows indicate direction of influence; thus, there is an interaction among behavior, personal variables, and the environment.

through observing the consequences of other people's actions. As described in Chapter 7, learning of the latter kind is termed **observational learning.** Observational learning, personal success, emotional arousal, and verbal persuasion from others influence a person's *self-efficacy,* which refers to one's perceived ability to perform behaviors appropriate to a given situation. Self-efficacy determines the probability that an individual will act to change (and improve) his or her world, persistence in the face of difficulty, and emotional reactions. Bandura (e.g., 1986) believes that effective therapy, regardless of how it is performed, strengthens the client's perceived self-efficacy. Therapies with this intended goal have proven useful in treating phobias and anxiety disorders (e.g., Bandura & Adams, 1977). Social learning theory also has formed the basis of a popular self-control program (D. L. Watson & Tharp, 1989).

For Watson and Tharp (1989), self-control occurs when a person comes to emit a desired behavior in place of what was formerly a higher-probability, but undesired, behavior. For example, an overweight person exercises self-control when he or she stops eating rich desserts in favor of more nutritional foods. In many cases, self-control involves foregoing an immediately available but inferior reward in order to receive a more delayed but qualitatively or quantitatively superior reward (cf., Logue, 1995). Watson and Tharp (1989) stress the importance of a data-driven approach to self-control, which entails carefully defining and monitoring the behaviors that are to be changed. Self-reinforcement, self-punishment, and behavioral contracting are among the procedures that may be used to change responding such that self-control occurs. Such an approach to improving human behavior is consistent with the tenets of social learning theory, and with the general dictates of scientific psychology as described throughout this book.

The personality theories described above differ in the details with which they attempt to understand and, explain human behavior. Nevertheless, they share, to varying degrees, one common feature: they all infer unobservable entities and processes (e.g., id, ego, and superego; inferiority complex, personal and collective unconscious; actualizing tendency; expectancies), and then use those entities and processes to explain the very behavior from which they were inferred. Sometimes, theories with questionable scientific validity are used to make decisions about individuals with undesirable consequences (see Sidebar 12-2). Such explanations are, thus, not scientifically adequate. This is not to say that such theories are completely useless. In many instances, the terms used within a particular theory may help to describe or summarize classes of behavior as, for example, when we describe behavior in terms of characteristics such as inferiority, or when we describe someone's behavior as defensive. Toward that end, personality theorists have produced a variety of tests or assessment tools that involve collecting information that allows an individual's general patterns of behavior to be classified and predicted.

Assessing Personality

Personality assessment involves collecting information that allows an individual's general patterns of behavior to be predicted, especially to help in the diagnosis of various forms of mental illness. Most of the major personality the-

---

Sidebar 12-2
Constitutional Personality Theory and the Ivy League Nude Posture Photo Scandal

In January, 1995, an article in the *New York Times Sunday Magazine* titled "The Great Ivy League Nude Posture Photo Scandal" described how, beginning as early as the 1920s, but especially during a period of time from the 1940s to the 1960s, thousands of nude photographs were taken of entering freshman students at many prestigious colleges and universities, including Yale, Princeton, Smith, Mt. Holyoke, and Vassar, to name only a few. Some of the individuals who were photographed include Hillary Rodham Clinton, Diane Sawyer, Meryl Streep, Robert Woodward, and George Bush. These photographs were taken under the guise of scientific research. W. H. Sheldon (1898–1977), the psychologist who developed a constitutional personality theory, convinced leaders of intellectual institutions across the country that much about a person's personality could be predicted by his or her particular body type, or somatotype (*soma* is the Greek word for "body").

Sheldon designed very specific procedures for assessing a person's somatotype. Over many years, Sheldon took photographs of thousands of men and women in order to study their physical characteristics. Using standardized camera equipment and lighting, he first obtained three photographs of each subject, one each from the front, back, and side. Subjects were photographed naked to permit a clear view of the entire body. He then evaluated the physical structure of each subject according to the relative presence of three classes of characteristics, termed endomorphy (endomorphs are rounded and spherical in appearance, with well-endowed abdomens), mesomorphy (mesomorphs are upright, sturdy, and rectangular, with large blood vessels, thick skin, and an upper chest area that is more developed than that of endomorphs), and ectomorphy (ectomorphs are thin, with long appendages and fine bone structures) (Sheldon, 1942). After careful study of the photographs, Sheldon assigned a number from 1 to 7 that reflected the presence of each of the three components; the higher the number, the more that component was represented in the person's physique. The resultant three-digit scores represented the person's somatotype.

Sheldon also needed to assess the personalities of his subjects to see if his prediction about the correspondence of morphology (the structural characteristics of the body) and behavior was justified. Sheldon identified 650 personality traits of interest. After condensing these to a series of 50, Sheldon interviewed 33 men. From these interviews and subsequent refinements, he identified three clusters of behavioral characteristics, or traits. Each cluster had 20 traits. Traits within clusters were often found together in a person, while traits from different clusters were not. Behavioral assessments that consisted of in-depth interviews with each subject were conducted with the Scale for Temperament.

Having devised a way to assess body type and behavioral characteristics (he called the latter "temperament"), Sheldon examined the extent to which somatotypes and behavior were associated. The results of his efforts suggested a relation between physique and behavioral characteristics. As a case in point, Sheldon found a relation between somatotype and antisocial behavior. From 1939 to 1946, he observed 200 juvenile delinquents who were referred to a Boston social agency. The results showed that the delinquents had more mesomorphic characteristics than did a collection of nondelinquent subjects. Moreover, Sheldon suggested that there was a relation between particular somatotypes and specific psychiatric disturbances. He posited, for instance, that manic-depressive patients (who experience wild swings of emotion) suffer from a lack of restraint and control, a characteristic typical of an absence of ectomorphic characteristics.

Like many other psychological theories, including personality theories, Sheldon's theory lacks scientific merit. At best, Sheldon showed nothing more than that certain features of physique and behavior may be correlated. He did not show that one caused the other, nor explain the mechanism through which they might vary together. At worst, Sheldon perpetrated a kind of pseudoscience that at least for many college freshmen proved to be insulting and humiliating. If there is in fact a relation between physique and behavior, does physique influence behavior? Or does behavior influence physique? In the former explanation, people with mesomorphic characteristics will be more successful in athletics and may, therefore, "love exercise" and be "competitive." In the latter,

(continued)

Sidebar 12-2
(Continued)

a child encouraged by her parents to engage in athletics may, as a result, develop the mesomorphic characteristics of a well-muscled body. Or perhaps both are a product of heredity, environmental factors, or a combination of the two (see Hall & Lindsey, 1985). The point is that a *correlation* between two variables does not imply a particular *causal relation* between them.

If there is a moral of the nude posture photo scandal, it is that any theory that lacks a scientific foundation should be viewed with extreme skepticism and should be subjected to experimental verification, especially before we permit outselves to change cultural practices because of it.

---

orists have developed their own strategies for assessing personality. Freud, for example, assumed that most important behaviors are controlled by unconscious processes which cannot be revealed by straightforward questioning of individuals. Given this orientation, psychoanalytic theorists developed **projective tests,** in which an individual is shown an ambiguous stimulus and asked either to report what she or he "sees," or to create stories based on the stimulus. The Rorschach Inkblot test (see Figure 12-3) and the Thematic Apperception Test (TAT) are well-known projective tests.

Individuals' responses to ambiguous stimuli, like those in the Rorschach test, often differ substantially across time and situations, and there is little agreement about what, if anything, these responses reveal about behavior (or personality) in other contexts (Anastasi, 1988; Greenwald, 1990; Lanyon & Goodstein, 1982). Although some writers continue to argue that projective tests are useful in revealing hidden causes of behavior (e.g., Watkins, 1991), it appears that precedent is the primary justification for their continued popularity.

Objective tests characteristically involve multiple-choice and true–false questions that are easy to score. The most common objective personality test is the Minnesota Multiphasic Personality Inventory (MMPI), which was revised and restructured as the MMPI-2 in 1989. The MMPI-2 comprises 567 true–false questions. Like intelligence tests, it is a norm-referenced test, which means that an individual's performance is compared to that of other people who have taken the test. The MMPI was developed to help in the diagnosis of psychological disorders (Hathaway & McKinley, 1943). This goal was accomplished by administering many questions to groups of individuals with different diagnoses (e.g., depression, schizophrenia) and to control groups consisting of friends and relatives of the diagnosed individuals. Questions to which people with a particular diagnosis responded differently from other people became part of the assessment scale for that disorder. If, for example, people diagnosed with depression were more likely to answer true to "I usually feel hopeless and forlorn," that question became part of the clinical scale for depression. Comparing an individual's scores on the various scales to norm values helps a psychologist to characterize that individual in terms of a diagnostic category, and to select an appropriate treatment strategy.

The various personality tests vary substantially in reliability, meaningfulness, and predictive validity. As with intelligence tests, personality tests sample only a limited range of behaviors, under a limited (and often artificial) range

Figure 12-3. An inkblot similar to a Rorschach Inkblot. What does it look like to you?

of conditions. Although the resultant information may be useful in predicting how a person will behave in other settings, accuracy of prediction is imperfect and often low. Even when the accuracy of prediction is high enough to be of practical value, the information obtained with the personality test does not explain the predicted behavior.

Consider a hypothetical study reporting that people who score high on a depression scale are in the next year more likely to commit suicide, take antidepressant medications, and lose their jobs than are people who score low on the same scale. One way to interpret these findings is to say that the scale revealed that some people (high scorers) had depression, which caused some of them to seek treatment (take drugs), lose a job, or even commit suicide. But what is the nature of this depression? Where is it located? What causes it? The simple finding that there is a correlation between scores on a depression scale and subsequent behaviors does not provide an answer. In fact, the scores on the test, losing jobs, taking antidepressant medications, and committing suicide are related behaviors, all of which are labeled with the term "depression." Depression in this sense is a descriptive, not an explanatory, concept.

Discovering the ultimate causes of depression either in the individual's past environment (ontogenetic history) or genes (phylogenetic history) is a difficult task. Moreover, the same variables that control reactions to the instruments used to measure depression also control the depressive behaviors (suicide, taking antidepressants, losing a job in our example) that the instruments are used to predict. Depression as measured by a personality test refers to *what* a person does, not *why* he or she does those things. The same is true of other personality traits, and of personality in general.

For scientific psychologists, the task in understanding personality is to look at the behaviors from which personality is inferred, and then to attempt to explain those behaviors in more parsimonious terms, that is, according to the laws of scientific psychology.

Social Behavior

The ways that people act with respect to one another—that is, **social behavior**—are a big part of what we commonly call their personalities. As discussed in Chapters 10 and 11, social interactions begin very early in life and play a crucial role in the formation and maintenance of many important human behaviors, especially those that involve language (Chapter 7). We are first and foremost social beings. Consider your daily activities. You probably live with someone, you may have your meals in a cafeteria or restaurant surrounded by diners, you attend classes with fellow students, and you engage in recreational and social activities with friends. It should come as no surprise that other people powerfully influence your behavior—and that you influence theirs.

Social isolation early in life can be devastating to the development of a child. The "Wild Boy of Aveyron," Victor, is a case in point. Victor had apparently been abandoned by his family many years before he was captured by hunters in the Cauned Woods near Aveyron, France. When captured in 1799, Victor was about 11 years old, and his behavior more closely resembled that of a wild animal than a typical human child. He was brought to Jean Marc Gaspard Itard (1774–1838), a prominent French physician, who spent five years attempting to educate the feral (i.e., wild or untamed) child. Itard's main concern was to transform Victor from "savagery to civilization, from natural to social life" (Kanner, 1964). Itard is reported to have named the boy Victor as a sign of the victory that education should achieve in him over brute nature (Sequin, 1966). Itard's teaching methods were based primarily on intensive interaction with the child and systematic consequences for his behavior. Over time, Victor developed relatively good manners and self-care skills. He could recognize objects, identify letters of the alphabet, and comprehend the meanings of many words and phases. However, because Victor did not develop speech, Itard considered his efforts a failure. We now know that infancy and early childhood is an especially sensitive time for the acquisition of social behaviors in general, and verbal behavior in particular, and that if such behaviors are not acquired by the age of six or seven, they will be very difficult to learn.

Fortunately, for most people lack of social interaction is not a problem: Our behaviors are constantly molded by the actions of others. How this occurs is the subject matter of **social psychology**, which encompasses the study of the effects of other people on the behavior of the individual. Social psychology deals with the structure of all human interactions, and is therefore one of the most diverse fields within psychology. Virtually all social situations have been subjected to scrutiny by social psychologists. As B. Guerin (1994) explains, social psychologists traditionally have (1) categorized patterns of interaction, (2) given those behavioral phenomena names, and (3) attempted to isolate the conditions under which they occur.

This strategy has revealed a number of interesting patterns of behavior. We know, for instance, that people sometimes work harder in a group than alone, a phenomenon known as *social facilitation.* Of course, in some situations, being part of a group reduces productivity; this phenomenon is called *social loafing.* Hundreds of studies have attempted to distinguish the conditions under which social facilitation and social loafing occur, and many theories have been advanced to explain these patterns (B. Guerin, 1993). B. Guerin (1994) proposed that social facilitation, and other subjects of interest to social psychologists, can best be understood as operant behaviors, which are controlled primarily by their consequences (see Chapter 6). He noted: "Behaviors have consequences in certain contexts which can affect the likelihood of occurring again in that context or in similar contexts" (p. 18). The contingencies between contexts, behaviors and consequences form the subject matter of scientific psychology as discussed in this book.

Many of the most important consequences of social behavior are mediated by other people. Groups of individuals who interact and arrange similar consequences for particular behaviors constitute communities or subcultures. Because they typically use (i.e., react to) language in similar fashion, they also are called verbal communities (Chapter 7). Communities often arrange consequences in a rather imprecise (and, as in the case of ritualistic behavior, sometimes arbitrary) fashion, which makes it difficult to describe precisely the contingencies that control social behavior. Doing so is further complicated by the fact that most social behaviors are controlled by complex and overlapping contingencies, which vary for different communities and, sometimes, for members of the same community. As Guerin (1994) points out:

> [Many] behaviors function merely to maintain the verbal communities, because of their many advantages. The function of such "symbolic" behaviors therefore has little to do with what is done: the doing of the symbolic behavior or ritual is itself the function, since it acts to maintain the group as a whole. For example, the function of taking bread in the Catholic Mass should not be analyzed in terms of eating food; the function is one of maintaining the community [of Catholics] itself. (p. 19)

Finally, social behavior often is controlled by rules as well as direct-acting contingencies, and our understanding of the origin and function of rules is only rudimentary (see Chapter 7). It is no easy task to analyze the contingencies responsible for human social behavior. But contingencies clearly determine, in large part, how humans interact, and must be emphasized in a natural-science approach. The alternative, which involves describing the social context in which particular behavioral phenomena (e.g., social loafing, social facilitation) occur, has neither led to a general theory of social behavior nor generated a technology for improving how we interact.

In the remainder of this section, we describe three patterns of interaction that social psychologists call *social influence:* conformity, compliance, and obedience; they are amenable to a scientific interpretation.

Conformity

Look at the two sets of lines in Figure 12-4. Which of the three comparison lines is most like the standard line? Chances are quite good that you can make the right choice. Now imagine that you are seated alongside four other people who, like you, are participating in an experiment. The first time the group is asked which line matches the standard line, all of you give the correct answer. The second time everyone again answers correctly. The third time, however, the first person gives an answer inconsistent with what you think is correct. The second, third, and fourth persons all give the same answer as the first person. It is now your turn. Do you give the answer that the four others gave or the one that you believe is correct? If you are like most people you are much less likely to answer correctly in this situation than if you were asked the question with no one else around. Solomon Asch (1956) performed this classic experiment and found that persons who answered alone gave correct answers 99 percent of the time. When seated in a group of others who were answering incorrectly, the correct answers dropped to 63 percent. Thus, even though the subjects "knew" the correct answer, they often behaved as others in the group had.

Conformity is defined as a change in behavior as a result of implicit group pressure. Behavior is considered an example of conformity only if it differs from what it would be if the person were alone. For instance, cheering for your favorite team in a crowded bar provides no evidence of conformity, but cheering for a team you dislike does.

Conformity is a part of all of our lives. Even groups that expressly emphasize nonconformity may foster conformity. For example, the hippies of the 1960s were nonconformists with respect to the general culture or "establishment," but they obviously conformed to their own "counterculture" in terms of dress, language, drug use, and sexual practices. Each fall, conformity may be observed on college campuses as the behavior of newly arriving freshmen changes to resemble (i.e., conform with) that of other students.

Four major factors affecting conformity have been identified: the size of the group, ambiguity with respect to appropriate behavior, the perceived expertise

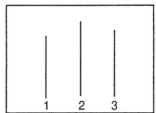

Figure 12-4. In the study by Asch (1956), subjects were shown two cards similar to those above. The subject's task was to choose the line in the group of three that was the same length as the single line on the other card. (From *Psychology: A Behavioral Overview* [p. 263], by A. Poling, H. Schlinger, S. Starin, and E. Blakely, 1990, New York: Plenum Press. Copyright 1990 by Plenum Press. Reprinted with permission.)

of group members, and the presence of an ally. With small groups, the greater the number of people, the greater the degree of conformity. After group size reaches six or seven, however, further increases in size have little effect on conformity (Roediger, Rushton, Capaldi, & Paris, 1984).

As a rule, degree of conformity increases when it is difficult to formulate clear rules about appropriate behavior, that is, when the situation is ambiguous. It also increases when members of the group are perceived to be experts. A fourth factor shown to affect conformity is the presence or absence of another person who resists pressure to conform. One is less likely to conform when there is another person present who resists conformity (Roediger et al., 1984).

Why does conformity occur? One reason is that most people have a history in which behaving as others behave was in many situations more successful (i.e., produced reinforcing consequences) than behaving differently. A second is that most people also have a history in which following rules consistent with the norm has been reinforced. "When in Rome, do as the Romans do" is not idle advice; our behavior is typically more successful in novel situations if it mimics the behaviors that occur around us.

Conformity obviously does not occur in all situations. Most of us have experienced occasions in which going with the flow has been counterproductive. In such cases, the probability of conforming in similar circumstances weakens. An adolescent who, for example, engages in vandalism in the presence of friends is less likely to repeat the act if caught and immediately punished. Moreover, many people have histories that foster noncompliant behaviors in certain situations. For instance, some drug-naive adolescents do not try drugs even though they are in the presence of drug users. This reflects in large part a history that fosters rule-governed behavior incompatible with drug use (see Chapter 13). Of course, adolescents trying drugs in the presence of drug users is described as conforming behavior.

Compliance

Whereas conformity involves behavior change as a result of indirect pressure to behave in a certain manner, **compliance** involves behaving in a manner consistent with a direct request for a certain form of behavior. For example, if someone asks if he may go ahead of you in a checkout line and you allow him to do so, your behavior demonstrates compliance. One learns to comply with requests because (a) doing so at least occasionally yields a positively reinforcing outcome (e.g., a "thank you"), and (b) failing to do so at least occasionally yields an aversive outcome (e.g., a scowl or frown) which can only be terminated by complying (negative reinforcement).

Although the mechanisms responsible for compliance are at one level simple, the variables that determine whether or not it occurs are complex. For example, Freedman and Fraser (1966) found that once someone complies with a relatively small request, they are much more likely to comply with a larger request. In their study, California women were approached and asked to place a small sign in their window or to sign a petition to keep California beautiful. Later, the women were asked to place in their yards a very large billboard promoting safe driving. Seventy-six percent of the women agreed. In contrast, only 17% of the members of a control group who were only asked to place the billboard in their yard agreed to do so. Freedman and Fraser called this method of obtaining compliance the "foot-in-the-door technique."

Cialdini and colleagues (1975) developed a different technique for inducing compliance. They called it the "door-in-the-face technique." With this approach, subjects are first asked to comply with a request that requires a considerable expenditure of money, time, or effort. Most refuse. The subjects are then asked to comply with a much less costly request. Most comply. For example, Cialdini and colleagues first asked college students if they would commit two years to be a counselor for delinquent children (large request). All refused. They then asked whether the students would agree to take a delinquent child to the zoo. Fifty-six percent of the them agreed to the smaller request. Only 32% of a control group, who were asked only to take children to the zoo, agreed. These data suggest that asking for something very large and then "settling" for something smaller is another method through which compliance can be achieved.

Obedience

Although the phenomena are similar, social psychologists often differentiate compliance and obedience. As usually conceived, compliance involves doing as requested by any other person, whereas **obedience** involves doing as ordered by a person of some authority. Although obedience may be necessary for the survival of a culture, blind obedience can be troublesome. One of the most devastating examples of obedience was the extermination by the Nazis of 8 million Jews, Gypsies, homosexuals, and other "undesirables." During the Holocaust, hundreds of German citizens routinely participated in torture and killing of these individuals. When questioned at the Nuremberg war crime trials, these people characteristically argued that they were "only following orders." Why did they do so? Could such a thing happen in other cultures? Would most people knowingly inflict injury on another person simply because they were ordered to do so?

In one of the most famous—and infamous—experiments in social psychology, Stanley Milgram (1963) investigated obedience to authority in 40 men who agreed to participate in what was described as a study of the effects of punishment on learning being conducted at Yale University. The experimenter explained to each subject that the procedure would involve a "teacher" and a "learner." The learner's task was to memorize a list of words, the teacher's task was to punish incorrect responses with electric shock. Subjects drew cards to determine which role they would play. Unbeknownst to them, all of the cards read "TEACHER" and the people who served as learners were confederates of the experimenter.

After roles had been assigned, the subject was shown an imposing shock generator with a row of 30 switches and given a sample shock to show that it worked. The subject also saw the learner being strapped into a chair with electrodes placed on his arm. The switches were labeled to indicate voltage, and signs above the switches from left to right read Slight Shock, Moderate Shock, Strong Shock, Very Strong Shock, Intense Shock, Extreme Intensity Shock, and Danger: Severe Shock. The last two switches were designated simply XXX.

The teacher was instructed to read a list of questions to the learner through a microphone. The learner supposedly responded through a microphone placed in his room. Each time the learner made a mistake, the teacher was told to administer a shock to him. The lowest intensity shock was to follow the first mistake, the second-lowest intensity shock was to follow the second mistake, and so on. Actually, answers were standardized on tape and no shocks were delivered; the learner behaved, however, as if shocked. At 75 volts he began to grunt and moan. At 150 volts the learner demanded to be let out of the experiment. At 180 volts he cried that he could not stand the pain. At 300 volts he pounded on the wall. At 330 volts he became silent (and taped answers ceased). At this point the subject was instructed to treat no answer as an incorrect answer and to administer the shock. If at any point the subject began to hesitate or question giving the shock, he was told that he had no choice in the matter and that he must continue.

Milgram (1963) was interested primarily in how far subjects would go before refusing to administer any more shocks. His results are summarized in Figure 12-5. One-hundred percent of the subjects gave shocks through the intense

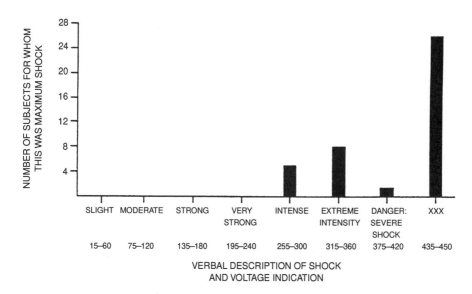

Figure 12-5. The number of subjects in Milgram's (1963) study for whom the listed value was the maximum shock intensity delivered. This figure was prepared from data presented in tabular form by Milgram. (From *Psychology: A Behavioral Overview* [p. 267], by A. Poling, H. Schlinger, S. Starin, and E. Blakely, 1990, New York: Plenum Press. Copyright 1990 by Plenum Press. Reprinted with permission.

level, and 65% delivered the full range of shocks. These findings show clearly that ordinary people will in some cases knowingly inflict injury upon another when ordered to do so. Another finding of interest is that many of the subjects were obviously in considerable distress but nevertheless continued delivering the shocks:

> I observed a mature and initially poised businessman enter the laboratory smiling and confident. Within 20 minutes he was reduced to a twitching, stuttering wreck, who was rapidly approaching a point of nervous collapse. He constantly pulled on his earlobe, and twisted his hands. At one point he pushed his fist into his forehead and muttered: "Oh God, let's stop it." And yet he continued to respond to every word of the experimenter, and obeyed to the end. (377)

Subsequent research by Milgram and others has revealed several variables that affect obedience. Having the learner within sight of the subject reduced the number of persons completing the entire sequence of shocks to approximately 40%. Requiring the subject to hold the learner's arm on the shock plate further reduced obedience to 30%. In another study in which the experimenter left the room and communicated with the subject via the phone, obedience was approximately 23%.

The prestige associated with Yale University in contributing to the obtained effects was shown in another experiment. Here, the location of the experiment was moved to a run-down neighborhood and only 48% of subjects delivered the entire range of shocks (65% did so at Yale). Finally, the presence of two nonobedient allies decreased the obedience to approximately 10%. Gender and country of citizenship were unrelated to probability of obedience.

Milgram's studies raise important ethical issues. Should researchers be allowed to conduct investigations in which subjects experience strong emotional distress? Should all aspects of the experiment be revealed beforehand to subjects? Milgram argued that his experiment was ethical because all of the subjects were debriefed and the experiment was explained in full after their participation. They were told that no shocks actually had been delivered and were allowed to meet the learner to see that he was unhurt. Eighty-four percent of the subjects reported that they were happy to have participated in the study. Nevertheless, it is unlikely that studies similar to Milgram's could be conducted today. Human subjects review boards, which characteristically evaluate all institutional (e.g., university, government) research with respect to costs and benefits to subjects, undoubtedly would find the protocol unacceptable. Moreover, contemporary researchers characteristically are required to obtain informed consent from all subjects. Securing informed consent involves apprising subjects of the purpose of, and any potentially harmful effects that may result from, a study. Milgram's procedure relied on subterfuge—had the subjects been informed that they weren't really delivering shocks, the results would have been meaningless—but such a practice is inconsistent with informed consent.

Apart from the ethical issues that it raises, Milgram's work is interesting in demonstrating that although there are general consistencies in behavior among people from the same culture, individual differences were nonetheless evident. Although all of the subjects in his 1963 study administered shocks through the intense level, 35% were unwilling to go to higher levels. What variables probably accounted for the difference in their behavior? Would it be possible to predict accurately on the basis of a personality test who would and would not administer intense shocks?

The Appeal and Peril of Nominal Psychologies

Before psychologists can understand behavioral phenomena they must categorize them (i.e., group them together because of what appear to be common features). As behaviors are categorized, they typically are assigned names. Personality theorists, for example, have named many different personality traits and types (e.g., introversion and extroversion), and social psychologists have classified many different social relations, including persuasion, altruism, love, and aggression. As you will see in the next chapter, clinical psychologists and psychiatrists have named hundreds of "mental disorders," which are more or less specific kinds of troublesome behaviors.

Trouble arises when (a) names are assumed to explain behavioral phenomena (nominal fallacy), or (b) the same name is assigned to unlike behaviors. The nominal fallacy, that is, the false notion that naming something explains it, was considered in Chapter 2. The problem that arises when the same name is assigned to unlike behaviors is evident if one considers "aggression," which is a topic of interest to many types of psychologists, including social psychologists, personality theorists, and clinical (applied) psychologists. No single definition of aggression is generally accepted; the term is applied to a wide and varied range of behavioral interactions. In most cases, **aggression** is used to describe situations where one organism emits behavior directed toward harming another (e.g., Hinde & Stevenson-Hinde, 1973). The harm may be direct or indirect, physiological or psychological, but it must not be "accidental."

Consider the following scenarios:

1. A red-tailed hawk kills and eats a blue jay.
2. A baseball player crashes into the catcher on a close play at home.
3. A youth strikes an elderly woman in the face, grabs her purse and runs away.
4. Two bighorn rams repeatedly slam into one another.
5. A U.S. navy pilot fires a missile, downing a Libyan warplane and killing all aboard.

Each statement describes a behavior that might be used as an example of aggression. But the behaviors in question are very different in form and in cause. The variables that control behaviors labeled as "aggressive" are many and complex; there is no single cause of aggression and it is useless to ask "What causes aggression?" It may, of course, be possible to determine the variables that control specific "aggressive" behaviors, such as the five examples listed above, and there may be some overlap in the causal variables. There is good reason to group together behaviors that have common controlling variables, perhaps as specific forms of aggressive behavior (e.g., operant aggression or predatory aggression). But it must be recognized that "operant aggression" or "predatory aggression," like aggression in general, is not a cause of anything. A bully who beats other people does not do so because he or she is aggressive; rather, she or he is called "aggressive" (and a "bully") by virtue of beating people. Aggression has no legitimate status as a causal variable. The same is true of that vast majority of behavior names developed by psychologists. At the risk of redundancy, it is worth reemphasizing that the only legitimate causes of behavior are environmental, genetic, and physiological variables. Scientific psychologists have discovered some of the variables that influence behaviors labeled as "aggressive."

For the most part, psychologists have focused on within-species aggression, with a particular interest in our own species. Several variables are known to affect the likelihood that one person will act to harm another. One is exposure to an aversive stimulus. As Hutchinson (1977) notes, "Numerous studies have shown that the delivery of an intense aversive, noxious, or unpleasant stimulus will produce, in a variety of species, movement toward, contact with, and possibly destruction of, animate or inanimate objects in the environment" (p. 418). If, for example, two rats are placed on a metal floor through which

Painful stimulation of one rat will elicit aggressive behavior if another rat is present. Photo courtesy of Roger Ulrich. (From *Psychology: A Behavioral Overview* [p. 273], by A. Poling, H. Schlinger, S. Starin, and E. Blakely, 1990, New York: Plenum Press. Copyright 1990 by Plenum Press. Reprinted with permission.)

electric shock is delivered, the rats will fight. This is termed *pain-elicited aggression*. In a human demonstration of the phenomenon, Berkowitz and Frodi (1977) had experimental subjects put their hand in ice water for seven minutes (the ice water was painful but caused no tissue damage). The control group placed their hands in cool (i.e., not painful) water. Members of both groups were then allowed to either reinforce or punish (with shock) the behavior of a (nonexistent) person waiting in the next room. Subjects in the experimental group delivered more shocks than persons in the control group. Moreover, they also reported more feelings of annoyance and anger. You may have observed pain-elicited aggression in your own repertoire: Have you ever harmed something just after it injured you? And have you ever struck a vending machine that failed to deliver either a snack or a refund? If so, your aggressive behavior was extinction-induced (e.g., Azrin, Hutchinson & Hake, 1966; Rilling & Caplan, 1973). *Extinction-induced aggression* occurs when a response that was previously reinforced ceases to produce a reinforcing consequence (see Chapter 6). Such situations often produce the emotional state that we label as "frustration," and some social psychologists have posited that aggression is frustration-induced (e.g. Dollard, Dobb, Miller, Morer, & Sears, 1939). In actuality, both aggression and frustration are probably reactions to the same environmental variables (e.g., extinction), including those that occur within the person's skin (e.g., covert self-talk).

In many cases, aggressive behavior is learned through operant conditioning. When this occurs, the consequences of behavior labeled as aggressive serve to increase its future probability. Skinner (1974) states:

> Aggressive behavior may be innate and released by specific circumstances in which survival value is plausible. An infant or child may bite, scratch, or strike if physically restrained when it could not have learned to do so. Or the behavior may be shaped and maintained because people are susceptible to reinforcement by signs of damage to others. The capacity to be reinforced when an opponent cries out or runs away would have survival value because a person so endowed would quickly learn to defend himself. Or, third, the behavior may be reinforced by consequences not explicitly related to aggression. Food and sexual contact, reinforcing for other reasons, may reinforce an attack on a competitor if food or a sexual partner is thus obtained. (p. 43)

Interestingly, in some situations, stimuli that elicit or evoke aggressive behavior serve as positive reinforcers. For example, laboratory mice will run mazes for the opportunity to fight with other mice (Lagenspetz, 1964). And male Siamese fighting fish and gamecocks will respond to produce visual access to a male conspecific, to which they will aggressively display (Thompson, 1963, 1964). How these findings relate to human behavior is uncertain, but it is clear that in some situations harming another person is reinforcing.

"Aggression" was considered at some length for three reasons: (1) aggression and other social relations (e.g., cooperation, altruism, attraction) have long interested social psychologists; (2) the ambiguities inherent in the term illustrate the problems of meaningfully classifying behaviors; and (3) ambiguities and the temptation of the nominal fallacy notwithstanding, it is possible to analyze the variables that control important human behaviors, including those we label aggressive. Classifying and naming behaviors, though arduous, is but the first stage in understanding human behavior from a natural science perspective. The second step is isolating the genetic, physiological, and environmental variables responsible for interesting classes of behavior. Unfortunately, many areas of psychology are stuck at stage one.

Summary

1. Although the term "intelligence" is used in many different ways, as characteristically used today, *intelligence* refers to the ability of an individual to learn, to remember information and use it appropriately, to solve problems, to acquire and use language, to exercise good judgment, to find similarities and differences, and generally to behave in ways that are deemed appropriate by the culture.

2. The first standardized intelligence test was developed in France by Alfred Binet for the purpose of detecting which school children were likely to need special services. Subsequent versions of Binet's intelligence test, for example, the Stanford-Binet scale, were used for purposes other than those suggested by Binet, for example, to support innate theories of intelligence and to rank children according to their presumed intelligence.

3. The intelligence tests most often used by psychologists today are the Wechsler scales, which were designed to provide a measure of global intelligence.

4. Today, instead of expressing IQ as a ratio of mental age to chronological age, most scales yield a *deviation IQ,* which expresses a given person's score in relation to scores earned by other people of the same age.

5. Although the reliability of intelligence tests is quite good, such tests are useful primarily as devices for predicting success in school. Still, it must be remembered that intelligence is not a thing, but rather a descriptive term, and, thus, cannot cause behavior.

6. For the same reasons, personality is as difficult to define as intelligence, although in general, when psychologists study *personality,* they are attempting to identify consistencies in behavior across time and situations and to explain those consistencies.

7. Well known personality theories have been proposed by Freud (psychoanalysis) and his intellectual relatives Adler (individual psychology) and Jung (analytical psychology); Rogers (phenomenological, or humanistic, psychology); and Bandura (social learning theory), to mention some of the more prominent ones.

8. Although the language of personality theories may help to describe or summarize classes of behavior, the behavior is not thereby explained. The task for scientific psychologists is to attempt to explain behavior in more parsimonious terms, that is, according to the laws of scientific psychology.

9. Personality assessment, usually through some kind of test such as the MMPI (Minnesota Multiphasic Personality Inventory), involves collecting information that allows an individual's general patterns of behavior to be pre-

dicted. Personality tests vary substantially in reliability, meaningfulness, and predictive validity, and usually sample only a limited range of behaviors, under a limited (and often artificial) range of conditions. Although personality tests may permit fairly accurate prediction of someone's behavior the tests do not explain the predicted behavior.

10. How people act with respect to one another—that is, *social behavior*—is a big part of what we commonly call their personalities. Social psychologists study the effects of other people on the behavior of the individual and have revealed several interesting patterns of behavior. Three such patterns are *conformity*, defined as a change in behavior as a result of implicit group pressure; *compliance*, defined as behaving in a manner consistent with a direct request for a certain form of behavior; and *obedience*, which involves doing as ordered by a person of some authority.

11. Although psychologists have categorized behaviors according to common features and have given the categories names (e.g., conformity, compliance, aggression), this by no means explains the behaviors. Explaining behavioral similarities and differences requires theorizing about objective variables. Aggression provides a good example. Once behavior is classified and named as *aggressive*, the next step is to attempt to isolate the genetic, physiological, and environmental variables responsible for the behavior. Scientific psychologists have discovered some of the variables responsible for behavior we call aggressive.

Study Questions

1. How is the term *intelligence* typically used by psychologists and how is it measured?

2. Who devised the first standardized intelligence test, for what purpose, and how was the test generally constructed?

3. What were the three principles Binet insisted on for his tests?

4. How are intelligence tests useful and what are some problems with them?

5. Is the concept of intelligence itself useful and, if so, how? Does intelligence cause behavior?

6. How is defining personality like defining intelligence? How do psychologists usually conceptualize it?

7. In what ways was Hippocrates's model of personality like many of those that followed?

8. How did Freud account for personality? What does the term *psychoanalysis* refer to? What is the id, ego, and super ego and what role do they play in personality?

9. What was the goal of Freud's therapy and how did this relate to his theory?

10. How does Freud's theory of personality stand up to scientific scrutiny?

11. Who were Alfred Adler and Carl Jung, how did their theories of personality deviate from Freud's, and were their theories any more scientifically adequate?

12. What was Carl Rogers's approach to explaining human behavior, termed *phenomenological* (or *humanistic*) psychology?

13. How did Rogers and other humanists conceptualize the individual, and what role did the self play? What was Rogers's form of therapy and how did it generally work?

14. How could it be said that B. F. Skinner developed a theory of personality and how could it be said that he didn't?

15. What is Bandura's social learning theory, how is it similar to Skinner's general conception of the role of consequences of behavior, and how is it different?

16. What kind of therapy did Bandura's theory generate and what is the popular self-control program that grew out of it?

17. What is the one common feature all personality theories share?

18. In what way are personality theories useful and in what way are they not?

19. What does personality assessment involve, and what are the two reasons psychologists carry it out?

20. What are projective tests, including an example, and what are objective tests, including an example?

21. How do psychologists use the term "social behavior" and how does the example of Victor illustrate the importance of early social interaction?

22. What is the subject matter of social psychology and what three things do social psychologists traditionally do?

23. How do social psychologists use the terms *conformity, compliance,* and *obedience* and what do the studies by Asch (1956) on conformity and Milgram (1963) on obedience show?

24. What are some of the variables that influence whether a person conforms, complies, or obeys, and how would scientific psychology approach each of these social relationships?

25. What is the point of the section titled "The Appeal and Peril of Nominal Psychologies," and how does the topic of aggression illustrate it?

Troublesome Behavior

13

Human behavior is remarkably diverse; no two of us behave in precisely the same way. The adjective "abnormal" designates any departure from the typical, therefore "abnormal behavior" is any pattern of responding that is rare or unusual. Psychologists, however, usually restrict the term to patterns of responding that constitute a problem for the person who emits them, or for other people. When used in this sense, **abnormal behavior** can also be called **troublesome behavior.** The present chapter considers the diagnosis, etiology (i.e., causes), and treatment of troublesome behaviors associated with mental illness, drug abuse, and mental retardation.

A wide range of behavior is tolerated in most societies, but certain actions cause trouble and require intervention. Consider the hypothetical case of Jerry, based on events that occur in schizophrenic disorders.[1] Jerry was born near Cleveland and had a normal childhood. A good student and a fair athlete, he was popular throughout high school. Jerry experienced most of the difficulties characteristic of youth, but his parents, teachers, and friends considered him generally warm and well adjusted. In the fall of 1995, Jerry, at 19 years of age, enrolled in the sociology program at the state university. Shortly thereafter, his behavior began to change. At first, the change was subtle: Jerry started spending more time alone in his dorm room, reading and listening to music. Over time, his attendance at classes and social events became increasingly sporadic and, on those rare occasions when he did venture out, he appeared preoccupied with the threat of a nuclear war initiated by Panama.

By the end of fall semester, Jerry spent almost all of his time in his room and rarely spoke with other people. At home for the Christmas holiday, Jerry avoided his family and old friends. When interactions did occur, they were often painful. This was the case on Christmas eve, the traditional time for his family to decorate the tree. Instead of helping his parents and four siblings with the task, as he had always done, Jerry chastised his family for constructing a graven image, then delivered a largely senseless monologue on the failings of humanity in general and his family in particular, and on the Armageddon soon to come. Attempts to calm him failed. Jerry eventually burst into tears, ran upstairs, and locked himself into a bedroom. He was quiet but caused no real problems on Christmas, and the family had a good holiday. Jerry received his grades two days later. The arrival of three Fs, a D, and a B precipitated a long and bitter argument. When Jerry's parents asked for an explanation of his poor performance, their son cursed them, something he had never done, and proclaimed them damned in a nuclear holocaust. He did so, however, in peculiar phrases: "You'll fry with me, won't you? Panama Canal, good-bye now. It wasn't like this before. They tell me, make us all deliver. I've read all of the papers and listened to it mostly, except when you lie. Lions lie with sheep, but who lies to me? A million megatons, on the shipping lanes."

On New Year's eve, Jerry's parents took their son to a local hospital, where professionals determined that he was in the active phase of a schizophrenic disorder. Two years after Christmas 1995, Jerry is living at home. He takes 15 mg of

---

[1]This example originally appeared in Gadow and Poling (1988).

the antipsychotic drug haloperidol (Haldol) every day and sees a clinical psychologist once a month. He makes no mention of nuclear war, and has little trouble with his parents. But he seldom interacts with other people, and most of his time is spent alone. Jerry occasionally talks about getting a job or returning to school, but he has made little real progress toward either.

Why is Jerry's case noteworthy? It is tempting to answer "because of his schizophrenia." And that is true. But it is important to recognize that schizophrenia is a label for a set of troublesome behaviors that meet certain diagnostic criteria. Jerry was labeled as schizophrenic because of what he did: Over time, his speech became progressively more bizarre; he failed to meet responsibilities; and his interactions with other people diminished. In essence, Jerry caused a problem for himself and for those around him because he stopped behaving in desirable ways. It was on the basis of his behavior and nothing more that he was diagnosed as schizophrenic. In a very real sense, schizophrenia is a behavior disorder.

Both public events and private events can provide evidence of behavior disorders.[2] Crying, for example, is a public indication of depression. So, too, is failing to call friends and family who once were a source of pleasure. Feelings of despair and hopelessness, on the other hand, are private indications of depression. That is, they are directly accessible only to the individual who experiences them. Of course, their existence is revealed to a psychologist (or any person other than the one experiencing them) only through public behavior, usually in the form of a verbal description.

Behavior disorders include all conditions in which individuals cause a problem for themselves or for other people because they exhibit behavior that is unacceptable or they fail to function appropriately. The disorder might be limited to one or two discrete responses, as in nighttime bed-wetting (enuresis) or self-injurious face-slapping, or it might involve a broad range of both private and public events, as in schizophrenia.

What Is Mental Illness?

When much if not most of an individual's behavior is troublesome, it is common to consider the specific behavior problems indications of a clinical disorder. Psychiatric (or psychological) diagnosis involves categorizing people according to the troublesome things they say and do. It is on this basis that the various forms of "mental illness" are distinguished. Although the distinction is no longer favored by some clinicians, the various forms of mental illness have for decades been divided on the basis of severity into psychoses and neuroses. **Psychoses** involve severe and pervasive behavioral problems and pronounced functional impairment and often involve *thought disorders* (thinking and

---

[2]Public indications of a behavior disorder are sometimes called signs, whereas private indications are termed symptoms. This convention is not always followed, however, and both private and public indications are often called symptoms.

speaking illogically), *hallucinations* (reporting objects and events not actually present), and *delusions* (making statements obviously contrary to facts). *Unusual affect* (emotion) is also common. All of these indications of psychosis are, of course, inferred on the basis of actual behavior.

Neuroses are less pervasive and debilitating behavior disorders than psychoses, although they can also cause great suffering. **Neuroses** do not involve substantial loss of behavioral control by environmental events (i.e., "contact with reality" is maintained), and they often appear to be exaggerations of normal reactions. Like psychoses, neuroses are mental illnesses only in the sense that a part of their symptomatology involves reporting a world within the skin that differs from that familiar to most people.

Before we describe them in more detail, we should point out that the mind cannot be responsible for psychoses or neuroses. The "mind" has no physical status, it does not control behavior, and it cannot become ill. From a scientific standpoint, the same classes of variables that are legitimate causes of "normal" behavior—genetic, physiological, and environmental variables—are also the only legitimate causes of "abnormal" behavior. Of course, environmental variables include stimuli and responses that occur "within the skin," and are commonly considered "cognitive" variables.

Mental disorder is an approximate synonym of mental illness. The American Psychiatric Association (1994) favors the former term and uses it in the *Diagnostic and Statistical Manual of Mental Disorders* (4th ed.; *DSM-IV*). *DSM-IV* provides a widely used nosological system (**nosology** is the branch of medicine that deals with the classification of diseases). In *DSM-IV*, each of the mental disorders is conceptualized as a clinically significant behavioral or psychological syndrome or pattern that occurs in an individual and that is associated with present distress (a painful symptom) or disability (impairment in one or more important areas of functioning) or with a significantly increased risk of suffering death, pain, disability, or an important loss of freedom (American Psychiatric Association, 1994).

The diagnostic system presented in *DSM-IV* is complex. It requires that each case be assessed on five dimensions, or "axes." These are (1) clinical disorders and other conditions that may be a focus of clinical attention; (2) personality disorders and mental retardation; (3) general medical condition; (4) psychosocial and environmental problems; and (5) global assessment of functioning. The first two axes determine the official *DSM-IV* diagnosis; the last three provide supplemental information. Hundreds of disorders are described in *DSM-IV,* and each is given a label. Table 13-1 lists the major diagnostic categories of *DSM-IV.*

One criticism of *DSM-IV* is that it does not describe precisely what an individual must do (or fail to do) in order to receive a particular diagnosis (see Sidebar 13-1 for an old but interesting example). A second criticism is that too many disorders are distinguished, and many of them have similar defining characteristics. A third criticism, related to the first two, is that clinicians often disagree with respect to the diagnosis properly assigned to a particular person.

Table 13-1
Major *DSM-IV* Categories

Disorders Usually First Diagnosed in Infancy, Childhood, or Adolescence
    Mental Retardation
    Learning Disorders
    Motor Skills Disorder
    Communication Disorders
    Pervasive Developmental Disorders
    Attention-Deficit and Disruptive Behavior Disorders
    Feeding and Eating Disorders of Infancy or Early Childhood
    Tic Disorders
    Elimination Disorders
    Other Disorders of Infancy, Childhood, or Adolescence
Delirium, Dementia, and Amnestic and Other Cognitive Disorders
    Delirium
    Dementia
    Amnestic Disorders
    Other Cognitive Disorders
Mental Disorders Due to a General Medical Condition Not Elsewhere Classified
Substance-Related Disorders
    Alcohol-Related Disorders
    Amphetamine (or Amphetamine-like)–Related Disorders
    Caffeine-Related Disorders
    Cannabis-Related Disorders
    Cocaine-Related Disorders
    Hallucinogen-Related Disorders
    Inhalant-Related Disorders
    Nicotine-Related Disorders
    Opioid-Related Disorders
    Phencyclidine (or Phencyclidine-like)–Related Disorders
    Sedative-, Hypnotic-, or Anxiolytic-Related Disorders
    Polysubstance-Related Disorder
    Other (or Unknown) Substance–Related Disorders
Schizophrenia and Other Psychotic Disorders
Mood Disorders
    Depressive Disorders
    Bipolar Disorders
Anxiety Disorders
Somatoform Disorders
Factitious Disorders
Dissociative Disorders
Sexual and Gender Identity Disorders
    Sexual Dysfunctions
    Paraphilias
    Gender Identity Disorders
Eating Disorders
Sleep Disorders
    Primary Sleep Disorders
    Sleep Disorders Related to Another Mental Disorder
    Other Sleep Disorders
Impulse-Control Disorders Not Elsewhere Classified
Adjustment Disorders

(continued)

Table 13-1
(Continued)

Personality Disorders
Other Conditions That May Be a Focus of Clinical Attention
    Psychological Factors Affecting Medical Condition
    Medication-Induced Movement Disorders
    Other Medication-Induced Disorders
    Relational Problems
    Problems Related to Abuse or Neglect
    Additional Conditions That May Be a Focus of Clinical Attention
    Additional Codes

Note: From *Diagnostic and Statistical Manual of Mental Disorders* (4th ed., pp. 13–24), by American Psychiatric Association, 1994, Washington, DC: American Psychiatric Association. Copyright 1994 by American Psychiatric Association. Reproduced with permission.

Even when a diagnosis is consistently applied, however, the diagnostic label does not explain why an individual behaves as he or she does, or what treatment that person should receive. In fact, some have noted that psychiatric diagnosis doesn't provide much more information about behavior than was known before the diagnosis was made. In other words, little information about causes, treatment of choice, or prognosis is given (Craighead, Kazdin, and Mahoney, 1981). Some (e.g., Szasz, 1960, 1987) have even gone so far as to recom-

---

Sidebar 13-1
Who's Schizophrenic?

Perhaps clinicians cannot even tell a normal person from a mentally ill one. A study by Rosenhan (1973) suggests that this may be so. Rosenhan had volunteers determined to be in no way psychotic seek admission to psychiatric hospitals by complaining of a single symptom. The symptom was hearing a voice that said "empty," "hollow," and "thud." With the exception of reporting this symptom, the volunteers behaved normally. Most of them were diagnosed as psychotic (schizophrenic) and were hospitalized. Once there, they stopped reporting hearing voices (hallucinations), behaved well, and even took public notes on ongoing events. Nonetheless, mental health professionals failed to realize that the volunteers were not mentally ill. Treatment was provided, and when the volunteers were released, they were usually given the diagnosis of "schizophrenia in remission." Interestingly, some mentally ill patients did recognize the volunteers as normal. One patient observed, "You're not crazy. You're a journalist or a professor. You're checking up on the hospital" (Rosenhan, 1973, p. 252).

Does it follow from Rosenhan's study that clinicians cannot tell schizophrenics from normal people, and that psychiatric diagnosis is therefore absurd? Not really. Rosenhan did not require clinicians to distinguish between schizophrenics and normal people. Instead, he required them to detect normal people pretending to suffer from schizophrenia. This is not a part of conventional diagnostic procedures, and says nothing about the adequacy of those procedures. Moreover, as Spitzer (1975) has argued, the clinicians in Rosenhan's study behaved in reasonable fashion given the data available to them. Each of the volunteers requested admission to a hospital, and such a request is in and of itself reason for clinical concern. Finally, the pseudopatients were quite passive after admission. They never told the clinicians "There's nothing wrong with me—I just pretended to hear voices. Let me go." A patient who was normal would be expected to say that.

mend that all attempts to classify mental disorders be abandoned, because labeling has done more harm than good.

Classifying behavior problems, however, cannot be avoided; it does allow for meaningful communication among researchers and clinicians. In addition, at least when pharmacological treatments are being considered, psychiatric diagnosis is useful in selecting appropriate treatments. A diagnosis of schizophrenia, for instance, suggests that an antipsychotic drug such as thioridazine (Mellaril) should be useful, whereas an antidepressant, perhaps fluoxetine (Prozac), would be more likely to produce the desired effect in treating depression.

Recently, Kessler and colleagues (1994) determined the prevalence of various mental disorders in the United States by interviewing more than 8,000 urban people. They found that the most common disorders, in descending order of prevalence, were substance use disorder, anxiety disorders, mood disorders, antisocial personality disorder, and schizophrenia and other psychotic disorders. The prevalences of these disorders are 26.6%, 24.9%, 19.3%, 3.5%, and 0.7%, respectively. Men reported higher prevalence rates for substance use disorders and antisocial personality disorder than did women, whereas mood and anxiety disorders were more common among women than men. The remainder of the chapter provides an overview of schizophrenia, anxiety disorders, mood disorders, drug abuse, and mental retardation.

Schizophrenia

Diagnosis and Etiology of Schizophrenia

It is common to distinguish positive and negative symptoms of schizophrenia. The primary *positive symptoms* are hallucinations, thought disorders, and delusions. They are called positive because they are present. The primary *negative symptoms* are flattened affect, impoverished speech, anhedonia (inability to experience pleasure), lack of motivation, and social withdrawal. They are called negative because they are absent. Clinicians commonly differentiate four subtypes of schizophrenia:

Catatonic schizophrenia is characterized by motor disturbances. These disturbances range from wild and excessive activity to complete immobility.

Disorganized schizophrenia is characterized by incoherence, inappropriate emotion, and grossly disorganized behavior. Speech is loosely organized and nonsensical; some have aptly described it as "word salad."

Paranoid schizophrenia is characterized by preoccupation with systematic delusions. "Paranoid" is used in the vernacular to mean unreasonably suspicious, but a person diagnosed as a paranoid schizophrenic might, for instance, believe that she is Helen Keller, but feel neither persecuted nor suspicious.

Undifferentiated schizophrenia includes cases that do not meet the diagnostic criteria for the other three categories.

The term *schizophrenia* comes from two Greek words, *schizein* (to split) and *phren* (mind). The man who coined the term, Eugen Bleuler (1911–1950), believed that the disorder resulted from a splitting, or disorganization, of mental functions. The result was disturbed thoughts, feelings, and overt behavior. This analysis, like all analyses that assign a causal status to the mind, is inadequate.

Researchers have some clues to the many causes of schizophrenia. For example, research has shown that drugs that are effective in treating the disorder act by blocking receptors in the brain for the neurotransmitter dopamine. In addition, drugs that increase dopamine (e.g., amphetamines, cocaine) can with prolonged exposure produce behaviors that closely resemble those characteristic of schizophrenia. These findings led researchers to speculate that the positive symptoms of schizophrenia are caused proximately by either (a) overproduction of dopamine in the limbic system or cortex or (b) production of an endogenous amphetamine-like compound (Baldessarini, 1990). This **dopamine hypothesis** of schizophrenia remains popular but unproved (e.g., Davis, Kahn, Ko, & Davidson, 1991). You may remember from Chapter 7 that neurons that secrete dopamine were also implicated as proximate causes of reinforcement. Thus, it has been suggested that the positive symptoms of schizophrenia may occur because these reinforcement mechanisms become activated independently of any normal reinforcement and at times when schizophrenic individuals may, like the rest of us, occasionally have a delusional or disordered thought (Carlson, 1995).

A possible proximate cause of the negative symptoms of schizophrenia is abnormalities in brain structure which have been detected in some, but not all, people diagnosed with schizophrenia. In particular, many schizophrenics have less tissue in thalamic regions and the prefrontal cortex than other people, and correspondingly enlarged ventricles (Andreasen et al. 1994). Viral infections such as the flu (perhaps leading to autoimmune disorders) and birth traumas may also play a role in causing schizophrenia (Mednick, Machon, & Huttunen, 1990; Schwarzkopf, Nasrallah, Olson, Coffman, & McLaughlin, 1989), although how they do so is yet unknown.

In terms of ultimate causes, there is evidence that some individuals may inherit a predisposition toward schizophrenia (e.g., Farmer, McGuffin, & Gottesman, 1987; Gottesman, 1991). For example, concordance rates for schizophrenia (i.e., the probability that both members of a pair of twins will either exhibit or not exhibit the condition) are more than twice as high for monozygotic twins (about 50%) as for dizygotic twins (about 20%). Moreover, the probability that a relative of a person diagnosed with schizophrenia will also exhibit the disorder increases the more closely related the two relatives are. Finally, even if they are adopted, the children of schizophrenic parents are more than 10 times as likely to develop the condition as are the children of nonschizophrenic parents (Kety et al., 1994). Nonetheless, even if both parents are schizophrenic, the probability of their having a schizophrenic child is only about 25%. It is likely that even if a genetic basis for schizophrenia is found, it will not be a single gene. Thus, discovering the actual genes will be a very difficult task. And that will not tell the whole story of schizophrenia, because both environmental and genetic variables contribute to schizophrenia.

Environmental (ontogenetic) variables clearly play a role in the development and maintenance of the specific problem behaviors characteristic of schizophrenia. Bleuler distinguished two forms of schizophrenia, *reactive* and *process,* based on whether the onset of the disorder was obviously correlated with an important environmental event, such as the loss of a loved one. If such an event occurred, the disorder was reactive; if not, it was process. Momentous environmental events can trigger psychotic reactions. More mundane events appear to play a role in determining the specific behaviors involved in such reactions. For example, delusions typically involve objects and events with which the patient has some familiarity, although they are described in a fashion that does not correspond to objective reality.

Moreover, contingencies of reinforcement and punishment exercise control over much of the bizarre behavior of psychotic individuals. Although the contingencies that operate to engender abnormal behavior in a particular patient are rarely evident, such behavior can in most cases be altered by changing its consequences. This indicates that the behavior is operant. Behavioral treatments of schizophrenia and other psychoses rest on this assumption.

Treatment of Schizophrenia

Although the treatment of schizophrenia has had a long history, the treatment of psychotic individuals was literally revolutionized in the 1950s with the introduction of a new drug, chlorpromazine (Thorazine). Chlorpromazine revolutionized psychiatry for a single reason: It reduced the undesirable behaviors of most psychotic patients. Many well-controlled studies have shown that chlorpromazine and related antipsychotic drugs are generally useful for managing schizophrenia and other psychoses, although not all psychotic individuals benefit from the drug, some improve without it, and all who receive it are at risk for developing motor dysfunctions and other deleterious side effects (Baldessarini, 1990).

Although use of antipsychotic drugs is the primary treatment for schizophrenia, nonpharmacological interventions are also important. One intervention that has proven ethical, practical, and effective in treating psychotic inpatients in institutional settings is the token economy. In a **token economy,** generalized conditioned reinforcers (tokens) are delivered dependent on the performance of appropriate behaviors. In most systems, inappropriate behaviors result in token loss. Accumulated tokens can be exchanged at predetermined times for back-up reinforcers, which usually include preferred objects (e.g., foods, clothing, cosmetics) and the opportunity to perform preferred behaviors (e.g., watch television, bowl). A token economy requires three ingredients (Kazdin, 1981):

1. *Tokens.* These consist of objects (e.g., poker chips, stars, cards) that are delivered dependent on appropriate performance.
2. *Back-up reinforcers.* These are reinforcing objects or activities for which tokens are exchanged; they are responsible for the reinforcing efficacy of the tokens.

3. *Rules describing the relation between behavior and tokens and between tokens and back-up reinforcers.* An effective token economy is dependent on rules that clearly specify how and when tokens can be earned, lost, and spent. Clients are usually informed verbally of the rules of the token system. This rule-governed behavior brings the patient's behavior into contact with the contingencies of the token economy, and these contingencies serve to control it further.

Token economies have been used successfully in many studies with psychiatric inpatients. Subsequent studies also documented the value of token economies. For example, Nelson and Cone (1979) used a token system to improve 12 behaviors in each of 16 chronic psychiatric inpatients, 13 of whom were diagnosed as psychotic, the remainder as mentally retarded. The behaviors were grouped into four classes: personal hygiene, personal management, ward work, and social skills. Results indicated that reinforcing appropriate behaviors with tokens resulted in "abrupt and substantial increases in performance of most target behaviors, significant improvements in global individual functioning, positive changes in general ward behavior, and increases in social interaction during off-ward activities" (p. 255).

Token economies and other behavioral strategies can of course be combined with pharmacological interventions, and such combined treatments may be especially effective. For example, Hersen, Turner, Edelstein, and Pinkston (1975) report the case of a schizophrenic who did not respond well to a social skills training program until a *neuroleptic* (antipsychotic) drug was prescribed. After the drug was administered, the behavioral intervention was quite effective. Behavioral interventions are not always a viable alternative to pharmacological interventions in the management of psychoses. Instead, they are valuable adjuncts.

There has been in recent years a major move toward deinstitutionalizing mentally ill (and mentally retarded) people. Therapeutic procedures based on behavioral principles are no less effective outside institutions than inside them, but they can be difficult to arrange when placements are relatively unstructured. Procedures based on operant conditioning have proven useful in community mental health centers (e.g., Liberman, King, & DeRisi, 1976).

Mood Disorders

Diagnosis and Etiology of Mood Disorders

Mood disorders, also known as affective disorders, are disorders of emotion, primarily elation or depression. Emotion is inferred on the basis of self-report and other overt behaviors; a person who makes self-deprecating statements, says she or he is unhappy, and rarely interacts with other people is described as depressed.

Four important mood disorders are **Major Depressive Disorder, seasonal affective disorder, Bipolar Disorder**—depressive episode, and **Bipolar Disor-**

der—manic episode. Major depression is relatively common; Kessler and colleagues (1994) estimate the lifetime prevalence rate at 21% in females and 13% in males. A person experiencing a major depressive episode reports feeling sad and guilty. Objects and events that once reinforced behavior control little behavior during a major depressive episode; therefore, behavior is generally suppressed. For example, a depressed person may rarely if ever go out, have sex, or call friends even though these activities were enjoyed and often performed prior to the depressive episode. A major depressive episode is severe, disruptive, and even life-threatening because of the elevated risk of suicide.

Seasonal affective disorder generally occurs during winter, when days are short and nights long. It is characterized by depression, craving for carbohydrates (often leading to weight gain), lethargy, and increased sleeping. Interestingly, the condition resembles hibernation and responds well to treatment with bright lights.

It is convenient to think of mania as the opposite of depression. During manic episodes, mood is abnormally elevated, the person is active and frequently irritable, overestimates personal ability, and behaves irresponsibly. She or he seems to be relatively insensitive to normally punishing consequences and acts to maximize momentary payoffs without regard to delayed consequences. For example, during a manic episode the person may take drugs, have sex, and spend money without regard to the consequences. Bipolar Disorder involves alternation between mania and depression. In this disorder, the time-course of the alternation varies and periods of normal affect also occur.

Several theories have been developed in an attempt to explain the development of mood disorders; none are fully adequate. As in schizophrenia, there appears to be an inherited susceptibility to mood disorders (e.g., M. G. Allen, 1976), but the mechanism of inheritance is unknown. Based on the neuropharmacological actions of clinically effective drugs, scientists have hypothesized that depression results from lowered amounts of certain neurotransmitter substances (e.g., serotonin) in the brain, whereas mania results from an excess of these neurotransmitter substances. But direct confirmation of this hypothesis is lacking (Baldessarini, 1990). A link between mood disorders and the brain mechanisms that control sleep cycles also has been proposed (e.g., Ehlers, Frank, & Kupfer, 1988) but not proven. Interestingly, depriving depressed people of rapid eye movement (REM) sleep is beneficial in many cases, and drugs that are effective in treating depression reduce REM sleep (Wu & Bunney, 1990).

Beginning with Charles Ferster (1965), several scientific psychologists have proposed that insufficient positive reinforcement plays a major role in the development of depression. The notion appears plausible: A major symptom of depression is a reduction in operant behavior, and one way that operant behavior can be reduced is by a lack of adequate reinforcement. Moreover, absence or loss of significant reinforcers, for instance those associated with a job or a lover, produces feelings and negative self-statements indicative of depression: "I'm no good, I can't even keep a job." When they first occur, such statements are likely to be reinforced, albeit inadvertently, by a sympathetic audience. Over time, however, associates may come to avoid contact with the depressed person, who isn't much fun to be around. This will decrease available reinforcers for appropriate as well as inappropriate behavior, and strengthen the depression (Lewinsohn, 1975).

The insufficient-reinforcement hypothesis has been extended in several directions. Moss and Boren (1972) speculated that depression does not result from insufficient positive reinforcement alone, but also requires "aversive control" (exposure to escape, avoidance, or punishment contingencies). Costello (1972) proposed that depression occurs because objects and events that were once reinforcing lose their ability to maintain behavior. These objects and activities continue to be available, but are not reinforcing, perhaps due to endogenous biochemical or neurophysiological events. This analysis appears to be generally consistent with clinical evidence.

Martin Seligman and his colleagues have proposed an alternative to the insufficient reinforcement analysis of depression. The **learned helplessness model** involves learning that something bad cannot be escaped or avoided. The phenomenon was first demonstrated in dogs exposed to inescapable and unavoidable electric shocks and then tested in an escape/avoidance procedure (Overmeier & Seligman, 1967). Results of this and many similar studies unequivocally demonstrated that exposure to uncontrollable shocks disrupts the acquisition of avoidance responding (Seligman, Klein, & Miller, 1976). Seligman and his colleagues (1976) proposed that learning that shocks are uncontrollable has three effects: (1) operant escape behavior is weakened (punished) and the organism appears passive (a motivational effect), (2) acquisition of responses that escape or avoid shocks is impaired (a cognitive effect), and (3) responses indicative of fear and anxiety are exhibited (an affective or emotional effect). These processes may be involved in the genesis of human depression. Seligman and colleagues (1976) observed:

> Some of the events which typically produce depression are: failure in work or school; death, loss, rejection or separation from loved ones; physical disease; and growing old. We believe that the depressed patient has learned that he cannot control those elements of his life which relieve suffering or bring him gratification. In short, he believes that he is helpless. (p. 196)

Over time, Seligman modified and refined his notions about the relation of learned helplessness to human depression. The refinements made the model more mentalistic. For example, Abramson, Seligman, and Teasdale (1978) proposed that a history of exposure to uncontrollable events causes a person to ask, "Why am I helpless?" This leads to an attribution about the cause, which in turn determines one's expectancies about the outcome of subsequent behavior. These expectancies influence behavior; for instance, "Nothing I can do has any effect, so why do anything?" Eventually, this process deflates self-esteem, and full-blown depression ensues.

In this analysis, attributions and expectancies are construed as mental events that control behavior. It is more scientific, however, if expectancies are considered overt or covert verbal responses. The covert verbal behavior of depressed individuals (i.e., what they say to themselves), like their overt behavior, differs from that of other people. On the basis of these differences in verbal behavior, Aaron Beck (e.g., 1976) argued that depression is a cognitive disorder, and developed a **cognitive-distortion theory.** Four cognitive distortions, or errors, cause depression: *arbitrary inference* (drawing unwarranted conclusions), *selective abstraction* (not considering all aspects of a situation), *magnification/minimization* (over- or underestimating the significance of events and behavior), and *overgeneralization* (reaching conclusions on the basis of inadequate information). Although behaviors indicative of cognitive distortions are often evident in depression, they are more likely a part of the disorder, and not its cause. Nonetheless, as described in the following section, studies have demonstrated that treatments designed to alter a patient's "cognitions" (covert verbal statements, especially those relevant to self-worth and ability to control the environment) can be useful in treating depression (e.g., Beck, 1976).

Treatment of Depression

Several kinds of interventions for depression have proven useful, including treatment with *antidepressant drugs, various forms of behavior and cognitive-behavior therapy,* and **electroconvulsive therapy (ECT).** ECT involves electrically inducing a seizure; it is used primarily to treat depression insensitive to other interventions.

The treatment of choice for depression is the use of antidepressant drugs. Antidepressants, like antipsychotics, are classified according to the way in which they affect certain neurotransmitters in the brain. The most recent class of antidepressants is called selective serotonin re-uptake inhibitors, or SSRIs for short. The popular antidepressant Prozac (fluoxetine) was the first SSRI to be marketed. The SSRIs are so called because they selectively inhibit or prevent serotonin from being taken back up into the terminal buttons of the neurons that secrete them (see Chapter 7). As a result, more serotonin is left in the synapse and available to affect other neurons. In fact, because all antidepressants affect the amount of serotonin that is either produced or released by neurons, many researchers believe that a major proximate physiological cause of depression is a deficiency of serotonin.

The decision about which type of antidepressant to try first is usually a "shot in the dark" approach based more on comparing the kinds of side effects produced by the drug (Preston, O'Neal, & Talaga, 1994). Because the SSRIs are relatively "clean," that is, they produce fewer undesirable side effects, they are more often the drug treatment of choice for a wide range of depressive disorders. Even when antidepressants improve life for depressed individuals, it is important to remember that "the combined approaches of pharmacotherapy and psychotherapy offer the best chance of successful recovery from depression" (Preston et al., 1994, p. 71).

One form of psychotherapy that has been shown to be particularly effective, especially in combination with antidepressant medication, is cognitive-behavior therapy. As indicated above, cognitive-behavior therapy is based on the assumption that one of the main problems for depressed individuals is negative thinking. Such individuals frequently report obsessive, irrational thoughts that often produce anxiety. Such thinking can be described as distorted, because it does not match reality. Several other styles of distorted thinking have been classified in addition to the four types of cognitive distortions described previously. Two of these are catastrophizing and mind reading (Copeland, 1992). In *catastrophizing*, the individual turns everything into a catastrophe as, for example, when a young person says, "I didn't get the job, so how am I going to live? How will I ever be able to buy a house? And, what about retirement?" In *mind reading*, the individual bases his assumptions and conclusions on what he imagines other people are thinking as, for example, when he thinks, "That woman is looking at me. She must think I am ugly." The goal of cognitive-behavior therapy is to change or eliminate such negative thoughts.

One specific method for changing negative thought is a procedure called thought-stopping. **Thought-stopping** is a self-control procedure designed to eliminate repetitive thought patterns that are unrealistic and that either inhibit the performance of a desired behavior or evoke undesirable behaviors (Wisocki, 1985). In the therapy sessions, the client is instructed to intentionally say the negative statement to himself and to raise a finger when he begins to make the self-statement. At that point the therapist, yells "STOP!" This causes a startle response and simultaneously causes the client to stop the negative self-statement. The therapist also teaches the client to perform the thought-stopping procedure himself so that he can apply it outside the therapy setting. When effective, the thought-stopping procedure eliminates negative thoughts and the anxiety and maladaptive overt behaviors that accompany them. Although this procedure is effective alone, it is more effective in conjunction with other behavioral procedures such as desensitization (Wisocki, 1985).

Other, more straightforward behavioral interventions have been used to treat depression, and most are relatively complex. As stated previously, an important assumption of many behavioral approaches is that depression results from a sudden and dramatic decrease in positive reinforcement (Lewinsohn, 1975), perhaps as a result of the loss of a loved one, job, or home. As a result, the person will be sad, pessimistic, and generally inactive. Hersen, Eisler, Alford, and Agras (1973) studied ways to increase activity level in the hope that by virtue of increased activity the depressed person would obtain much-needed reinforcement. The depressive behavior of three clients was first assessed in a baseline condition. In this condition, they received blue index cards for completing tasks (e.g., work, personal hygiene) and reward activities were delivered independent of their performance. In the treatment condition, the rewards were dependent on the number of cards they earned. The results showed that when the reward activities were dependent on performance, there was an increase in tasks completed and a corresponding decrease in depressive behaviors. The authors suggested that the card system increased opportunities for reinforcement of social (i.e., nondepressive) behavior.

Other researchers who assume that depressed people experience a lack of reinforcement have taken a different tack by teaching depressed clients how to obtain social reinforcers. For instance, Hersen, Bellack, and Himmelhoch (1980) identified clients' deficits in interactions with family and friends, with strangers, and with co-workers. Particular situations were then identified that caused trouble for each client. Through instructions, role-playing, feedback, and reinforcement from the therapist, the clients learned how to obtain social reinforcement in these situations. The results showed decreases in depression, as measured by both rating scales and self-report inventories.

Behavior therapy and pharmacotherapy each appear to be generally effective in managing depression, and there is emerging evidence that the two can, in some cases, be combined to produce effects superior to either alone (Hollon, Spoden, & Chastek, 1986).

Anxiety Disorders

Diagnosis and Etiology of Anxiety Disorders

The *DSM-IV* lists under the general category of anxiety disorders the following conditions: Panic Disorder With (or Without) Agoraphobia (fear of being alone in, and avoidance of, public places), Agoraphobia Without History of Panic Disorder, Specific Phobia(s), Social Phobia, Obsessive-Compulsive Disorder, Posttraumatic Stress Disorder, Acute Stress Disorder, Generalized Anxiety Disorder, Anxiety Disorder Due to (various medical conditions), Substance-Induced Anxiety Disorder, and Anxiety Disorder Not Otherwise Specified. All of these disorders involve "anxiety," although they differ with respect to the conditions that evoke it and the patterns of behavior taken to be indicative of its occurrence.

Although **anxiety** is difficult to define, it generally involves an unpleasant subjective state aptly described as "fearful," physiological arousal, and troublesome overt behavior that minimizes contact with certain stimuli. Those stimuli might be publicly accessible things (e.g., spiders) or private responses of the anxious person (e.g., thoughts of spiders). Anxiety has three components: (1) a self-reported component (e.g., "I'm scared to death of spiders"), (2) a physiological arousal component (e.g., increases in heart rate and blood pressure when a spider is sighted), and (3) a motor component (e.g., screaming and running away when a spider appears). Interestingly, these three measures of anxiety do not always correlate well (Nietzel & Bernstein, 1981). For instance, a person may report being deathly afraid of ordering from a restaurant menu but nevertheless do so regularly and exhibit only minimal physiological arousal when doing so. The component of anxiety that is of primary interest to a clinician is the one that causes trouble for the patient.

You will recognize that anxiety is not a thing, but only a label assigned to describe certain kinds of behavioral and physiological responses emitted under the control of certain kinds of stimuli. The same is true of phobias, obsessive-compulsive disorder, and all related terms. Consider a quiet autumn day at school. You're listening to a lecture when a horsefly buzzes in through an open window. Suddenly, the person to your left screams, "God, bees," and runs wildly from the room. A bit odd; perhaps a bee phobia? Now consider the same student hiking through the woods and accidentally stepping on a hornets' nest. Same verbal response, "God, bees," same wild running. No phobia there, just simple and reasonable fear. Therefore, it is important to remember that clinicians, like lay people, assign diagnostic labels on the basis of what people do and the conditions under which they do them.

Anxiety disorders *are* behavior problems; they do not *cause* behavior problems. In fact, from a scientific perspective,

> We have to deal not with . . . anxiety, but with the conditions giving rise to anxiety. . . . The concept of anxiety is superfluous in dealing directly with people rather than with theories. In a clinical intervention we deal with what is being avoided, with what a person needs to learn or unlearn or relearn. . . . [Accepting the concept of anxiety] makes us think we know something when we do not and should be looking harder. (Krasner & Ullmann, 1973, pp. 98–99)

There is no single specifiable cause of anxiety disorders. With the exception of simple and social phobias, anxiety disorders appear to "run in families," suggesting there may a genetic predisposition to them (e.g., Kendler et al., 1995; Pauls, Alsobrook, Goodman, Rasmussen, & Leckman, 1995) (although this also suggests a learning mechanism). The mechanism through which genotype influences susceptibility to anxiety disorders is unknown, however.

Environmental variables play a significant role in the development of anxiety disorders. The stimuli that produce anxiety disorders are part of the person's environment; these stimuli produce a subjective state that is unpleasant and the stimuli are avoided in a manner that is troublesome. How stimuli control these responses is not as simple as it might seem. A temptingly simple analysis is based on the proposition that stimuli evoke anxiety by being paired with other, unpleasant objects or events. Many years ago, J. B. Watson and Rayner (1920) successfully produced "fear" in a young boy through a process of classical conditioning. In that study, a tame white rat (NS) (which initially elicited no adverse responses) was paired with a loud noise (US), which aroused the boy and caused him to cry (UR). After a few pairings, the rat alone (CS) did the same. Moreover, objects and events that induce crying often serve as negative reinforcers. Hence it is likely that the boy would have responded to escape or avoid the rat. If this occurred, and the avoidance responses, physiological arousal, and emotional responses produced by visual contact with the rat were strong and continued over many exposures, a rat phobia would be observed.

Could this be a model for all phobias? Perhaps. But you will recall that a CS (e.g., the rat) controls behavior only by virtue of being at least occasionally paired with a US (e.g., the loud noise). We know, however, that clinical phobias endure for long periods even when the CS is not correlated with an external object or event with aversive properties. For example, an adult may have been bitten by a spider only once, long ago, but still exhibit a serious spider phobia. How can that be? One possibility is that the person, after being bitten, rarely, if ever, encountered a spider. That is, she or he was quite successful in avoiding them; hence there was no possibility for classical extinction to occur. Another possibility is that, although simple classical conditioning is important in producing a phobia, other processes are involved in maintaining it. For example, the adult just described may have seen many spiders and never have been bitten, but nonetheless repeatedly verbalized to himself and other people how hideous spiders are, and how important it is to avoid them. It is possible that the overt verbal responses, like the behavior intended to avoid spiders, were reinforced by a sympathetic audience. Moreover, both overt and covert verbal responses could help to maintain the phobia as a form of rule-governed, albeit undesirable, behavior. A person with a spider phobia might, for instance, regularly state to him- or herself, "I must stay out of places where spiders live so they won't bite me." This rule states a behavior (staying out of places where spiders live) and a consequence for this behavior (avoiding being bitten). The rules that one generates and follows depend on historical and current variables, and these variables are, in principle, subject to analysis. They are likely to be complex, interactive, and difficult to discern retrospectively.

Treatment of Anxiety Disorders

In most cases, the cause(s) of a phobia or some other kind of anxiety disorder cannot be determined precisely. Given this, it is fortunate that effective treatment does not require known causes. Systematic desensitization, a treatment developed by Joseph Wolpe (1958), is one procedure widely employed in the treatment of phobias. It is based on the reciprocal-inhibition principle, the essence of which is captured in a statement by Wolpe (1958): "(I)f a response antagonistic to anxiety can be made to occur in the presence of anxiety-evoking stimuli so that it is accompanied by a complete or partial suppression of the anxiety responses, the bond between these stimuli and the anxiety responses will be weakened" (p. 71). In essence, **systematic desensitization** is a treatment that teaches a person to relax in the presence of stimuli that once produced anxiety. Leitenberg (1976) describes the three major components of effective systematic desensitization:

> (1) construction of a graduated hierarchy of anxiety-provoking scenes, and arrangement of these in an order such that the first scene elicits minimal anxiety and the last scene evokes considerable anxiety; (2) training the patient in deep muscle relaxation . . . although hypnotic induction techniques, drugs, and biofeedback have also been employed for this purpose; (3) having the patient visualize each of the scenes while in the relaxed state. (pp. 127–128)

After the client can envision each of the scenes in the hierarchy without feeling anxious, he or she may be required to actually participate in the activities represented in those scenes. For instance, a person with a dog phobia might first be trained until she or he is able to relax while envisioning close contact with a large dog. When this occurs, the client is introduced to a small (and friendly!) living dog at ever-decreasing distances. If anxiety is reported, the distance increases; if not, the dog is brought closer. When the client can pet the dog without feeling anxiety, a larger dog would be brought in. Eventually, the client should show no fear of any friendly dog, and treatment would be considered a success. Treatments similar to systematic desensitization have shown success with people who suffer from posttraumatic stress disorder (see Sidebar 13-2).

Many other behavioral procedures are useful in treating phobias and other anxiety disorders. They include systematic reinforcement procedures and mod-

---

Sidebar 13-2
Use of Imaginal Flooding in the Treatment of Posttraumatic Stress Disorder

Victims or observers of a violent act, such as war veterans or rape victims, sometimes manifest a **posttraumatic stress disorder (PTSD).** Sufferers experience dreams, flashbacks, or other intrusive recollections that are related to the event; they also avoid stimuli associated with the event and exhibit other behaviors such as insomnia, hypervigilance, outbursts of anger, and anxiety reactions to stimuli associated with the event (American Psychiatric Association, 1994). According to many therapists, PTSD results from a respondent conditioning process in which trauma is paired with other stimuli. Keane, Zimmering, and Caddell (1985) suggest that

> humans exposed to a life threatening experience can become conditioned to a wide assortment of stimuli present during the trauma. For example, sounds, smells, terrain, time of day, the people present, and even cognitions can become conditioned to the traumatic event. Thus, each stimulus can evoke anxiety responses similar to those experienced during the event. (p. 10)

A treatment for this syndrome, which gained notoriety by publicity associated with the Vietnam War, was reported by Fairbank and Keane (1982). They treated a Vietnam veteran who reported anxiety and depression as a result of recurring nightmares and flashbacks to combat experiences. Treatment was an *imaginal flooding* procedure in which the man repeatedly imagined the combat scenes, and then imagined a positive, relaxing scene. Results showed that when a particular scene was involved in treatment, there was a decrease in self-reported anxiety when he imagined that combat scene (see Figure 13-1), and a corresponding decrease in nightmares and flashbacks. Fairbank and Brown (1987) suggest that such treatment procedures involve classical extinction (see Chapter 6) wherein the troublesome stimuli (CSs) are presented without the traumatic events (USs) until they no longer evoke distress and anxiety. Moreover, repeated presentation of the CSs also decreases their aversiveness, thereby decreasing behavior that avoids these stimuli.

---

eling. In **modeling,** a therapeutic technique made popular by Albert Bandura (e.g., 1969), the client observes another person responding appropriately in a situation where the client fails to do so (e.g., one in which an anxiety-arousing stimulus is present). Modeling is effective to the extent that the client has a history in which behaving as others (models) behave has been reinforced. When they have such a history, it represents a simple and cost-effective intervention.

Drug Abuse

Recreational use of legal and illegal substances is widespread; and drug-related problems are perhaps the most common form of behavior disorder (Kessler et al., 1994). For instance, figures published by the World Health Organization (1995) indicate that roughly 70%–90% of adults in developed countries consume alcohol, and perhaps 5%–10% of them develop problems related to use of the drug. Rice, Kelman, Miller, and Dunmeyer (1990) estimate that in 1988 alone, alcohol abuse cost U.S. citizens $85.8 billion.[3] Costs in-

---

[3]A billion dollars is difficult for most people to envision. It may become easier if you know that a person who spent $1,000 a day, every day of the year, would take over 3,000 years to spend a billion dollars.

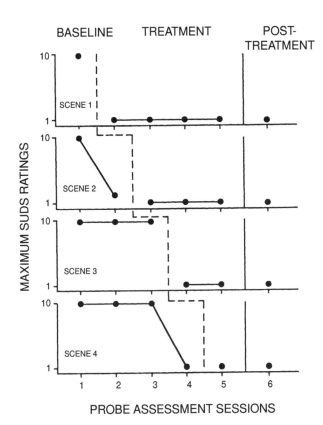

BASELINE   TREATMENT   POST-
TREATMENT

Figure 13-1. Maximum SUDS ratings in probe sessions during baseline, treatment, and posttreatment conditions. SUDS are subjective units of distress reported by the subject. (From "Flooding for Combat-Related Stress Disorders: Assessment of Anxiety Reduction Across Traumatic Memories," by J. A. Fairbank and T. M. Keane, 1982, *Behavior Therapy, 13,* p. 499–510. Copyright 1982 by Association for Advancement of Behavior Therapy. Reproduced with permission.)

clude those related to criminal activities, accidents, lost productivity, treatment, and incarceration.

Worldwide, about 1.1 billion cigarette smokers smoke around 6 trillion cigarettes each year. The World Health Organization estimates, "If current smoking trends persist, about 500 million people currently alive (about 9% of the world's population) will eventually be killed by tobacco, and half of them will be in middle age when they die, losing about 20–25 years of life" (1995, p. 16). In 1991, cigarette smoking became the number one cause of death in the United States, claiming more than 157,000 victims (Abadinksy, 1993). In addition, the annual cost of treating smoking-related illnesses is between $350 billion and $400 billion.

Alcohol and tobacco obviously are not the only drugs that are used by substantial numbers of people or that cause problems. For example, results of a national survey of drug use (L. D. Johnston, O'Malley, & Bachman, 1994) revealed that, in 1993:

- By their late twenties, roughly 80% of young people had tried an illicit (illegal) drug. Roughly 50% had tried a substance other than (but often in addition to) marijuana.
- Roughly one-third of the respondents had tried cocaine by age 28 (4.3% had tried crack).
- About one in forty high school seniors smoked marijuana daily; the prevalence was very similar in people 19 to 28 years of age.
- When compared to results for the previous decade, eighth-graders' use of marijuana, cocaine, LSD and other hallucinogens, and inhalants increased.

The greatest cost of drug abuse is not measured in dollars, but in human suffering. Most of us know someone whose life has been devastated by alcohol, tobacco, or an illegal drug. It is erroneous to assert, however, that "drugs are bad" and that anyone who uses any drug for recreational purposes is bound to experience problems. The vast majority of adults who consume drugs like marijuana or alcohol do so in moderation and experience no deleterious effects.

Although the term historically has been used in many different ways, we use the term **drug abuse** to refer to any pattern of drug self-administration that produces harmful behavioral or physiological effects without producing compensatory medical benefit. The term encompasses an immense and heterogeneous set of problems. A college freshman busted twice for driving under the influence of alcohol has a drug-related problem, but it differs from that of a prostitute physically dependent on heroin or an executive whose excessive cocaine use has led to financial ruin. There is, however, one element common to these and all other examples of drug abuse: *Inappropriate drug-seeking and drug-taking behaviors harm someone, and, thus, are considered troublesome.* The harm can be lessened only if these behaviors are changed. As we will see, however, there are a variety of genetic, physiological, and environmental factors that make it very difficult to change the behaviors that lead to drug abuse.

Etiology of Drug Use

Historically, drug abuse has been considered an ethical weakness, a sin, or a reflection of a particular type of personality, such as antisocial personality. But the majority of drug abusers do not fit only one type of personality. In fact, "no single recognized addictive personality or constellation of traits has been identified that is equally applicable to all varieties of compulsive drug users" (Jaffe, 1990, p. 530). As you may recall, using a particular personality type as an explanation for any type of behavior is an example of the inadequate explanation known as reification. In short, personality-based models of drug-abuse lead attention away from the inappropriate drug-taking and drug-seeking behaviors that are the crux of all drug abuse, and ignore the objective variables that cause these behaviors to occur.

Environmental Variables

In the last 30 years or so, scientific psychologists have concluded that the behavior of using drugs, called drug self-administration, is an operant response that can be studied and explained in the same manner as other operant responses. At the heart of this conclusion is the discovery that self-administered drugs can function as positive reinforcers; that is, they strengthen responses that lead to their delivery. Numerous laboratory studies have demonstrated that rats or monkeys will self-administer most of the same drugs that humans self-administer if a particular response, such as a lever press, results in the drug being administered. In testing more than 100 drugs, researchers have found that, in general, those that are self-administered and abused by humans will serve as positive reinforcers in nonhumans (Griffiths, Bigelow, & Henningfield, 1980). These include opiates (e.g., heroin), CNS depressants (e.g., alcohol), stimulants (e.g., amphetamine), and other drugs. Hallucinogenic compounds such as LSD, mescaline, and psilocybin are exceptions to this pattern.

All of these drugs establish and maintain the drug taking of nonhumans in environments without obvious predisposing factors. In other words, rats and monkeys need not be stressed, food-deprived, provided with nondrug reinforcement, or treated in any unusual manner to establish drug self-administration. All that is needed is exposure to a situation in which a response leads to drug delivery. Given this, the behavior leading to drug delivery occurs often and results in high levels of intake. For example, monkeys allowed to press a bar producing intravenous injections of morphine will self-administer enough of the drug to produce physical dependence (Thompson & Schuster, 1964). Furthermore, unless arrangements that limit drug intake are in place (which is the case in almost all studies), monkeys under some conditions will self-administer enough morphine or *d*-amphetamine to overdose and die (Johanson, Balster, & Bonese, 1976).

Studies of drug self-administration by nonhumans are important for two reasons. First, they provide information about the possible causes of human drug use and abuse. Second, they indicate that many drugs can exercise powerful control over behavior in the absence of any obvious psychopathology. For instance, it does not appear reasonable to assume that the average rat or monkey is mentally ill, weak-willed, or aberrant in personality development.

Even though scientific psychologists know that most drugs of abuse can maintain behavior as potent reinforcers, the question remains as to why someone will use the drug in the first place. The first thing to remember is that no one abuses a drug without having been exposed to it. Given that a drug is available, then, the initial decision to use the drug and the early pattern of use depends on at least three factors: (1) the kind of rules concerning appropriate drug intake and expected drug effects given to or generated by the person, (2) the extent to which historical events favor following these rules, and (3) the degree to which current circumstances (i.e., contingencies of reinforcement and punishment) support or weaken drug-taking behavior. Consider an example of a college sophomore to whom a date offers cocaine at a party, saying, "It's great stuff: max rad, no hangover. Try it." This isn't quite like Mom and Dad's rule: "Cocaine use is bad—it's an expensive road to ruin. Just say no." Which rule is followed, that is, whether or not the sophomore tries cocaine, depends on the individual's experience with respect to drugs and parents' versus dates' pronouncements, as well as the circumstances in which the drug is offered. If all party goers are snorting cocaine and encouraging the novice to do so, the likelihood that the response will occur is increased (an instance of conformity).

The variables that are responsible for the maintenance of drug abuse (reinforcers) often differ from those responsible for initial use. In fact, many drugs that are not positively reinforcing upon early exposure come to be so if self-administration continues. Cigarette smoking is a case in point. If you ever tried to smoke a cigarette, you undoubtedly remember what it was like the first time you inhaled the smoke. It certainly did not reinforce the behaviors leading up to that first attempt. Thus, early exposures to cigarettes are not in themselves positively reinforcing. Nevertheless, many people will try smoking again and again largely because of peer praise associated with the experience. Also, in our culture it is still considered "cool" to smoke, at least in some circles, as is evidenced by the number of movies in which characters smoke. Thus, there is some automatic reinforcement associated with seeing oneself look like a movie star or rock star. With continued exposure to cigarettes, tolerance (a reduced drug effect due to repeated exposure) develops to certain unpleasant effects of smoking (e.g., nausea), and cigarette use may become positively reinforcing. Nicotine plays a big role in the repeated use of cigarettes because, despite what the CEOs of the major tobacco companies claim, nicotine is addictive. Self-talk may also play a role in early drug use, as when a young person praises his or her own smoking, perhaps saying, "Cigarette smoking is great. It makes me look cool and grown-up." It is important to note that there is nothing accidental in how someone responds when first offered a drug; this behavior is a function of historical (ultimate) and current (proximate) variables that, although complex, act in lawful fashion.

Other variables, such as discriminative stimuli and motivational variables, continue to control self-administration once a drug is serving as a positive reinforcer. Discriminative stimuli, which nearly always include individuals who have provided the drug in the past, are correlated with successful drug seeking, and their presence increases the likelihood that such behavior will occur.

Physical Dependence

One strong determinant of the reinforcing effectiveness of a given drug, especially in physically dependent users, is the degree of drug deprivation, a motivational variable (see Chapter 6). **Physical dependence** describes the state of an organism in which abrupt termination of chronic (repeated) drug administration is followed by a withdrawal syndrome. The **withdrawal syndrome** is a confluence of signs (observable changes) and symptoms (changes reported by the individual) that emerge following abrupt termination of drug administration. As levels of drug in the bloodstream fall and withdrawal symptoms ensue, the value of the drug as a positive reinforcer grows. An implication of the term physical dependence is that the chronic presence of the drug has altered the individual in such a way that normal functioning requires continued presence of the drug. Disruption of normal activity induced by drug withdrawal includes physiological responses (e.g., diarrhea and vomiting when heroin administration is discontinued), overt behavioral responses (e.g., drug-seeking behavior), and subjective responses (e.g., self-reported craving for the drug).

Withdrawal symptoms result not only from falling levels of the drug in the bloodstream, but also from classical conditioning. As we described in Chapter 5, greater tolerance is observed under conditions in which the drug has been regularly taken in the past. Specifically, the sights and sounds associated with the drug-taking environment become CSs which elicit a compensatory response opposite to that of the drug, in other words, withdrawal symptoms. Thus, as the drug user enters the environment in which he or she as regularly used the drug (CS), the withdrawal symptoms (CR) become more acute. The withdrawal symptoms then function as a motivational variable in the sense that they can be escaped immediately only by self-administering more drug (negative reinforcement).

Changes in drug level (i.e., relative deprivation) can also influence patterns of self-administration in the absence of physical dependence. Studies with rats and humans given limited access to cocaine show, for example, that typical subjects rapidly self-administer enough drug to reach a moderately high drug level, then space administrations so that this level is maintained. When constantly available, cocaine and similar stimulants are usually self-administered in a cyclic pattern in which periods of high drug intake alternate with periods of low intake during which much time is spent eating and sleeping (Griffiths et al., 1980). Other drugs are associated with different patterns of self-administration. Opioids, for example, when constantly available are typically administered in increasing quantities over a period of several weeks, after which a fairly stable level of intake is maintained.

Like other operant responses, drug-seeking and drug-taking behavior is controlled in part by the schedule of delivery. With illegal drugs that are scarce or expensive, much behavior may be required prior to drug delivery. Consider that an average heroin user can easily self-administer $100 or $200 worth of the drug each day. Much of such a person's time is necessarily devoted to a long chain of drug-seeking behavior. For instance, theft, fencing stolen items, contacting a dealer, and preparing a fix may all precede drug injection. Therefore, abuse of heroin affects not only the user, but also the society in which the user acts to obtain the drug. In such cases, it is interesting to note that most of the harm caused by heroin addiction is not due to the drug itself but, rather, to the fact that it is illegal.

Nonpharmacological Consequences of Drug Use

Nonpharmacological consequences of drug seeking and drug taking can also strongly affect these behaviors. In some instances, drug use provides access to valued objects or activities that otherwise would not be available. The seducer's maxim, "Flowers are good, but liquor is quicker," emphasizes that, in certain circles, drug (alcohol) use is associated with increased likelihood of a particular kind of nonpharmacological reinforcer, sexual activity. Although this need not be the case, it sometimes is. Moreover, the rule "alcohol + potential partner = sex" can foster drinking in a person for whom sexual activity is a potent reinforcer, even if the rule is untrue. Add to the equation the fact that females get drunk more quickly than males because their bodies metabolize alcohol slightly differently, and you may begin to understand why men frequently offer women alcoholic drinks.

Nonpharmacological consequences also play a major role in the development and maintenance of nonabusive drug use. Even though studies with nonhumans show beyond a reasonable doubt that many drugs are very potent reinforcers, not all humans who come into contact with such drugs abuse them. Why? The general answer is straightforward: Environmental contingencies foster responsible use by many people. These contingencies, which are arranged by society at large as well as by families and friends of the drug user, involve short-term consequences of drug-seeking and drug-taking behaviors: Responsible drug use (or abstinence) is reinforced, irresponsible drug use is punished. In addition, rules describing appropriate drug use are provided, and voicing and following these rules is reinforced. Finally, behaviors that are incompatible with drug abuse are encouraged and reinforced. The contingencies a group arranges to prevent abusive drug intake by its members are effective to the extent that they involve consequences more powerful than those working to produce abusive self-administration.

Unfortunately, the reinforcing properties of a drug, coupled with a lack of rules and consequences sufficiently powerful to reduce drug use, sometimes lead to drug abuse. As drug use increases, drug-related behaviors can weaken contingencies that otherwise would discourage abuse. Envision a newly married couple, one of them recently employed as a construction laborer. Neither has a drug abuse problem, but the newly hired spouse begins to stop regularly after work to have a few beers with fellow workers. At first, the stops use up little time or alcohol, because the reinforcers associated with home and spouse are preferred to those associated with bar and friends. As days pass, however, the homebound mate wearies of waiting and begins to behave differently when the companion returns from work. No longer is dinner cooked or are romantic evenings planned. Arguments beginning with "Where the hell have you been?" become commonplace, and the evening hours grow less pleasant for both partners. As the home environment becomes less rewarding, the bar grows relatively more so. Hence, more time is spent at the bar and more beer is drunk. This, in turn, further increases marital discord which might end in a drug-abuse problem.

The scenario just described is oversimplified, but it does emphasize an important point: Drug-related behaviors may reduce an individual's access to other reinforcers and thereby increase the relative time and effort directed to drug seeking and drug taking. Moreover, many individuals who experience drug-related problems, for example, those raised in poverty, have never acquired a behavioral repertoire adequate for attaining any of a range of significant positive reinforcers, including those associated with a good education and job, and all the reinforcers that follow. In the absence of strong competing reinforcers, the relative power of drugs to control behavior is magnified immensely. Therefore, as Ray (1983) notes, "treatment for many drug abusers is habilitation, not rehabilitation" (p. 28).

Physiological Variables

In Chapter 7, we described how abused drugs affect behavior at the neurophysiological level by altering neurotransmission, either by binding directly to receptors of receiving neurons, as with opiates such as heroin and morphine, or by directly altering the amount of neurotransmitter substance, as with cocaine and amphetamines. In either case, most drugs of abuse affect the same parts of the brain as do natural reinforcers such as food and sex. Thus, two important points need to be made. First, whether or not humans have inherited a susceptibility to a particular drug, such as alcohol (see the following section), it is clear that we have all inherited a brain that is sensitive to drugs of abuse. Second, drugs act as potent reinforcers in all of us due to specific features of our nervous system.

Genetic Variables

The foregoing discussion has emphasized that environmental variables acting through certain physiological mechanisms play a major role in drug abuse. This should not be taken to mean that everyone is equally sensitive to these variables, or is equally likely to develop drug-related problems. A substantial body of information, overviewed in Chapter 4, suggests that genetic variables play a role in determining the risk of a person's developing drug-related problems, at least with respect to alcohol. Support for this notion comes from adoption studies and twin studies with humans, and from selective breeding studies in laboratory animals (Begleiter & Kissin, 1995). In 1990, researchers even reported having isolated a specific gene that leads to alcoholism (Blum, Noble, Sheridan, Montgomery, & Richie, 1990), although subsequent work called that conclusion into question (Gelernter, Goldman, & Risch, 1993). Although there appears to be a genetic predisposition toward alcohol abuse, the gene(s) that controls this predisposition and the mechanism responsible for it are unclear. As Petrakis (1985) indicated in a review of the role of genetics in alcoholism:

> The studies described in preceding sections observed only a behavioral phenomenon—alcoholism—and provided strong evidence that it can have a genetic basis. But

strictly speaking, behavior, as such, cannot be inherited. Only genes can, and the immediate products of genes are proteins. Behavioral characteristics arise from the genes and their products, but remotely, and furthermore they are strongly influenced by environment.

It is therefore insufficient merely to say that the risk of the behavior pattern, alcoholism is inherited and let it go at that. We need to know what *physical* characteristics people inherit that make them vulnerable to develop the alcoholic behavior pattern. Specifically, how do their anatomical, physiological, and biochemical systems differ from those of people who are not susceptible? And by what mechanisms do these differences become expressed as alcoholism? Such questions have more than theoretical importance; they can lead to discoveries that help us understand how alcoholism develops and devise better ways to treat and prevent it. Merely proving that alcoholism can have a genetic basis, and asking no further questions, gets us nowhere. (p. 18; emphasis in original)

Further questions are being asked, and we may someday understand fully the biochemical and genetic bases of alcoholism and other forms of drug abuse, and be able to develop treatments that work at these levels. At the present time, however, there are no genetic treatments and few biochemical ones, but there are many "psychological" approaches to the treatment of drug abuse. It is beyond our purpose to detail specific drug abuse treatment programs or to consider their efficacy. Those programs that are consistent with the scientific orientation presented in this book are based on the assumption that drug abuse results in large part from exposure to a particular kind of environment, one in which contingencies support a troublesome pattern of drug self-administration. Altering these contingencies must therefore be a part of treatment.

Treatment of Drug Abuse

Treatment of drug abuse characteristically begins with detoxification. **Detoxification** involves safely weaning a physically dependent person away from a drug, and can be accomplished easily with current technology (Jaffee, 1990). After an individual is detoxified, dramatic steps must be taken to alter the consequences of drug taking such that abusive patterns of intake are not supported. Abusive patterns of intake typically harm the user, but the harm often is much delayed relative to the time of drug intake. In contrast, the positively reinforcing effects of drug administration occur with little delay. In light of this, effective approaches to the treatment of drug abuse focus on four tactics. First, since delayed consequences have little direct effect on behavior, most effective approaches attempt to arrange short-term consequences that weaken inappropriate drug use and strengthen appropriate drug-related behavior. Second, treatment programs attempt to teach appropriate rule-governed behavior (see Chapter 8) concerning drugs. Third, training new responses appropriate for gaining nonpharmacological reinforcers may be necessary. Finally, conditioning factors in the client's daily environment that foster inappropriate drug usage will have to be altered. These include aspects of the environment acting as discriminative stimuli and establishing operations for, as well as nonpharmacological reinforcers associated with, drug self-administration. For many drug users, this means changing the people he or she associates with and the settings in which these interactions occur. Obviously, this means a dramatic change in the lifestyle of the drug user and explains why reducing drug-taking behaviors is such an intractable problem.

It follows, then, that it is easier to eliminate inappropriate drug use in inpatient than outpatient settings (Griffiths et al., 1980). Like other operant behavior, drug self-administration is sensitive to punishment. For example, delivering shock or imposing a time-out dependent on drinking suppresses alcohol intake in a research ward setting. Extinction, which can involve pharmacological blockage of a drug's effects or simple failure to deliver the drug, also reduces drug self-administration. Pairing the taste of a drug with nausea and vomiting in a conditioned taste aversion procedure is also effective, and this procedure is sometimes used to stop cigarette smoking and ethanol abuse.

Although punishment, extinction, and taste aversion conditioning are effective in reducing drug intake, the clinical utility of these procedures outside controlled settings is limited. None of these procedures produce permanent effects unless they are kept in effect; like all contingency management procedures, they affect behavior when they are operative and for a limited time thereafter. Once punishment or extinction ends, or the pairing of drug and nausea ceases, behavior typically returns to pretreatment levels. Moreover, humans can discriminate conditions correlated with particular contingencies and behave accordingly. For instance, an alcohol abuser who is taking disulfiram (Antibuse) as part of a treatment program may learn that drinking alcohol leads to sickness in the presence of disulfiram, but not in its absence. Sickness can be avoided by not drinking after taking disulfiram, or by not taking disulfiram before drinking. In the latter case, the client circumvents the intended treatment. Clients' avoiding therapeutic contingencies is a major problem in the outpatient treatment of drug abuse.

One approach that can be taken to increase the likelihood that clients will be exposed to therapeutic contingencies is to make these contingencies positively reinforcing. A study by McCaul, Stitzer, Bigelow, and Liebson (1984) provides a good example of the use of positive reinforcement in treating drug abuse. This investigation involved 20 male opiate abusers who were enrolled in an outpatient detoxification program in which methadone doses were gradually decreased over time. Contingency management treatment, which was arranged for 10 men (the experimental group), involved giving a patient $10 and a take-home methadone dose each time he produced an opiate-free urine specimen, and requiring him to participate in an intensive clinical procedure when an opiate was present in urine. As shown in Figure 13-2, this treatment slowed the relapse to illicit opiate use relative to control subjects who were paid for providing a urine sample regardless of drug content.

Several other researchers have shown that contingency management procedures similar to those used by McCaul and colleagues (1984) are effective in reducing abusive drug intake. **Contingency contracting,** wherein a therapist and client formally agree that specified patterns of drug-related behavior (e.g., abstinence for a one-week period) will lead to particular consequences, has, for

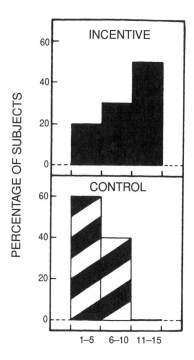

Figure 13-2. The longest opiate-free period achieved by patients in experimental and control groups, expressed as the number of consecutive opiate-free urine specimens. Patients provided two specimens per week during the 10-week intervention period; thus they could achieve a maximum of 20 consecutive opiate-free specimens. Patients in the experimental group received money and methadone contingent on producing an opiate-free specimen, control patients did not. (From "Contingency Management Interventions: Effects on Treatment Outcome During Methadone Detoxification," by M. E. McCaul, M. L. Stitzer, G. W. Bigelow, and I. A. Liebson, 1984, *Journal of Applied Behavioral Analysis, 17*, p. 35–43. Copyright 1984 by The Society for the Experimental Analysis of Behavior. Reproduced with permission.)

example, been demonstrated effective in reducing cigarette smoking, excessive caffeine intake, cocaine intake, alcohol consumption and, as shown in Figure 13-3, barbiturate use by inpatient sedative abusers.

Numerous other examples of the use of behavioral procedures to treat abusive drug intake are available (e.g., Harris, 1981). On balance, it is clear that altering the consequences of drug-related behaviors is an effective method for treating drug abuse in a variety of situations. The primary shortcoming of such procedures is that it is often difficult to arrange the environment so that appropriate consequences occur. Although this can be done within a treatment facility, return to the client's normal environment too often results in exposure to the same contingencies that originally produced the drug abuse.

A compelling example of the importance of the posttreatment environment in the reinstatement of drug abuse involves American military personnel who

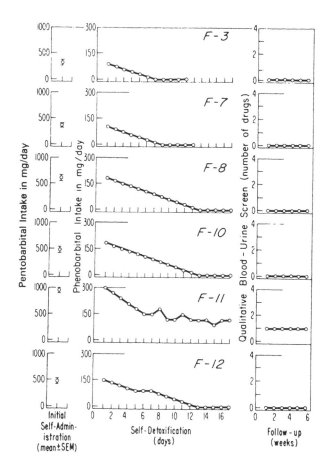

Figure 13-3. The effects of contingency contracting on drug intake of six subjects with confirmed histories of sedative abuse. Graphs along the left side indicate levels of pentobarbital intake per day prior to treatment. At the start of detoxification, phenobarbital was substituted for pentobarbital (15 mg phenobarbital for 50 mg pentobarbital) for three days of self-administration. Subjects were then given points (exchangeable for a variety of reinforcers) for successfully reducing drug intake but lost points for failing to do so. Five of the six subjects met the requirements of the contract and became drug-free. Follow-up data (right panels) indicate that these patients had not returned to drug use two months after detoxification. [From Pickens, R., 1979. A behavioral program for treatment of drug dependence. In N. A. Krasnegor (Ed.), *Behavioral analysis and treatment of drug abuse,* pp. 44–54. Washington, DC: U.S. Government Printing Office. Reproduced with author's permission.]

returned from Vietnam with a heroin abuse problem. After treatment and return to their home country, the vast majority did not return to heroin abuse (Robins, 1974). This occurred because the environmental variables that fostered abuse in Vietnam were not present in the posttreatment situation.

Mental Retardation

Three general features characterize people with mental retardation (Hodapp & Dykens, 1996). First, these individuals have subaverage general intellectual functioning, as evidenced by intelligence test scores below a designated level. Second, they exhibit deficits in adaptive behavior, which involves activities necessary to care for oneself and to function in society. Third, the deficits in general intellectual functioning and adaptive behavior are evident early in life. It is the deficits in adaptive behavior that constitute much of the troublesome behavior for many mentally retarded individuals.

Most definitions of mental retardation agree that mental retardation occurs prior to 18 years of age. The overall prevalence of mental retardation is unknown, but several estimates place it somewhere between 1% and 3% (Gadow & Poling, 1988). People diagnosed as mentally retarded are a remarkably heterogeneous group; one obvious difference is the degree of impairment in adaptive behavior and intelligence test scores. Mental retardation typically is classified according to severity, although other modes of classification (e.g., by clinical symptoms or by etiology) are sometimes used. The system used most often today classifies mental retardation as *mild, moderate, severe,* or *profound,* in increasing order of severity. Approximately 90% of people with mental retardation are classified as mildly mentally retarded (American Psychiatric Association, 1994). Most of these individuals look and act much like other people and, with appropriate support, can live relatively independent and profitable lives.

More than 250 conditions are known to cause, or at least increase the risk of, mental retardation, including chromosomal aberrations, metabolic and nutritional disorders, brain disease, trauma, sensory deprivation, and psychosocial disadvantage (Grossman, 1983). Nonetheless, causal mechanisms are unknown in most cases, because mild mental retardation (the most prevalent form) is often determined by the same complex maze of variables that influence ability and performance in nonretarded people (MacMillan, 1982).

Although psychologists use a variety of interventions to help people with mental retardation, procedures based on the principles of operant conditioning are especially successful in dealing with their troublesome behaviors. In fact, hundreds of studies have demonstrated that "through the monitoring and systematic manipulation of antecedents and consequents, it has been possible to develop rudimentary self-help skills and complex vocational assembly tasks while controlling inappropriate responses such as aggression and self-injurious behavior . . ." (Scibak, 1983, p. 339).

A good example of the behavioral approach to dealing with troublesome behavior is provided by Azrin and Foxx (1971), who taught nine profoundly mentally retarded institutionalized adults (20 to 62 years of age) appropriate toileting skills. Prior to the institution of treatment, each of them regularly urinated and/or defecated in their clothing. Within a few days of exposure to treatment, incidents of incontinence were reduced by about 90%, and by the

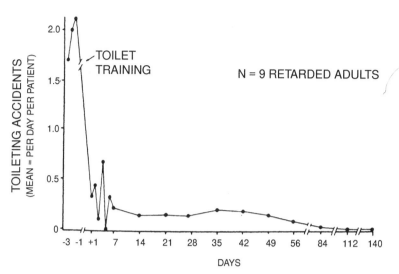

Figure 13-4. The effects of a toilet training program on the mean frequency of accidents (urinating and defecating in clothing) by nine profoundly mentally retarded adults. (From "A Rapid Method of Toilet Training the Institutionalized Retarded," by N. H. Azrin and R. M. Foxx, 1971, *Journal of Applied Behavior Analysis, 4,* pp. 89–99. Copyright 1971 by the Society for the Experimental Analysis of Behavior, Reproduced with permission.)

end of treatment incontinence was almost totally eliminated (Figure 13-4). Thus the treatment obviously benefited the residents and the staff who cared for them.

The procedures used by Azrin and Foxx (1971) involved (1) increasing the frequency of urination (by having the residents drink water) to increase the opportunities for learning, (2) providing positive reinforcement for correct toileting, (3) using an automatic apparatus to signal elimination, (4) shaping independent toileting, and (5) training the residents to emit hygienic behaviors. Steps were also taken to ensure the maintenance of appropriate toileting. These procedures, based largely on principles of operant conditioning, are noteworthy for their completeness and efficacy.

That procedures based on operant conditioning have proven to be especially effective in helping people with mental retardation should not be interpreted to mean that such procedures are intrinsically more effective with this population than with other people. If it is possible to use operant conditioning procedures systematically, then it is possible to change a wide range of behaviors in any human. Such procedures have been widely used to treat people with mental retardation for two reasons: (1) Some people with mental retardation exhibit problem behaviors that are resistant to other treatments; and (2) the residential, educational, and vocational placements of some people with mental retardation are structured so that it is possible to use the procedures systematically.

Conclusion

The depth and breadth of troublesome human behavior is both tragic and fascinating. Problems can crop up in any area of endeavor, including learning, sleeping, eating, working, raising children, and making love, to name a few. Behaviors considered as troublesome vary; diagnostic categories come and go, and particular categories generate different degrees of interest across time and cultures. In fact, some troublesome behaviors appear to be caused by what might be reasonably termed "cultural" variables. As a case in point, eating disorders, including *anorexia* (self-induced starvation) and *bulimia* (binge eating followed by inappropriate compensatory behaviors, such as vomiting) appear to have become more prevalent over time (Fairburn, Hay, & Welch, 1993). Such disorders now occur rather frequently in Western cultures, although they are rare among males and occur most frequently in young, educated women of high socioeconomic status (G. T. Wilson, Heffernan, & Black, 1996). Both disorders are rare in cultures that do not emphasize thinness as a highly desirable characteristic in females, but what, exactly, causes young women to starve themselves, or to binge and purge, remains to be discovered (G. T. Wilson et al., 1996). Moreover, although reasonably effective treatments of bulimia are available, anorexia is largely resistant to current therapies (Hsu, 1990). Clearly, there is work for psychologists in understanding, treating, and preventing eating disorders. Continued development of a science of behavior appears to be a prerequisite for success in each of these areas, and in dealing with the multitude of other troublesome behaviors that beset us.

Summary

1. *Troublesome behavior* refers to patterns of responding that constitute a problem for the person who emits them or for other people.

2. Psychiatric (or psychological) diagnosis involves categorizing people according to the troublesome things they say and do. On this basis, two general forms of *mental illness* have been identified. *Psychoses* involve severe and pervasive behavioral problems, pronounced functional impairment and *thought disorders, hallucinations,* and *delusions.* Less pervasive and debilitating behavior disorders, termed *neuroses,* often appear to be exaggerations of normal reactions and do not involve substantial loss of behavioral control by environmental events.

3. Even though the term mental illness is used, the mind cannot control behavior and, hence, it cannot become ill. From a scientific standpoint, the same classes of variables that cause "normal" behavior—genetic, physiological, and environmental—also cause "abnormal" behavior.

4. The most widely used classification system for mental disorders is the *Diagnostic and Statistical Manual of Mental Disorders* (4th ed.; *DSM-IV*). Because the criteria for diagnosing a particular disorder are somewhat vague, however, the *DSM-IV* has been criticized.

5. Schizophrenia is characterized by *positive symptoms,* which include hallucinations, thought disorders, and delusions, and *negative symptoms,* which include flattened affect, impoverished speech, anhedonia (inability to experience pleasure), lack of motivation, and social withdrawal. Although there is no one cause of schizophrenia, there is evidence that physiological (overproduction of dopamine), genetic (as studied in twins) and environmental (prenatal stress or illness, contingencies of reinforcement) variables play a role.

6. The treatment of choice for schizophrenia is antipsychotic drugs (e.g., chlorpromazine), although nonpharmacological interventions, such as token economies and applied behavior analysis, are also important.

7. *Mood disorders,* also known as affective disorders, are disorders of emotion, and include Major Depressive Disorder, seasonal affective disorder, and Bipolar Disorder, including mania. *Major Depressive Disorder* is characterized by episodes in which the individual reports feeling sad and guilty, and objects and events that were once rewarding control little behavior; behavior is generally suppressed.

8. As with schizophrenia, there is evidence of physiological (e.g., lowered amounts of neurotransmitter substances in the brain), genetic, and environmental (insufficient positive reinforcement, learned helplessness) causes of depression.

9. The treatment of choice for major depression is the use of antidepressant drugs, although *electroconvulsive therapy* (ECT), which involves electrically inducing a seizure, is still used in rare cases that are insensitive to other treatments. Also effective are behavior and cognitive-behavior therapies.

10. *Anxiety Disorders* include Panic Disorder, Phobias, Obsessive-Compulsive Disorder, and Posttraumatic Stress Disorder. Although difficult to define, *anxiety* generally involves an unpleasant subjective state aptly described as "fearful," physiological arousal, and troublesome overt behavior that minimizes contact with certain stimuli. However, anxiety is not a thing, but only a label assigned to describe certain kinds of behavioral and physiological responses emitted under the control of certain kinds of stimuli.

11. Although there may be a genetic predisposition to anxiety disorders, environmental variables play a significant role in their development, most likely through classical conditioning, avoidance learning, rules, and observational learning.

12. Effective treatments of anxiety disorders include *systematic desensitization,* in which a person is taught to relax in the presence of stimuli that once produced anxiety, and *modeling,* a therapeutic technique in which the client observes another person responding appropriately in a situation where the client fails to do so (e.g., one in which an anxiety-arousing stimulus is present).

13. The term *drug abuse* is used to refer to any pattern of drug self-administration that produces harmful behavioral or physiological effects without producing compensatory medical benefit. Scientists now know that drug abuse is a set of behaviors that are controlled by the same kinds of variables that influence other important human activities.

14. Laboratory studies have demonstrated with nonhuman subjects that many abused drugs (e.g., cocaine, amphetamine, caffeine, nicotine, opiates) serve as powerful positive reinforcers for the behavior that results in their administration. However, the initial decision to self-administer and the early pattern of use depends on the kinds of rules concerning drug use given to or generated by the person, the extent to which historical events (i.e., reinforcers) favor following these rules, and the degree to which current circumstances support or weaken drug-taking behavior.

15. Treatment of drug abuse characteristically begins with *detoxification,* which involves safely weaning a physically dependent person away from a drug. Thereafter, steps must be taken to alter the consequences of drug taking such that abusive patterns of intake are not supported, in part by teaching appropriate rule-governed behavior concerning drugs, training new responses for gaining nonpharmacological reinforcers, and by altering conditioning factors in the client's daily environment that foster inappropriate drug usage.

16. People with mental retardation typically exhibit deficits in adaptive behavior, which involves activities necessary to care for oneself and to function in society. Hundreds of studies have shown that procedures based on the principles of operant conditioning are successful in dealing with their troublesome behaviors.

Study Questions

1. What is abnormal behavior and why is it better termed "troublesome behavior"?

2. Why is the example of Jerry noteworthy?

3. When is the term *mental illness* used, what is the distinction between psychoses and neuroses, and what is the point about the mind causing illness?

4. What is the *DSM-IV,* how is it used, how is it related to explanation, and what are the pros and cons?

5. What are the two types of symptoms of schizophrenia and the four subtypes?

6. What are the possible proximate physiological causes of schizophrenia (i.e., dopamine hypothesis and abnormalities in brain structure), and the possible ultimate causes (i.e., genetic and environmental variables)?

7. What is the primary (pharmacological) treatment of schizophrenia and the example of token economy as a nonpharmacological treatment?

8. What are mood disorders, including the four types?

9. What are the possible causes of mood disorders, especially as in the insufficient positive reinforcement hypothesis and its more recent incarnation, the learned helplessness model? How is the cognitive-distortion theory related?

10. What are the major treatments of depression, including antidepressant medications and cognitive-behavior therapy?

11. What are SSRIs and how do they work?

12. How does cognitive-behavior therapy approach the treatment of depression and how does the thought-stopping procedure work?

13. What kinds of behavior therapy procedures have been generated by the insufficient reinforcement hypothesis?

14. What are the types of anxiety disorders and how is the term *anxiety* defined, especially as troublesome behavior; what is the point about anxiety as a thing that causes behavior?

15. What are some of the possible causes of anxiety disorders, especially environmental (learning) causes?

16. What are systematic desensitization and modeling and how are they used to treat anxiety disorders?

17. How is the term *drug abuse* used (defined)?

18. What is wrong with saying that drug abuse is a sign of weakness or of a dysfunctional personality?

19. How is drug self-administration viewed as an operant response and what kinds of nonhuman studies have shed light on this view? For what two reasons are studies of drug self-administration by nonhumans important for humans?

20. What are some of the variables that cause drug use (and abuse) in humans? What is tolerance and how does it develop, especially to drugs (e.g., nicotine) that are not initially reinforcing?

21. What is detoxification and what other methods are effective in treating drug abuse, including contingency contracting? What is the difference between in- and outpatient settings?

22. What troublesome behaviors do people with mental retardation have and what is the most successful form of treatment for such behaviors?

Glossary

abnormal behavior   (see *troublesome behavior*)

accommodation   In the cognitive developmental theory of Piaget, a process of adaptation whereby exisiting knowledge (cognitive structures) must be modified to adapt to new experiences which cannot be assimilated (see *assimilation*).

action potential   The wave of electrical activity along an axon of a neuron, caused by the influx of sodium ions, that lasts less than three milliseconds, and passes rapidly, without diminishing until it reaches the terminal buttons (see *nerve impulse*).

affective disorders   (see *mood disorders*)

afferent nerves   Sensory nerves that go from sensory receptors to the central nervous system.

aggression   Name applied to a wide range of social interactions in which one organism emits behavior directed toward harming another but not accidentally.

agnosia   Term that refers to the inability of an individual to identify or recognize an object by means of a particular sensory modality. For example, people with visual agnosias are often unable to recognize objects visually even though they can recognize them by touch or sound.

agonist   Drugs that facilitate (or mimic) the effects of neurotransmitter substances.

amygdala   Part of the forebrain (limbic system); involved in learning and memory and plays a role in emotional (e.g., aggressive, fearful) and stress-related behavior.

animism   (see *vitalism*)

antagonist   Drugs that inhibit (or retard) the effects of neurotransmitter substances.

antecedent stimulus   A stimulus that precedes the response it controls.

anthropomorphism   Describing nonhuman characteristics with terms usually used to describe human characteristics.

anxiety   Anxiety involves an unpleasant subjective state aptly described as "fearful," physiological arousal, and troublesome overt behavior that minimizes contact with certain stimuli.

aphasia   An impairment of language production or speech (Broca's aphasia) or comprehension (Wernicke's aphasia) produced by brain damage.

archival studies   A type of research design that makes use of existing documentation as a data source. Examples include clinical records, quarterly reports, census banks, or any other permanent records kept by clinics, hospitals, businesses, governments, or other organizations.

artificial intelligence   Term used to refer to output by a computer that if displayed by a human would be considered intelligent.

assimilation   In the cognitive developmental theory of Piaget, a process of adaptation whereby new experiences are interpreted in terms of existing knowledge (cognitive structures).

attachment   Term used to describe special kinds of parent–child interactions, specifically those that indicate that the child seeks to be close to and in other ways prefers the parent over other people.

automatic reinforcement   Reinforcement that is a natural result of behavior when such behavior operates upon the behaver's own body or the surrounding world. Automatic reinforcers thus do not require direct mediation by other persons (see ecological reinforcers).

autonomic nervous system (ANS)   The branch of the peripheral nervous system that regulates the cardiac muscle, and the smooth muscles and glands.

axon   Structure of the neuron that carries nerve impulses away from the cell body toward the terminal buttons.

backward conditioning   A classical conditioning procedure in which the CS occurs after the US.

behavior disorder   All conditions in which individuals cause a problem for themselves or for other people because they exhibit behavior that is unacceptable or they fail to function appropriately.

behavior genetics   The (correlational) study of the relation between differences in genotype and differences in behavior (phenotype) in a population.

between-subjects experimental design   Each subject is exposed to only one level of the independent variable and the effects of the independent variable are determined by comparing the behavior with that of each subject who has been exposed to different conditions.

bipolar disorder   Mood disorder characterized by the alternation between mania and depression.

Broca's area   An area on the left side of the frontal lobe responsible for the memories of speech that if damaged results in a type of speech aphasia called Broca's aphasia.

Cartesian dualism   The view of Descartes that humans possess both a physical body and a nonphysical mind (soul) (see also mind–body dualism).

central nervous system (CNS)   Division of the nervous system that consists of the brain and spinal cord.

cerebral cortex   A layer of neurons approximately 2 millimeters thick that covers the cerebrum.

cerebrum   The outermost and largest portion of the human brain; consists of a right and left hemisphere.

chaining   (see *response chaining*)

chromosomes   Long strands of deoxyribonucleic acid (DNA). Humans have 46 (23 pairs).

circular reasoning   A type of inadequate explanation of behavior in which the only evidence for the explanation is simply the behavior to be explained.

classical discrimination training   (see *discrimination training*)

classical extinction   (see *extinction*)

cognition   Term for the cognitive or mental processes by which one acquires knowledge of the world.

cognitive-distortion theory   Theory of depression in which depression is characterized by distortions in thinking (self-talk) about the world that don't match reality.

cognitive psychology   An approach to the study of behavior in which behavior is observed and measured in order to infer unobservable (cognitive or mental) processes.

collateral responses   Term used to refer to overt (public) changes in behavior that occur in conjunction with a private event.

common descent   The view that all life forms descended from a common ancestor (see also species continuity).

comparative psychology   The study of nonhuman behavior to learn about human behavior.

compliance   A type of social relation studied by social psychologists that is defined as behaving in a manner consistent with a direct request for a certain form of behavior.

concurrent reinforcement schedule   A schedule of reinforcement in which reinforcement is arranged simultaneously for two or more response classes.

conditional discrimination   An operant discrimination procedure in which a response that is reinforced (and therefore subsequently occurs) in the presence of one stimulus depends on the presence of a second stimulus.

conditional reflex   A learned relation in which a CS comes, through classical conditioning, to elicit a conditional response.

conditional response (CR)   The response elicited by a CS after classical conditioning.

conditional stimulus (CS)   A (previously neutral) stimulus that, after being paired with a US in classical conditioning, elicits a response that is usually, but not always, similar to the UR.

conditioned reinforcers   Reinforcers that gain their ability to strengthen behavior through learning (also called secondary reinforcers).

conformity   A type of social relation studied by social psychologists that is defined as a change in behavior as a result of implicit group pressure.

consciousness   (see *self-awareness*).

conservation   A term used by Piaget to refer to situations in which a person responds to an object as unchanged despite transformations performed on that object.

contingency   In classical conditioning the probability of the US occurring must be higher immediately after CS presentation than at any other time. In operant conditioning the probability of the consequence (reinforcer or punisher) occurring must be higher immediately after a response than at any other time.

contingency contracting   A contingency management technique wherein a therapist and client formally agree that specified patterns of drug-related behavior (e.g., abstinence for a one-week period) will lead to particular consequences.

contingency-governed behavior   Behavior that is affected by directly contacting environmental relations, for example, by operant conditioning.

control processes   Processes (e.g., encoding, chunking, rehearsal) assumed by information theory to orchestrate the flow of information through the three levels (structural components) of memory.

corpus callosum   The largest and most important bundle of nerve fibers that connects the two cerebral hemispheres that, when severed surgically in some patients with epilepsy, results in split-brain phenomena.

correlational research   A research strategy in which the researcher attempts to determine the relationship between two existing variables in a population without manipulating independent variables.

crossing experiments   Experiments on the genetic bases of behavior in which organisms that differ with respect to a particular behavior are crossed (mated) while holding environmental factors as constant as possible.

data   The (plural) term used for the kind of information obtained by scientists. (*Datum* is the singular form.)

deductive ordering   The general principles, laws, and other statements of a science are established such that accurate statements about particular happenings are possible (general to particular).

delayed conditioning   A classical conditioning procedure in which the CS begins shortly before the US and is terminated after the US is presented.

dendrites   Branchlike structures that extend from the cell body of neurons and synapse on terminal buttons of sending neurons.

deoxyribonucleic acid (DNA)   The self-replicating physical carrier of genetic information found in the nuclei of all cells.

dependent variable   In an experiment, it is the behavior of interest that may or may not reflect systematic changes in the independent variable.

depression   (see *major depression*)

deprivation   Term used to describe a momentary increase in the reinforcing efficacy of a stimulus as a result of withholding presentations of that stimulus (see *establishing operation*).

determinism   The philosophical doctrine that events (in psychology, behavior) are caused; that the universe is lawful and orderly (vs. random and chaotic).

detoxification   A treatment for drug abuse that involves safely weaning a physically dependent person away from a drug.

development   In its most general meaning it refers simply to change related in an orderly fashion to time. As used in this book it means progressive (i.e., systematic) changes in interactions between the behavior of individuals and the events in their environment.

deviation IQ   A statistic which expresses a given person's score on an intelligence test in relation to scores earned by other people of the same age.

differential reinforcement   A response is reinforced in the presence of one stimulus and is extinguished in the presence of one or more other stimuli.

direct replication   In research a study or studies that essentially duplicate conditions of the original investigation.

discrimination training   In classical conditioning, a procedure in which a CS is repeatedly paired with a US, whereas another stimulus (which differs physically from the CS along a specifiable dimension) is repeatedly presented without such pairing. In operant conditioning, a procedure in which a response is more successful in the presence of the stimulus, subsequently called a discriminative stimulus (S^D), than in its absence.

discriminative stimulus (S^D)   A stimulus that evokes a response because in the past that kind of response has been more successful in the presence of that stimulus than in its absence.

dopamine hypothesis (of schizophrenia)   Hypothesis that the positive symptoms of schizophrenia are caused by an overproduction of the neurotransmitter substance dopamine in various regions of the brain.

double helix   Watson and Crick's term for the structure of the DNA molecule which looks like a spiral staircase.

Down syndrome   A chromosome disorder in which there is an extra 21st chromosome. Afflicted individuals have upward slanting eyelids, small (epicanthal) folds of skin over the inner corners of the eyes, thick protruding tongues, a higher than average incidence of hearing problems, respiratory infection, heart problems, leukemia, and mental retardation.

drug abuse   Any pattern of drug self-administration that produces harmful behavioral or physiological effects without producing compensatory medical benefit.

ecological reinforcers   Reinforcers that result from the successful manipulation of the environment (see also automatic reinforcers).

effectors   Cells that receive input from efferent nerves (from the brain) and when activated affect the internal or external environment. They include muscles and glands.

efferent nerves   Motor nerves that go from the central nervous system to effector organs (muscles, glands).

electroconvulsive therapy (ECT)   A last-resort treatment for major depression that involves electrically inducing a seizure; it is used primarily to treat depression insensitive to other interventions.

embryonic period   Period of prenatal development that begins technically when the zygote reaches the uterus and attaches to the uterine wall. It is at this time that the woman is technically considered to be pregnant.

empirical phenomena   Objects and events that can be detected through observation or experimentation.

endorphins   Endogenous (i.e., produced within the body) substances in the brain that combine and activate the same receptors as drugs such as morphine and heroin.

environment   Used by scientific psychologists to refer to all of the stimuli that affect an organism's sensory receptors at a given moment.

establishing operation (EO)   A general label for operations such as deprivation that (1) increase (or decrease) the effectiveness of a particular consequence and (2) evoke (or suppress) the occurrence of behavior that has in the past been followed by that consequence (also called motivational variables).

ethology   The study of species-specific behaviors, that is, relatively stereotyped behaviors that distinguish one species from another.

eugenics   Term coined by Francis Galton to describe attempts to improve the human species through the selective breeding of certain "desirable" characteristics.

evolution   Term that refers to gradual changes in species (gene pools) over time.

evolutionary psychology   A recent approach to human behavior which is based on theorizing about human psychology using modern evolutionary principles.

experimental question   A brief but specific statement of what the researcher wants to learn from conducting the experiment.

experimentation   Research strategy in which one variable, called the independent variable, is systematically altered, and the resulting changes in another variable, called the dependent variable, are observed.

explanation   Literally meaning "to give the cause of," in science it is a statement that points to causes of some phenomenon. An explanatory statement is scientifically adequate if it points to variables that can be potentially observed and manipulated.

exteroceptive stimuli   Energy changes originating in the external environment.

extinction   In classical conditioning, the cessation of the CR to the CS due to presentation of a CS not paired with a US. In operant conditioning, cessation of responding to a motivational variable or a discriminative stimulus due to a response occurring without reinforcement.

extraneous variables   Variables in an experiment other than the independent variable that might alter the dependent variable. Experimenters attempt either to eliminate them or at least to hold them constant across experimental conditions.

facilitated communication   A procedure in which a facilitator provides physical assistance to enable a client with severe communication impairments (usually someone diagnosed with autism) to spell words by touching letters on a computer keyboard or similar device.

family resemblance studies   Studies (usually with humans) in which a behavioral trait is observed in one individual and his or her biological relatives are observed for the same trait.

fatalism   Philosophical doctrine that all events are predetermined by fate and therefore unalterable.

fetal alcohol syndrome   Disorder produced by the prenatal effects of alcohol in which afflicted infants are born with facial, heart, and limb defects, and are likely to be mentally retarded and hyperactive.

fetal period   Usually said to begin between the sixth and eighth week when the first bone cells appear or when primitive reflexive movement of the fetus first occurs.

fixed action patterns (FAPs)   Complex patterns of behavior in a species that are evoked by certain stimuli and are usually studied by ethologists.

forebrain   The largest part of the human brain and the most recent to evolve; includes the limbic system, hypothalamus, thalamus, and cerebrum.

four-term contingency   Refers to an operant relation (contingency) between an establishing operation, a discriminative stimulus, an operant response, and a reinforcer.

functional relationship   A relationship between two (or more) variables in which the value of one variable determines the value of a second variable (if A, then B).

gene   The basic unit of heredity, comprising a unique sequence of amino acids on the DNA molecule which code for the production of a single protein.

generalized conditioned reinforcers   Conditioned reinforcers (e.g., money, praise) that are paired with many other reinforcers.

genotype   Mendel's term for all of the genes an organism possesses (vs. its physical appearance).

generality   Term that refers to whether results similar to those in one experiment can be produced under conditions that differ in one or more aspects from those of the original study.

geocentric view   The view that the earth was the center of the universe and that the sun and all the planets and stars revolved around it.

glands   Specialized groups of (effector) cells that manufacture and secrete chemicals that affect the function of other parts of the body.

gustation   The term for the sensation called taste, which results from chemical changes that affect receptors in the tongue.

habituation   Term for the diminished tendency of an unconditional stimulus to elicit an unconditional response as a result of repeated exposures (i.e., frequency of presentation).

higher-order conditioning   Name for a classical conditioning procedure in which a neutral stimulus is paired with an already established CS (also called second-order conditiong).

hindbrain   The oldest and most primitive part of the brain. It connects the spinal cord with the mid- and forebrain and consists of three major subdivisions—the medulla, pons, and cerebellum—which, together, control activities important for basic survival.

holophrases   Term used by linguists for single words that sometimes have more complex meanings for a language-learning child.

hormones   Chemicals released into the bloodstream by endocrine glands that travel to and affect target cells in other organs.

humanistic psychology   (see *phenomenological psychology*)

hypothalamus   Part of the forebrain that plays a crucial role in regulating the internal environment of the organism; maintains proper temperature, fluid balance, and food stores by controlling the pituitary gland and the autonomic nervous system. It is also involved in controlling the species-specific behaviors.

imprinting   The term refers to the fact that in precocial animals (i.e., those that can move around independently after birth or hatching), the first moving object seen will either be followed or will determine the nature of the sexual preferences of the mature animal.

independent variable   The event that is manipulated in an experiment in an attempt to alter the dependent variable (in scientific psychology, behavior).

individual psychology   The name for Alfred Adler's theory of personality.

information-processing analysis   Approach used by modern cognitive psychologists that involves tracing a sequence of mental operations and their products (the information) in the performance of a cognitive task.

inheritance of acquired characteristics   Term for Lamarck's theory that evolution proceeds when offspring inherit the changes that the parent(s) acquires during their lifetimes.

inherited trait   A trait (either behavioral or nonbehavioral) which has a genetic basis different from that of some alternative trait.

instruction   Term for the discriminative effect of verbal stimuli on behavior, such as when a parent's instruction "Pick up your toys" evokes the appropriate behavior.

intelligence   Term that refers to the ability of an individual to learn, to remember information and use it appropriately, to solve problems, to acquire and use language, to exercise good judgment, to find similarities and differences, and generally to behave in ways that are deemed appropriate by the culture.

internal consistency   The assumptions, laws, and general principles of a science hold together and make sense in light of the observations it attempts to explain.

interoceptive stimuli   Energy changes originating inside an organism's body or internal environment.

intervention   (see *treatment*)

latent inhibition   Classical conditioning phenomenon in which repeatedly presenting a CS alone before it is paired with a US inhibits later conditioning.

law of effect   Law of behavior first named by Thorndike which states that behavior in a certain situation is determined by the effects (or consequences) of the behavior in that situation (see also *reinforcement*).

learned helplessness model   Model of depression that involves learning that something bad cannot be escaped or avoided.

learning   Relatively permanent changes in relationships between behavior and environmental stimuli due to certain types of experience.

long-term memory   The third structural component of memory in which information exists as an encoded version of short-term memory information and which has an unlimited storage capacity.

major depression   A person experiencing a major depressive episode reports feeling sad and guilty. Objects and events that were once rewarding control little behavior during a major depressive episode; therefore, behavior is generally suppressed (see *mood disorders*).

mania   The opposite of depression, mania is characterized by abnormal elevation of mood, frequent irritability, overestimation of personal ability, and irresponsible behavior (see *mood disorders*).

manic depressive disorder   (see *bipolar disorder*)

maturation   Refers to a genetically determined plan of biological development that is relatively independent of experience (i.e., environment).

mechanistic physiology   Descartes's view that all of the body's (physiological) functions can be understood according to natural laws.

modeling   A therapeutic technique for the treatment of anxiety in which the client observes another person responding appropriately in a situation where the client fails to do so (e.g., one in which an anxiety-arousing stimulus is present).

monosynaptic reflex   A reflex, such as the patellar reflex, in which there is only one synapse between a sensory neuron and a motor neuron.

mood disorders   Also known as affective disorders, mood disorders are disorders of emotion, primarily elation or depression, and include *major depression, seasonal affective disorder, bipolar disorder*, and *mania.*

motivational variables   (see *establishing operations*)

muscles   Effector organs which include skeletal muscles that move the bones relative to each other, and smooth muscles that control movement in internal organs.

mutations   Actual changes in the structure of the DNA molecule which can be produced by errors in DNA self-replication or external agents (mutagens) such as radiation.

natural science   Any of the sciences, such as physics, chemistry, and biology, that deal with objectively measurable phenomena.

natural selection   Term for Darwin's theory of evolution which states that some individuals will be more successful in producing offspring because of specific traits they inherited from their parents.

naturalism   The view that all natural entities, including humans, are to be understood in the same basic, naturalistic, terms.

nature–nurture   Phrase coined by Sir Francis Galton to distinguish between what a person is born with, or inheritance (nature), and what he or she acquires as a result of experience, or learning (nurture).

negative reinforcer (S^{R-})   A reinforcer that is subtracted (taken away) following a response.

negative reinforcement   The procedure of strengthening a response by subtracting or taking away a stimulus following a response.

neonate   The term for infants during the first two weeks of life.

nerve impulse   A chemically initiated electric signal conducted along neurons, otherwise described as the neuron "firing" (also called *action potential* contrasted with *resting potential*).

neuron   The basic structural and functional unit (cell) of the nervous system.

neurophysiology   The study of the physiology of the nervous system.

neuroses   A classification of mental illness that involves behavior disorders that are less pervasive and debilitating than psychoses, do not involve substantial loss of behavioral control by environmental events, and often appear to be exaggerations of normal reactions.

neurotransmitters   Chemical substances such as norepinephrine, dopamine, acetylcholine, serotonin, and gamma aminobutyric acid (GABA) that are released into the synaptic cleft by neurons and which stimulate receptors in adjoining neurons.

neutral stimulus (NS)   Stimulus that does not elicit a response similar to that elicited by the US, although it may elicit other responses.

nominal fallacy   A type of inadequate explanation of behavior in which the behavior to be explained is simply named.

normative research   A form of correlational research, often used in the study of child development, in which changes in behavior are correlated with changes in age.

nosology   The branch of medicine that deals with the classification of diseases.

obedience   A type of social relation studied by social psychologists involving doing as ordered by a person of some authority.

objective   Term used by scientists to refer to events that can be observed by more than one person.

objective tests   Personality tests, such as the Minnesota Multiphasic Personality Inventory (MMPI), that characteristically involve multiple-choice and true–false questions that are easy to score.

observational learning   Learning that occurs as a result of one person observing another person's behavior (also called social learning).

observational study   A type of research design in which no experimental manipulation occurs and data are simply recorded under the conditions that occur in the natural environment.

Ockham's (Occam's) razor   (see *parsimony*)

olfaction   The term for the sensation called smell which results from chemical changes that affect receptors in the nasal cavity.

ontogeny   The development or course of development of an individual organism.

operant conditioning   A form of learning in which behavior is determined primarily by its consequences.

operant discrimination training   (see *discrimination training*)

operant extinction   (see *extinction*)

operant response class   All behaviors that produce the same consequence, regardless of their form.

operational definition   Defining variables in an experiment in terms of how they are measured.

operations   Piaget's term for internalized, symbolically represented schemes that can be viewed as a set of rules or plans of problem solving and classification.

optokinetic nystagmus   A kind of reflexive focusing wherein lateral movement of the eyes is elicited by passing a series of fine vertical stripes past the infant's eyes.

overcorrection   An operant punishment procedure in which a person is made to engage in a low-probability behavior each time a higher-probability, and undesired, response occurs (see *Premack principle*).

paradigm   Term that refers to the conceptual framework and body of assumptions, methods, and values adhered to by scientists.

parasympathetic nervous system   Division of the autonomic nervous system that is involved in increasing the body's supply of stored energy.

parsimony   The view that, given any two explanations of some phenomenon, the one that explains it with the fewest assumptions is to be preferred.

perception   Term that refers to the behavior controlled by sensory stimulation.

peripheral nervous system (PNS)   Division of the nervous system that consists of all sensory and motor nerves.

person-centered therapy   Form of psychotherapy used by humanistic psychologists, such as Carl Rogers, based on establishing warm and nurturing client–therapist relations.

personality   Term used by psychologists to refer to consistencies in behavior across time and situations.

phenomenological psychology   Theory of personality of Carl Rogers in which humans are conceptualized as being inherently good, and their lives are characterized by choices, creativity, and growth (see also humanistic psychology).

phenotype   Mendel's terms for an organism's physical appearance (vs. its genetic makeup, or genotype).

phenylketonuria (PKU)   A genetic disorder caused by a single recessive gene that results in the inaction or absence of the enzyme phenylalanine hydroxylase, which converts the amino acid phenylalanine (found in most protein sources) into the amino acid tyrosine. Afflicted infants show increasing signs of mental retardation, irritability, poor coordination, and convulsions.

phonoreceptors   Specialized auditory sensory receptors located in the inner ear.

photoreceptors   Specialized visual sensory receptors (rods and cones) located in the retina of the eye.

phylogeny   The evolution (development) of a genetically related group of organisms.

physical dependence   Term that describes the state of an organism in which abrupt termination of chronic (repeated) drug administration is followed by a withdrawal syndrome.

polygenic   Term (literally, many genes) that refers to (behavioral) traits that result from the integrated action of many genes.

positive reinforcement   The procedure of strengthening a response by presenting or adding a stimulus following a response.

positive reinforcer (S^{R+})   A reinforcer that is added following a response.

Premack principle   The principle that high-probability behaviors can be used to reinforce (increase) lower-probability behaviors and, conversely, that low-probability behaviors can be used to punish (decrease) higher-probability behaviors.

private events   Stimuli and responses that occur inside the body.

proactive interference   Memory (actually forgetting) phenomenon in which previously learned material interferes with recall of newly learned material (see *retroactive interference*).

projective tests   Personality test in which an individual is shown an unambiguous stimulus and asked either to report what she or he "sees" or to create stories based on the stimulus (e.g., Rorschach Inkblot test).

prosopagnosia   A form of visual agnosia (see *agnosia*) in which those afflicted are unable to say who a familiar face belongs to even though they can say they are looking at a face and can say who the person is after hearing his or her voice.

proximate causes   Behavioral causes that occur immediately before behavior and can be of two types; physiological, in which the causes are to be found in the central nervous system, and environmental, in which the causes are environmental stimuli.

psychoanalysis   Freud's term for both his form of psychotherapy which includes a set of clinical procedures (e.g., dream analysis, free association) and his theory of personality.

psychological (or behavioral) development   Progressive changes over time in behavior–environment interactions (see development).

psychology   The scientific study of the interactions between the behavior of organisms and the environment in which it occurs.

psychoses   A classification of mental illness that involves severe and pervasive behavioral problems that are marked by pronounced functional impairment and often involve thought disorders, hallucinations, and delusions.

public accompaniments   Term used by B. F. Skinner to refer to public non-behavioral events that may occur in conjunction with private events.

punishment   An operant conditioning process in which stimuli that follow behavior (called punishing consequences, or punishers) produce a decrease in the frequency of that behavior under similar circumstances.

quantitative   Data are quantitative if they can be scaled in physical units along one or more dimensions.

receptor cells   (see *sensory receptors*)

reduction   (or reductionism) Term used to refer to attempts to explain some phenomena in terms of simpler phenomena.

reflex   Term that refers to automatic, stereotyped responses to specific stimuli (see also unconditional reflex).

reification   A type of inadequate explanation of behavior in which the behavior is named (see nominal fallacy), but then the name is assumed to refer to a real entity somewhere inside the behaving individual.

reinforcement   An operant conditioning process in which stimuli that follow behavior (called reinforcing consequences, or reinforcers) produce an increase in the frequency of that behavior under similar circumstances.

releasers   The stimuli that evoke fixed action patterns (also called sign stimuli).

reliability   Term that refers to whether results similar to those of one experiment can be reproduced under conditions essentially equivalent to those of the original study.

reliable   Term used by scientists to refer to independent observers agreeing that objective events (data) have occurred.

research   A systematic way of asking questions and gaining information. The purpose of *basic research* is to gain information about behavior and the variables that affect it, and the purpose of *applied research* is to gain information that directly and immediately benefits others.

respondent behaviors   The collective name for reflexive responses (i.e., conditional and unconditional responses).

response   An objectively quantifiable unit of behavior selected for study.

response chaining   An operant conditioning procedure of developing new behavior–environment relationships in which a sequence of behaviors must be emitted before the unconditioned reinforcer is delivered.

response cost   An operant punishment procedure in which a positive reinforcer that a person has earned is removed contingent upon some misbehavior.

resting potential   The normal state of neurons when they are not firing in which there is a "potential" for movement of ions across the cell membrane that would result in firing (also called the membrane potential).

resurgence   An effect of operant extinction in which previously extinguished behaviors that once produced the same kind of reinforcer as the behavior currently being extinguished reappear.

retroactive interference   Memory (actually forgetting) phenomenon in which learning new material interferes with recalling previously learned material (see *proactive interference*).

rule   Term for the (verbal) descriptions of relations between stimuli, or between stimuli and behavior, that alter the control of stimuli over behavior as a result.

rule-governed behavior   Behavior affected by verbal instructions describing environmental relations that a person has not directly contacted.

satiation   Term used to describe a momentary reduction in the reinforcing efficacy of a stimulus as a result of repeated presentations of that stimulus (see *establishing operation*).

schedule of reinforcement   The term for relations among (discriminative and/or reinforcing) stimuli, responses, and the passage of time that lead to an increase in response strength.

schemes   Piaget's term for different mental activities that are used by children to organize and to respond to experiences.

science   A form of human activity characterized by the search for regularities in the natural world.

scientific law   The mathematical or verbal description of cause-and-effect relationships between different sets of variables.

schizophrenia   Psychotic disorder characterized by *positive symptoms,* such as hallucinations, thought disorders, and delusions, and *negative symptoms,* such as flattened affect, impoverished speech, anhedonia (inability to experience pleasure), lack of motivation, and social withdrawal.

scientific theory   A system of rules and assumptions used to explain and predict observations.

seasonal affective disorder   Disorder that generally occurs during winter, when days are short and nights long, and is characterized by depression, craving for carbohydrates (often leading to weight gain), lethargy, and increased sleeping (see *mood disorders*).

selection experiment   A type of experiment in which individuals from a genetically varied population are tested for a particular behavioral trait and then males and females with extreme scores are selectively mated over a number of generations, thus creating two distinct behavioral lines.

self-awareness   The ability of individuals to describe their own behavior (both public and private) or (interoceptive) stimuli that originate within their bodies.

sensation   Term that refers to the basic effects of stimuli on sensory receptors, in other words, the transduction of environmental energy by sensory receptors into nerve impulses.

sensitive (or critical) period   Time period during which an individual is exceptionally susceptible to the effects of a particular experience.

sensory memory   The first of the three structural components of memory, with a temporary but large capacity, in which stimuli exist in the same form as in the environment.

sensory receptors   Specialized nerve cells (neurons) that are stimulated by stimuli (energy changes) and whose main function is to transform that energy into neural impulses (also called receptor cells).

sex-linked disorders   Chromosome disorders that result from problems with the 23rd pair of chromosomes, the so-called sex chromosomes.

shaping   An operant conditioning procedure of developing new behavior–environment relationships in which successively closer approximations to a given operant response are reinforced.

short-term memory   The second structural component of memory which holds information with which the person is in immediate contact. The form of the stimuli is an encoded, or transformed, version of those first entered into sensory memory (also called working memory).

simultaneous conditioning   A classical conditioning procedure in which the CS and US are presented at the same time.

social behavior   Behavior of an individual that is determined by stimuli, as either antecedents or consequences (called social stimuli), that arise from other persons.

social environment   The term used to describe all of the social stimuli that affect the behavior of an individual at a given time.

social learning theory   Personality theory of Albert Bandura in which both the actual consequences of behavior and an individual's beliefs about the consequences of behavior, termed *expectancies,* determine behavior.

social psychology   Branch of psychology which encompasses the study of the effects of other people on the behavior of the individual.

sociobiology   Term coined by the biologist E. O. Wilson to refer to the systematic study of the biological basis of all social behavior.

somatic nervous system   The branch of the PNS that receives information from the sensory organs and controls the skeletal muscles.

somatosenses   Sensory system (also called body senses) which includes sensory receptors that detect changes on the surface of the body and inside it; includes the cutaneous and organic senses and kinesthesia.

species   A group of actually or potentially interbreeding organisms, which do not interbreed with other organisms.

species continuity   The view that all species are related.

species-specific behaviors   Behaviors of members of one species that differ from those of another species because each species has different genes.

spinal reflex   When a stimulus elicits a response without the involvement of the brain.

spontaneous recovery   In classical conditioning, if a considerable period of time (e.g., a day) passes from the end of one series of extinction trials (CS presentations) to the beginning of a second series of trials, the strength of the CS–CR relation increases measurably (recovers spontaneously). In operant conditioning, if after a time period following extinction the operant reappears in circumstances similar to those in which it was previously reinforced.

stimulus (the plural is **stimuli**)   The term used by neurophysiologists to refer to any change in energy that affects the sensory receptors of an organism. As used by scientific psychologists a stimulus must also affect behavior.

stimulus control   Term that refers to the fact that behavior differs in the presence and absence of a stimulus.

stimulus generalization   In classical conditioning, after a stimulus is established as a CS, stimuli that are physically similar to it may elicit the same CRs, even though these stimuli have never been paired with the US. In operant conditioning, when stimuli that differ along a given dimension (e.g., wavelength) evoke the same response because one of the stimuli was present when the response was reinforced.

structural components   Functionally distinct kinds of memory systems (sensory, working or short-term, and long-term memory) assumed by information-processing theory to exist.

subjective   Terms used to refer to events that can be observed by only one person, for example, private events.

survey   A type of nonexperimental investigation in which information is directly obtained from people by asking them questions concerning their current and historical practices, opinions, and demographic characteristics.

sympathetic nervous system   Division of the autonomic nervous system which is involved in the expenditure of energy.

synapse   A very small fluid-filled gap between the terminal buttons of one neuron and the dendrites or cell body of adjoining cells.

synaptic transmission   A chemical process through which neurons communicate with other neurons.

synaptic vesicles   Sac-like structures located inside the terminal buttons of neurons, which, when stimulated, release chemical substances called neurotransmitters.

systematic desensitization   A behavioral treatment that teaches a person to relax in the presence of stimuli that once produced anxiety; the method uses imagery and a gradual fading of more and more anxiety-arousing thoughts.

systematic replication   An experimental arrangement in which the independent and dependent variables are similar to those examined in the original investigation, but the studies differ in at least one significant aspect. Used to determine the generality of the results.

target behavior   The dependent variable in applied research.

taste aversion learning   Phenomenon, first demonstrated experimentally in the 1950s by John Garcia and his colleagues, in which a taste (as a NS) is paired (often only once) with a strong US, such as nausea, and thus becomes a CS that also elicits feelings of nausea. It is measured by active avoidance of the substance.

telegraphic speech   Term used by linguists for two-word combinations that have the same meaning (produce the same effect) as more complex sentences.

teleological explanation   A type of inadequate explanation in which a future event is assumed to cause a current event.

teratogens   Agents, such as drugs, viruses, and toxic chemicals, that cause abnormal prenatal development.

terminal buttons   Structures located at the end of the axon which contain synaptic vesicles.

thalamus   Part of the forebrain where most incoming sensory impulses are relayed to the cerebral cortex.

theory   In science, a system of (verbal/mathematical) rules and assumptions used to organize, predict, and explain a set of facts or observations.

thought-stopping   Self-control procedure designed to eliminate repetitive thought patterns that are unrealistic and that either inhibit the performance of a desired behavior or evoke undesirable behaviors.

threshold of excitation   The beginning of a neuron firing that occurs when depolarization is sufficiently strong and the membrane becomes very permeable to positively charged ions, which then begin to enter the neuron.

time-out   An operant punishment procedure in which a period of time in which one or more positive reinforcers are unavailable occurs contingent on some behavior (the full name is time-out from positive reinforcement).

token economy   A structured behavior modification program in which generalized conditioned reinforcers (tokens) are delivered dependent on the performance of appropriate behaviors.

tolerance   Term used for the diminished effects of a drug as a result of repeated exposure to that drug.

trace conditioning   A classical conditioning procedure in which a measurable period of time (called the trace interval) elapses between the offset of the CS and the onset of the US. In other words, the CS begins and ends before the US is presented.

transduction   The process, carried out by sensory receptors in the nervous system, of converting environmental energy into the energy of nerve impulses.

treatment   The independent variable in applied research (also called intervention).

troublesome behavior   Patterns of responding that constitute a problem for the person who emits them, or for other people.

ultimate causes   Behavioral causes that establish proximate causes and can be of two types: phylogenetic ultimate causes, which result from the evolution of the species, and ontogenetic ultimate causes, which result from experiences (learning) in the lifetime of the individual.

unconditional reflex   Term for the relationship between an unconditional stimulus (US) and an unconditional response (UR).

unconditional response (UR)   The response elicited by an unconditional stimulus in the absence of a special learning history.

unconditional stimulus (US)   Any stimulus that elicits a reflexive response in the absence of a special learning history.

unconditioned reinforcers   Reinforcers that strengthen behavior in organisms without any particular history, that is without learning (also called primary reinforcers).

verbal behavior   Term for behavior that is reinforced through the mediation of other persons who are trained (though not formally) to mediate and reinforce such behavior (traditionally called language).

vestibular system   Sensory system in which changes in the head's orientation and angular acceleration are detected by receptors in the semicircular canals and vestibular sacs; this system is responsible for maintaining posture and balance.

visible spectrum   Wavelengths in the electromagnetic radiation spectrum between approximately 380 and 700 nm that can be detected by the human eye. We call such wavelengths "light."

vitalism   The view that all living things contain a life force or soul that cannot be explained by natural laws.

vocal apparatus   That portion of the human anatomy that produces speech which includes the lips, mouth, tongue, nasal cavity, pharynx, larynx, and diaphragm.

Wernicke's area   An area of the brain located between the primary auditory cortex and a structure called the angular gyrus that is responsible for language comprehension and, if damaged, results in a deficit in language comprehension called Wernicke's aphasia.

withdrawal syndrome   Terms used for the confluence of signs (observable changes) and symptoms (changes reported by the individual) that emerge following abrupt termination of drug administration.

within-subject experimental design   An experimental arrangement in which each subject is exposed to different levels of the independent variable and the effects of the independent variable on the subject's behavior are determined by comparing that subject's behavior across different conditions.

working memory   (see *short-term memory*)

zygote (or ovum)   The single fertilized cell that, in humans, contains 46 chromosomes.

References

Abadinsky, H. (1993). *Drug abuse.* Chicago: Nelson-Hall.

Abramson, L. Y., Seligman, M. E. P., & Teasdale, J. D. (1978). Learned helplessness in humans: Critique and reformulation. *Journal of Abnormal Psychology, 87,* 49–74.

Adler, A. (1924). *The practice and theory of individual psychology.* New York: Harcourt, Brace.

Adler, A. (1929). *The science of living.* New York: Greenberg.

Adler, R. (1981). Behavioral influences on immune responses. In S. M. Weiss, J. A. Herd, & B. H. Fox (Eds.), *Perspectives on behavioral medicine* (pp. 163–182). New York: Academic Press.

Adler, R., & Cohen, N. (1975). Behaviorally conditioned immunosuppression. *Psychosomatic Medicine, 37,* 333–340.

Adler, R., & Cohen, N. (1982). Behaviorally conditioned immunosuppression and murine systemic lupus erythematosis. *Science, 215,* 1534–1535.

Adler, R., Cohen, N., & Bovjberg, D. (1982). Conditioned suppression of humoral immunity in the rat. *Journal of Comparative and Physiological Psychology, 96,* 517–520.

Alcock, J. (1984). *Animal behavior: An evolutionary approach.* Sunderland, MA: Sinauer Associates.

Alessi, G. (1992). Models of proximate and ultimate causation in psychology. *American Psychologist, 47,* 1359–1370.

Allen, K. D., Loiben, T., Allen, S. J., & Stanley, R. T. (1992). Dentist-implemented contingent escape for management of disruptive child behavior. *Journal of Applied Behavior Analysis, 25,* 629–636.

Allen, M. G. (1976). Twin studies of affective illness. *Archives of General Psychiatry, 33,* 1476–1478.

Alling, K., & Poling, A. (1995). The effects of differing response-force requirements on fixed-ratio responding of rats. *Journal of the Experimental Analysis of Behavior, 63,* 331–346.

Allport, G. W. (1937). *Personality: A psychological interpretation.* New York: Holt, Rinehart & Winston.

American Heritage Dictionary of the English Language. (1984). New York: Houghton Mifflin.

American Psychiatric Association. (1994). *Diagnostic and statistical manual of mental disorders* (4th ed.). Washington, DC: American Psychiatric Association.

Anastasi, A. (1988). *Psychological testing.* New York: Macmillan.

Anderson, J. R. (1985). *Cognitive psychology and its implications* (2nd ed.). New York: Freeman.

Andreasen, N. C., Arndt, S., Swayze, V., II, Cizadleo, T., Flaum, M., O'Leary, D., Ehrhandt, J. C., & Yuh, W. T. C. (1994). Thalamic abnormalities in schizophrenia visualized through magnetic resonance image averaging. *Science, 266,* 294–298.

Asch, S. E. (1956). Studies of independence and conformity: A minority of one against a unanimous majority. *Psychological Monography, 70* (Whole No. 546).

Atkinson, R. C., & Shiffrin, R. M. (1968). Human memory: A proposed system and its control processes. *The Psychology of Learning and Motivation, 2,* 89–195.

Azrin, N. H., & Foxx, R. M. (1971). A rapid method of toilet training the institutionalized retarded. *Journal of Applied Behavior Analysis, 4,* 89–99.

Azrin, N. H., & Holz, W. C. (1966). Punishment. In W. K. Honig (Ed.), *Operant behavior: Areas of research and application* (pp. 380–447). New York: Appleton-Century-Crofts.

Azrin, N. H., Hutchinson, R. R., & Hake, D. F. (1966). Extinction-induced aggression. *Journal of the Experimental Analysis of Behavior, 9,* 191–204.

Baars, B. J. (1986). *The cognitive revolution in psychology.* New York: Guilford.

Bachrach, A. J. (1972). *Psychological research: An introduction.* New York: Random House.

Baldessarini, R. J. (1990). Drugs and the treatment of psychiatric disorders. In A. G. Filman, T. W. Rall, A. S. Nies, & P. Taylor (Eds.), *The pharmacological basis of therapeutics* (pp. 345–382). New York: Pergamon.

Baldwin, J. D., & Baldwin, J. I. (1988). *Behavior principles for everyday life.* Englewood Cliffs, N J: Prentice-Hall.

Bandura, A. (1969). *Principles of behavior modification.* New York: Holt, Rinehart & Winston.

Bandura, A. (1977). *Social learning theory.* Englewood Cliffs, NJ: Prentice-Hall.

Bandura, A. (1986). *Social foundations of thought and action: A social cognitive theory.* Englewood Cliffs, NJ: Prentice-Hall.

Bandura, A., & Adams, N. E. (1977). Analysis of self-efficacy theory of behavioral change. *Cognitive Therapy and Research, 1,* 287–310.

Barash, D. P. (1977). *Sociobiology and behavior.* New York: Elsevier.

Barber, T. X. (1976). *Pitfalls in human research.* New York: Pergamon.

Barlow, D. H., Hayes, S. C., & Nelson, R. O. (1984). *The scientist practitioner.* New York: Pergamon.

Barnard, C. J. (1983). *Animal behavior: Ecology and evolution.* New York: Wiley.

Bates, E., O'Connell, B., & Shore, C. (1987). Language and communication in infancy. In J. D. Osofsky (Ed.), *Handbook of infant development* (pp. 149–203). New York: Wiley.

Beaumont, J. G. (1983). *Introduction to neuropsychology.* New York: Guilford.

Beck, A. T. (1976). *Cognitive therapy and the emotional disorders.* New York: International Universities Press.

Begleiter, H., & Kissin, B. (1995). *The genetics of alcoholism.* New York: Oxford University Press.

Bell, S. M., & Ainsworth, M. D. S. (1972). Infant crying and maternal responsiveness. *Child Development, 43,* 1171–1190.

Belluzzi, J. D., & Stein, L. (1983). Operant conditioning: Cellular or systems property? *Society for Neuroscience Abstracts, 9,* 478.

Berkowitz, L., & Frodi, A. (1977). Stimulus characteristics that can enhance or decrease aggression. *Aggressive Behavior, 3,* 1–5.

Berndt, T. J. (1992). *Child development.* Orlando, FL: Harcourt Brace Jovanovich.

Bernstein, I. L. (1978). Learned taste aversions in children receiving chemotherapy. *Science, 200,* 1302–1303.

Bijou, S. W. (1979). *Behavior analysis of the infantile stage of development.* Unpublished manuscript.

Bijou, S. W., & Baer, D. M. (1978). *Behavior analysis of child development.* Englewood Cliffs, N.J: Prentice-Hall.

Biklen, D. (1990). Communication unbound: Autism and praxis. *Harvard Educational Review, 60,* 291–315.

Blakely, E., & Schlinger, H. (1987). Rules: Function-altering contingency-specifying stimuli. *Behavior Analyst, 10,* 183–187.

Bloomfield, L. (1933). *Language.* New York: Holt.

Blum, K., Noble, E. P., Sheridan, P. J., Montgomery, A., & Ritchie, T. (1990). Allelic association of human dopamine D2 receptor gene in alcoholism. *Journal of the American Medical Association, 263,* 2055–2060.

Blum, N. J., Mauk, J. E., McComas, J. J., & Mace, F. C. (1996). Separate and combined effects of methylphenidate and a behavioral intervention on disruptive behavior in children with mental retardation. *Journal of Applied Behavior Analysis, 29,* 305–319.

Bobvjerg, D. H., Redd, W. H., Maier, L. S., Holland, J. C., Lesko, L. M., Niedzwiecki, D., Rubin, S. C., & Hakes, R. B. (1990). Anticipatory immune suppression and nausea in women receiving cyclic chemotherapy for ovarian cancer. *Journal of Consulting and Clinical Psychology, 58,* 153–157.

Bolles, R. C. (1993). *The story of psychology: A thematic history.* Pacific Grove, CA: Brooks/Cole.

Boring, E. G. (1950). *A history of experimental psychology* (2nd ed.). New York: Appleton-Century-Crofts.

Bowlby, J. (1969). *Attachment and loss: Vol. 1. Attachment.* New York: Basic Books.

Bowlby, J. (1973). *Separation and loss.* New York: Basic Books.

Brazelton, T. B. (1982). Behavioral competence in the newborn infant. In J. K. Gardner (Ed.), *Readings in developmental psychology* (pp. 79–90). Boston: Little, Brown.

Brewer, W. F. (1974). There is no convincing evidence for operant or classical conditioning in adult humans. In W. B. Wimer & D. S. Palermo (Eds.), *Cognition and the symbolic processes* (pp. 1–42). Hillsdale, NJ: Erlbaum.

Brower, L. P., & Brower, J. V. (1964). Birds, butterflies, and plant poisons: A study in ecological chemistry. *Zoologica, 49,* 137–159.

Brown, J. L. (1975). *The evolution of behavior.* New York: Norton.

Brown, R. (1973). *A first language: The early stages.* Cambridge, MA: Harvard University Press.

Brown, R., & Bellugi, U. (1964). Three processes in the child's acquisition of syntax. *Harvard Educational Review, 34,* 133–151.

Buss, D. M. (1994). *The evolution of desire: Strategies of human mating.* New York: Basic Books.

Campbell, B. G. (1985). *Humankind emerging.* Boston: Little, Brown.

Campos, J. J., Langer, A., & Krowitz, A. (1970). Cardiac responses on the visual cliff in prelocomotor human infants. *Science, 170,* 196–197.

Carew, T. J., Pinsker, H. M., & Kandel, E. R. (1972). Long-term habituation of a defensive withdrawal reflex in Aplysia. *Science, 175,* 451–454.

Carew, T. J., Hawkins, R. D., & Kandel, E. R. (1983). Differential classical conditioning of a defensive withdrawal reflex in *Aplysia californica, Science, 219,* 397–400.

Carlson, N. R. (1984). *Psychology: The science of behavior.* Boston: Allyn & Bacon.

Carlson, N. R. (1986). *Physiology of behavior.* Boston: Allyn & Bacon.

Carlson, N. R. (1988). *Discovering psychology.* Boston: Allyn & Bacon.

Carlson, N. R. (1995). *Foundations of physiological psychology* (3rd ed.). Needham Heights, MA: Allyn & Bacon.

Carter, E. N. (1973). The stimulus control of a response system in the absence of awareness. Unpublished doctoral dissertation, University of Massachusetts.

Castellucci, V. , & Kandel, E. R. (1974). A quantal analysis of the synaptic depression underlying habituation of the gill-withdrawal reflex in *Aplysia. Proceedings of the National Academy of Sciences* (USA), *71,* 5004–5008.

Catania, A. C. (1992). *Learning* (3rd ed.). Englewood Cliffs, NJ: Prentice-Hall.

Chance, P. (1994). *Learning and behavior* (3rd ed.). Pacific Grove, CA: Brooks/Cole.

Chomsky, N. (1957). *Syntactic structures.* London: Mouton.

Chomsky, N. (1965). *Aspects of the theory of syntax.* Cambridge, MA: MIT Press.

Chugani, H. T., & Phelps, M. E. (1986). Maturational changes in cerebral function in infants determined by 18FDG positron emission tomography. *Science, 231,* 840–843.

Cialdini, R. B., Vincent, J. E., Lewis, S. J., Catalan, J., Wheeler, D., & Darby, B. L. (1975). Reciprocal concessions procedure for inducing compliance: The door-in-the-face technique. *Journal of Personality and Social Psychology, 31,* 206–215.

Clark, L. (1996). *SOS: Help for parents.* Bowling Green, KY: Parents Press.

Cohen, L. B., & Gelber, E. R. (1975). Infant visual memory: Basic visual processes. In L. B. Cohen & P. Salapatek (Eds.), *Infant perception: From sensation to cognition* (Vol. 1, pp. 347–403). New York: Academic Press.

Cooper, J. O., Heron, T. E., & Heward, W. L. (1987). *Applied behavior analysis.* New York: Macmillan.

Cooper, L. A., & Shepard, R. N. (1973). Chronometric studies of the rotation of mental images. In W. G. Chase (Ed.), *Visual information processing.* New York: Academic Press.

Copeland, M. E. (1992). *The depression workbook.* Oakland, CA: New Harbinger.

Cosmides, L., & Tooby, J. (1987). From evolution to behavior: Evolutionary psychology as the missing link. In J. Dupré (Ed.), *The latest on the best essays on evolution and optimality.* Cambridge, MA: MIT Press.

Costello, C. G. (1972). Depression: Loss of reinforcers or loss of reinforcer effectiveness? *Behavior Therapy, 3,* 240–247.

Council Report. (1983). *Fifth special report on alcohol and health.* Washington, DC: U.S. Government Printing Office.

Craighead, W. E., Kazdin, A. E., & Mahoney, M. J. (1981). *Behavior modification: Principles, issues, and applications.* Boston: Houghton Mifflin.

Crossman, E. K. (1985). The kiss and the promise: A review of Hubert L. Dreyfus' *What computers can't do: The limits of artificial intelligence. Journal of the Experimental Analysis of Behavior, 44,* 271–277.

Cuny, H. (1965). *Ivan Pavlov: The man and his theories.* New York: Eriksson.

Daly, M., & Wilson, M. (1988). *Homicide.* New York: De Gruyter.

Damasio, A. R. (1985). Prosopagnosia. *Trends in Neuroscience, 8,* 132–135.

Darley, J. M., Glucksberg, S., Kamin, L. J., & Kinchla, R. A. (1981). *Psychology.* Englewood Cliffs, NJ: Prentice-Hall.

Darwin, C. (1859). *On the origin of species by means of natural selection, and selection in relation to sex.* (2nd ed). London: Murray.

Darwin, C. (1879). *The descent of man.* London: Murray.

Darwin, C. (1872). *The expression of the emotions in man and animals.* London: Murray.

Davidson, R. J. (1992). Anterior cerebral asymmetry and the nature of emotion. *Brain and Cognition, 20,* 125–151.

Davis, K. L., Kahn, R. S., Ko, G., & Davidson, M. (1991). Dopamine in schizophrenia: A review and reconceptualization. *American Journal of Psychiatry, 148,* 1474–1486.

Dawkins, R. (1976). *The selfish gene.* New York: Oxford University Press.

Dawkins, R. (1986). *The blind watchmaker.* New York: Norton.

Dayton, G. O., Jones, M. H., Aiu, P., Rawson, R. H., Steele, B., & Rose, M. (1964). Developmental study of coordinated eye movements in the human infant. *Archives of Opthamology, 71,* 865–870.

Deguchi, H. (1984). Observational learning from a radical-behavioristic viewpoint. *The Behavior Analyst, 7,* 83–96.

Delgado, J. M. R. (1969). *Physical control of the mind.* New York: Harper & Row.

Dennett, D. C. (1991). *Consciousness explained.* Boston: Little, Brown.

De Toffol, B., Autret, A., Gaymard, B., & Degiovanni, E. (1992). Influence of lateral gaze on electroencephalographic spectral power. *Electroencephalography and Clinical Neurophysiology, 82,* 432–437.

de Villiers, J. G., & de Villiers, P. A. (1978). *Language acquisition.* Cambridge, MA: Harvard University Press.

Dickenson, A. M., & Gillette, K. L. (1993). A comparison of the effects of two individual monetary incentive systems on productivity: Piece rate pay versus base pay plus incentives. *Journal of Organizational Behavior Management, 14,* 3–82.

Dickerson, R. E. (1978). Chemical evolution and the origin of life. *Scientific American, 239,* 70, 1–9.

Dobzhansky, T. (1964). *Heredity and the nature of man.* New York: Harcourt, Brace & World.

Dollard, J., Dobb, L., Miller, N., Morer, O., & Sears, R. (1939). *Frustration and aggression.* New Haven, CT: Yale University Press.

Donahoe, J. W., & Palmer, D. C. (1994). *Learning and complex behavior.* Boston: Allyn and Bacon.

Dowling, H. F. (1977). *Fighting infection.* Cambridge, MA: Harvard University Press.

Drake, R. A. (1985). Lateral asymmetry of risky recommendations. *Personality and Social Psychology Bulletin, 11,* 409–417.

Drake, R. A., & Seligman, M. E. P. (1989). Self-serving biases in causal attributions as a function of altered activation asymmetry. *International Journal of Neuroscience, 45,* 199–204.

Dreyfus, H. L. (1979). *What computers can't do: The limits of artificial intelligence.* (Rev. ed.). New York: Harper Colophon.

Dworetzky, J. P. (1996). *Introduction to child development* (6th ed.). St. Paul, MN: West.

Eacker, J. N. (1972). On some elementary physiological problems of psychology. *American Psychologist, 27,* 553–565.

Ehlers, C. L., Frank, E., & Kupfer, D. J. (1988). Social zeitgebers and biological rhythms. *Archives of General Psychiatry, 45,* 948–952.

Eisenson, J., Auer, J. J., & Irwin, J. V. (1963). *The psychology of communication.* New York: Appleton-Century-Crofts.

Ewen, R. B. (1988). *An introduction to theories of personality.* Hillsdale, NJ: Erlbaum.

Fairbank, J. A., & Brown, T. A. (1987). Current behavioral approaches to the treatment of posttraumatic stress disorder. *The Behavior Therapist, 3,* 57–64.

Fairbank, J. A., & Keane, T. M. (1982). Flooding for combat-related stress disorders: Assessment of anxiety reduction across traumatic memories. *Behavior Therapy, 13,* 499–510.

Fairburn, C. G., Hay, P. J., & Welch, S. L. (1993). Binge eating and anorexia nervosa: Distribution and determinants. In C. G. Fairburn & G. T. Wilson (Eds.), *Binge eating: Nature, assessment, and treatment* (pp. 123–143). New York: Guilford.

Fancher, R. E. (1996). *Pioneers of psychology* (3rd. ed.). New York: Norton.

Fanselow, M. S., & Baakes, M. P. (1982). Conditioned fear-induced opiate analgesia on the formalin test: Evidence for two aversive motivational systems. *Learning and Motivation, 3*, 200–221.

Fantino, E., & Logan, C. A. (1979). *The experimental analysis of behavior: A biological perspective.* San Francisco: Freeman.

Fantz, R. L. (1961). The origin of form perception. *Scientific American, 204*, 66–72.

Farmer, A., McGuffin, P., & Gottesman, I. (1987). Twin concordance in DSM-III schizophrenia. *Archives of General Psychiatry, 44*, 634–641.

Farris, H. E. (1967). Classical conditioning of courting behavior in the Japanese quail, *coturnix coturnix japonica. Journal of the Experimental Analysis of Behavior, 10*, 213–217.

Feldman, R. S., Meyer, J. S., & Quenzer, L. F. (1997). *Principles of neuropharmacology.* Sunderland, MA: Sinauer.

Ferster, C. B. (1965). Classification of behavior pathology. In L. K. Krasner & L. P. Ullman (Eds.), *Research in behavior modification* (pp. 87–109). New York: Holt, Rinehart & Winston.

Finlay, D., & Ivinkis, A. (1984). Cardiac and visual responses to moving stimuli presented either successively or simultaneously to the central and peripheral visual fields in 4-month-olds. *Developmental Psychology, 20*, 29–36.

Flanagan, D. P., Genshaft, J. L., & Harrison, P. L. (1997). *Contemporary intellectual assessment.* New York: Guilford.

Foster, T. M., Temple, W., Robertson, B., Nair, V., & Poling, A. (1996). Concurrent schedule performance in dairy cows: Persistent undermatching. *Journal of the Experimental Analysis of Behavior, 65*, 57–80.

Franklin, K., & McCoy, S. N. (1979). Pimozide-induced extinction in rats: Stimulus control of responding rules out motor deficit. *Pharmacology, Biochemistry, and Behavior, 11*, 71–75.

Freedman, J. L., & Fraser, S. C. (1966). Compliance without pressure: The foot-in-the-door technique. *Journal of Personality and Social Psychology, 4*, 195–202.

Freud, S. (1933). *New introductory lectures on psychoanalysis.* New York: Norton.

Freud, S. (1938). *The basic writings of Sigmund Freud.* New York: Modern Library.

Futuyma, D. J. (1979). *Evolutionary biology.* Sunderland, MA: Sinauer.

Futuyma, D. J. (1986). *Evolutionary biology* (2nd ed.). Sunderland, MA: Sinauer.

Gadow, K. D., & Poling, A. (1988). *Pharmacotherapy and mental retardation.* Boston: College-Hill.

Gallahue, D. L. (1989). *Understanding motor development: Infants, children, adolescents* (2nd ed.). Indianapolis: Benchmark.

Gallistel, C. R., & Karras, D. (1984). Pimozide and amphetamine have opposing effects on the reward summation function. *Pharmacology, Biochemistry, and Behavior, 20*, 73–77.

Gantt, W. H. (1966). Conditional or conditioned, reflex or response. *Conditioned Reflex, 1*, 69–74.

Garcia, J., Kimeldorf, D. J., & Koelling, R. A. (1955). Conditioned aversion to saccharin resulting from exposure to gamma radiation. *Science, 122*, 157–158.

Gardner, H. (1983). *Frames of mind: The theory of multiple intelligences.* New York: Basic Books.

Gardner, H. (1985). *The mind's new science.* New York: Basic Books.

Gardner, R. A., & Gardner, B. T. (1978). Comparative psychology and language acquisition. *Annals of the New York Academy of Sciences, 309*, 37–76.

Gelman, R. (1969). Conservation acquisition: A problem of learning to attend to relevant attributes. *Journal of Experimental Child Psychology, 7*, 167–187.

George, F. R. (1987). Genetic and environmental factors in ethanol self-administration. *Pharmacology, Biochemistry, and Behavior, 27*, 379–384.

George, F. R. (1990). Genetic approaches to studying drug abuse. *Alcohol, 7*, 207–211.

Gelernter, J., Goldman, D., & Risch, N. (1993). The A1 allele at the D2 dopamine gene and alcoholism. *Journal of the American Medical Association, 269*, 1673–1677.

Geschwind, N. (1979). Specializations of the human brain. *Scientific American, 241*, 180–199.

Gewirtz, J. L. (1977). Maternal responding and the conditioning of crying: Directions of influence within the attachment-acquisition process. In B. C. Etzel, J. M. LeBlanc, & D. M. Baer (Eds.), *New developments in behavioral research: Theory, method, and application* (pp. 31–57). Hillsdale, NJ: Erlbaum.

Gewirtz, J. L., & Boyd, E. F. (1977). Does maternal responding imply reduced infant crying? A critique of the 1972 Bell and Ainsworth report. *Child Development, 48,* 1200–1207.

Gibson, E. J., & Spelke, E. S. (1983). The development of perception. In P. H. Mussen, J. H. Flavell, & E. M. Markman (Eds.), *Handbook of child psychology: Vol. 3. Cognitive development* (4th ed., pp. 1–76). New York: Wiley.

Gibson, E. J., & Walk, R. D. (1960). The "visual cliff." *Scientific American, 202,* 64–71.

Gilovich, T. (1991). *How we know what isn't so: The fallibility of human reason in everyday life.* New York: Free Press.

Ginsburg, H. P., & Opper, S. (1988). *Piaget's theory of intellectual development* (3rd ed.). Englewood Cliffs, NJ: Prentice-Hall.

Glanzer, M., & Cunitz, A. R. (1966). Two storage mechanisms in free recall. *Journal of Verbal Learning and Verbal Behavior, 5,* 351–360.

Goddard, H. H. (1912). *The Kallikak family: A study in the heredity of feeble-mindedness.* New York: Macmillan.

Goddard, H. H. (1928). Feeblemindedness: A question of definition. *Journal of Psycho-Asthenics, 33,* 219–227.

Goleman, D. (1995). *Emotional intelligence.* New York: Bantam.

Gorczynski, R. M., Macrae, S., & Kennedy, M. (1982). Conditioned immune response associated with allogenic skin grafts in mice. *Journal of Immunology, 129,* 704–709.

Gottesman, I. (1991). *Schizophrenia genesis: The origins of madness.* New York: Freeman.

Gould, S. J. (1981). *The mismeasure of man.* New York: Norton.

Gould, S. J. (1987–88). The verdict on creationism. *Skeptical Inquirer, XII,* 184–187.

Green, G. (1994). Facilitated communication: Mental miracle or sleight of hand? *Behavior and Social Issues, 4,* 69–85.

Greenough, W. T., & Green, E. J. (1981). Experience and the aging brain. In J. L. McGaugh, J. G. March, & S. B. Kiesler (Eds.), *Aging: Biology and behavior.* New York: Academic Press.

Greenwald, D. F. (1990). An external construct validity study of Rorschach personality variables. *Journal of Personality Assessment, 55,* 768–780.

Griffin D. R. (1981). *The question of animal awareness.* Los Altos, CA: Kaufman.

Griffiths, R. R., Bigelow, G. E., & Henningfield, J. E. (1980). Similarities in animal and human drug-taking behavior. In N. Mello (Ed.), *Advances in substance abuse* (pp.1–90). Greenwich, CT: JAI.

Grobstein, C. (1988). *Science and the unborn.* New York: Basic Books.

Grossman, H. J. (1983). *Classification in mental retardation.* Washington, DC: American Association on Mental Deficiency.

Grubb, H. J., & Dozier, A. (1989). Too busy to learn: A "competing behaviors" explanation of cross-cultural differences in academic ascendancy. *Journal of Black Psychology, 16,* 23–45.

Guerin, B. (1993). *Social facilitation.* Cambridge, England: Cambridge University Press.

Guerin, B. (1994). *Analyzing social behavior.* Reno, NV: Context Press.

Guerin, G. F., Goeders, N. E., Dworkin, S. L., & Smith, J. E. (1984). Intracranial self-administration of dopamine into the nucleus accumbens. *Society for Neuroscience Abstracts, 10,* 1072.

Gustafson, G. E. (1984). Effects of the ability to locomote on infants' social and exploratory behaviors: An experimental study. *Developmental Psychology, 20,* 397–405.

Haith, M. M. (1966). The response of the human newborn to visual movement. *Journal of Experimental Child Psychology, 3,* 235–243.

Haith, M. M. (1969). Infrared television recording and measurement of ocular behavior in the human infant. *American Psychologist, 24,* 279–283.

Haith, M. M. (1976). Visual competence in early infancy. In R. Held, H. Leibowitz, & H. L. Teuber (Eds.), *Handbook of sensory physiology* (Vol. 8). New York: Springer-Verlag.

Hall, C. S., & Lindsley, G. (1985). *Introduction to theories of personality.* New York: Wiley.

Harlow, H. F. (1958). The nature of love. *American Psychologist, 13,* 673–685.

Harlow, H. F. (1967). Love in infant monkeys. In J. L. McGaugh, N. M. Weinberger, & R. E. Whalen (Eds.), *Psychobiology: The biological bases of behavior* (pp. 100–106). San Francisco: Freeman.

Harlow, H. F., & Suomi, S. J. (1970). The nature of love—simplified. *American Psychologist, 25,* 161–168.

Harlow, H. F., & Zimmerman, R. R. (1959). Affectional responses in the infant monkey. *Science, 130,* 421–432.

Harris, L. S. (1981). *Problems of drug dependence, 1981.* Washington, DC: U.S. Government Printing Office.

Hart, B., & Risley, T. R. (1995). *Meaningful differences in the everyday experience of young American children.* Baltimore: Brookes.

Hathaway, S. R., & McKinley, J. C. (1943). *Manual for the Minnesota Multiphasic Personality Inventory.*

Hawking, S. W. (1988). *A brief history of time: From the big bang to black holes.* New York: Bantam.

Hayes, C. (1952). *The ape in our house.* London: Gollancz.

Hegel, M. T., Ayllon, T., Vanderplate, C., & Spiro-Hawkins, H. (1986). A behavioral procedure for increasing compliance with self-exercise regimens in severely burn-injured patients. *Behaviour Research and Therapy, 24,* 521–528.

Helms, J. E. (1997). The triple quandary of race, culture, and social class in standardized cognitive ability testing. In D. P. Flanagan, J. L. Genshaft, & P. L. Harrison, (Eds.), *Contemporary intellectual assessment* (pp. 517–532). New York: Guilford.

Herrnstein, R. J., & Murray, C. (1994). *The bell curve: Intelligence and class structure in American life.* New York: Free Press.

Hersen, M., Eisler, R. M., Alford, G. S., & Agras, W. S. (1973). Effects of token economy on neurotic depression: An experimental analysis. *Behavior Therapy, 4,* 392–397.

Hersen, M., Turner, S. M., Edelstein, B. A., & Pinkston, S. G. (1975). Effects of phenothiazines and social skills training in a withdrawn schizophrenic. *Journal of Clinical Psychology, 31,* 588–594.

Hersen, M., Bellack, A. S., & Himmelhoch, J. M. (1980). Treatment of unipolar depression with social skills training. *Behavior Modification, 4,* 547–555.

Hess, E. H. (1958). Imprinting in animals. *Scientific American, 198,* 81–89.

Hester, P., & Hendrickson, J. (1977). Training functional expressive language: The acquisition and generalization of five-element syntactical responses. *Journal of Applied Behavior Analysis, 10,* 316.

Hetherington, E. M., & Parke, R. D. (1986). *Child psychology: A contemporary viewpoint* . New York: McGraw Hill.

Higgins, S. T., Delaney, D. D., Budney, A. J., Bickel, W. K., Hughes, J. R., Foerg, F., & Fenwick, J. W. (1991). A behavioral approach to achieving cocaine abstinence. *American Journal of Psychiatry, 148,* 1218–1224.

Hinde, R., & Stevenson-Hinde, J. (1973). *Constraints on learning: Limitations and predispositions.* New York: Academic Press.

Hjelle, L. A., & Ziegler, D. J. (1992). *Personality theories.* New York: McGraw-Hill.

Hodapp, R. M., Dykens, E. M. (1996). Mental retardation. In E. J. Mash & R. A. Barkley (Eds.), *Child psychopathology* (pp. 362–389). New York: Guilford.

Hoebel, B. G. (1988). Neuroscience and motivation: Pathways and peptides that define motivational systems. In R. C. Atkinson, R. J. Herrnstein, G. Lindzey, & R. D. Luce (Eds.), *Steven's handbook of experimental psychology* (2nd ed., pp. 547–625). New York: Wiley.

Hoebel, B. G., Monaco, A. P., Hernandez, L., Stanley, W. G., Aulisi, E. P., & Lenard, L. (1983). Self-injection of amphetamine directly into the brain. *Psychopharmacology, 81,* 156–163.

Hoff-Ginsburg, E., & Shatz, M. (1982). Linguistic input and the child's acquisition of language. *Psychological Bulletin, 92,* 3–26.

Hollard, V. D., & Delius, J. D. (1982). Rotational invariance in visual pattern recognition by pigeons and humans. *Science, 218,* 804–806.

Hollon, S. D., Spoden, F., & Chastek, J. (1986). Unipolar depression. In M. Hersen (Ed.), *Pharmacological and behavioral treatment: An integrative approach* (pp. 199–239). New York: Wiley.

Horgan, J. (1993). Eugenics revisited. *Scientific American, 268,* 123–131.

Horgan, J. (1995). The new social Darwinists. *Scientific American, 273,* 174–181.

Horowitz, F. D. (1987). *Exploring developmental theories: Toward a structural/behavioral model of development.* Hillsdale, NJ: Erlbaum.

Howard, D. V. (1983). *Cognitive psychology: Memory, language, and thought.* New York: Macmillan.

Hsu, L. K. G. (1990). *Eating disorders.* New York: Guilford.

Hubel, D. H. (1979). The brain. *Scientific American, 241,* 45–53.

Hubel, D. H., & Wiesel, T. N. (1979). Brain mechanisms of vision. *Scientific American, 249,* 150–162.

Hunt, M. (1982). *The universe within: A new science explores the human mind.* New York: Simon & Schuster.

Hutchinson, R. R. (1977). By-products of aversive control. In W. K. Honig & J. E. R. Staddon (Eds.), *Handbook of operant behavior* (pp. 415–431). New York: Appleton-Century-Crofts.

Isreal, A. C., & Brown, M. S. (1977). Correspondence training, prior verbal training, and control of nonverbal behavior via control of verbal behavior. *Journal of Applied Behavior Analysis, 10,* 333–338.

Jaffee, J. H. (1990). Drug addiction and drug abuse. In A. G. Gilman, T. W. Rall, A. S. Nies, & P. Taylor (Eds.), *The pharmacological basis of therapeutics* (pp. 522–573). New York: Pergamon.

Jarema, K., LeSage, M., & Poling, A. (1995). Schedule-induced defecation: A demonstration in pigeons exposed to fixed-time schedules of food delivery. *Physiology and Behavior, 58,* 195–198.

Jaynes, J. (1976). *The origin of consciousness in the breakdown of the bicameral mind.* Boston: Houghton Mifflin.

Johanson, C. E., Balster, R., & Bonese, S. (1976). Self-administration of psychomotor stimulant drugs: The effects of unlimited access. *Pharmacology, Biochemistry, and Behavior, 4,* 45–51.

Johnson, E. I., & Tversky, A. (1983). Affect, generalization, and the perception of risk. *Journal of Personality and Social Psychology, 45,* 20–31.

Johnston, J. M., & Pennypacker, H. S. (1993). *Strategies and tactics of scientific research.* Hillsdale, NJ: Erlbaum.

Johnston, L. D., O'Malley, P. M., & Bachman, J. G. (1994). *Overview of key findings.* In: *National survey results on drug use* (pp. 11–25). Bethesda, MD: National Institute on Drug Abuse.

Jung, C. G. (1928). *Contributions to analytical psychology.* New York: Harcourt, Brace.

Kagan, J. (1970). The distribution of attention in infancy. In D. H. Hamburg (Ed.), *Perception and its disorders.* Baltimore: Williams & Wilkins.

Kallman, W. M., Hersen, M., & O'Toole, D. H. (1975). The use of social reinforcement in a case of conversion reaction. *Behavior Therapy, 6,* 411–413.

Kalnins, I. V., & Bruner, J. S. (1973). The coordination of visual observation and instrumental behavior in early infancy. *Perception, 2,* 307–314.

Kamin, L. J. (1974). *The science and politics of IQ.* Potomac, MD: Erlbaum.

Kandel, E. R., & Hawkins, R. D. (1992). The biological basis of learning and individuality. *Scientific American, 267,* 79–86.

Kandel, E. R., & Schwartz, J. H. (1982). Molecular biology of learning: Modulation of transmitter release, *Science, 218,* 433–443.

Kanner, L. (1964). *A history of the care and study of the mentally retarded.* Springfield, IL: Thomas.

Kazdin, A. (1981). The token economy. In G. Davey (Ed.), *Applications of conditioning theory.* London: Methuen.

Keane, T. M., Zimmering, R. T., & Caddell, J. M. (1985). A behavioral formulation of posttraumatic stress disorder. *Behavior Therapist, 8,* 9–12.

Keller, F. S. (1973). *The definition of psychology* (2nd. ed.). Englewood-Cliffs, NJ: Prentice-Hall.

Keller, F. S., & Schoenfeld, W. N. (1950). *Principles of psychology.* New York: Appleton-Century-Crofts.

Keller, H. (1908). *The world I live in.* New York: Century.

Kendler, K. S., Kessler, R. C., Walters, E. E., MacLean, C., Neale, M. C., Heath, A. C., & Eaves, L. J. (1995). Stressful life events, genetic liability, and onset of an episode of major depression in women. *American Journal of Psychiatry, 152,* 833–842.

Keogh, J., & Sugden, D. (1985). *Movement skill development.* New York: Macmillan.

Kessler, R. C., McConagle, K. A., Zhao, S., Nelson, C., Hughes, M., Eshleman, S., Wittchen, H., & Kendler, K. (1994). Lifetime and 12-month prevalence of *DSM-III-R* disorders in the United States. *Archives of General Psychiatry, 51,* 8–19.

Kettlewell, H. B. D. (1973). *The evolution of melanism.* Oxford, England: Clarendon.

Kety, S. S., Wender, P. H., Jacobsen, B., Ingraham, L. J., Jansson, L., Faber, B., & Kinney, D. K. (1994). Mental illness in the biological and adoptive relatives of schizophrenic adoptees. *Archives of General Psychiatry, 51,* 442–455.

Kitcher, P. (1985). *Vaulting ambition: Sociobiology and the quest for human nature.* Cambridge, MA: MIT Press.

Klatzky, R. L. (1980). *Human memory: Structures and processes* (2nd ed.). San Francisco: Freeman.

Kleber, H. (1995). Pharmacology, current and potential, for the treatment of cocaine dependence. *Clinical Neuropharmacology, 18,* 96–109.

Knapp, T. J. (1987). Perception and action. In S. Modgil & C. Modgil (Eds.), *B. F. Skinner: Consensus and controversy* (pp. 283–294). New York: Falmer.

Kolb, B., & Wishaw, I. W. (1985). *Fundamentals of human neuropsychology.* New York: W. H. Freeman.

Koob, G. F., & Bloom, F. E. (1988). Cellular and molecular mechanisms of drug dependence. *Science, 242,* 715–723.

Krasner, L., & Ullmann, L. P. (1973). *Behavior influence and personality: The social matrix of human action.* New York: Holt, Rinehart & Winston.

Kroll, N. E. A., Parks, T., Parkinson, S. R., Bieber, S. L., & Johnson, A. L. (1970). Short-term memory while shadowing: Recall of visually and of aurally presented letters. *Journal of Experimental Psychology, 85,* 220–224.

Kuhn, T. (1970). *The structure of scientific revolutions.* Chicago: University of Chicago Press.

Lagenspetz, K. (1964). Studies on the aggressive behavior of mice. *Suomalainen Tudeakatemia* (Helsinki), *131,* 1–131.

Lamb, M. E., & Bornstein, M. H. (1987). *Development in infancy: An introduction* (2nd ed.). New York: Random House.

LaMere, J. M., Dickinson, A. D., Henry, G., & Poling, A. (1996). Effects of a multi-component monetary incentive program on the performance of truck drivers: A longitudinal study. *Behavior Modification, 20,* 385–405.

Lanyon, R. I., & Goodstein, L. D. (1982). *Personality assessment.* New York: Wiley.

LaPiere, R. T. (1934). Attitudes and actions. *Social Forces, 13,* 230–237.

Lattal, K. A., & Gleeson, S. (1990). Response acquisition with delayed reinforcement. *Journal of Experimental Psychology: Animal Behavior Processes, 16,* 27–39.

Lavelle, J. M., Hovell, M. F., West, M. P., & Wahlgren, D. R. (1992). Promoting law enforcement for child protection: A community analysis. *Journal of Applied Behavior Analysis, 25,* 885–892.

Leahey, T. H. (1987). *A history of psychology: Main currents in psychological thought* (2nd ed.). Englewood Cliffs, NJ: Prentice-Hall.

Leitenberg, H. (1976). Behavioral approaches to treatment of neuroses. In H. Leitenberg (Ed.), *Handbook of behavior modification and behavior therapy* (pp. 124–167). New York: Appleton-Century-Crofts.

Lempert, H., & Kinsbourne, M. (1982). Effect of laterality of orientation on verbal memory. *Neuropsychologia, 20,* 211–214.

Lenneberg, E. H., Rebelsky, F. G., & Nichols, I. A. (1965). The vocalizations of infants born to deaf and hearing parents. *Human Development, 8,* 23–37.

Lerner, R. M. (1984). *On the nature of human plasticity.* New York: Cambridge University Press.

LeSage, M., Byrne, T., & Poling, A. (1996). Effects of d-amphetamine on free-operant response acquisition with immediate and delayed reinforcement. *Journal of the Experimental Analysis of Behavior, 66,* 349–367.

Lester, B. M., & Zeskind, P. S. (1982). A biobehavioral perspective on crying in early infancy. In H. E. Fitzgerald, B. M. Lester, & M. H. Yogman (Eds.), *Theory and research in behavioral pediatrics* (Vol. 1, pp. 133–180). New York: Plenum.

Levant, R. F., & Schlein, J. M. (1984). *Client-centered therapy and the person-cetered approach: New directions in theory, research, and practice.* New York: Praeger.

Lewinsohn, P. M. (1975). The behavioral study and treatment of depression. In M. Hersen, R. M. Eisler, & P. M. Miller (Eds.), *Progress in behavior modification* (pp. 335–372). New York: Academic Press.

Lewontin, R. C., Rose, S., & Kamin, L. J. (1984). *Not in our genes.* New York: Pantheon.

Liberman, R. P., King, L. W., & DeRisi, W. J. (1976). Behavior analysis and therapy in community mental health. In H. Leitenberg (Ed.), *Handbook of behavior modification and behavior therapy* (pp. 566–603). Englewood Cliffs, NJ: Prentice-Hall.

Liedloff, J. (1977). *The continuum concept.* Reading, MA: Addison-Wesley.

Logue, A. W. (1995). *Self-control*. Englewood Cliffs, NJ: Prentice-Hall.

Lord, C. (1975). Is talking to baby more than baby talk? A longitudinal study of the role of linguistic input to young children. Unpublished paper presented at the Biennial Conference of the Society for Research in Child Development, Denver, CO.

Lovaas, O. I. (1987). Behavioral treatment and normal educational and intellectual functioning in young autistic children. *Journal of Consulting and Clinical Psychology, 55*, 3–9.

Lovaas, O. I. (1993). The development of a treatment-research project for developmentally disabled and autistic children. *Journal of Applied Behavior Analysis, 26*, 617–630.

Mackintosh, N. (1974). *The psychology of animal learning*. New York: Academic Press.

MacMillan, D. L. (1982). *Mental retardation in school and society*. Boston: Little, Brown.

Maisto, M. A., Galizio, R., & Connoer, G. J. (1995). *Drug use and abuse*. New York: Harcourt.

Malamed, E., & Larsen, B. (1977). Regional cerebral blood flow during voluntary conjugate eye movements in man. *Acta Neurologica Scandinavica, 56*(Suppl. 64), 530–531.

Malsbury, C. W. (1971). Facilitation of male rat copulatory behavior by electric stimulation of the medical preoptic area. *Physiology and Behavior, 7*, 797–805.

Maslow, A. H. (1970). *Motivation and personality*. New York: Harper & Row.

Mayr, E. (1978). Evolution. *Scientific American, 239*, 46–55.

McCain, G., & Segal, E. M. (1988). *The game of science*. Pacific Grove, CA: Brooks/Cole.

McCaul, M. E., Stitzer, M. L., Bigelow, G. W., & Liebson, I. A. (1984). Contingency management interventions: Effects on treatment outcome during methadone detoxification. *Journal of Applied Behavior Analysis, 17*, 35–43.

McFarland, R. A., & Kennison, R. (1986). Sex, handedness, and hemispheric asymmetry in the emotional and skin temperature responses to music [Abstract]. *Psychophysiology, 23*, 451.

Meadows, J. C. (1974). The anatomical basis of prosopagnosia. *Journal of Neurology, Neurosurgery, and Psychiatry, 37*, 489–501.

Medawar, P. B. (1984). *The limits of science*. New York: Harper & Row.

Mednick, S. A., Machon, R. A., & Huttunen, M. S. (1990). An update on the Helsinki influenza project. *Archives of General Psychiatry, 47*, 292.

Merckelbach, H., & van Oppen, P. (1989). Effects of gaze manipulation on subjective evaluation of neutral and phobia-relevant stimuli. *Acta Psychologica, 70*, 147–151.

Metzler, J., & Shepard, R. N. (1974). Transformational studies of the internal representation of three dimensional objects. In R. L. Solso (Ed.) *Theories of cognitive psychology: The Loyola Symposium*. Hillsdale, NJ: Erlbaum.

Michael, J. L. (1975). Positive and negative reinforcement, a distinction that is no longer necessary; or a better way to talk about bad things. *Behaviorism, 3*, 33–44.

Michael, J. L. (1982). Distinguishing between discriminative and motivational functions of stimuli. *Journal of the Experimental Analysis of Behavior, 37*, 149–155.

Milgram, S. (1963). Behavioral study of obedience. *Journal of Abnormal and Social Psychology, 67*, 371–378.

Miller, G. A. (1956). The magical number seven, plus or minus two: Some limits on our capacity for processing information. *Psychological Review, 63*, 81–97.

Miller, L., & Milner, B. (1985). Cognitive risk-taking after frontal or temporal lobectomy—II. The synthesis of phonemic and semantic information. *Neuropsychologia, 23*, 371–379.

Miltenberger, R. (1997). *Behavior modification: Principles and procedures*. Pacific Grove, CA: Brooks/Cole.

Moerk, E. L. (1990). Three-term contingency patterns in mother–child verbal interactions during first-language acquisition. *Journal of the Experimental Analysis of Behavior, 54*, 293–306.

Moore, K. L. (1989). *Before we are born* (3rd ed.) Philadelphia: W. B. Saunders.

Moss, G. R., & Boren, J. J. (1972). Depression as a model for behavioral analysis. *Comprehensive Psychiatry, 13*, 581–590.

Mulick, J. A., Jacobson, J. W., & Kobe, R. H. (1992). Anguished silence and helping hands: Miracles in autism with Facilitated Communication. *Skeptical Inquirer, 17*, 270–280.

Murray, D. J. (1988). *A history of western psychology* (2nd ed.). Englewood Cliffs, NJ: Prentice–Hall.

National Institute on Alcohol Abuse and Alcoholism (1983). *Biological and genetic factors in alcoholism*. Research Monograph No. 9. Rockville, MD: Author.

Neisser, U. (1976). General, academic, and artificial intelligence. In L. B. Rescind (Ed.), *The nature of intelligence* (pp. 135–144). Hillsdale, NJ: Erlbaum.

Nelson, G. L., & Cone, J. E. (1979). Multiple-baseline analysis of a token economy for psychiatric inpatients. *Journal of Applied Behavior Analysis, 12,* 255–272.

Nevin, J. A. (1973). Stimulus control. In J. A. Nevin (Ed.), *The study of behavior: Learning, motivation, emotion, and instinct* (pp. 114–152). Glenview, IL: Scott Foresman.

Nietzel, M. T., & Bernstein, D. A. (1981). Assessment of anxiety and fear. In M. Hersen & A. S. Bellack (Eds.), *Behavioral assessment* (pp. 215–245). New York: Pergamon.

Olds, J. (1965). Operant conditioning of single-unit responses. *Excerpta Medica International Congress Series, No. 87,* 372–380.

Olds, J., & Milner, P. (1954). Positive reinforcement produced by electrical stimulation of septal areas and other regions of rat brains. *Journal of Comparative and Physiological Psychology, 41,* 419–427.

Olds, M. E., & Forbes, J. L. (1981). The central basis of motivation: Intracranial self-stimulation studies. *Annual Review of Psychology, 32,* 523–574.

Overmeier, J. B., & Seligman, J. E. P. (1967). Effects of inescapable shock upon subsequent escape and avoidance learning. *Journal of Comparative and Physiological Psychology, 63,* 23–33.

Owens, R. E. (1984). *Language development: An introduction.* Columbus, OH: Merrill.

Palmer, D. C. (1986). Chomsky's nativism: A critical review. In L. J. Hayes & P. N. Chase (Eds.), *Psychological aspects of language* (pp. 44–60). Springfield, IL: Thomas.

Palmer, D. C. (1991). A behavioral interpretation of memory. In L. J. Hayes, & P. N. Chase (Eds.), *Dialogues on verbal behavior* (pp. 261–279). Reno, NV: Context Press.

Parton, D. A., & DeNike, L. D. (1966). Performance hypotheses of children and response to social reinforcement. *Journal of Personality and Social Psychology, 4,* 444–447.

Patterson, C. (1978). *Evolution.* Ithaca, NY: Cornell University Press.

Patterson, F., & Linden, E. (1981). *The education of Koko.* New York: Holt, Rinehart & Winston.

Pauls, D. L., Alsobrook, J. P., II, Goodman, W., Rasmussen, S., & Leckman, J. F. (1995). A family study of obsessive-compulsive disorder. *American Journal of Psychiatry, 152,* 76–84.

Pavlov, I. P. (1927). *Conditioned reflexes.* (G. V. Anrep, Trans.). Oxford, England: Clarendon.

Peterson, L. R., & Peterson, M. J. (1959). Short-term retention of individual verbal items. *Journal of Experimental Psychology, 58,* 193–198.

Peterson, N. (1960). Control of behavior by presentation of an imprinted stimulus. *Science, 132,* 1395–1396.

Petrakis, P. L. (1985). *Alcoholism: An inherited disease.* Washington, DC: U.S. Government Printing Office.

Pfaff, D. W., & Sakuma, Y. (1979). Deficit in the lordosis reflex of female rats caused by lesions in the ventromedial nucleus of the hypothalamus. *Journal of Physiology, 288,* 203–210.

Phares, E. J. (1984). *Introduction to personality.* Columbus, OH: Merrill.

Phillips, J. R. (1973). Syntax and vocabulary of mother's speech to young children: Age and sex comparisons. *Child Development, 44,* 182–185.

Piaget, J. (1952). *The origins of intelligence in children.* New York: International Universities Press.

Pickens, R. (1979). A behavioral program for treatment of drug dependence. In N. A. Krasnegor (Ed.), *Behavioral analysis and treatment of substance abuse* (pp. 44–54). Washington, DC: U.S. Government Printing Office.

Pinel, J. P. J. (1990). *Biopsychology.* Needham Heights, MA: Allyn and Bacon.

Poling, A. (1986). *A primer of human behavioral pharmacology.* New York: Plenum.

Poling, A., Gadow, K. D., & Cleary, J. (1991). *Drug therapy for behavior disorders: An introduction.* New York: Pergamon.

Poling, A., Methot, L. L., & LeSage, M. G. (1995). *Fundamentals of behavior analytic research.* New York: Plenum.

Popper, K. (1978). Natural selection and the emergence of the mind. *Dialectica, 32,* 339–355.

Premack, D. (1959). Toward empirical laws: I. Positive reinforcement. *Psychological Review, 66,* 219–233.

Preston, J, O'Neal, J. H., & Talaga, M. C. (1994). *Handbook of clinical psychopharmacology for therapists.* Oakland, CA: New Harbinger.

Prior, M., & Cummins, R. (1992). Questions about facilitated communication and autism. *Journal of Autism and Developmental Disorders, 22,* 331–337.

Pryor, K. W., Haag, R., & O'Reilly, J. (1969). The creative porpoise: Training for novel behavior. *Journal of the Experimental Analysis of Behavior, 12,* 653–661.

Puig-Antich, J., & Ryan, W. (1986). *Schedule for affective disorders and schizophrenia for school-age children.* New York: New York Psychiatric Association.

Rachman, S., & Hodgson, R. J. (1968). Experimentally-induced sexual fetishism: Replication and development. *Psychological Record, 18,* 25–27.

Rall, T. W. (1990). Hypnotics and sedatives: Ethanol. In A. G. Gilman, T. W. Rall, A. S. Nies, & P. Taylor (Eds.), *The pharmacological basis of therapeutics* (pp. 345–382). New York: Pergamon.

Ray, O. (1983). *Drugs, society, and human behavior.* St. Louis, MO: Mosby.

Ray, O., & Ksir, C. (1995). *Drugs, society, and human behavior.* St. Louis, MO: Mosby.

Reschly, D. (1979). Nonbiased assessment. In G. Phye & D. Reschly (Eds.), *School psychology: Perspectives and issues* (pp. 215–253). New York: Academic Press.

Reschly, D. J., & Grimes, J. P. (1995). Best practices in intellectual assessment. In A. Thomas & J. Grimes (Eds.), *Best practices in school psychology—III* (pp. 763–773). Washington, DC: National Association of School Psychologists.

Rescorla, R. A. (1968). Probability of shock in the presence and absence of CS is fear conditioning. *Journal of Comparative and Physiological Psychology, 66,* 1–5.

Reynolds, A. G., & Flagg, P. W. (1977). *Cognitive psychology.* Boston: Little, Brown.

Rheingold, H. L., Gewirtz, J. L., & Ross, H. W. (1959). Social conditioning of vocalizations in the infant. *Journal of Consulting and Clinical Psychology, 52,* 67–73.

Rice, D. P., Kelman, S., Miller, L. S., & Dunmeyer, S. (1990). *The economic costs of alcohol and drug abuse and mental illness: 1985.* San Francisco: Institute for Health and Aging.

Rilling, M., & Caplan, H. (1973). Extinction-induced aggression during errorless discrimination learning. *Journal of the Experimental Analysis of Behavior, 20,* 85–91.

Robins, L. N. (1974). *The Vietnam drug user returns.* Washington, DC: U.S. Government Printing Office.

Roediger H. L., III, Rushton, J. P., Capaldi, E. D., & Paris, S. G. (1984). *Psychology.* Boston: Little, Brown.

Rogers, C. R. (1951). *Client-centered therapy: Its current practice, implications, and theory.* Boston: Houghton Mifflin.

Rollin, B. E. (1986). Animal consciousness and scientific change. *New Ideas in Psychology, 4,* 141–152.

Rosenhan, D. L. (1973). On being sane in insane places. *Science, 179,* 250–258.

Rosenzweig, M. R. (1966). Environmental complexity, cerebral change, and behavior. *American Psychologist, 21,* 321–332.

Rosenzweig, M. R., & Bennet, E. L. (1970). Effects of differential environments on brain weights and enzyme activities in gerbils, rats, and mice. *Developmental Psychobiology, 2,* 87–95.

Rothenbuhler, W. C. (1964). Behavior genetics of nest cleaning in honeybees: IV. Responses of F1 and backcross generations to disease-killed brood. *American Zoologist. 4,* 111–123.

Rovee, C. K., & Fagen, J. W. (1976). Extended conditioning and 24-hour retention in infants. *Journal of Experimental Child Psychology, 21,* 1–11.

Rovee-Collier, C., Griesler, P. C., & Earley, L. A. (1985). Contextual determinants of retrieval in three-month-old infants. *Learning and Motivation, 16,* 139–157.

Rovee-Collier, C. K., Morrongiello, B. A., Aron, M., & Kupersmidt, J. (1978). Topographical response differentiation and reversal in 3-month-old infants. *Infant Behavior and Development, 1,* 323–333.

Rumbaugh, D. M. (1977). *Language learning by a chimpanzee.* New York: Academic Press.

Russell, M., Dark, K. A., Cummins, R. W., Ellman, G., Callaway, E., & Peeke, H. V. S. (1984). Learned histamine release. *Science, 225,* 733–734.

Salapatek, P. (1975). Pattern perception in early infancy. In L. B. Cohen & P. Salapatek (Eds.), *Infant perception: From sensation to cognition* (Vol. 1). New York: Academic Press.

Sarason, S. B., & Doris, J. (1969). *Psychological problems in mental deficiency.* New York: Harper & Row.

Salzinger, K. (1978). Language behavior. In A. C. Catania & T. A. Brigham (Eds.), *Handbook of applied behavior analysis: Instructional processes.* New York: Irvington.

Schlinger, H., & Blakely, E. (1987). Function-altering effects of contingency-specifying stimuli. *The Behavior Analyst, 10,* 41–45.

Schlinger, H. D. (1992). Intelligence: Real or artificial. *Analysis of Verbal Behavior, 10,* 125–133.

Schlinger, H. D. (1995). *A behavior analytic view of child development.* New York: Plenum.

Schlinger, H. D. (1996a). How the human got its spots: A critical analysis of the just so stories of evolutionary psychology, *Skeptic, 4,* 68–76.

Schlinger, H. D. (1996b). What's wrong with evolutionary explanations of human behavior. *Behavior and Social Issues, 6,* 35–54.

Schneider, A. M., & Tarshis, B. (1975). *An introduction to physiological psychology.* New York: Random House.

Schoenfeld, W. N., & Cumming, W. W. (1963). Behavior and perception. In S. Koch (Ed.), *Psychology: A study of a science* (pp. 213–252). New York: McGraw Hill.

Schultz, D. P. (1975). *A history of modern psychology.* New York: Academic Press.

Schultz, F. (1971). Pragung des sexual Verhaltens von Enten und Gansen durch Sozialeindrucke wahrend der Jugendphase. *Journal of Neurovisceral Relations, Supplementum, 10,* 357–399.

Schwarzkopf, S. B., Nasrallah, H. A., Olson, S. C., Coffman, J. A., & McLaughlin, J. A. (1989). Perinatal complications and genetic loading in schizophrenia: Preliminary findings. *Psychiatry Research, 27,* 233–239.

Scibak, J. W. (1983). Behavioral treatment. In J. L. Matson & J. A. Mulick (Eds.), *Handbook of mental retardation* (pp. 339–350). New York: Pergamon.

Searle, J. (1984). *Minds, brain and science.* Cambridge, MA: Harvard University Press.

Searle, L. V. (1949). The organization of hereditary maze-brightness and maze-dullness. *Genetic Psychology Monographs, 39,* 279–335.

Sears, R. R., Maccoby, E. E., & Levin, H. (1957). *Patterns of childrearing.* Evanston, IL: Row, Peterson.

Seligman, M. E. P., Klein, D. C., & Miller, W. R. (1976). Depression. In H. Leitenberg (Ed.), *Handbook of behavior modification and behavior therapy* (pp. 168–210). New York: Appleton-Century-Crofts.

Sequin, E. (1966). *Idiocy, and its treatment by the physiological method.* New York: William Wood.

Sheldon, W. H. (with the collaboration of S. S. Stevens) (1942). *The varieties of temperament: A psychology of constitutional differences.* New York: Harper & Row.

Shepard, R. N., & Metzler, J. (1971). Mental rotation of three-dimensional objects. *Science, 171,* 701–703.

Shirley, M. M. (1933). *The first two years.* Minneapolis: University of Minnesota Press.

Sidman, M. (1960). *Tactics of scientific research.* New York: Basic Books.

Sigel, I. F., Roeper, A., & Hooper, F. H. (1966). A training procedure for acquisition of Piaget's conservation of quantity: A pilot study and its replication. *British Journal of Educational Psychology, 36,* 301–311.

Siegel, S. (1984). Pavlovian conditioning and heroin overdose: Reports by overdose victims. *Bulletin of the Psychonomic Society, 22,* 428–430.

Siegel, S. (1989). Pharmacological conditioning and drug effects. In A. J. Goudie, & M. W. Emmett-Oglesby (Eds.), *Psychoactive drugs: Tolerance and sensitization* (pp. 115–180). Clifton, NJ: Humana Press.

Siegel, S., Hinson, R. E., Krank, M. D., & McCully, J. (1982). Heroin "overdose" death: Contribution of drug-associated environmental cues. *Science, 216,* 436–437.

Skinner, B. F. (1938). *The behavior of organisms.* Englewood Cliffs, NJ: Prentice-Hall.

Skinner, B. F. (1945). The operational analysis of psychological terms. *Psychological Review, 52,* 270–277.

Skinner, B. F. (1953). *Science and human behavior.* New York: Macmillan.

Skinner, B. F. (1957). *Verbal behavior.* Englewood Cliffs, NJ: Prentice-Hall.

Skinner, B. F. (1969). *Contingencies of reinforcement.* New York: Meredith.

Skinner, B. F. (1974). *About behaviorism.* New York: Random House.

Skinner, B. F. (1978). *Reflections on behaviorism and society.* Englewood Cliffs, NJ: Prentice-Hall.

Slater, P. J. B. (1985). *An introduction to ethology.* Cambridge, England: Cambridge University Press.

Snelson, J. S. (1995). The ideological immune system: Resistance to new ideas in science. *Skeptic, 1,* 44–55.

Snyder, J. J. (1989). *Health psychology & behavioral medicine.* Englewood Cliffs, NJ: Prentice Hall.

Sperling, G. (1960). The information available in brief visual presentations. *Psychological Monographs, 74* (Whole No. 498).

Spitzer, R. L. (1975). On pseudoscience in science, logic in remission, and psychiatric diagnosis: A critique of Rosenhan's "On being sane in insane places." *Journal of Abnormal Psychology, 84,* 442–452.

Springer, S. P., & Deutsch, G. (1984). *Left brain, right brain.* San Francisco: Freeman.

Spyraki, C., Fibiger, H. C., & Philips, A. G. (1982a). Attenuation by haloperidol of place preference conditioning using food reinforcement. *Psychopharmacology, 77,* 379–382.

Spyraki, C., Fibiger, H. C., & Philips, A. G. (1982b). Dopaminergic substrates of amphetamine-induced place preference conditioning. *Brain Research, 253,* 185–193.

Stein, L., & Belluzzi, J. D. (1985). Operant conditioning of hippocampal neurons: Chlorpromazine blocks reinforcing actions of dopamine. *Society for Neuroscience Abstracts, 11,* 873.

Stein, L., & Belluzzi, J. D. (1988). Operant conditioning of individual neurons. In M. Commons, R. M. Church, J. R. Stellar, & A. Wagner (Eds.), *Quantitative analyses of behavior: Biological determinants of reinforcement* (pp. 249–264). Hillsdale, NJ: Erlbaum.

Sternberg, R. J., & Detterman, D. K. (Eds.). (1986). *What is intelligence? Contemporary viewpoints on its nature and definition.* Norwood, NJ: Ablex.

Sternberg, R. J., Wagner, R. K., Williams, W. M., & Horvath, J. A. (1995). Testing common sense. *American Psychologist, 50,* 912–926.

Stock, L. Z., & Milan, M. A. (1993). Improving dietary practices of elderly individuals: The power of prompting, feedback and social reinforcement. *Journal of Applied Behavior Analysis, 26,* 379–387.

Stroufe, L. A., & Cooper, R. G. (1988). *Child development: Its nature and course.* New York: Knopf.

Symons, D. (1992). On the use and misuse of Darwinism in the study of human behavior. In J. Barkow, L. Cosmides, & J. Tooby (Eds.), *The adapted mind: Evolutionary psychology and the generation of culture* (pp. 137–159). New York: Oxford University Press.

Szasz, T. S. (1960). The myth of mental illness. *American Psychologist, 15,* 113–118.

Szasz, T. S. (1987). *Insanity: The idea and its consequences.* New York: Wiley.

Terrace, H. S. (1979). *Nim: A chimpanzee who learned sign language.* New York: Washington Square Press.

Thomas, C. L. (1981). *Taber's cyclopedic medical dictionary.* Philadelphia: F. A. Davis.

Thompson, T. (1963). Visual reinforcement in Siamese fighting fish. *Science, 141,* 55–57.

Thompson, T. (1964). Visual reinforcement in fighting cocks. *Journal of the Experimental Analysis of Behavior, 7,* 45–49.

Thompson, T. (1993). A reign of error: Facilitated Communication. *Kennedy Center News, 22,* 3–5.

Thompson, T., & Schuster, C. R. (1964). Morphine self-administration, food-reinforced, and avoidance behaviors in rhesus monkeys. *Psychopharmacologia, 5,* 87–94.

Thorndike, E. L. (1898). Animal intelligence. *Psychological Review Monographs, 29*(8).

Thorndike, E. L. (1911). *Animal intelligence.* New York: Macmillan.

Tinbergen, N. (1951). *The study of instinct.* Oxford: Oxford University Press.

Tooby, J., & Cosmides, L. (1989). Evolutionary psychology and the generation of culture, Part II. *Ethology and Sociobiology, 10,* 51–97.

Trivers, R. (1985). *Social evolution.* Menlo Park, CA: Benjamin/Cummings.

Tryon, R. C. (1940). Genetic differences in maze-learning in rats. *Yearbook of the National Society for the Study of Education, 39,* 111–119.

U.S. Department of Health and Human Services. (1993). National household survey on drug abuse: Highlights 1991. Washington, DC: Substance Abuse and Mental Health Services Administration.

Vaughan, M. E., & Michael, J. L. (1982). Automatic reinforcement: An important but ignored concept. *Behaviorism, 10,* 217–227.

Vetter, H. J. (1963). *Language behavior and communication: An introduction.* Itasca, IL: Peacock.

Walker, E., Wade, S., & Waldman, I. (1982). The effect of lateral visual fixation on response latency to verbal and spatial questions. *Brain and Cognition, 1,* 399–404.

Wardhaugh, R. (1977). *Introduction to linguistics.* New York: McGraw-Hill.

Watkins, C. E. (1991). What have surveys taught us about the teaching and practice of psychological assessment? *Journal of Personality Assessment, 56,* 426–437.

Watson, D. L., & Tharp, R. G. (1989). *Self-directed behavior: Self-modification for personal adjustment.* Pacific Grove, CA: Brooks/Cole.

Watson, J. B. (1930). *Behaviorism.* New York: Norton.

Watson, J. B., & Rayner, R. (1920). Conditioned emotional reactions. *Journal of Experimental Psychology, 3*, 1–14.

Watson, J. D., & Crick, F. H. C. (1953). Molecular structure of nucleic acid: A structure for deoxyribose nucleic acid. *Nature, 171*, 737–738.

Watson, J. S., & Ramey, C. T. (1972). Reactions to responsive contingent stimulation in early infancy. *Merrill-Palmer Quarterly, 18*, 219–227.

Wechsler, D. (1991). *Wechsler Intelligence Scale for Children—Third Edition.* San Antonio, TX: Psychological Corporation.

Werle, M. A., Murphy, T. B., & Budd, K. S. (1993). Treating chronic food refusal in young children: Home-based parent training. *Journal of Applied Behavior Analysis, 26*, 421–433.

Wheeler, D. L., Jacobson, J. W., Paglieri, R. A., & Schwartz, A. A. (1993). An experimental assessment of facilitated communication. *Mental Retardation, 31*, 49–60.

White, B. L. (1967). An experimental approach to the effects of environment on early human behavior. In J. P. Hill (Ed.), *Minnesota symposium on child psychology* (Vol. 1, pp. 201–225). Minneapolis: University of Minnesota Press.

White, B. L., & Held, R. M. (1966). Plasticity of sensorimotor development in the human infant. In J. Rosenblith & W. Allinsmith (Eds.), *The causes of behavior: Readings in child development and educational psychology* (pp. 60–70). Boston: Allyn & Bacon.

White, B. L., Castle, P., & Held, R. M. (1964). Observations on the development of visually directed reaching. *Child Development, 35*, 349–364.

Whitehurst, G. J. (1972). Production of novel and grammatical utterances by young children. *Journal of Experimental Child Psychology, 13*, 502–515.

Wilford, J. N. (1985). *The riddle of the dinosaur.* New York: Knopf.

Willis, M. G. (1989). Learning styles of African American children: A review of the literature and interventions. *Journal of Black Psychology, 16*, 47–65.

Wilson, E. O. (1975). *Sociobiology: The new synthesis.* Cambridge, MA: Harvard University Press.

Wilson, E. O. (1978). *On human nature.* Cambridge, MA: Harvard University Press.

Wilson, G. T., Heffernan, K., & Black, C. M. D. (1996). Eating disorders. In E. J. Mash & R. A. Barkley (Ed.), *Child psychopathology* (pp. 541–571). New York: Guilford.

Wilson, M. S., & Reschly, D. J. (1996). Assessment in school psychology training and practice. *School Psychology Review, 25*, 9–23.

Winograd, T. (1975). Frame representations and the declarative-procedural controversy. In D. Bobrow & A. Collins (Eds.), *Representation and understanding: Studies in cognitive science.* New York: Academic Press.

Wisocki, P. (1985). Thought stopping. In A. S. Belack and M. Hersen (Eds.) *Dictionary of behavior therapy techniques* (pp. 219–222). New York: Pergamon.

Wolpe, J. (1958). *Psychotherapy by reciprocal inhibition.* Stanford, CA: Stanford University Press.

Woolverton, W. L., & Johnson, K. M. (1992). Neurobiology of cocaine abuse. *Trends in Pharmacological Science, 13*, 193–200.

World Health Organization. (1995). Facts, figures and estimates about substance use. *World Health, July/August*, 16–17.

Wright, R. (1994). *The moral animal: The new science of evolutionary psychology.* New York: Pantheon.

Wright, R. (1995, March). The biology of violence. *New Yorker*, 69–77.

Wu, J. C., & Bunney, W. E. (1990). The biological basis of an antidepressant response to sleep deprivation and relapse: Review and hypothesis. *American Journal of Psychiatry, 147*, 14–21.

Zeiler, M. (1977). *Schedules of reinforcement.* In W. K. Honig & J. E. R. Staddon (Eds.), *Handbook of Operant Behavior* (pp. 201–232). Englewood Cliffs, NJ: Prentice-Hall.

Zelazo, P. R., Zelazo, N. A., & Kolb, S. (1972). "Walking" in the newborn. *Science, 176*, 314–315.

Zimbardo, P. G. (1988). *Psychology and life.* Glenview, IL: Scott, Foresman.

Index

385